George L. Fox was considered the funniest man of his time. As a comic actor who did his most acclaimed work in pantomime, he reflected the culture and events of the mid-nineteenth century and was a major force in the development of a distinctly American brand of theater. Later popular entertainment forms such as silent film comedy, animated cartoons, and slapstick owe much to his genius. Yet until now there has been no full-length biography of this man known almost exclusively through brief accounts and footnotes.

Laurence Senelick uses family papers, manuscript scenarios, and contemporary newspaper and periodical accounts to recreate Fox's theatrical career in the context of the historical forces that influenced it. This amply illustrated biography is both an account of one man's life and a history of evolving popular tastes during a turbulent period when America moved from a Jacksonian agrarian culture to the urban industrialism of the Gilded Age. "Fox seemed, invariably, to be at the crux of whatever major changes were happening in American life; what he did on stage often reflected a popular *mentalité* and accounted for his great success," writes Senelick. The events of the day affecting his shows included the temperance movement, the rebirth of Evangelical Protestantism, abolitionism, the Civil War, and Grant Era corruption.

Fox's career had its beginning in puritanical Boston, where "a respectable family would no more be seen entering [a theater] than it would a brothel." He and his family eventually moved to New York, introducing the first successful adaptation of *Uncle Tom's Cabin* to this pro-slavery city. As manager of two Bowery playhouses, Fox gradually lured middle-class audiences to lower-class theaters and evolved a distinctly American style of pantomime, remarkable for its action, violence, and topical satire. He was the first to demonstrate that "a clown could occupy as high a position in the esteem of the public as a tragedian . . .

nd familiar in
nd elevated it,
realism of violent
se," writes

with his master-
which he played
Boss Tweed and
n guise, Fox as
amiliar figure in
appearing in
effigies, and chil-
death. Senelick
h of Humpty
d into one
rming innocence
of nineteenth
d of American
ough characters
ression half a
f Laurel and
ster Keaton, and
til now, Fox him-
in history as he

her Professor of
His most recent
nov (1985),
rt of Mikhail
award-winning
Gordon Craig's Moscow Hamlet (1982).

The Age
and Stage of
GEORGE L. FOX

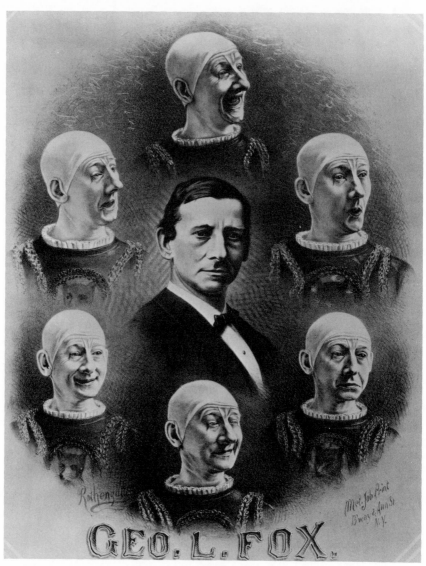

Frontispiece. G. L. Fox and his alter ego, Humpty Dumpty. A lithograph by Rothengutter, based on photographs by Napoleon Sarony, c. 1869. (Courtesy Harvard Theatre Collection)

The Age
and Stage of
GEORGE L. FOX

1825-1877

LAURENCE SENELICK

PUBLISHED FOR TUFTS UNIVERSITY
BY UNIVERSITY PRESS OF NEW ENGLAND
HANOVER AND LONDON
1988

© 1988 by Trustees of Tufts University

Printed in the United States of America

LIBRARY OF CONGRESS CATALOGING-IN-PUBLICATION DATA
Senelick, Laurence.
The age and stage of George L. Fox, 1825–77.

Bibliography: p.
Includes index.
1. Fox, George Lafayette, 1825–1877.   2. Mimes—
United States—Biography.   3. Comedians—United States—
Biography.   I. Title.
PN1986. F68 S46   1988   792.3′028′0924 [B]   87–23162
ISBN 0–87451–433–9

5   4   3   2   1

For MMM,
Who has lived in the period

CONTENTS

ILLUSTRATIONS

ACKNOWLEDGMENTS

This work has benefited over the years from the encouragement and assistance of a great many persons. I should like first to acknowledge the enthusiastic support I have received from institutions and libraries. Pride of place must go to the John Simon Guggenheim Foundation, which awarded me a grant to carry out preliminary research; but close on its heels come the many librarians and libraries who selflessly aided me. These include Jeanne Newlin, Curator, Martha Mahard, former Assistant Curator, and the staff of the Harvard Theatre Collection; Dorothy Swerdlove, Curator, Paul Myers, former Curator, and the staff of the Billy Rose Theatre Collection, Lincoln Center, New York; Louis A. Rachow, Curator and Librarian of the Walter Hampden-Edwin Booth Theatre Collection and Memorial Library, Players Club, New York; Mary Ann Jensen, Curator of the William Seymour Theatre Collection, and her staff at Princeton University who let me explore the McCaddon Collection of pantomime scripts; Ellen S. Dunlap, Research Librarian, and the staff of the Hoblitzelle Theatre Collection in the Humanities Research Center of the University of Texas at Austin, who opened the G. P. Howard Collection to me; Mary Henderson, former Curator, and her staff at the Theatre Collection of the Museum of the City of New York; Brigitte Kueppers, former Curator, and the staff of the Shubert Archive, New York; Laetitia Yeandle of the Folger Shakespeare Library, Washington, D.C.; John Lancaster, Special Collections Librarian and Archivist, Amherst College Library, Amherst, Mass.; Ladd Macmillan, Curator, Arts and Crafts, Heritage Plantation of Sandwich, Mass.; Barbara Luck, Registrar, and Ann Barton Brown, Research Associate, Addy Aldrich Rockefeller Folk Art Collection, Williamsburg, Va.; and Mary Leen, Librarian, The Bostonian Society, Boston, Mass. In addition, I am grateful to the staffs of the Massachusetts Historical Society; the Boston Public Library; the Enthoven Theatre Collection of the Victoria and Albert Museum, London; the New-York Historical Society; the Cambridge Public Library; and the Boston Athenaeum.

Further thanks are warmly extended to A. H. Saxon, who first suggested that my thumb-nail sketch of Fox should become a full-length portrait; Brooks McNamara and the Conference on the History of American Popular Entertainment, which gave me the opportunity to unveil that early sketch to a receptive audience of scholars; J. Wearing and L. W. Conolly, who published that sketch in *Nineteenth Century Theatre Research*; Barbara Barker and Al Pichel for allowing me to pore over unpublished material on the Kiralfys; George Speaight, Charlie Stewart, William C. Darrah, and the late Marian Hannah Winter who provided material from their collections; my brother, Dr. Richard Senelick, who tried, unsuccessfully, to pry open the jealously guarded files of McLean's Hospital; Robert Healy, who photocopied endlessly; and Michael McDowell, who typed and copy-read assiduously. Helpful commentary and assistance were also offered by David Grimsted, David Mayer III, John Preston, Paul Schoenfeld, Yvonne Shafer, and Don B. Wilmeth at various stages of the process. Charles Backus and Janet B. Pascal of the University Press of New England have been encouraging in their circumstantial interest and involvement, which brought this work to fruition. At the last minute, Elizabeth Howard Linzee, a collateral descendant of the Howard-Foxes, shared family lore with me, and bestowed her "blessing" on the enterprise. Ultimately, however, any errors and questions of interpretation must be laid at my door.

October 1987   L. S.

INTRODUCTION

A pantomime may have been the first original play staged in New York. When the *New Pantomime Entertainment in Grotesque Characters, called the Adventures of Harlequin and Scaramouch, or the Spaniard Trick'd* played at Henry Holt's Long Room east of Broadway on 12 February 1738/9, a style of comic spectacle was initiated that came to stay, although it took its time getting naturalized.[1]

By the second half of the eighteenth century, English troupes such as the Hallams, as well as native entrepreneurs, had added pantomimes as welcome leavening to heavier bills. Garrick's *Harlequin's Invasion* and Sheridan's *Robinson Crusoe*, for instance, were seen at the John Street Theater, New York, in 1786. For the most part, the American version of a pantomime clove closely to the English, the same scripts and the same performances appearing on both sides of the Atlantic. That some attempt was made to acclimate the form is apparent from such titles as *Harlequin Traveller and The Temple of the Sun* (1800) and *Harlequin Panattahah or The Genii of the Algonquins* (1810),[2] fanciful counterparts to Sheridan's *Pizarro* and Rogers's *Ponteach*. But in shape and content the pantomime remained a foreign transplant, suitable merely for rounding out an evening or celebrating the holiday season.

The term *pantomime* is so loosely used to mean "mute performance" that it may be worth specifying what the genre was like at this time. French fairground performers had presented so-called "dark scenes," short *commedia dell'arte* scenarios, to London in the early eighteenth century. As anglicized by the actor-manager John Rich, these were expanded into comic afterpieces, structured into two distinct halves. The opening, based roughly on classical mythology, featured spectacular mechanical tricks and dialogue in rhymed couplets. At a critical moment in the plot, the characters were transformed into the *commedia* types of Pantaloon, Columbine, and Harlequin; they engaged in a balletic harlequinade, dominated by the trickery of Harlequin and his magic bat. In the 1780 pantomime *The Genius of Nonsense*, George Colman, perhaps responding to a less classically grounded public, drew his opening not from mythology but from nursery tales. This became standard, although the nursery tales were, to a large degree, nominal, only the characters' names and the broadest outlines of the original stories being preserved.

The Regency pantomime, perfected by Thomas Dibdin, grew from an afterpiece to a full evening's entertainment. In the process, the purely

English character of Clown edged out Harlequin, whose function became more acrobatic than balletic. The talent and prestige of the great buffoon Joseph Grimaldi made the expanded harlequinade a glorious vehicle for Clown's mischief, and plot became subservient to song, slapstick, and topical satire. The opening dwindled into a brief introduction, to leave more time for the elaborate tricks of construction and athletic mayhem of the harlequinade. Gradually, a number of unalterable traditions adhered, including the comic "dame" role played by a male comedian.[3]

Lacking a Grimaldi or, possibly, a theatre-going public urbane enough to appreciate high-grade nonsense, the English pantomime never really caught on in the early republic. The toy theatre sheets from Elton's Theatrical Print Warehouse in Nassau Street depicted Clown, Pantaloon, Harlequin, and Columbine in their traditional costumes and poses, but neither fashionable nor demotic American audiences took to the genre. When New York's most prestigious theatre, the Park, declined in its fortunes, it stooped to full-length pantomime under the tutelage of John Grimaldi Wells, but even there the experiment failed.[4] The English pantomimist E. J. Parsloe sailed to New York in the 1831 Christmas season to repeat at the Bowery Theatre his success in *Mother Goose*, but he was so dismayed by the audience's silence, "broken only by the cracking of peanuts," that on the fourth night of the run, during his transformation from Squire Bugle to Clown, he burst into tears.[5]

Greater enthusiasm was shown for the French *ballet-pantomime* perfected by Mazurier, when it was introduced to America by the Ravels, whose name for thirty years meant pantomime. Mazurier's most famous creation, Jocko the Brazilian Ape, had appeared at the Bowery impersonated by the Englishman Gouffe the same season as Parsloe's fiasco, and it had proved so successful that he played it in a number of variations throughout the season.[6] The Ravels, who arrived the next year (1832), offered more sophisticated versions of Jocko and other Mazurier scenarios, such as *The Magic Trumpet, Mazulme the Night Owl,* and *The Green Monster,* loading the original low-key and delicate work of Mazurier with elaborate tricks of transformation and full-scale ballets to cover the more difficult scene changes. Heightening these balletic fables with rope-dancing, acrobatics, and spectacular leaps, the Ravels made a smash at Niblo's Garden in the summer months, and so came to popularize what was known erroneously as "the Italian style" of pantomime, which used no dialogue. The sentiments were genteel and the pathos strong, and tears flowed freely at the death of the apes in *Jocko* and *Pongo*. With this emphasis on gymnastics, scenic display, and refined feeling, the Ravels were half-way to the musical comedy *The Black Crook,* and, as Hannah Winter has noted, "what the Ravels began, the Kiralfys would finish," for those brother impresarios inflated pantomime to the level of spectacular extravaganza.[7]

However, between the French Ravels and the Hungarian Kiralfys, there appeared an American performer who imitated the former and imported the latter, bringing pantomime to a pitch of success it was never again to enjoy in the United States. George Lafayette Fox, though heralded in his day as the "American Grimaldi" and "the Talma of pantomime," and remembered for a generation afterwards as the funniest man of his time, has remained as mute in history as he was in panto. So well known was his *vis comica*, so well attended were his best productions that critics and chroniclers thought it supererogatory to go into detail. Laurence Hutton could write in 1891 that "[Fox] was never properly appreciated during his life, and [never]—not even in William Winter's usually complete *Brief Chronicles*—has received more than a passing notice in the long records of the stage he did so much to adorn."[8]

My own interest in Fox dates to childhood, when I read in the article on "Makeup" in the *Encyclopœdia Britannica* that the white lead he used on his face had brought about his insanity and death. The accompanying photograph of a grimacing clown labelled "Humpty Dumpty" was confusing; he did not look like an egg, certainly not Tenniel's in *Through the Looking-Glass*. What or who precisely was "Humpty Dumpty"? When I had become a student of theatre history, I found fugitive references to Fox in most histories of the American stage, but they took it for granted that their readers could reconstruct from memory Fox's achievements as a comedian. Or perhaps they chose to evade the difficult task of making what had been hilariously funny in the theatre equally amusing in description. As Max Beerbohm notes in an essay, when Hamlet refers to Yorick setting the table on a roar, he wisely refrains from giving illustrations of the gags the jester used to do it.

But when I launched into an intensive study of Fox, I discovered another reason for this silence. As a private individual he had left very little memorabilia; there were no caches of correspondence, no autobiographical fragments, almost no personal reminiscences of him by others. The specific details of his domestic life and even of his earliest performances had to be laboriously pieced together from all sorts of ephemeral sources. As is so often the case with remarkable performers, the man was less than the sum of his performances, and the performances, although among the greatest of his time, had not been interpretations of scripts and thus would not profit from the kind of analysis the biographer of a Shakespearean tragedian practices.

However, in the course of my research, a curious phenomenon kept recurring. Fox seemed, invariably, to be at the crux of whatever major changes were happening in American life; what he did on the stage often reflected a popular *mentalité*, which helps account for his great success. His career was rooted in the Jacksonian era, when America was developing from a traditional agrarian society to an industrial and capitalist society, eager to accept innovation. Born in New England at a time when theatres were shunned by most respectable citizens, he and his family were largely responsible for giving stage performances a good name and enticing a new audience to them. Laying their stress on moral drama and sentiment, they managed to appeal to both a sedate middle-class public and a new urban proletariat.

On his own, Fox, both as manager and actor, was a man for all seasons. The poster for one of his benefits touts him as "Fox the Candidate, Our Fox, Fox the comedian, Fox the pantomimist, Fox the Irish Comedian, Fox the Yankee Comedian, Fox the Ethiopean Delineator, Fox the nautical performer, Fox the dancer, Fox the great vocalist, Fox the soldier, Fox the stage manager."[9] Amid this plethora of capacities, he distinguished himself by concentrating on pantomime, transforming it from a peripheral foreign import to a native article of high quality and topical relevance. At a time when much legitimate American drama imitated French and English formats, he won enormous popularity by stressing the indigenous humor of his pantomime, making it a not-too-distorting mirror of the values and concerns of his audience. The physical violence of the comedy, its down-to-earth ruthlessness, embodied the conflicts rampant in the growing cities and yet rendered them safely absurd by artistic means. "Humpty Dumpty," the title and leading character of his most successful piece, became the generic term for all such efforts, and the image of Fox in the role entered American folk iconography as the symbol for "clown."

Even in his decline, his career mirrored the macrocosm of American society. Pantomime, which had reached its zenith after the Civil War, during a time of national expansion, succumbed to this very expansionism. It was swamped by the taste for "better and bigger," for "more and more," the vaudeville acts, burlesque, and musical comedy that appealed to a more heterogeneous audience. Having located the spectator's funny bone, Fox was left behind when other portions of audience anatomy demanded attention. The legitimate drama's growing realism could not house his aggressively grotesque comedy, while at the same time the disjunct vaudeville failed to provide the modicum of structure his talent required.

Similarly, Fox's physical and mental breakdown can be attributed in part to his lack of business acumen in an age that worshipped the shrewd operator as a kind of financial frontiersman; in recouping lost fortunes and slaving under crooked contracts for shady managers, Fox was a paradigm of the average American victimized by the trusts and

stock swindles of the Gilded Age. He was all the more average in thinking himself the type of shrewd dealer his times admired, even as he got
entangled in his own sorry attempts to emulate the crooks around him.
He failed most when he was most unscrupulous. While those members
of his family who had "gone legit" by entering politics or management
continued to thrive, he remained the bohemian mummer, instinctively
brilliant on stage but incapable of controlling his fate offstage.

Therefore, I have chosen to title this work "the age and stage" of
George L. Fox. The causes of his phenomenal success and abrupt failure are to be sought not merely in the sparse details of his own life, but
in the broader society to which the theatre makes appeal in its function
as *speculum mundi*. On the face of it, Fox's case might seem the classic
cliché of the clown who makes others laugh while his own heart is
breaking. But if we adjust to a wider focus, we find that his biography is
exemplary in another way, shedding light not only on private vicissitudes
but on public attitudes.

1

On Stage in Boston

(1825-38)

The Boston of 1820, still unincorporated as a city, possessed all the features of an attractive country town. Its narrow houses, never more than two stories high, were trimmed with gardens front and rear. The Common was an untended pasture where cattle grazed behind wooden palings. The town crier, the night watchman, and the ambulant oyster-vendor still patrolled the winding streets, emitting their several calls. The town had become rich from Yankee trading and newly founded factories, but extremes of poverty were also conspicuous. As the population swelled, Boston's resources could not keep up with it, and living conditions were worse than Spartan for those of low incomes. Wells continued to provide drinking water for the forty thousand inhabitants since no plumbing had yet been laid down.[1]

"There was but one theater in Boston at that time," recalled an old inhabitant, "and we had never heard of it. We knew nothing of dramas, and had never witnessed a tableau."[2] The Puritan scorn of amusements was a long time dying in Boston, although towns of comparable size, such as Charleston, New York, and Philadelphia had boasted play-houses for years. It was 1794 before the imposing brick structure of the Boston Theatre, at the corner of Federal and Franklin streets, opened its neoclassical portals. The acting company was English, the repertory genteel, and the attendance sparse. By the season's end, the management had gone bankrupt. This did not prevent the erection of the Haymarket Theater in 1796. The two playhouses competed until the Boston Theatre was destroyed by fire two years later. The Haymarket's victory was Pyrrhic, for it too failed to turn a profit and was demolished in 1803.[3]

The reason for these failures was twofold: inexperience and lack of business acumen on the part of the managers were compounded by a scarcity of theatregoers. Playhouses were regarded by the godly as the devil's chapels, and a respectable family would no more be seen entering one than it would a brothel. Weekdays were given over to labor, and in a town where sabbatarianism was so intense that, for many households, the reading of anything but the Bible on the Lord's Day was thought sacrilegious, weekend amusements were out of the question.

Still, despite these discouraging factors, and over the angry protests of citizens who took the demise of earlier theatrical enterprises to be a sign of divine displeasure, the Boston Theatre was rebuilt by the eminent architect Charles Bulfinch and reopened in 1798. For the next thirty years it maintained its monopoly as the only permanent, well-appointed playhouse in the city. It was to the Federal Street Theatre, as it came to be known, that great tragedians such as Junius Brutus Booth, Edmund Kean, and Edwin Forrest played in the works of Shakespeare and lesser but equally admissible dramatists.

This was the Boston to which Emily Cecilia Wyatt, a woman of twenty, came upon marrying George Howe Fox of Mendon on 10 March 1824.[4] She hadn't far to come, being a native of Westboro, Massachusetts, where her parents, Lott and Martha Forbes Wyatt, continued to reside with Emily's three sisters and one brother. One of Emily's children, who much later became the mayor of Cambridge, took the trouble to inquire into his family's antecedents. The Forbes connection was Scottish and would be represented in Massachusetts after their emigration by a state congressman and a chief justice of the Superior Court. As for the Foxes, they could be traced back to a strain in Lincolnshire, and numbered among their illustrious forebears the author of *The Acts and Boke of Martyres*. Such, at any rate, was the genealogy provided when a politician went seeking a prestigious lineage.[5]

George and Emily Fox were living on Hanover Street when their first child was born on 3 July 1825. According to the family Bible, he was christened George Lafayette, but his full appellation was George Washington Lafayette, a suitably patriotic set of surnames for someone born, like George M. Cohan, on the day before the Fourth of July. No member of his family ever called him by these given names; he was simply known as "Laff," the *a* pronounced in the broad Boston manner.[6]

That same year had seen a reversion of bad feeling toward the Federal Street Theatre, stimulated by the riots following Edmund Kean's second appearance or rather, non-appearance, there. It had been suffering, too, from a paucity of public, whose need for recreation could now be slaked by lectures and other entertainments that were not so questionable morally. For, like most early nineteenth century playhouses, the Federal Street had a separate entrance for prostitutes who plied their trade in the boxes.[7] Assignations and the alcohol sold at the bars provided supplements to the box office, but they helped keep the god-fearing away. A sharp rift developed between the theatre's proprietors and its managers. The actor William Pelby, piqued that his demand for a salary raise had not been met, rallied his friends round and established a rival playhouse.

When the new competitor, the Tremont Theatre, opened on 24 December 1826, the Federal Street responded by recruiting English stars; the Tremont company was deliberately composed of the native born. Two years of intense rivalry ensued, featuring "prize poems, free tickets, balloon ascensions, extravagant orchestras, humorous ads" as lures;[8] the concomitant costs resulted in exhaustion. Boston could not support two theatres, and so the proprietors of the establishments reached a compromise: "The Federal Street retired in favor of the younger rival, which leased the old historic building—and kept it closed."[9]

The ascendancy of the Tremont over its rival could be attributed more to its novelty and elegance than to any substantial superiority. Its first and second tiers of boxes seated no more than 264 persons, producing hardly enough income to cover expenses. It was, however, the first Boston theatre to install gas lighting (in 1832); its orchestra was excellent and its accommodations for actors unusually luxurious, with two greenrooms, one for leading players and another for the rank and file. It also provided what was known as a "nigger heaven," a gallery to which blacks were admitted for fifty cents. But for some reason, perhaps its opulent interior, the theater was regarded strictly as the resort of wealth and fashion and never caught on with the common people.[10]

The history of the Tremont and that of the Foxes are closely interconnected, for during this period George H. Fox became a stage carpenter there and his wife joined in some capacity as well, probably wardrobe-mistress-*cum*-walking-gentlewoman.[11] Two incomes helped support a growing family. Emily's father and her younger sister Martha Cordelia had died shortly after the birth of little Laff, and it is likely that her mother and brother George moved from Westboro to join the Foxes in Boston. Emily's other surviving sister, Susan, had married Lemuel G. Aiken in 1826, and their sons George and Frank were to become close friends and associates of the Fox children. For Laff now had a number of siblings: James Augustus (born 11 August 1827), Caroline Emily (born 10 March 1829) and Mary Ann (born and died in 1830).[12]

One of the best ways to supplement the slender wages of the parents was to put the children on the stage. The early 1830s was the great period for child prodigies in the American theatre; Master Burke the "Irish Roscius," Miss and Master Russell, Master Baker, Clara Fisher Maeder, and Louisa Lane all exploited their precocity to financial advantage. Later came Master Hughes, "The Welsh Paganini," his violin accompanied by four child harpists and an accordionist; Master and Mrs. Booth, two midgets who passed themselves off as children in *Richard III;* and the moppets Kate and Ellen Bateman who thrilled audiences as Gloster battling Richmond, Portia pleading with Shylock, and Macbeth conspiring with his lady. Modern historians have exclaimed at this taste for miniature thespians, but our own society whose pedophilia battens on a black dwarf impersonating a child on a T.V. sitcom and a popular musical about orphaned waifs is in no position to assert superior taste.

The popularity of these *Wunderkinder* in the early republic was, in fact, a sign of the infiltration of Puritanism by a romantic view of the child. The gloomy doctrine of original sin, promulgated in the opening verses of the earliest colonial primers—"In Adam's fall / We sinned all"—had regarded children as limbs of Satan, to be straightened and pruned into responsible Christians through privation, self-control, and corporal punishment. Even innocent frolics like skipping and jumping had been condemned as evidence of a wanton nature.

But Rousseau's belief that childhood was the period most closely corresponding to an innocent "state of Nature" had begun to take hold in many American minds by the early nineteenth century. Moral education was no longer intended to amend a child's non-existent innate corruption but to develop discipline through common sense and "natural wisdom," to preserve as long as possible the child's wholesome unspoilt impulses. With industrialization, the adult world took on an even more sordid appearance, and children, particularly girls, were respected as embodiments of innocent, unsullied morality.[13]

Juvenile stars like the Bateman sisters thus benefited from both the old tradition and the new conception. On stage they behaved like the miniature adults that the seventeenth and eighteenth centuries had approved, and yet, by their infantile naturalness, purified the stage of its corrupting influence. They were performers who commanded high salaries. A child used simply to swell a progress or dress forth a scene, on the other hand, was paid only twenty-five cents a week at the Tremont.[14]

According to T. Allston Brown, Laff Fox first appeared on stage at age five in *The Hunter of the Alps* at a benefit for Charles Kean,[15] though the earliest playbill from the Tremont to cite a member of the Fox-Aiken clan is for a 26 March 1832 performance of *Cinderella,* with one

"Aikin" appearing among the fairies. Possibly this was two-year-old cousin George. Laff did not lag behind, for on 19 September the cast list of *102 or The Veteran and his Progeny* includes "Theodore, Master Fox." On 14 December, the seven-year-old boy showed up again as a page in the train of King Lear, as portrayed by Junius Brutus Booth.[16]

It is ironic that Laff Fox, whose last year on stage would be tainted by madness, should begin his career under a tragedian whose erratic behavior became a byword. Booth had first exhibited symptoms of derangement in public at the Tremont in December 1829. As Ludovico in *Evadne*, he had startled a packed house by his negligence and lack of preparation. In the third act he turned to the audience, explaining that he did not know his lines and would either read the rest of the part or have the prompter do so. This evoked a wave of hissing and booing, met by Booth with a broad grin that broke into an open laugh. He had to be led off the stage, as he cried, "I can't read—I am a charity boy; I can't read. Take me to the Lunatic Hospital!"[17] No such outburst, however, seems to have marred his Lear two years later.

Laff's rapid acclimation to the stage led his parents to launch another child, and on 13 February 1833, little Caroline appeared as Annette in *The Stranger.* From this point on, Laff and Caddie (as the girl was known) showed up regularly in the Tremont playbills as Master and Miss Fox, with an occasional stint at the Warren Theatre, remodelled in 1832 from an equestrian amphitheatre. They were used in tragedy, comedy, and farce with both the stock company and the touring stars.

A major event in Boston theatrical history occurred in May 1833, when the English tragedian Charles Kemble and his daughter Frances came to the Tremont. Fanny Kemble reported in her journal that Boston audiences were "upon the whole, cold—very still and attentive, however, and when they do warm it is certainly very effectually, for they shout and hurrah like mad."[18] She had nothing but praise for the acting company, "the very prettiest collection of actresses I ever saw" and the strongest actors "I played with *any where* outside of London . . . the ladies and gentlemen of the Tremont theatre . . . do not seem to despise their work, and it is, generally speaking, well done therefore. Our pieces were all remarkably well got up there; and the green-room is both respectable and agreeable."[19] The Kembles's arrival caused a run on the box-office, and Fanny, watching the crush from a window in the Tremont House across the street, was bemused by the tactics of the ticket-scalpers.

I was surprised to see men of a very low order pressing foremost to obtain boxes, but I find that they sell them again at an enormous increase to others who have not been able to obtain any; and the better to carry on their traffic, these worthies smear their clothes with molasses, and sugar, &c., in order to prevent any person of more decent appearance, or whose clothes are worth a cent, from coming near the box office: this is ingenious, and deserves a reward.[20]

On this first Boston run, Laff and Caroline did not appear with the Kembles, but in *Mr. & Mrs. Pringle*, the afterpiece to *Macbeth*, one reads the names of Billy Robinson (Master Fox) and Tommy Robinson (J. Fox), indicating that five-and-a-half-year-old James Augustus had been recruited. There is also a family legend that when Fanny Kemble's cue came as Lady Macbeth, she handed her shawl to Emily Fox in the wings; pregnant Emily, encumbered by the shawl, hung it on a nail projecting from a flat and forgot it. After a scene-change, Lady Macbeth came to retrieve her property; Emily reached up only to find that it and the flat had been flown into place. Center stage, in full view of the audience, the colorful Indian shawl was dangling from the corner of a painted cloud.[21]

This contretemps sealed a growing affection between the English stars and the Boston clan, for when Emily gave birth to a baby boy on 15 August, she named him Charles Kemble Mason Fox. The Kembles returned to the Tremont in September and enlisted Caddie to play the child in Kotzebue's *The Stranger*, at which time the box office took in the extraordinary sums of $634.75 and $942.75.[22] Laff was charged with the responsible role of Donalbain when the Kembles revived *Macbeth*, and his Shakespearean roster was enlarged the next month when he first appeared as the Duke of York to C. H. Eaton's *Richard III*. This part was to be Laff's exclusive property for some years; from 1833 to 1837 he was periodically murdered at the behest of Eaton, W. C. Forbes, Junius Brutus Booth, and even Mrs. Henry Lewis.

Backstage, the Kembles would toss Caddie back and forth like a ball, and "all three would get in gales of laughter." Fanny presented the child with some of her stage jewelry, telling her to wear it when she became a grown-up actress, an injunction that Caddie faithfully carried out in later years.[23]

The impact of the Kembles had barely sunk in when the impressive bulk of Edwin Forrest towered over the Fox children. Acknowledged by this time to be the preeminent American-born tragedian, he appeared in his repertory at the Tremont in November 1833, and the Foxes were employed in almost every play. Laff assumed the boys in *The Gladiator* and *The Ancient Briton*, and Donalbain again, this time with his lines cut; while Caddie was seen and occasionally heard as Page to Goneril in *King Lear*, Child in *Metamora*, a singing witch in *Macbeth*, and Damon's son, a part with several lines, in *Damon and Pythias*.[24] Once again, family lore preserves an anecdote of this engagement. Forrest is recalled to have come across little Caddie at the tender age of four-and-a-half strutting before the greenroom mirror.

"What's the little Fox trying to be?"

"A gate bid actress wid a long train." (The baby-talk is a transcription from the Howard family tradition.)

"Indeed?" Forrest pulled out a capacious bandanna handkerchief and draped it on her as a train. "There now, give us an imitation of Fanny Kemble." And he taught her to lisp, "Out, damned spot!" On another occasion the child was pouting, and when Forrest inquired what ailed "Fanny Kemble," Caddie replied, "Mama won't buy me a 'mate-up' box." Whereupon the generous tragedian handed her ten dollars to procure the coveted piece of professional equipment.[25]

While they earned their living on stage, the Foxes had not neglected their education. Boston had one of the best public school systems in the new republic; basic literacy was taught in primary schools to four-to-seven-year olds, before the child moved up to more intensive grammar schools. Any child admitted to school had to have a certificate of vaccination,[26] so we may assume the Fox boys had undergone that trial. Laff and James attended the Mayhew School on Hawkins Street, which had 364 scholars under two principals, two ushers and two female attendants. The pupils were not coddled; each room was heated by a grated coal fireplace near the door and a cast-iron stove at the other end of the room, but there were no washrooms or ventilation, and infrequent recesses. The more advanced curriculum included English prose and poetry, penmanship, arithmetic, ancient and modern history, English grammar and composition, and rhetoric, with optional studies in natural philosophy, geometry, algebra, and natural sciences.[27]

The textbooks were an improvement over early primers. They had been prepared by the Reverend John Pierpont, who emphasized the inclusion of American authors such as Irving, Bryant, Patrick Henry, Jefferson, and Webster. Despite his clerical vocation, Pierpont (a grandfather of J. P. Morgan) was stage-struck. He had pseudonymously and with great mystery written the prize poem for the opening of the Tremont and would later be a motivating force in the success of the theatre known as the Boston Museum.[28]

The faculty was, to put it mildly, Dickensian. The reading-master, Parker, was slim, bespectacled, and a severe executant of the rattan cane, the writing-master, Holt, a thickset, brutal wielder of the cowhide. But the ushers were known to be gentle and patient, willing to train candidates in declamation for the Franklin medals handed out on examination day.[29] The Fox boys might have had an insider's edge in recitation, but no record of any academic awards has survived.

Book-learning did not seem to "take" with Laff; in later life, he seldom penned a line if he could help it and had no sense of numbers. Brother James, on the other hand, must have shown diligence and promise, for he continued his studies at the classical school of Amos Baker, near the Old South Chapel in Spring Lane, where he acquired little Latin and less Greek.[30] The contrast between the tedious academic routines by day, and the gas-lit excitement and backstage magic by night must have struck the Fox boys and made adjustment to the classroom even more difficult than usual.

Although they were histrionic veterans at an early age, they were probably as much enthralled as the rest of Boston by the arrival of the Ravel family. The old Boston Theatre had featured spectacular pantomimes, rope-dancers, and acrobatic entertainments over the years,[31] and the Tremont had followed suit with occasional offerings such as "the laughable Pantomime, called the Imaginary Sick Man, or Harlequin Dead or Alive" and *The Pastry Cook of Madrid or Harlequin Deserter.*[32] Ordinarily, these were presented as afterpieces to a more sober bill. The ten-person Ravel troupe, which made its first appearance in Boston on 6 November 1832,[33] was a self-contained unit. It had built upon the *ballets-pantomimes* of Charles Mazurier, an amalgam of fairy-tale spectacle and melodrama that it popularized by coarsening the comedy and adding spectacular feats of acrobatic skill. After a successful career in France, the Ravels had arrived in New York during the cholera epidemic, and yet so great was their acclaim that fear of contagion could not keep the crowds from cramming the Park Theatre, attracted by the novelty of the presentation and the finesse of the performers.[34]

In Boston they became immediate favorites, the *Atlas* reporting:

The feats of this family at the Tremont Theatre are truly surprising. Having always had an aversion to Circus exhibitions, it was with no little regret that we heard of their engagement at this fashionable theatre. Our regret was changed, however, to feelings of a very different character on witnessing their performances.[35]

Expecting the rough-and-tumble of the circus ring, the critics were taken unaware by the Gallic polish of the Ravels and the intricacy of their stunts, which seemed incredible. Much of their precision derived from the self-sufficiency of the inter-married troupe, in the tradition of the great fairground dynasties of Europe. They had no need to recruit unskilled extras or members of a resident stock company to assist in their shows. Moreover, "the legitimate drama is very often a bore, and the Ravels pantomimes never are."[36]

The managers of the Tremont were quite unprepared for the enthusiastic welcome given the Ravels, and, to accommodate the demand, re-opened the Federal Street Theatre on 13 November. The Ravels played alternately at both theatres until 5 December, when they followed Charles Kean as King John at the Tremont. The Boston engagement was longer than any they had yet enjoyed in America and initiated a long-standing love affair between them and the Boston public.[37]

The Ravels customarily began their runs with simple exhibitions of their prowess and gradually proceeded to more elaborate and ambitious pantomimes. Their earliest Boston performance began with dances and exercises with the balance-pole, an *allemande* and *pas de deux* danced by Jean and Madame Ravel upon two parallel cords, and a pantomime ballet, *The Invisible Harlequin*. Later in the run, the Infant Ravels, aged three and four, played *The Conscript and the Soldier*, Jean Ravel demonstrated Herculean feats and academical postures, and a "mimic and plastic tableau illuminated by Gregorian fire," *The Death of Abel or The First Fratricide*, involving Dominique Ravel as Cain, Jérôme Ravel as Abel, Antoine Ravel as Adam, and Madame Ravel as Eve.[38]

However, it was the extended pantomimic ballets, usually featuring the comic graces of young Gabriel, that captivated the spectators' imagination. In *Le Carnaval de Venise*, he staggered them as Polichinelle with a drunk scene on stilts, outdoing the limber mime and dancer, Charles Mazurier, according to French reports. In *Monsieur Molinet or A Night of Adventures*, adapted from a ballet of J. B. Blache, Gabriel's character, Vol-au-Vent, in a white costume and red wig, performed a complicated stunt on the *barre cerrique*, propelling a primitive pogo stick around the stage in minuscule circles. Another adaptation from Blache, *Godenski or The Skaters of Wilna*, began with mimed slapstick.

The scene took place in a Russian inn where Godenski liked the innkeeper's daughter. When the clumsy Godenski enters the scene, he causes general mayhem; he plants his hunting gun down on the toes of Katrin, the mother of his beloved; the gun accidentally goes off, his cigar explodes and breaks a window. To get [him] out of the way, Godenski is thrust into a chicken coop. When he is finally let out, he discovers that Lodoiska, his beloved, is going to wed another fellow named Lowenski. In despair, he tears his hair out, and when he looks into the mirror and sees only his bare skull, frantically tries to put it back on.[39]

Godenski concludes with an ice-skating scene of comic falls and tumbles into frigid water; it introduced "parlour" skates (roller skates disguised as ice-skates) to an American audience seventeen years before Dutchmen glided across the stage of the Paris Opéra in Meyerbeer's *Le Prophète*. The Fox boys no doubt revelled in these antics,

Figure 1. The Ravel family in their pantomimic farce about conscription, *Jeannette and Jeannot.* A wood engraving from *Gleason's Pictorial*, 9 August 1851. Malingering peasants are forced to join up despite their acrobatic stratagems. (Courtesy Harvard Theatre Collection)

tried to imitate them, and stored away the slapstick in their impressionable minds.

It is worth dilating on these early appearances of the Ravels in Boston because, throughout Laff Fox's stage career, he imitated, learned from, and was regularly compared with Gabriel Ravel. Nowhere else could he have observed the overwhelming effect of silent physical comedy in reducing a large audience to helpless laughter. Much of Fox's talent was later directed toward absorbing and overcoming the Ravel influence and devising for himself an individual technique that was purely American.

The Ravels had one other material effect on the life of the Foxes. When the managers of the Tremont Theatre, where George H. Fox was property man, reopened the Federal Street Theatre, they charged him with the same function there and allowed him to move his family onto the premises.[40] The entrance to their living quarters was on Theatre Alley, a no-thoroughfare 343 feet deep on land belonging to the theatre. The Boston City Directory for 1834 lists George H. Fox at that address, one of the few contemporary allusions to his shadowy existence. His name is preserved in the records of the theatre only by an undated receipt:

> The Proprietors of the Federal Theatre, Dr
> to Fox & Duffey
> to Painting fence Front of Theatre $2.00
> Rec'd payment   Fox & Duffey[41]

The walk to the Mayhew School was several blocks longer than it had been from Hanover Street, but in recompense the Fox children and their Aiken cousins had free run of the stage all day long.[42] And they were only a few steps from "Marm" Dunlap's shop. Grace Dunlap sold snuff and confectionary in her eating-house adjacent to the stage-door in Theatre Alley and was a household word to members of the profession from 1830 to 1866. "During that period there were few Boston boys, who had not reveled in Marm Dunlap's gingerbread."[43] Living in such proximity, the Fox brothers must have been regular customers.

The Fox children carried on as attendant sprites and miscellaneous progeny at the theatres, but as one peruses the bills, it becomes apparent that Caddie was in greater demand than Laff, and her roles were more variegated. They included daughter Gertrude to James Hackett's Rip Van Winkle, a housemaid in *Love in a Village*, a peasant in *Der Freischütz*, Cora's child in *Pizarro*, and Mrs. Stanley in *The Wreck Ashore*.

Confronted with competition, the Tremont began increasingly to lean away from legitimate drama toward popular entertainment, reducing its prices in the process. When it attempted an English pantomime on 13 January 1834, Laff made his panto debut as Glowglisten, Herald of the Moon, while his mother appeared as Glimmer, Herald of the Dog Star. Another sibling came before the footlights on 31 December 1834, when Charles Mathews, Sr., the English mimic and protean comedian, on his last voyage to America, starred in *The May Queen*. His sons were impersonated by Master L. Fox and Master A. Fox, with Caroline as his daughter. Since Laff was billed by his middle initial, A. Fox may be James Augustus, whose appearances were becoming more frequent. James later stated he too had played the Boy to Edwin Forrest's Rolla in *Pizarro*.[44] But it was Wallack, not Forrest, who starred in that play during the 1834/35 season at the Tremont, with Laff regularly appearing as the manhandled child.[45] James also remembered appearing in *The Children of the Wood* and may very well be the Master Fox listed in that play on 7 November 1834, with Caddie typecast as his sister.

Caddie was procuring individual engagements as well, as her skill as a dancer improved. In the summer of 1835 she was a member of a stock company of twelve in Portland, Maine. Her parents must have realized that if the children could be trained to perform specialties they would become independent of the standard repertories of the theatres. Consequently, at the Warren Theatre on 12 May 1835, Dumas's melodrama *The Tower of Nesle* was followed by "a PAS DE TROIS FROM GOODY TWO SHOES BY THE THREE FOXES" along with a *pas de deux* by Miss Fox [*sic*]. Caddie's success earned her a New York debut, on 10 July, at Mrs. Hamblin's Franklin Theatre, following *Richard III* as Little Red Riding Hood.[46]

Yet another Boston playhouse took advantage of the talents of the little Foxes; the Lion Theatre, opened by William Barrymore on 11 January 1836. In February and April, Caroline made frequent appearances there, and at her benefit performance on 14 April teamed with Laff and James in a dance of the Coriphee [*sic*]. Then, when the Warren Theatre changed its name to the National and opened its freshly gas-lit premises on 15 August, sure enough, Caddie was displaying her terpsichorean abilities in the company of an Angelica Fox unknown to the family archives (but who had also appeared at the Franklin Theatre debut as the Duke of York). Perhaps other juvenile performers temporarily adopted the name, since sister acts were more attractive than nondescript duos. Her brothers joined Caddie at the National on 19 December for a *pas de trois* in the masked ball scene of Scribe's *Gustave III* (the basis for Verdi's *Ballo in maschera*).

One last Fox had come to swell the ranks: Henry Nelson, born on 27 September 1836. With another mouth to feed, the Foxes departed from their routine schedule and launched into an enterprise that would set the style for their later excursions. They took part in the Lion Theatre's touring company of ten men and four women, which was the first theatrical troupe to appear in New Bedford, Massachusetts. New Bedford was a Quaker town and had no proper playhouse, so the performances had to be given in a circus building. The New Bedford *Mercury* announced that a Master Fox would dance a "Sailor's Hornpipe" between the plays and, on 17 April, it informed the public of "Miss C. Fox's benefit and positively her last appearance . . . a grand double hornpipe in the character of Miss Caroline and Master Fox . . . Grand Scotch Dance of Miss C. Fox to conclude with burletta of Tom Thumb."[47] It was James who stooged for his starring sister on this foray. Laff, in the tertiary role of Donalbain, continued in Boston to support such English Macbeths as J. K. Field, Thomas Barry (with Charlotte Cushman as his lady), and George Vandenhoff. He was storing up material for his later parodies of the thane. He also played the Count's child to the English star Ellen Tree's Mrs. Haller in *The Stranger*, from Kotzebue.

By 1838 Caddie had moved almost exclusively to the National The-

atre, where she danced, played fairies or other minor parts, and garnered considerable acclaim as a special turn. At a Juvenile Gala night
on 12 April for her own benefit and that of Miss F. Jones, another infant
phenomenon, she displayed her versatility as Distaffina in an all-tot
burlesque, *Bombastes Furioso* (with James as General Bombastes and
Laff as Artaxomines), young Norval in acts 4 and 5 of the tragedy
Douglas, and Little Pickle in the farce *The Spoiled Child*. There was no
question who the star was in the Fox family.

2

The Little Foxes

(1838-46)

Laff was eclipsed on stage not only by his sister but, in 1838, by his younger brother James, his mother's pet.[1] The older boy was growing up gawky and losing those dimpled contours that constitute cuteness. The twenty-five-cent pieces that he could earn on stage were insufficient in a time of economic depression, for Boston, like the rest of the nation, was short of cash, in the wake of the Panic of 1837.

The money problem had begun when President Jackson, to end the runaway speculation in public lands, had issued his "Specie Circular" in July 1836, directing land agents to accept payment only in gold and silver. Slaves, soap, railroad tickets, bank shares, and even shoes, whose prices had been set in imaginary paper currency, were brought down in value by the Panic, although the worldwide depression was only tangentially related to Jackson's decree. Three English banks with large American holdings had failed; the subsequent collapse of Lancashire cotton mills caused a drop in cotton prices and, in true domino fashion, New Orleans firms caved in. The Midwestern wheat crop had been poor for two years running, disenabling farmers from repaying the merchants who had made them cash advances. Factories in the east were compelled to lay off workers for want of customers, and by September 1837 they had all shut down. Every bank in the U.S. suspended specie payment, and 618 of them failed.[2]

Among those stricken were the banks of Boston. Provisions in the

Commonwealth became very dear, with flour at the unheard-of price of $15.00 a barrel.[3] An extant account book of the Fox family for 1840 has them running up a weekly grocery bill of $22.52, expended chiefly on such New England staples as salt-fish and salt-pork, but also on a surprising quantity of chocolate, raisins, and currants, no doubt to prepare those heavy fruitcakes that had long been part of Massachusetts's British heritage. "Nowhere is the stomach of the traveller or visitor put in such constant peril as among the cake-inventive housewives and daughters of New England," Charles Joseph Latrobe had warned in 1836.[4] Emily Fox was no exception to the rule of homemakers.

To keep such regional fare on the Fox table, Laff was taken out of school and made errand-boy for a department store, and then a clerk for Charles A. Smith, merchant tailor at 12 Washington Street, a post he held for about seven years.[5] In 1835, the Federal Street Theatre had been sold, over the protests of the actors, to become a place-of-worship-*cum*-lecture-room, under the name of the Odeon. Most likely the Foxes were evicted at this time, and the need to pay a regular rent contributed to the necessity of Laff's extra-theatrical earnings. His mother may have also been forced to take in lodgers. When John Gough, later a world-renowned temperance lecturer, was acting in low comedy parts at the Lion Theatre in 1837, he lodged with a Mrs. Fox and when he was unemployed, she offered him room and board gratis until he could obtain work.[6]

With Laff's withdrawal to the world of commerce, the Little Foxes meant Caddie and James, who appeared regularly at the Tremont and National Theatres through 1838, occasionally accompanied by their uncle George Wyatt. James had inherited his brother's repertory of legitimate roles at the Tremont and he, not Laff, played the son to Forrest's Spartacus in *The Gladiator* by Robert Montgomery Bird, Donalbain to Charles Kean's Macbeth and the Boy to "Yankee" Hill's *Yankee in Spain* in the 1839/40 season.[7] Although these activities continued through 1842, the siblings' identity as a variety team grew steadily. The reason is not far to seek. Their innocence was at a premium at a time when the anti-theatrical prejudice had been fortified by the nation-wide upsurge of Evangelical Protestantism that produced the Sunday School movement.[8]

The influential minister Lyman Beecher regularly railed against playhouses, vowing to extirpate every last one in Boston, and his daughter Harriet Stowe feared that "if the barrier which now keeps young people of religious families from theatrical entertainments is once broken down by the introduction of respectable and moral plays, they will then be open to all the temptations of those which are not such."[9] The sanctification of the Federal Street Theatre as the Odeon was a sign of the times, and although Mrs. Fox's boarder, Gough, had made his stage debut in 1837 as the keeper of a temperance house in *The Departed Spirits, or The Temperance Hoax*, a play in which Beecher and his ilk were ridiculed,[10] such shafts were ineffectual against the serried ranks of evangelism.

After the Panic of 1837, theatrophobic ministers took heart, mistakenly assuming that the drop in box-office receipts corresponded to a spiritual awakening, when it simply reflected a decline in private incomes.[11] Yet families who would not cross the threshold of a playhouse had fewer compunctions about attending a mixed bill of songs and recitations, performed in a nondescript hall by children. The tender age of the performers guaranteed the moral immaculateness of the entertainment.

By 1840, eleven-year-old Caddie was being billed as "The Juvenile Prodigy!" and brother James, her elder by two years, as "The Young American Drollerist." She performed the dances, he the comic monologues and impersonations, and together they sang duets and recited dialogues. A typical programme of this period reads:

DUET: The Two Lovers
Song, Charming Woman
Comic Song, Gawkey Shanks.
Grand Scarf Dance.
The Faithless Fair One.
Wooden Shoe Dance.
Lubin & Louise
Humorous Double Dance.
Comic Dialogue.
Funny Duett.
Comic Song "The Little Dutchman."
The Scotch Strathspey.
Recitation: Napoleon's Campaign to Moscow:
But oh! what conflagration gleamed,
When wrapt in flames, fair Moscow seemed
One awful sea of living fire
That levelled every lofty spire.
Dance: The Little Corporal with the manual exercise[12]

On occasion, they presented a Quaker dialogue of Ephraim and Ruth singing "Dost thou love me, Sister Ruth." The usual charge for their performances was twenty-five cents, with half prices for children.

Wyzeman Marshall, sensing the need for amusements in the summer when Boston theatres were closed, opened Boylston Hall as the Vaudeville Saloon in July 1840, and the Fox Children were on the very first bill, playing primarily to tourists.[13] That same summer they travelled to Maine, appearing in Portland, Waldborough, and Belfast, probably chaperoned by their mother. A law of 1806 had still prohibited the building of any house in Portland for theatrical exhibitions, under threat of a heavy fine, when a Mr. Powell, the Bostonian manager of a regular summer company, had tried to erect a permanent theatre in the western section of town. In 1820, he had fitted up Union Hall in the middle of the commercial district as a playhouse, and public opinion had prevented the 1806 law from coming into force. It was at Union Hall that the Fox children played. The local newspapers considered the advent of the Foxes of sufficient importance to warrant detailed coverage that stressed the respectability of the spectators and the "splendor" of the exhibition. Caddie was especially cited for the elegance of her dancing, and the Waldboro' *Patriot* assured its readers with more enthusiasm than syntax that her Highland Fling "would do credit to the most experienced actor, as also the Sailors Hornpipe . . . conducted with the utmost decorum, and the most fastidious could feel no compunction of conscience by sitting through an exhibit of this kind."[14]

Unbeknownst to her, Caddie had attracted an admirer during her earlier visit to New Bedford in 1837, when she had acted with her brother and mother in the Lion Theatre troupe. A young Canadian actor had been passing through at the time, and when he joined the Tremont Theatre for the 1842/43 season he renewed his acquaintance with the adolescent danseuse. George Howard Cunnabell had been born in Halifax, Nova Scotia on 6 September 1815.[15] Boston had seen him first as an amateur with the Hawley Street Thespians in 1836, when he assumed Lord Randolph and Norval in *Douglas* and Wilford in *The Iron Chest*, juvenile leads on which most aspiring actors of the period cut their teeth. The next year he was at Julian Hall, at the corner of Congress and Milk streets, emoting his way through Jaffier in *Venice Preserved*, Frank Hardy in *Paul Pry*, and similar "first lovers." Because he realized that his name left him open to bad puns (later, even serious sources give it as "Cannibel"), and because his family was chagrined by his choice of profession, the young actor billed himself as George C. Howard, adopting his maternal grandmother's name. Eventually he made the alteration legal.[16]

Most of Howard's earliest professional engagements were as a walking gentleman in Philadelphia (Old Chestnut St. Theatre, 1838–42; Arch St. and Burton's, 1841; Walnut St., 1842; McAron's Garden, 1842) and Baltimore (Museum, 1839; Holiday St. Theatre 1841/42), with a summer stint in Portland in 1842.[17] These appearances are worth enumerating because Howard's early career is hopelessly garbled in most biographical sources; Claire McGlinchee's *First Decade of the*

Boston Museum compounds the error by confusing him with the English actor Charles Howard, who also came to the Tremont in 1843, attributing to George Cunnibell appearances in London and New York that he never made.[18]

The word that recurs throughout reviews of George Howard's acting and memoirs of his private life is "gentlemanly." That trait is to be found in the earliest notice we have of him, a critique of his performance in *Cinderella* at the Baltimore Museum: "Mr. Howard is a young man whose merits cannot but be appreciated; in the first place, he is handsome; secondly, he comprehends the author; and in the third, knows his part and performs it with care and judgement."[19] What must the run-of-the-mill actor have been like if Howard was praised for knowing his part and understanding his lines? Many years later, in a eulogy, his sister-in-law Mary Hewins recalled that "He was courteous and kindly to all he met, but not a man to be intimate with anyone."[20] At a time when actors fulfilled only too well the caricatures of bombastic Crummleses and alcoholic bohemians, George C. Howard's gentility and sweet tenor voice were appealing and marketable.

His sister-in-law also recollects that "Caroline Fox and George Howard were lovers at first sight." This *coup de foudre* may have struck in New Bedford in 1837, but more likely took place when Howard joined the Tremont in 1842 to play Sir Charles Crosland in *The Poor Gentleman*. At that time he was a fresh-looking twenty-seven and she a demure thirteen. He seems to have made very little impression as an actor, but definitely knew his business; his starting salary was $8.00 a week, and by the time the theatre closed the next year he had made $251.95.[21] Whereas his namesake Charles Howard was frequently absent, imperfect in his part, sick (for which read drunk), and consequently often cited in the Forfait [*sic*] Book kept by the stage manager, George Howard appears there only twice: once to replace Charles Howard as Jim Jib in *The Battle of Lake Erie*, because on the previous evening the English actor had been hit by a wing-piece, and once on account of an absence from the crowd scene finale of *Paris in London*, "notwithstanding a notice put in the Glass case requesting every Lady and Gentleman to be on in Dominoes and Masks."[22] The Forfait Book also reveals that during a performance of *King Henry IV*, the property man could not be found to clear the scene, causing a considerable stage wait at the start of act 3.[23] Was George Howe Fox growing remiss in his duties as his children took over as the family breadwinners?

The Tremont had fallen on evil days. Despite the hefty admission fees of one dollar for boxes, seventy-five cents for the third tier, fifty cents for the pit, and twenty-five cents for the gallery,[24] the limited seating prevented expenses from being met even when houses were crowded.

The third tier had been closed to prostitutes in the hope of appeasing censure of the theatre, but that had resulted only in reducing the audience. During his seven-year management, Thomas Barry had assiduously tried to promote legitimate drama, but his importation of stars entailed extraordinary expenses, and the practice of ticket-scalping further reduced his takings. Moreover, the city fathers had limited the use of the theatre's bars so much that concessionaires' rentals fell from twenty-five hundred to one thousand dollars. Following the 1837 Panic, reported the theatre's directors, "the theatrical business in Boston . . . has been, and still is, in a state of extraordinary depression."[25]

On 23 June 1843, the final performance was given at the Tremont Theatre. The building had been sold for fifty-five hundred dollars to the Baptists and became the Tremont Temple. The gloating among the godly was gruesome to behold. When another theatre had burned down, Lyman Beecher had commented, "Another gateway to Hell has been destroyed by the direct intervention of Providence"; of the Tremont, he had boasted, "I shall preach there yet."[26] At the Temple's opening service, the Rev. Nathaniel Colver intoned

> *Satan has here held empire long—*
> *A blighting curse—a cruel reign—*
> *By mimic scenes, and mirth and song,*
> *Alluring souls to endless pain.*[27]

It was a harrowing indictment of the fairy dances and comic skits whereby the Little Foxes had unknowingly lured their fellow Bostonians to damnation. In a short space, the new tenants had vandalized the elegant neoclassic façade by renting it out for shops, and the auditorium was soon leased by the week to mesmerists and blackface minstrels.

The dispossessed Foxes had, as "The Juveniles," enjoyed a benefit at the Boston Museum on 8 April, which marked the debut of yet another cub, Henry, youngest of the siblings. He obliged with a Sailor's Hornpipe, James delivered a lecture on animal magnetism, operating upon two "Graham-fed subjects," and both joined Caroline in an Irish lilt. Unlike many theatrical satirists, James Fox was relatively up-to-date in his spoofs of Grahamism and animal magnetism. Or, more correctly, the towns to which he would take his comedy were just catching up with the latest fads and were ripe to appreciate the gibes.

Sylvester Graham, a Presbyterian minister and temperance lecturer, had reached the height of his fame in 1835–36 for preaching the gospel of dietary reform. He advocated hard mattresses, open bedroom windows, cold showers, looser clothing, daily exercise, and cheerfulness at mealtimes. Such tenets in themselves would not attract mockery, but his nutritional program was crankier. Graham prohibited condiments, fats, gravies, seafood, and unfiltered water, and strongly advocated the use of unbolted whole wheat flour. This last precept caused a bakers's riot in Boston when the Marlborough Hotel, where Graham was urging housewives to do their own baking and boycott public bakeries, was mobbed. His followers rescued "the poet of bran bread and pumpkins," as Emerson uncharitably called him, by pouring unslaked lime on the heads of the rioters. Graham moved to Northampton, leaving only the Graham cracker in his wake.[28]

As for animal magnetism, it enjoyed a revival in the early nineteenth century and was particularly popular in the 1840s. Dr. J. Rodes Buchanan, a "phrenological cartographer," promulgated in 1843 a theory of nerve-aura organs as a connecting link between will and consciousness. The Reverend La Roy Sunderland, who had begun his career as a revivalist preacher at the age of eighteen, published a magazine, *The Magnet*, in 1842 to expound his phreno-mesmerical discoveries, which included no less than 150 new phrenological organs, and his theory of pathetism, based on a "universal law of nature," which he claimed was instrumental in curing a score of ailments from tic douloureux to blindness.

The New Hampshire clockmaker Phineas Parkhurst Quimby had also experimented with animal magnetism, practising a laying-on of hands. He soon turned to faith healing, his most illustrious patient being Mary Baker Eddy. At the time, however, a more influential quack was Andrew Jackson Davis, a cobbler known as the Poughkeepsie Seer, who in 1844 went into a semi-trance and wandered forty miles from home. His *Principles of Nature, her Divine Revelations and a Voice to Mankind* was a best seller teaching that there was no mind, only matter. But when in the late 1840s he put his faith in the more domestic and solacing cult of Spiritualism, most of his disciples and competitors in Phreno-Mesmerism followed suit.[29] It would seem that the dire economic situation of the United States had driven citizens to look to supernatural aids for some kind of security.

James Fox's lampoon of these vagaries has not survived, but it probably resembled the "Magnetic Lecture" that the platform performer Ossian E. Dodge was delivering. In the course of this act, Dodge put a complicitous boy into a magnetic sleep in which he was only "physically dead," and expatiated on the benefits of this somnolent state in such lucid terms as "carryoliverous," "verokulationary," "dorryophrigulous," and "falbuguziptionary."[30]

Clearly, the Little Foxes's repertory was expanding. Caddie was capable of dancing a Tyrolienne and a Cracovienne, James added a lecture on phrenology, and they began to evolve more extended sketches, including one in which brother Laff was brought in to play an old man.[31]

When the Tremont got religion, they took to the road once more, appearing that summer at the Masonic Hall in Middlebury, Vermont, and at Lowell, Massachusetts, accompanied by "Yankee" Addams. John P. Addams (1815–85), a Bostonian, had taken up acting as one of several pursuits and specialized in the shrewd "bodacious" Yankee caricature. In 1850 he would lead a Mormon colony of about six hundred to Beaver Island in Lake Michigan.[32] At this time, he was content to shepherd a couple of talented children.

The Foxes had refurbished their "Concert of Gaieties and Gravities" to offer an entirely new program:

Duet (Mr. & Mrs. Smith)	Master J. and Miss C. Fox
Song (What Shall We Do for Change)	Mast. J. Fox
Song (I'm Too Young to Marry Yet)	Miss C. Fox
Address to the Firemen of Lowell	Mr. J. P. Addams
Shawl Dance	Miss C. Fox
Comical Wooden Shoe Dance	Master J. Fox
Dialogue (Sam Patch)	Mr. Addams, Mast. and Miss Fox
Punchenello	By the Little Foxes
Dialogue—With Duett	Mast. J. and Miss Fox
Scotch Strathspey	Miss C. Fox
Yankee Story—with comic song	Mr. J. P. Addams

The whole to conclude with Humorous Double Dance by
Master J. and Miss C. Fox
12 1/2 cents to all.[33]

In addition to its ampleness, this bill deserves examination for the timeliness of its offerings. Caddie's strathspeys and shawl dances belong to the school made popular in America by Augusta Maywood and Madame Celeste. The Punchenello was presumably a grotesque *ballet d'action* in the tradition of Mazurier and the Ravels (later Henry Fox and Uncle George Wyatt would join them in it). "What Shall We Do for Change?" was a topical song, taking as its tag-line a commonly heard phrase in that period of tight money:

> *The mischievous banks are at their pranks,*
> *Our specie to restrange,*
> *'tis every body's cry as they pass by—*
> What shall we do for Change![34]

Seven verses ring variations on the inability to get change from one's washerwoman, barber, penny-postman, butcher, barman, and fiddler, with the comic burden of "Ri toll loll, ri toll loll loll loll." In short, the

Little Foxes were providing the same fare as adult performers on a variety bill, with the added attraction of their evanescent precocity.

The Foxes had to perform at "museums" and Masonic halls because no towns in New England, other than the largest, countenanced permanent theatres. On the other hand, the new organizations that were supplanting older bonds of church and community—mechanics' institutions, political clubs, and charitable societies—were voluntary and egalitarian in their memberships, and more welcoming to entertainers. In the process, they threatened the establishment.

Typical was tension between conservatives and liberals in the industrial shanty-town of Lowell, Massachusetts, whose government was particularly adamant in its rejection of theatre. A Boston and Lowell stock company had built the Lowell Street Theatre in 1833, and a new liberal faction in the town meeting was formed solely to agitate for its licensing, but the playhouse was denounced by nearly every churchgoer in Lowell and censured from every pulpit. Anyone connected with the theatre in any way, including the playbill printer, was threatened with prosecution, but the house was ready, the company hired, the play advertised. Some prominent Lowell citizens guaranteed that they would see the entrepreneur Barrett was financially unscathed, so he resolved to raise the curtain. When the actors went ahead and performed, Barrett was summoned the next day to answer charges of high crime and misdemeanors, in acting without a license. After a few more performances, he was found guilty. The speculators gave up and turned the building into a tenement for Irish immigrants.[35]

Rendered cautious by these events, the shrewd entrepreneur Moses Kimball fitted up Wyman's Exchange as a museum with dioramas and a stage for magic shows, and eschewed plays. The enterprise faltered and he eventually sold it in 1845;[36] but in the meantime he moved to Boston and capitalized on his experience by opening what he called The Boston Museum and Gallery of Fine Arts. Situated on Tremont Street, between Montgomery Place and Bromfield Street, a stone's throw from the Tremont Theatre, the museum contained a "musical saloon" or lecture room capable of seating twelve hundred. A capacity audience could cover the cost of light entertainments. For his first two seasons, Kimball presented only musical concerts and olios, but the demise of the Tremont, now known as "the deacon's theatre," emboldened him to become a theatrical impresario. Hiring William H. Sedley Smith as his stage manager, he offered his first dramatic entertainment on 4 September 1843. The company included the Little Foxes, their uncle George H. Wyatt, and George C. Howard, now acknowledged as Caddie's beau.[37]

Their Uncle Wyatt's grotesque dancing and the sketches he tailored to their abilities greatly aided the Little Foxes. One of his pieces, *The*

Figure 2. A Playbill for George C. Howard's benefit at the Lowell, Massachusetts Museum in 1845. Since Texas was annexed on 1 March, the Howards' speedy enterprise in adding a sketch on the subject is evident. (Courtesy Theatre Arts Library, the Harry Ransom Humanities Research Center, the University of Texas at Austin)

Odd Fellow or My Old Umbrella, gave Caddie protean opportunities; she appeared in it as Jenny Transit a young lady, Cornelia Clappergo a literary spinster, Deborah Criskin a pork butcher's widow, Bridget Buckthorn a rustic beauty, and Ensign Thaddeous O'Transit of the Kilkenny Lancers.[38] It was a miniature version of the quick-change entertainments that Charles Mathews, Sr., had made popular. At Wyatt's benefit on 22 December, George Howard and Caddie Fox appeared together in the same play, the afterpiece *The Angel of the Attic,* fueling rumors of their engagement.

Boston in 1840 was a city of ninety-three thousand souls that boasted twenty-nine benevolent associations, five circulating libraries, ten daily newspapers, twenty-seven weeklies, seven bi-weekly journals— and only three theatres, one of which succumbed to bad business and bigotry. Moses Kimball sought to attract to his museum audiences that had hitherto avoided the theatre, partly by emphasizing the cabinet of curiosities attached to the establishment and partly by mounting "family" entertainments that might prove irresistible. Among the latter were Christmas pantomimes, which had never been naturalized to Boston, having been played in the past by foreign troupes passing through or cheaply got up for a special occasion. Kimball spared no expense, and in the Christmas week of 1843 *The Christmas Gift, or The Golden Axe* by William Barrymore with music arranged by Thomas Comer was revealed to the public. It proved to be so popular that it ran well into February of the next year, and in following years was revived for a series of Saturday matinees.

This was succeeded by another Barrymore and Comer collaboration, *The Busy Bee, or Harlequin in the Hive of Industry.* By 1847, these homegrown pantomimes had been superseded by imitations of James Robinson Planché's elegant extravaganzas imported from London. But the original impact of the Barrymore-Comer pieces engaged the Boston public's affection. One critic who had been a boy at the time could recall

the wild joys which thrilled our little breasts when The Enchanted House, The Enchanted Beauty, The Forty Thieves, The Children of Cyrus, and Aladdin possessed the fairyland of the stage . . . All were real and true, just because it was far away and romantic. The 'cloud-cuckoo-land' of the imagination was the native heath of the healthy child of that day. And well I remember how tame, unimportant, and unnatural the characters appeared to me in The Drunkard,—to which I was taken for ethical reasons, no doubt, when it was produced at the Museum,—in contrast with the glorious, vital, and convincing figures of Ali Baba, Cogia Houssan, and Morgiana, of Cherry and Fair Star.[39]

The success of the pantomimes clinched the museum's popularity, and may have formed Boston taste to the detriment of more sophisti-

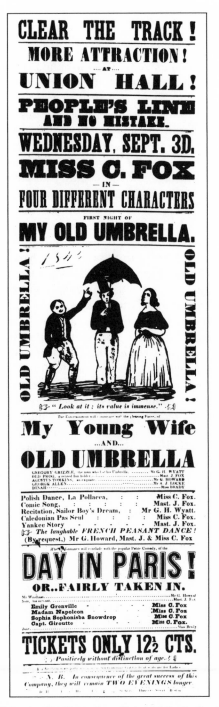

Figure 3. A Playbill for the Fox-Howards at Union Hall, Portland, Maine, in 1845, with Caroline Fox featured. (Courtesy Theatre Arts Library, the Harry Ransom Humanities Research Center, the University of Texas at Austin)

cated offerings. Such, at any rate, was the opinion of the English tragedian George Vandenhoff, who regretted that despite the city's reputation
for literary polish, the "Drama of Shakespeare, Sheridan, Knowles,
Bulwer, &c.—does not generally attract the Bostonians. Show and
spectacle, glitter, blue flame and pantomimic extravagance, have in-
finitely greater charm for them. Hamlet, Macbeth, the School for Scan-
dal, have no chance against the Ravels and pantomime."[40] What was
true for older, soberer heads was probably true for Laff Fox. In later
years, *The Golden Axe* was to be a staple of his repertory.

Caddie Fox and George Howard were prominently featured in *The
Golden Axe*, she as Sylva, Queen of the Fairies, and he as Colin, afterwards Harlequin; and throughout the season they were inseparable on
stage and off. They were also in the cast when Kimball pulled off his
next coup by opening on 25 February 1844 the aforementioned *Drunkard*, a blatant appeal to those very moralists who regarded the theatre
as a sinkhole of vice. It was a timely move.

From the days of the Pilgrim Fathers, New England had been a hard-
drinking settlement. But in the first years of the new republic, temperance became a burning issue. The Protestant ethic, which placed
such emphasis on the value of deeds, saw prohibition as the only means
of ensuring a perfect society, and, with the inveterate presumption of
organized religion, determined to fit its code of conventional morality to
the entire population—in the population's own interests, of course. The
majority of Americans in the early nineteenth century was pietistic and
favored legal interference in social issues; moral attitudes could best be
imposed on conduct by legislation. The unquenchable Lyman Beecher's
"Six Sermons on Intemperance," delivered and published in 1825,
gave total abstinence a social cachet and were much acclaimed. The
following year, the Reverend Justin Edwards, pastor of South Church at
Andover, Massachusetts, founded the American Society for the Promotion of Temperance, known more familiarly as the "American Temperance Union." He managed to organize over three thousand affiliated
societies in the northeastern states, closed fifty distilleries, and persuaded four hundred merchants to cease purveying Demon Rum. By
1833 there were four thousand branches and half a million members.[41]

The movements were strongest in the growing factory towns of eastern Massachusetts, where a new proletariat hoped to change society.
They were weakest in the port cities where conservatism lodged. Fired
by the notion of improving the moral world just as business and professional life were being modernized, prohibitionists were among the likeliest members of a community to join lyceums, public libraries, and
mechanics's institutes. They would probably frequent museums. In addition, there was a longstanding association between entertainment and

prohibition. The teetotal Washingtonians organized comic singsongs in the early 1840s as alternatives to the grog shops and theatres whose bars tipped the balance between profit and loss. Although many high-minded persons found the Washingtonians too low, a decade later the transition to respectability would be made by Ossian E. Dodge, the self-promoting one-man show, who netted eleven thousand dollars in his 1851 tour of New England.[42]

As early as 1838, the Massachusetts legislature passed a law forbidding the sale of "ardent spirits" in quantities of less than fifteen gallons, to be purchased and delivered at once. (Licensed apothecaries and practising physicians were exempted, thus beginning the association of the drugstore with bootleg liquor.) The rationale was that no man could possibly drink such an amount on the spot, although some tried. To get around this impossible ordinance, a clockmaker in Dedham painted black and red stripes on a white pig and exhibited the beast in a tent. Word soon went round that a free glass of grog was given with the price of admission. In no time at all, tents exhibiting "striped pigs" and "blind pigs" had sprung up all over New England. The fifteen-gallon law, so repugnant to notions of individual liberty, was repealed in 1840.[43]

This setback only hardened the temperance movement to the difficulties of its task, so that Kimball's presentation of *The Drunkard* was a brilliantly timed stroke both for the cause and for the museum's reputation. Compared with the more-or-less literary drama that had graced the stages of the Tremont and the Federal Street, *The Drunkard* was a crude, garishly colored cautionary tale, an overwrought pendant to George Cruikshank's novel-in-etchings *The Bottle*. Although devoid of wit, psychological subtlety, or literary style, it made a direct appeal to the inexperienced playgoer, and most members of the teetotal movement were that. It bore the name of Smith, the museum's genteel stage manager, as "arranger," but evidence points to the authorship of the Reverend John Pierpont, temperance advocate and abolitionist who had written the textbooks the Fox boys had conned. A stagestruck clergyman, he had to conceal his sacrifices to Thespis behind smoke-screens of great density. Ironically, three of the pillars of his Hollis St. Church were distillers, who stored their rum in his basement, which led the knowing to sing

> *Above the Spirit Divine,*
> *Below the Spirits of Wine.*[44]

One of the novelties of *The Drunkard* was that it filled an entire evening, dispensing with the curtain-raisers and afterpieces that customarily eked out the bill. No doubt George Howard bore this in mind years later when he made *Uncle Tom's Cabin* an unaccompanied feature

(*Uncle Tom* has mistakenly been assumed to have pioneered that innovation). Once again, Howard and the Foxes were in at the inception of a novelty. Caddie played Sallie Lawton, Howard, Farmer Stevens, little Master Fox (probably James), Henry Evans, and G. H. Wyatt, the villainous lawyer Cribbs.[45]

The Drunkard's popularity was phenomenal. During the Temperance Week festivities held in May after the play had opened, a "monster" march with twenty-three brass bands, a "Cold Water" Army of those who signed the pledge, a line of twelve thousand reformed alcoholics, and six pieces of fire equipment paraded through Boston. A Grand Total Abstinence Celebration took place on the Common with the ladies' auxiliaries shouting "The Teetotalers are coming!" and the Mayor delivered a speech. Banks closed for three days. As a culmination of the day's activities, both the Boston Museum and the backsliding Tremont Temple exhibited *The Drunkard*, "by all acknowledged to be the most successful play ever acted in Boston."[46]

At the season's end, Caddie once more took a benefit at the museum, dancing in the pastoral ballet *Little Red Riding Hood* and partnering George Howard in the well-named *Loan of a Lover*. The fall season began with important changes in the Foxes's domestic arrangements. On 31 October 1844, fifteen-year-old Caddie married George C. Howard, fourteen years her senior. It had been a foregone conclusion in theatrical circles and shed a glow of greater respectability on the museum. A month later, eight-year-old Henry was billed to appear with his uncle as Swizzle in *The Loan of a Lover*, singing "I'm too little for anything"; but on November 27 he died, and the printed playbill was never posted.

The surviving Fox children were now of an age to fend for themselves and they had, by marriage, annexed a leading man to their domestic troupe. On the following 14 June, Emily Fox's mother Martha Wyatt died of peritonitis and debility, following thirty visits from the doctor.[47] This freed the matriarch of the Foxes to accompany her children when they set off on a summer tour more ambitious than ever before, performing a number of abridged plays, including *The Gambler*, the museum's sequel to *The Drunkard*.

Caddie, still billed as Miss Caroline Fox, continued to dance polkas and tyroliennes, and brother James still recited comic songs, but the bulk of their program was now composed of farces such as *The Portland Depot! Or What Will Mrs. Jones Say to That?* (in which the family was abetted by an A. J. Locke and a Miss Brady), *The Lady in Black*, *The Artful Dodger or The Inventions of Lollypop*, *The Game of Love*, *My Wife's Come or John Prettyjohn & Co.*, *A Day in Paris, or Fairly Taken In* (with another set of Protean parts for Caddie), *The Maid of Croissey*, and a melodrama, *The Factory Girl*, an apt piece for the milltowns in which they appeared. One of their topical plays was *The Annexation of Texas or Uncle Sam's Courtship* in which Miss Texas (Caddie) was wooed by Uncle Sam (Uncle Wyatt) to the vexation of Santa Anna (brother James). The itinerary for summer 1845 included Mechanics Hall, Salem; Union Hall, Portland, Maine; Lyceum Hall, Lynn; and the Lowell Museum, still owned by Moses Kimball.

When the Foxes returned to Boston in the fall, they did not rejoin Kimball's other museum, but instead entered the new Howard Athenaeum. Contrary to the usual course of events, the Athenaeum had been converted from a chapel of the Millerites, yet another sect spawned by the pessimism of the times. William Miller, an old soldier and ex-deist, claimed to have rent the veil that obscured the meaning of the Scriptures; making his calculations in Low Hampton, New York, he computed that the Second Coming of Christ was to occur on 23 April 1843. As he travelled on his mission, his numerous followers prepared for the end and were somewhat bewildered when the fatal day came and went without incident. Miller explained that he had mistakenly calculated according to the Hebrew rather than the Roman chronology; his new reckoning set 22 October 1844 for the crack of doom. Obediently, when the day came, the Millerites gathered in white robes on hillside and housetop, including the roof of the temple that had opened in May 1843 on the south side of Howard Street. This time the disappointment was definitive, and "Muslin for Ascension Robes" rapidly declined in price. The Millerite Tabernacle was on the market until a quadrumvirate of managers fitted it up as a theatre and opened it on 13 October 1845.[48]

The Athenaeum's original stock company included Mr. and Mrs. George Howard and J. A. Fox, but whatever their intentions in moving to the new house—higher salaries, better roles, more benefits—they were thwarted when, the following February, the building burned to the ground. George Howard was an ambitious young man with managerial aspirations; his mother-in-law Emily Fox, "a woman of great energy and business tact,"[49] was no longer encumbered by an ailing mother and a small child. The paterfamilias, George Howe Fox, soon dropped out of the picture, unable to get on or keep up with his resourceful wife. Their summer tour had familiarized them with the tastes and capacities of New England townsfolk, and they hit upon the idea of extending their visits throughout the year, when the inhabitants of remote communities would be just as desirous of amusement and the competition less. Accordingly, the Little Foxes struck out on their own as Howard and the Foxes.

3

The Howards and the Foxes

(1846-50)

The year 1846 was a good time to venture on a new business enterprise. The country had pulled out of the slough of the Panic and was embarked on a wave of prosperity unparalleled in national experience; the good times would last a decade—until the next panic in 1857. The native element in the population of Boston had been varied by a large influx of "foreigners," who comprised 23.7 percent of its population; these outsiders were less intractable to the theatre than the descendants of the Puritans. Although unskilled laborers, mostly German and Irish immigrants, remained underprivileged, underpaid, and illiterate, the upper- and middle-classes enjoyed improved living conditions and economic security. The public now had the inclination and the leisure to become an audience.[1]

The newly organized Fox company absorbed the entire family, including Laff. His venture as a merchant tailor had not panned out, but he did feel sufficiently provident to marry one Caroline Gould of Watertown.[2] Like so much of G. L. Fox's private life, this marriage is obscure, even the date unnoted in the family records; the bride's personality remains a blank. She must have had a modicum of stage ability, however, for "Mrs. G. L. Fox" begins to appear in the company's bills in August 1846. It is unlikely that Laff married her simply to strengthen the troupe, but no family member was going unexploited. Even Emily

Fox, whose acting had primarily been a stopgap affair, now lent her matronly support to the plays.

Wasting very little time after the Athenaeum conflagration, the reconstituted Fox-Howard company appeared in March at the Cambridgeport Town Hall in some of their standard vehicles, billed as "The Foxes in Town." By April they were under way as "The Foxes and Mr. G. Howard." Caddie now appeared on the program as Mrs. G. Howard, no doubt because her pregnancy was too conspicuous to be ignored. On 10 May her daughter Adelia Ann was born. This child goes unmentioned throughout the rest of the Howards's career and it is safe to speculate that she died almost immediately. This is supported by the fact that although the company played through April and June, May was unbooked in their schedule.[3]

George Howard may have quit the Boston Museum, but he remained on good terms with its management and had secured the touring rights to not only *The Gambler* but *The Drunkard* as well. The version he toured, billed as *The Freedom of the Drunkard or His First and Last Pledge* by Charles H. Saunders, was condensed, with several characters omitted, and the remaining names changed; the cast was small enough to be filled by Uncle Wyatt, Howard, and the Foxes. James appeared as Sim Sprague a lively Yankee and Laff in the small role of Constable Higgins. Advertised as "having received the stamp of approval from a Boston audience and since been represented with much moral effect in nearly every city in the New England states," the miniaturized *Drunkard* could be presented in a mixed bill with songs and dances, and that was how the smaller towns of New England first became acquainted with it.[4]

Although Howard retained a handful of the comic one-acts that had been the bread-and-butter of the Little Foxes, he shrewdly put his emphasis on the moral dramas, hoping thereby to conquer the prejudices of the puritanical backwaters. To a large extent he succeeded, abetted not only by his gentlemanly manners but by the troupe's domestic flavor. Moreover, by making a virtue of necessity and appearing in nondescript halls rather than playhouses, he had obviated a major objection of the moral reformers. Lyman Beecher had complained that theatres forced the respectable to mingle with "the most debased and worthless portion of the community."[5] This would be less likely in a mechanics' institute.

One commentator has pointed out that

The annalists of the stage have failed to note that a great factor in eliminating the prejudice against the theatre that formerly existed, especially in New England, was the work done by Mr. Howard and his wife. Mr. Howard was a gentleman in the true sense of that much abused term, a man of high moral character, who recognized that the people wanted to be amused and that they should be given theatrical entertainments, but who tried to make those entertainments irreproachable, believing that the theatre could be made to convey as worthy lessons as the pulpit itself.[6]

The pulpit often felt the rivalry keenly and responded hostilely.

Beginning in the mill town of Lynn, the Foxes and Howards moved next to the Fall River Town Hall on 9 April, where, in addition to *The Gambler* and *The Lady in Black*, they astutely offered *The Factory Girl* to a public whose life revolved around mechanical looms and cotton prices. Their audiences were large and attentive, and they met with considerable success. Newspapers began to take notice, one of them commenting:

The dancing between the Gambler and the afterpiece was decidedly fine . . . There is a grace and delicacy in Mrs. Howard's dancing which renders her performance on the 'light fantastic toe' everywhere acceptable . . . Mr. Howard has a graceful figure, a good voice, and his attitudes are usually good . . . Mr. James Fox, in his particular line, bore off the palm. [He] bids fair to take a high rank in the profession he has chosen. He is every inch a *Yankee*, and he seems rather the *original* than the personator in the character of his line. Ten years hence, James Fox, in comedy, will stand no. 1. All the members of the company was [*sic*] courteous and well bred, and seemed to exert themselves to furnish a rational and innocent amusement. Their success was complete.[7]

This was the usual consensus. The company's gentility was always mentioned, and James received most of the plaudits, while Laff passed without special mention. James had learned his lessons well from Yankee Addams and the other regional comics he had supported. During this New England period he, rather than his elder brother, was the cynosure of critical commendation. But the reviewer's prescience was mistaken. Ten years later, James would be an ornament to the bar while Laff would be reducing audiences to helpless laughter.

From Fall River they moved west to Brown Hall on South Main Street in Providence, later one of their favorite resorts. This time *The Drunkard* was embellished with "a beautiful act drop presenting a correct view of Charlestown and Bunker Hill Monument."[8] This combination of homily and patriotism was becoming a trademark of the Fox-Howards. The Providence *Pledge and Standard*, edited by a local minister, sniffed that their "moral entertainment" did not find favor with a moral and intelligent citizenry; but another paper leapt to their defence, declaring, "we honestly believe that the people who go there, and who appear to be very much pleased with the performances are as moral and as intelligent as those who attend upon the editor's preaching on the

Sabbath."[9] Whenever assailed by a local newspaper, Howard always had the luck to be championed by a rival editor; the animosities of the provincial press had their useful aspect. In this particular case, the wilful secularization of American life by the press was also a potent factor.

The May hiatus in which Caroline became a mother was followed by a rapid recovery. In June the company headed for Newport. The only public meetinghouse there was the town hall at Thames Street and Long Wharf, a brick building whose upper story had been rented out for theatrical purposes for years. The city was beginning to lose its homogeneous character even as it prospered as a spa and industrial center. Irish immigration was alloying the purely Yankee character of the town.[10] A local advertisement for *The Drunkard* quoted reviews to the effect that "'The Fallen Saved' was excellent—the best Temperance Drama that we ever saw performed."[11]

"Thence they proceeded"—the formulaic beginnings of so many sentences in Xenophon's *Anabasis*—applies to this phase of the Fox-Howard progress rather neatly. From Newport, they made for the Quaker town of New Bedford, which had set its face against a permanent theatre building long before. The usual site for entertainments there was Mechanics Hall on William Street, built in 1834 by the Mechanics' Rifle Corp. A certain I. P. Adams had been granted a license for a concert of comic songs and narrations in September 1840, and a resolution had been entered at the town meeting to license the building permanently as a theatre. The vote against this measure had been conclusive; five hundred and sixty-six to twelve.[12] The Foxes gave only two performances there before moving on to Nantucket where they stayed from 29 June to 11 July.

Nantucket had undergone a severe economic slump, the long-term effect of the Panic and the gradual falling-off of the whaling trade on which it depended. Still, it heartily welcomed *The Drunkard* as staged at its Athenaeum, formerly a Universalist church and an institution in which the entire community took as much pride as if it were held in common ownership. The local paper noted that Howard was not above including a canine performer in his troupe:

The Temperance Drama has drawn full houses this week, and given universal satisfaction. Sculpin is a comic dog, and should be arrested at once, as he had caused the sides of several of the audience to distend to such a degree that they are afraid their ribs will never resume their proper position. However, as it is a part of the play we suppose they will have to grin and bear it.[13]

The season was unusually dry, and two days after the final performance, a great fire destroyed one third of the town, with a loss of over a

million dollars in property. The victims included the much-loved Athenaeum and "many were the sighs and heavy hearts, as we gazed on the
ruins of that favorite institution."[14] We do not know if any of the local
preachers saw the hand of God punishing theatregoers by this calamity.

By that time, the Fox-Howard company had sailed to Sandwich
on Cape Cod to play at the Town Hall. The chronicle reports that "Mrs.
G. Howard . . . is a beautiful woman, and she is a pattern of a drunkard's wife," whatever that may mean. "Tim [the role played by James
Fox] adds light to the picture, which without his drollery would be too
sombre."[15] His brother Laff was consigned to utility character parts,
such as the philanthropist Roseville in *The Gambler*, a lunatic-keeper
in *The Railroad of [this Town]* (the name of the town was changed according to the place of performance) and Sir Marmeduke Meadow in
Bamboozling! James specialized in comic parts such as "Prosperity
Pickerel, a Yankee ripe for trade, fighting, loving, inventing, argu-
menting, auctioneering, circumventing, up to a little more than everything and nothing else." Some historians have claimed, on scant evidence, that G. L. Fox honed his Yankee impersonations during his New
England period; but if so, it was probably by observing his younger
brother.

At Leyden Hall, Plymouth, the troupe played a benefit for the "Nantucket Sufferers" on 27 July, and, as if to lighten the occasion, stuck to
farces. After a return trip to Newport, they came home to Boston and
at the National Theatre on 8 August initiated three new comedies for
Caddie's benefit. Once again she was billed as Miss Caroline Fox, to jog
the memories of Boston playgoers. She appeared in *The Idiot Witness*
(in the role of a deaf-mute who communicates in mime), *Bamboozling!*
in which Mrs. G. L. Fox made her first appearance in the bills, and *The
Escapes of Sophia of Dresden*.

Nothing is heard of the Fox-Howards in September; perhaps they
were resting. But in October they sallied forth once more in Concord
coaches over the Newburyport turnpike, this time to occupy Salem's
Lyceum Hall. Of all the Massachusetts townships that regarded the
theatre as Satan's playground, Salem was, not surprisingly, the most
virulent. When a hall had opened on Crombie Street in 1828, meant
solely for shows, a general complaint arose; it was sold and became a
place of worship four years later. "From that time to the present," one
contemporary approved, "our citizens have found it a much more profitable mode of spending their time and money, to hear lectures on
interesting and useful subjects than to congregate for the purpose of
listening to actors."[16] The very year that the Foxes played there, an enterprising townsman, hoping the climate of opinion had grown more liberal, proposed that Mechanics Hall be fitted up for theatricals. "But the

proprietor of the building well knew that revenue from such a source would be very inadequate compensation for the moral injury which would be likely to come on some other portion of the community, if not on some of their own children. For such reasons, the scheme was relinquished."[17] This was an atmosphere to make showfolk tremble. The Fox-Howards stayed but a day in Salem, before proceeding to New Bedford.

Their bill in New Bedford is of some interest, for it reverted to the all-comedy program of their earlier days. Mr. and Mrs. C. W. Hunt replaced Emily, but Caddie, G. H. Wyatt, and Mr. and Mrs. G. L. Fox (playing Mr. and Mrs. Sourcrout in *The New Footman*) are well in evidence, and Jim Fox, as he is now styled, carries on his Yankee impersonations. The foot of the bill reads "The whole produced under the direction of G. Howard." Earlier bills had boasted that the troupe was from the Howard Athenaeum; now the manager's name was sufficient guarantee of wholesomeness and quality.[18]

Touring New England in the winter months was less attractive as a reality than it had been as a project, and manager Howard cast around for a more permanent situation. The capital of Rhode Island struck him as a likely seat for the company: Providence had responded enthusiastically to their earlier visit and boasted two halls capable of housing dramatic presentations. The prevailing mood was, in the tradition of Roger Williams, more tolerant, less churchy than in rural Massachusetts. So, on 21 December 1846, "Mr. Howard and the Foxes (James and G. L.) and the Company" opened at Cleveland Hall on North Main Street and, for the next four years, with occasional sorties in the off-season, they were the resident theatre of Providence.

"The Company" remained a family affair, which limited the scope of their offerings to casts of fewer than ten. One new member was cousin George L. Aiken who had been invited to dance with the understanding that he might act if he wanted to. The boy had left school in Boston at fourteen to work in Brewer's Carpet Warehouse and the offer to join a dramatic troupe was irresistible.[19] The clannish nature of the enterprise must have pleased Howard who was, by nature, a nester: "His was a home life, no matter where the Howards were, George made his rooms at hotels, or his section of a car, or his cabin on a steamer, take on the atmosphere of a home, where with his wife he passed the quiet life he loved to lead. He delighted in study."[20] At first, however, there was little time for repose. Cleveland Hall had to be fitted with scenery and a new repertory rehearsed. Touring from town to town the company could rely on a few standbys, but once permanent, it had to prevent staleness by varying the fare regularly.

Although they started out with the tried-and-true olios, moral dramas,

Figure 4. A Playbill for the Fox-Howards at the Cambridgeport Town Hall in 1846. George L. Fox has now joined the company, but the woodcut represents his brother James in a Yankee role. The striped trousers, elastic-sided boots, and top hat prefigure Uncle Sam. (Courtesy Theatre Arts Library, the Harry Ransom Humanities Research Center, the University of Texas at Austin)

and one-act farces that they never entirely gave up, the Fox-Howards were growing more ambitious, and as their position became more stable they were able to enlarge their casts and launch more spectacular stagings for even an old chestnut like *The Factory Girl.* Even at their grandest, however, the enterprise was a homely one. Admission cost twenty-five cents and seats were not reserved, "so many matrons used to come early, and bring their knitting" when the doors opened at 6:30.[21] Junius Brutus Booth, in a gesture of friendship, had offered to appear in his Shakespearean roles, and George Howard had difficulty dissuading him, for the postage-stamp-sized stage and youthful company would have been unable to accommodate his robust style.[22]

The lines of business remained the same. Jim, a great popular favorite, was still the company comic, while Laff appeared in unmemorable character parts; in one of his brother's magnetism lectures he did make a stab at burlesque in a drag role, the Sleeping Beauty.[23] For the most part, the local press showered them with praise for offering "Lots of fun,"[24] though as it grew more familiar with the company's abilities and stock-in-trade, the reportage began to cavil. Undoubtedly weary of a perpetual diet of *The Drunkard* and *The Gambler,* one paper, while granting that the Fox-Howards competed successfully with rival attractions, offered the "hint to our friends that they must keep up with the times by giving the patrons something new."[25]

The rigors of maintaining a diversified repertory evidently told on some of the members of the company:

In the main the "Six Degrees of Crime" was never better played than at Cleveland Hall last night . . . Mrs. Fox was very well as Madam Doucet, but she lacks much of giving the abduction scene its proper effect. Benson and Fox exhibited a shocking want of taste in the last act. A little more attention to the text on the part of the gentleman last named and the piece will then go off better.[26]

The rebuke of want of taste may well refer to Laff. In years to come he was constantly admonished by critics to refrain from vulgarity, particularly in improvisation or audience-pleasing. This trait was apparently not new when he went to work in the Bowery, though the Bowery may have fostered an inbred tendency to grossness.

The rebuke is all the more surprising since the troupe founded its appeal on its respectability. According to Providence folklore, one straitlaced old gentleman who had always preached to his family that the theatre was the turnpike to Hades, heard that his son had clandestinely spent an evening at "Howard and Foxes." Bent upon rescuing the lad from damnation, he entered the hall but once the curtain went up became so deeply interested in the play that he stayed till the end, and father and son went home together, "the father unable to reproach the son for being attracted by a diversion, by which he himself had been equally fascinated."[27]

The troupe flourished, and in early 1848 Howard closed the theatre for repairs, to enlarge the stage and have fresh scenery and decorations painted. It reopened on 12 March as the Cleveland Hall Vaudeville Saloon with a handsome act-drop presented by Moses Kimball of the Boston Museum to his former employee.[28] During the hiatus, more important domestic developments had occurred that would affect every member of the family.

Caddie had once again become a mother, and the baby girl born on 1 February was baptised Cordelia (a family name, not a Shakespearean reference). The mother returned to the stage on 3 April for the first time after her confinement, with all three of her brothers in the cast. It was not long before Cordelia was initiated into the profession, for at the age of six months, she replaced the rag-doll that had ordinarily been brought on to impersonate the baby in the farce *Peter White*. She was carried on by one of her uncles and, as she later wrote, "influenced no doubt by the bright lights, [when I] began to laugh and croon and to hold out [my] arms to the audience, of course it elicited a great round of applause, my first reception."[29]

The Fox-Howard repertory resembled that of almost every other theatre in America, presenting such popular fare as *Box and Cox*, *The Lady of Lyons*, *Luke the Labourer*, and *New York As It Is* (much as any regional theatre today adopts the latest hits of Broadway and the West End); but an extant 1848 promptbook for the old standby *The Iron Chest* drastically cuts any verbiage that clogs the plot and ruthlessly excises incidental characters. Such trimming probably accommodated the limitations of the actors and the patience of the public.[30] The company did strive to be timely. "Yankee" Addams had supplied Howard with a star-spangled "Grand National Drama," *The Battle of Buena Vista* in 1848. "This new play was calculated to finish the season with éclat as the near approach to the Fourth would naturally excite patriotic feelings in every American breast."[31] The few juicy characters were tailored to the family, in particular the free-and-easy Yankee Hezekiah Hartshorn, personated by George Wyatt, who performed surprising feats of derring-do against incredible odds. Young George Aiken and Charley Fox played the American army, and when the former lad tripped through a trap door, he had to be fished out by his cousin. The comic Irishman, Barney O'Flanigan, fell to Laff's lot. The occasion is noteworthy, first, because this was the earliest of many such chauvinistic pieces in which Laff would later appear, and second, because it

Figure 5. A daguerreotype of Caroline Fox-Howard and her mother Emily Wyatt-Fox, c. 1850. (Courtesy Theatre Arts Library, the Harry Ransom Humanities Research Center, the University of Texas at Austin)

is his earliest attempt at the Irish characters that would become a specialty.

The absence of Jim Fox from his wonted comic *emploi* also deserves explanation. Although he continued to make occasional appearances with his family, usually in tandem with Laff in *Box and Cox* or *Slasher and Crasher* as a fraternal sight-gag, he was gradually withdrawing from the theatre. Some time in 1848, James Augustus Fox had wed, and it may be conjectured that his in-laws were not overjoyed to see their daughter, a local heiress, marry into a family of mummers, whatever their comparative respectability. For James's bride was Julia Elizabeth Valentine, daughter of a colonel and, more important, granddaughter of William Valentine of Fall River, one of the wealthiest, most influential manufacturers of that city. James had invariably been singled out as the most promising of the Foxes, and newspapers had prophesied an illustrious stage career for him. By the age of twenty he had played Mercutio and Jacques, a gravedigger in *Hamlet* and a witch in *Macbeth*, young Wilford in *The Iron Chest* and grizzled Sergeant Austerlitz in *The Maid of Croissey*, gallant king Charles in *Faint Heart Never Won Fair Lady* and ancient Philip Gabois in *102*, not to mention all the comic phrenologists, sailors, and Yankees of the olios. But his in-laws distrusted the stage connection enough to make sure that the estate they bequeathed to their daughter would be entailed in perpetuity. To support his bride and win favor with his new relations, James had to resume his interrupted studies, entering Harvard Law School. On graduating, he joined the Boston law office of John C. Park, and in 1858 was admitted to the Suffolk Bar. This new career would culminate in the mayoralty of Cambridge, a position that would cast luster on the other Foxes, but spelled a loss to the American stage. Moreover, James seemed desirous of concealing his bohemian connections in later years; in sketching his career in 1861, when petitioning to the governor for customs house appointment, he described it simply as "a business life up to the age of twenty-five, three years of study—five years of practice as a lawyer." [32]

One immediate result of James's defection was the bestowal of his line of business on Laff, the variety of whose roles became staggering. While keeping his old miscellaneous character parts (Father Philipps in *The Castle Spectre*, the Governor in *Lola Montes*, Mr. Friendly in *The Drunkard*), he also slipped into the phrenological lecturer and the hypnotist and a proliferation of comic Irishmen. Significantly for the future, he also branched out into the fields of pantomime and burlesque. When he was only eleven, Laff may have seen Monsieur Gouffe play Marmozette in *The Dumb Savoyard and His Monkey* with Uncle Wyatt amid the crowd of peasants; now he got a chance to play the Mazurier-Ravel animal role himself. [33]

As for burlesques, in 1850 the troupe performed a travesty *Macbeth* with Laff as the Thane of Cawdor, George Howard as Duncan, James Fox as Macduff, and Caddie as Lady Macbeth. The first performance, on April Fool's Day, had been billed as Shakespeare's tragedy to trick the audience. Evidently it proved such a hit that it was revived in June at the Boston Odeon with the more revelatory title *The Admirable Burlesque of Macbeth! not by William Shakespeare*. The play "will be produced with the most startling effect . . . the piece concludes in a rough and tumble between Macbeth and Macduff, in which the latter is slain according to history."[34]

In essence, this kind of burlesque, though not unknown in England, was a logical extension of the Yankee character. Just as the Yankee, with his homespun common-sense, undercuts Old World pretention and snobbery, so the comic demolition of high art proclaims democratic values. Culturally insecure audiences, bored by over-exposure to the edifying—and many Victorians expected Shakespeare to be edifying—would leap to welcome a free-spirited chivvying of the sacred cow. The burlesque *Macbeth* was a dress rehearsal for those grotesque Shakespearean battles that G. L. Fox would later wage, reducing New York patricians and proles alike to tears of merriment.

The year 1848 was an *annus mirabilis* for the Howards and Foxes in less agreeable ways as well. For the first time during their tenure in Providence they were offered serious competition, by the new Providence Museum, which had better facilities and attracted touring stars with greater drawing power and novelty than the home team could boast. Throughout the 1848/49 and 1849/50 seasons, the Cleveland Hall company strove to maintain its popularity by changing its bill every other night. During this period, Laff played a minimum of seventy-two separate roles, from venerable old men to idiot boys, from druggists to highway robbers, from Mushapug the monkey to Joseph Surface. However superficial the results, it was an invaluable apprenticeship, schooling his memory, his ingenuity, and his stage knowhow.

The rest of the company had to display equal versatility, but by 1850 Howard was reduced to the crassest means of attracting the public. He lowered his admission to twelve-and-one-half cents; changed the curtain-time from seven to the more fashionable seven-thirty; cut down the repertory exclusively to farces and melodramas, dropping the moral dramas; and added G. H. Wyatt, his wife's aunt Julia Brady, and young Charles Kemble Fox (who had appeared in *Rob Roy* at Boston's Eagle Theatre the previous summer) to the permanent company. Family members might be more understanding if "the ghost failed to walk" on pay nights.[35] Presumably the patriarch, George H. Fox, was still with them, but no mention of him has survived. He was in Providence when he died in 1855 at the age of fifty, but there is something suspect in the fact that his family was in either New York or Cambridge at the time.

Howard's efforts were to no avail, and the season ended in hugger-mugger when the actor E. H. Dawes accidentally shot himself while hunting. All performances were cancelled until his widow was offered a benefit on 8 June. Pulling up stakes, Howard leased the Odeon Theatre in Boston for three weeks in June. This house on Sudbury Street had opened in 1848 as Bland's Lyceum and was dedicated to minstrelsy, a new, popular, but not entirely "legitimate" form of amusement. It was a comedown for Howard, who had hitherto played only in dramatic theatres or town halls, and, in keeping with his milieu, he presented only farces and vaudevilles interspersed with dance. Here it was that baby Cordelia got her first billing as a "Fairy Spirite" [*sic*] playing with granny Emily in *The Mountain Sylph*, a dramatic ballet. The burlesque *Macbeth* was revived and Laff, now headlined as G. L. Fox "Prince of Comedians," received a benefit on 28 June, in which he enacted three roles, including the old mesmerist fuddling his Graham-fed subjects.[36]

July saw them back in Providence with a bill of old favorites trotted out, while Howard was negotiating a new deal in Worcester, Massachusetts. He obtained a licence to produce dramatic entertainment there in a hall known as the Flagg Block, opposite the Bay State House hotel. By this time the company had been streamlined to himself, his wife, his mother-in-law, Charles, Laff and his wife, and a certain J. G. Burroughs.

Settling in Worcester was a gamble, for it too had a long history of opposition to the theatre. For decades, the only available entertainments had been West's Circus and occasional concerts, dioramas, and freak shows, with the odd equestrian exhibition. A showman named "Blind" Dexter annually displayed colored statuary in his van. But regular dramatic presentations were invariably opposed and when, in 1846, a Dr. Robinson put on a serious play called *The Reformed Drunkard*, he was refused a second permit, possibly because the local liquor interests had been offended. The Selectmen's report found the play "demoralizing . . . calculated [rather] to increase the vice there represented than to diminish it," and revealed that a French danseuse had exhibited herself in immoral postures. As supporting evidence, they reminded their fellow citizens that a lecture by a reformed gambler had increased the sale of playing cards. "Tableaux vivants" were introduced in 1848. This billing made plays sufficiently decent to permit ladies to attend in evening dress.[37]

In 1850, the newly-opened and Gothic-fronted Flagg Block contained a hall with a stage thirty-six feet by sixty feet and seating for 1,200 in three tiers and a parquet.[38] George Howard christened it the Worcester Dramatic Museum and opened it on 2 September. The previous year he had been jubilant when a son and heir was born to him in Providence, but the child had died a few months afterwards. The father was disconsolate and could easily sympathize when his brother-in-law James lost his first son. But Worcester saw the birth of a sturdy boy to the Howards: John G., who was to survive to the age of twelve. The family was changing in other ways; no sooner had the museum opened when, for reasons unknown, Laff and his wife left the company at the end of September and returned to Providence to join his Aiken cousin and Mr. and Mrs. Green C. Germon. Brother James had to be called away from his law studies to fill in and stayed till the season ended on 4 February 1851.[39]

Before following the fortunes of G. L. Fox, we must consider the unfortunate conclusion of Howard's venture into hostile Worcester. At first he was reasonably successful, dusting off the old moral dramas of *The Gambler* and *The Drunkard*, but almost immediately he ran into opposition, not from the church party but from "rum" elements and the new mayor, Peter Bacon. Worcester was not a temperance town, and the controversy over liquor issues raged hot and heavy there, the result of a basic clash of values within the citizenry. Almost all the town's lawyers, legislators, and professional men were pro-license and for the liquor interests. They feared that prohibition would create more problems than it would solve, by upsetting the social order. They meant to uphold the traditional caste system of New England society and frowned upon such plebeian movements as temperance.[40]

When George C. Howard sought to renew his theatrical licence in April 1851, the controversy was fanned by the newspapers. Under the heading "Juvenile Depravity," *The Daily Spy* reported that delinquents between the ages of eleven and sixteen, guilty of many burglaries

confessed that they were in the habit of visiting these exhibitions of coarse theatricals which for a number of months past have been alluringly held out to the public from Flagg's Hall under the title of Howard and Foxes' dramatic entertainment. The place has long been the resort of the reckless and unthinking, and no one who is a witness to the general aspect of the crowd that assembles there and the character of the plays, can for a moment hesitate in making up his mind that the tendencies of such an entertainment are demoralizing, and that the time has come for its suppression by withholding further licenses.[41]

This opinion was firmly seconded by the *Daily Morning Transcript*.

Howard had his defenders, however. One, who signed himself "An Old Citizen," pointed out that juvenile delinquency predated the performances at Flagg Hall and that

The proprietor Mr. Howard is a gentleman of sound moral principles and habits of agreeable and exemplary mind and correct views, and his aim seems

to be to blend useful moral instruction with popular gratification and amusement . . . Howard & Foxes have the merit throughout the New England States
of being truly respectable, exemplary in morals in private and upon the stage,
and as substantial and faithful in the discharge of all private and public pecuniary obligations and as such they are entitled to the respect and favorable
regards of the community. If a dramatic organization is to be tolerated here,
none more reliable or worthy of the same degree can be found in the country.[42]

Under this onslaught, the editor of the *Morning Transcript* apologized
that he had judged by hearsay, and, in recompense, published a letter
from Howard himself.

I have labored to present Dramatic exhibitions moral in their influences and
results, intermingled with humorous and popular lighter plays, and mainly
with the object of securing the approbation of the intelligent and respectable
portion of the community. I have also aimed strenuously to preserve a correct
state of order and manners in my exhibitions and to render them acceptable to
citizens of sound and refined taste, many of whom with their families have
constantly attended my performances.[43]

A further testimonial was furnished by the Worcester *Palladium* which,
in commending the Howards's morals in the face of a censorious community, also noted

Mr. Howard has established the fact, that there is a large class of our population—mostly working people—who decide for themselves that they need
some amusement; and that an evening at his entertainments is, for them a very
good and cheap substitute for a railroad trip to Boston, or New York, or Providence, to hear a few songs and see a few sights.[44]

This early defense of regional theatre failed to impress the city fathers, who did not choose to have the working classes deciding on their
own amusements, especially when those amusements portrayed the
evils of drink. Despite the glowing testimonials and his stated intention
of becoming a citizen of Worcester, Howard was denied a renewal. His
own probity in the choice of plays had worked against him. Not until
1857, when the Front St. Musée was built, would Worcester accept a
permanent theatre.

This controversy deserves a full exposition because it casts light on
the changing attitudes toward theatre in provincial New England, the
meaning of rational amusement in such communities, and the distinction of the Howard and Fox troupe. But the dubious honor of being a
pioneer was beginning to tell on the genteel manager. Worn out with
fighting the hidebound prejudices of Yankee strongholds, the Howards
and the Foxes now turned their gaze to New York.

4

New York Opportunities

(1850-52)

"New York," reported Lady Emmeline Stuart-Wortley who passed through the city in 1850, "is certainly altogether the most bustling, cheerful, lifeful, restless city I have yet seen in the United States. Nothing and nobody seems to stand still for half a moment in New York."[1] The streets were filled with ladies in elegant Parisian toilettes, long-haired, bearded prospectors newly returned from the California goldfields, and a vast number of recent immigrants from Germany and Ireland, escaping from poverty and political repression. Forty-eight percent of the city's population of 515,000 was foreign born. The Irish, who made up thirty percent of the total population, received seventy percent of the city's relief, and by 1851 it was estimated that one half of those arrested by the police were Irish. This supported the emerging stereotype of the New York Irish as drunken, disorderly, and indigent.[2]

The Irish were not alone in their poverty; one seventh of the city's residents lived on charity. But much of New York was undergoing a period of relative prosperity, and, as Coolidge once said of America, the business of New York was business. Expansion had reached as high as Fourteenth Street and was creeping up to Union Square. "The commercial spirit predominates over every other," noted the Scottish observer Alexander Mackay, "and largely infuses itself into the society of the city . . . It is gay to a degree, sprightly and cordial, but far less conventional than Philadelphia."[3]

The combination of gaiety and mercantilism was best seen in the speed with which theatres rose and fell in Manhattan. One of the most active theatre districts was also one of the least flattering to the city's reputation—the Bowery. Although the playhouses located there had so far failed to compete seriously with the city's most prestigious theatre, the Park, they were well patronized by local residents to whose tastes they catered. While more fashionable theatres imitated London styles in plays and players, the Bowery theatres cultivated a more indigenous and red-blooded repertory and performance technique. This guaranteed their survival, and in time they began to lure more westerly playgoers.

Mary Henderson, historian of Manhattan's theatre buildings, has written that "New York at mid-century was a city in transition . . . New York's streets were the dirtiest, its crime the vilest, its mansions the most vulgar, its poor the most exploited, its disease the most virulent, its death rate the highest." And, one may add, its police "the worst in the world."[4] The worst-policed area of a badly policed metropolis was the notorious Five Points, an intersection of Cross, Anthony, Little Water, Orange, and Mulberry Streets that debouched into a seedy, triangular half-acre "park," Paradise Square, grassless, unfenced, and sporting a dozen stunted trees, cluttered with carts, piles of stones, lines of drying linen, and, as everywhere else in the area, unwashed urchins at home in the dust. Charles Dickens had viewed it as the amalgam of all that was "loathsome, drooping and decayed" in the city.[5]

The local tenements housed brutal gangs like the Roach Guards, the Plug Uglies, and the Dead Rabbits, who terrorized the vicinity and were, in part, responsible for the demise of small trade. They had been conspicuous participants in the 1837 "flour riot" and the 1849 Astor Place riot, when "Young America," supporters of the native tragedian Forrest, rose against the English actor William Charles Macready, with a death toll of twenty-two ensuing. Even so, the Five Points was regarded as an entertainment district, deriving its reputation primarily from the famous Bowery Theatre, by choice the most popular resort of local thugs, newsboys, and prostitutes, although a quantum of respectable German families also attended.[6]

In time, Anthony Street stretched from Paradise Square to Chatham Square, within the purlieux of the Bowery. There to the north at 145–47 Chatham, between Roosevelt and James streets, the New Chatham Theatre opened on 11 September 1839, during one of the lowest ebbs of the economic depression. It had been erected by a local landowner to spite the evangelists who had converted the old Chatham beergarden and playhouse into the Chatham Temple. Despite its unpromising origins, the Chatham Theatre managed to survive by keeping its prices

low and offering spectacular novelties and a galaxy of stars, including
Booth, Forrest, and those popular performers in tights, Mme Celeste
and Adah Isaacs Menken. Its reputation remained as low as its price,
one memoirist calling it "a kind of sewer for the drainage of other establishments . . . some place for a certain class of people to effervesce in
their excitements of pleasure."[7] In 1848, the name was changed to the
New National, and, two years later, after a number of rapidly changing
managements, it passed into the hands of Alexander H. Purdy, who had
run the box-office during the tenures of his two predecessors.

Purdy, known as Captain for no apparent reason, was a man of Pickwickian rotundity and manner, no actor but a businessman of shrewdness, energy, and liberality.[8] He began his reign by entirely renovating,
painting, and carpeting the theatre, taking care not to increase prices.
He was also assiduous in mounting spectacles noteworthy not for great
acting or sophistication but for their appeal to pleasure seekers. Among
these was a lavish pantomime *The Magic Well*, "produced . . . in a very
superb manner," as afterpiece to "a pictorial drama" (that is, a series of
animated tableaux), *The Curate's Daughter*, which closely imitated *The
Drunkard*, also "put upon the stage most effectively." One reviewer remarked that *The Magic Well*, by following a drama about the evil effects
of intemperance, made a very "proper suggestion to people affected by
a weakness of the elbow."[9]

The "go-ahead" manager was put on his mettle because his chief
competition at the time was the irrepressible Ravels, lording it over
Niblo's Garden, which had become their New York home since their
first appearance there in 1832. Marzetti's hilarious yet pathetic impersonation of Jocko the Brazilian ape, the side-splitting pantomime, and
the graceful ballets of *Mazulme or The Night-Owl*, *Kim-Ka*, and *Jeannette and Jeannot* with its laughable military maneuvers, all these were
attractions so familiar and yet so sought-after that Purdy could not vie
with them. "The jumping through clocks, stone walls, men's bodies,
and into windows is truly astonishing," *Figaro* commented on the Ravels's *Green Monster*, "and makes one almost think witchcraft is indeed
concerned with their execution."[10] Purdy had no one in his troupe
equal to Gabriel Ravel in acrobatics, but he did possess, in the person
of Charles Burke, a first-class comedian.

As a child, Master Burke had been a major drawing-card at theatres
including the Tremont, when ticket-scalping had reached ridiculous
heights. Grown up, he was a well-known figure on the New York and
Philadelphia stages, sharing with his half-brother Joseph Jefferson the
roles of Paul Pry, Bob Acres, and Sir Andrew Aguecheek. He had a
special fondness for Washington Irving and fashioned his own drama-
tisations of Rip van Winkle and Ichabod Crane. Physically the latter

role suited him perfectly, for he was over six feet tall, angular and ema-
ciated, with long arms and a small round head set low on squared
shoulders. His rubbery face could supply a new countenance for every
part. Despite this grotesque exterior, Burke had an almost pointillistic
technique, painstakingly laying on slight strokes, delicately making
new points throughout his role. He was also a masterful violinist, which
enabled him to parody the Norwegian virtuoso Ole Bull, and a dramatist of works like *Metaroarer,* a lampoon of Edwin Forrest's *Metamora,*
and *The Revolution,* a saga of Bunker Hill spotlighting the Yankee role
of Mesopotamia Jenkins. According to rumor, Burke had been exiled to
the Bowery by William Burton who found him too much liked at his
own theatre. On the east side, Burke had to forgo the classic comedies
in which he made his name and stick to low farce, but the adjustment
was an easy one.[11]

Another ally of Captain Purdy in maintaining the quality of the National in Chatham Street was the veteran stage manager James "Irish"
Anderson, who had taken up the post during the earlier management of
Flynn and Willard. Cantankerous and disobliging, Anderson upheld
discipline by eccentricities of behavior and unexpected tyrannies. If,
during a performance, an actor walked into the wings to refresh his
memory by looking at the promptbook Anderson held, he would be
greeted with "Phat word do yez want?" and if the play were by Shakespeare, in whom Anderson was very proficient, the actor might discover
that the stage manager was holding not *Hamlet* or *Macbeth* but *The
Irish Tutor,* one of his personal favorites. On one occasion, Anderson
went to the dressing-room where an actor was telling an anecdote and
laughed at the punchline before remarking, "It's damned funny, but the
stage has been waiting five minutes for yez, and this will cost you five
dollars." When an intoxicated player fell twenty feet down from the
paint frame and lay immobile at Anderson's feet, the Irishman eyed him
coolly and said, "Bedad, I'll fine yez for damaging the stage."[12]

During his first season as lessee, Purdy sought to woo the actor John
Winans away from the Bowery Theatre. Whether or not Winans actually intended to be won over or simply played a trick on a rival manager
is unknown, but after letting himself be hired, he fell ill on the eve of
his first appearance. Purdy and Anderson were tearing their hair, when
someone suggested that they call in G. L. Fox.[13] This is one version.
Another is that Thomas Hampton had failed in *The Magic Well;* Purdy
advised him to go west and take up farming; and then Laff Fox, who was
already in the company, volunteered for Hampton's role.[14] Both stories
are dubious. Winans never was a member of the National, and it would
have taken more than a day for Fox to come to New York and learn the
role. Since Fox's first part at the National was in *The Magic Well,* he

could not already have been in the company before he played it. In any
case, Thomas Hampton did not work at the National until 1853.

Whatever the circumstances, sometime early in the fall season of
1850, a vacancy suddenly opened at the National and Purdy was advised to send for Laff Fox. "Who the devil is Fox? was "Irish" Anderson's response. When the New Englander showed up, he was a dismaying spectacle. He had arrived directly from Providence, still wearing a
Down Easterner's cap with earflaps; his gangling stance, wooden features, and provincial clothing marked him for a full-blown hayseed. He
had been hired as low comedian, and Anderson immediately prophesied
disaster. "Is this the clumsy lout that is going to do the work of Charley
Burke and Joe Jefferson?" he is reported to have asked Purdy in a tone
of bitter contempt. The rehearsals were hardly more reassuring, for Laff
was never at his best in practice, saving himself for the inspiration of a
real audience.

Billed as Lafayette Fox, he made his New York debut on 25 November 1850 as Giles in *The Magic Well*, Tobias Shortcut in *The Spitfire*
and, according to the chroniclers, though not the playbills, Christopher
Strop in *A Pleasant Neighbor*. He stepped on stage to dead silence, for
the audience had no intention of welcoming an unknown quantity with
applause, but within minutes he had gained the favor of the house. As
the actor Ben Ringgold, who was a boy in the pit on that occasion,
recalled

when Fox's pale physiognomy, with its comic long proboscis, appeared from
out the wings for his first entrance as Christopher Strop . . . the pit boys were
charmed,—and before the low comedian had made his first exit, they were
crying out, with tears trickling down their aching jaws, "He'll do. He's as
funny as Burke." [15]

His acting was received with rounds of applause, and at the end of each
act he was called before the curtain. By the evening's close, Fox had
made so solid a success that Anderson uncharacteristically apologized
to him. [16]

Burke had left the National the week before, and some rumors had it
that it was he who had recommended Fox to Purdy, although it is not
clear when he had ever seen the young man perform. The part of Christopher Strop had been especially associated with Burke's half-brother
Joe Jefferson, who left the National the following week. His departure
was not prompted by pique; the brothers crossed the East River to open
the Brooklyn Museum under the lesseeship of Frank Chanfrau. These
defections left Fox without serious competition in the realm of low comedy, and he was to remain at the National for the next seven years.

Fox's instant success was all the more surprising because of the adjustments it entailed. Although he had been on the stage almost from infancy, in the last few years he had played to very small provincial houses and callow, undemanding, god-fearing audiences. Only with his brother James's retirement from the stage had he been entrusted with large comic roles. The National held twenty-two hundred spectators who, if far from cultivated, were rabid playgoers and knew in no uncertain terms what they liked.

At the time, the Bowery was so remote from Broadway culturally that only the most remarkable spectacle or rumor of outstanding talent could draw the Gothamite to this *terra incognita* of raucous and volatile proles. A sharp line was drawn between the Broadway and the Bowery actor, and the former could lose caste by appearing on the east side. A reporter visiting the National shortly after Fox's debut was fascinated by the motley throng, so different from the fashionable uptown crowd at the Park.

We sat down in the 'dress circle,' a distinction arising from the fact that those occupying it generally had coats and hats on, while in other parts of the house coats, hats, and vests were often dispensed with.

The hour of performance being at hand, black spirits and white, blue spirits and gray, began to pour into the pit; some in red shirts, some in striped, some in suspenders, some without; but all noisy, and all in good humor. In the boxes came pretty Jewesses from Chatham Street, pretty milliners from the Bowery; 'short boys,' 'huge fisters,' 'Bowery Boys,' eastern 'young America,' in all its glory of misshapen beards, greasy hair and large cravats; and above all was the gallery thronged with our 'colored breatheren,' [*sic*] of all shades, from whity brown to jet black. [17]

These roughnecks and rowdies, when not interfering with municipal elections, spent their time chasing fire engines and engaging in rock fights with *aficionados* of rival engine companies. A local conflagration could result in a neighborhood war that went on for days, as the skirmishing moved from street to street like a lethal version of a floating crap game. "More than one New York lad," an old-timer recalled, "will remember the significant clutch of the throat, accompanied by a scowling enquiry, 'Wot's yer number?', an unfortunate reply being remarked with a crash over the head with a shillaleh—a favorite weapon in New York in those days—and a thorough drubbing." [18]

This uncouth crowd of butcher boys and harness makers was not easy to please; any performer had first to overcome the crowd's noise before he could make an impression. Punching their neighbors in the side or mashing down hats in their enthusiasm, Bowery spectators could be uproarious in approval and displeasure alike. Babies took suck at their mothers' breasts, while those who were weaned devoured pig's feet and peanuts during the performance; the shucking of goobers

Figure 6. The rebus, deciphered at the bottom, presents a portrait of Captain Purdy, the façade of the National Theatre, a skyline of Manhattan with Castle Garden at the left, and vignettes of a box and the pit. The actors shown are Junius Brutus Booth as Richard III, Barney Williams as Paddy O'Rafferty in *Born to Good Luck*. Charles Burke as Kasrac in *Aladdin*, and G. L. Fox as Rollabus in *Pizarrobus*. The black silhouette is of Thomas Dartmouth Rice as Jim Crow. (Courtesy Harvard Theatre Collection)

in the "peanut gallery" produced a low continuous growl throughout the show. Another old-timer recollected the unspoken hostility among the various social strata in the audience.

The backless seats in these old theatres, covered with some red stuff, were drolly uncomfortable, and the absolute separation of the low-priced pit from the boxes produced a sense of caste in the audience which has wholly disappeared in the later day. It was an unpardonable offence for the occupant of a box to turn his back to the pit between the acts—an offence of which he was promptly made aware by hisses and calls from the popular sovereigns. There was also a disreputable part of the auditorium, which has vanished long since, but which gave an ill-name to the theatre, from which it has not yet recovered.[19]

This is a discreet allusion to the prostitutes who were relegated to the upper gallery, no woman being allowed in the lower tiers or main floor unless accompanied by a man.

Of this audience, the most conspicuous and homogeneous segment was juvenile, the newsboys and bootblacks, spawn of urban poverty but not unlike the industrious little gamins of Horatio Alger's imagination. The cost of their admission to the gallery was hard-earned. Newsboys were up by four A.M. to crowd the folding-rooms of the morning newspapers and stayed on the streets till late at night. If a boy sold more than a hundred papers a day, he could count himself lucky, though his profits would amount to only fifty cents. "Generally ragged, often hatless and shoeless, or both, unclean in person and language," a newsboy might work fourteen hours a day to make a weekly wage of three dollars.[20] The bootblacks were more independent, not tied down to publication schedules, and more nomadic, but at best they made little more than five dollars a week, and the long intervals of leisure between clients tempted them to petty theft and vandalism. For these urchins, old before their time, the theatre provided color, excitement, a taste of beauty, and an emotional appeal that, on the street, they were too callous to admit.

As at the transpontine playhouses of London or the theatres of Paris's "Boulevard du Crime," the Bowery audiences called for blood-and-thunder. They wanted to feed fat on gruesome murders, racketty fights, and thefts distinctly professional. The criminous and the sulphurous were their favorite elements, and their only classical hero was Richard the Third who, on the Bowery, was interpreted in a writhing, ranting manner; his career culminated in a duel in which blue sparks were struck from the steel blades. "They don't affect anything humorous on the stage, unless it be in the shape of burnt cork or comic songs," commented one observer,[21] though he might have added slapstick and local allusions. At the same time, they had a sentimental streak that could be activated by the spectacle of virtue in distress, even if virtue had little currency outside the theatre. One reporter found the National "crammed full of attentive people . . . sailors, country-folks, and a pit full of boys, watchful, silent and on the keen lookout for any brave speech, relief of oppression, triumph of virtue and manhood against odds; and always applauding such successes to the roof." [22]

The enthusiastic reception this coarse-grained but sincere audience gave G. L. Fox guaranteed him the *emploi* of low comedian, and for the next two seasons he played a plethora of roles, appearing almost nightly in two parts. The range was as extensive as it had been in Providence, but he made a particular hit as Farmer Gubbins in *The Golden Axe*, a Christmas pantomime he knew well from its Boston run. At this time, the pantomime clown, a part Fox would later appropriate definitively, was in the care of W. A. Thompson. [23] Probably to counteract the Ravels, the National loaded its boards with pantomime during the holiday season, and Fox had the chance to appear in *The Frisky Cobbler, Old King Cole*, and similar offerings. This veteran of *The Drunkard* fit smoothly into *The Curate's Daughter*, which J. T. Haines had distilled and diluted from Hogarth's *Harlot's Progress*, and (shades of brother James!) was even called upon to deliver a mock lecture.

In February 1851, the tragedian J. G. Hanley arrived to star in a repertory of *Othello, Virginius, Macbeth*, and *Pizarro*. This last inspired Fox's first burlesque in New York, for every night Hanley's sonorous emoting was followed by *Pizarrobus, or Who Shot Rollabus?* It "made much fun," said *The Spirit of the Times*, [24] and Fox's participation as Rollabus apparently created so strong an impression that it inspired his first portrait in costume. In company with the National's other stars, J. B. Booth, Charles Burke, and Barney Williams, he is shown wearing a short tunic, a plumed turban, and a massive star-shaped amulet around his neck; waving a short sword, he looks like the village idiot applying for a job as a cigar-store Indian. The lineaments of Humpty Dumpty are already visible.

Fox's success is verifiable by circumstantial evidence as well. Unlike most New Yorkers, who dwelt in boarding houses, Fox and his wife moved into rented lodgings at 45 Allen Street sometime in 1851. The next year they went up the block to 51 Allen. [25] And he was provoking jealousy. The National's leading man, Harry Watkins, noted sourly in his journal in the summer of 1851, "A little warmer. Benefit of G. L. Fox, low comedian of the company and a very low one he is too, possessing little talent and less education, but an admirable substitute for both—plenty of impudence. The theatre is badly in want of a Low Comedian." [26] This is the earliest reference to Fox's churlishness, and, although the witness is partial, there were probably grounds for his remarks. Early success is a dizzying gift. On the other hand, Mrs. E. A. Eberle who acted at the Chatham when Fox had become its stage manager remembered him as "a wonderful man!" [27]

Throughout his first two seasons at the National, Fox gradually confirmed his popularity and increased his versatility, adding to his roster character parts like Solon Shingle the village lawyer and farcical roles like Downy Billy in *The Ragged School;* obstreperous schoolboys would become a specialty. He earned few press notices, for only the sporting journals deigned to cover Bowery houses. One of them, *The Spirit of the Times,* mentioned him by name in March 1853 as "more than ordinarily happy" in Irish characters. [28]

On the few days off he could obtain, Fox might have attended Niblo's Garden, to renew his acquaintance with the Ravels. Report has it that he became a keen student of their production techniques, with the idea of some day turning this knowledge to practical account. [29] Perhaps he was already trying out crude imitations of their tricks and knockabout routines in the many fairy plays and extravaganzas that highlighted the National bills.

Captain Purdy managed to secure a new six-year lease in 1852 and decided to refurbish the theatre. While it was closed for alterations, Fox took the opportunity to visit his relatives and offer his support as a star attraction. How had the Howards and the Foxes been faring while brother Laff made his reputation in the big city? Passably.

After their virtual expulsion from Worcester, the little troupe played in a Masonic hall somewhere in Rhode Island. [30] When, on 20 June 1851, Laff took the benefit that Watkins had complained of, he invited his family to share his honors: in *Box and Cox,* he and James, again playing hooky from Harvard Law School, were Mrs. Bouncer's tenants; in the burlesque *Macbeth,* James was Squire Macduff and Caddie Mrs. Macbeth; and in *The Actress of All Work,* she starred. It was her first New York appearance since *Little Red Riding Hood* at the age of six. Meanwhile, George Howard managed to take over the Troy Museum, and that September, the Howards, along with mother-in-law Emily, brother Charles, cousin George Aiken and a few others, settled in as Troy's resident acting company. The call-boy was James Lewis, later to become famous as a character comedian under Augustin Daly.

The temperance town of Troy, New York, boasted, in the late 1840s, twenty-five churches. They were in no way threatened in the spring of 1847 by a cabinet of curiosities housed in a new building on the northeast corner of River and Elbow Streets: Peale's Museum. The museum stayed open all day to display "Grand Cosmoramas, fifty Burmese figures in their native costumes and different castes, superior electrical machines, and admirable paintings of the great Sea Serpents."[31] At eight in the evening, vocal concerts and dramatic performances were put on for the public. Such versatility, the *raison d'être* of museums in American culture, spurred on Trojan journalists to brag, "Take it all in all, we have no hesitation in saying that *our museum*, in point of beauty, neatness, and elegance, is second to none."[32]

With its long experience of small-town sensibilities, the Howard troupe had little difficulty in acclimating itself while it boarded at the American Hotel. Howard was careful to advertise that they presented "entertainment adapted to juvenile visitors,"[33] and in time he was able to attract touring stars to the museum, where they were paired with Caddie, whose talent was recognized by the local papers.[34] Little Cordelia too was now a regular on stage, and virtually stole the show from her elders in *Oliver Twist*. Charlie Fox as the Artful Dodger and his mother as Mrs. Corney were thought excellent, although Howard as the dastardly villain Monks was found to be "a little too gentlemanly, respectable and bland for so great a rogue . . . but we suppose he couldn't help it."[35]

Four-year-old Cordelia got into the act when Howard conceived the notion of including in this adaptation from Dickens the role of Little Dick, the dying workhouse boy who bids a tearful farewell to Oliver when he runs away. It was meant to be a mute role, but in rehearsal the precocious actress came out with "Dood-by—tum again." Quick to exploit this effective ad lib, Caddie taught Cordelia four speeches; Uncle Charlie made up her chubby cheeks to look as consumptive as possible; they put a pair of pants on her legs and a spade in her hands to dig at a pile of dirt; and they sent her on stage. The following dialogue derives from family tradition.

OLIVER (Caddie Fox Howard) (coming upon Dick delving away in the prop dirt behind a paling): I'm running away, Dick.

DICK (omitting the rehearsed dialogue and improvising): Wunning away, is oo?

OLIVER: I'll come back and see you some day, Dick.

DICK (sobbing with intense emotion and excellent projection): It yont be no use, Ollie dear. When 'oo tum back, I yont be digging 'ittle graves, I'll be all dead an' in a 'ittle grave by myself.[36]

The enthusiastically lachrymose response to this bit of upstaging persuaded Howard that his little Delia was a born actress and he featured her, with the billing "The Youthful Wonder Generally Called the Child of Nature." In later life, Cordelia herself seconded this descrip-

Figure 7. Caroline Fox-Howard and her daughter Cordelia. A daguerreotype c. 1850.
(Courtesy Theatre Arts Library, the Harry Ransom Humanities Research Center, the University of
Texas at Austin)

tion, claiming that she had never had an acting lesson in her life but instinctively intuited what needed to be done on stage.

It was a month after Delia's debut that Uncle Laff, taking advantage of the National's temporary closure, travelled up to Troy as guest star, heralded as "the popular comedian from New York." For six days (April 12–17) he played thirteen different roles, never repeating himself, in such specialties as Tobias Shortcut, Jacques Strop, the hypnotist Dr. Guy, and Rollabus. Giving him his full complement of initials, *The Northern Budget* summed up his stay by saying that "G. W. L. Fox . . . has distinguished himself during his engagement . . . He will have a warm greeting from his many friends in Troy, and though they may regret that it is the last of him he will doubtless contrive to put them in good spirits."[37]

Fox's success among the Trojans brought him back on 5 June to play Rollabus at his mother's benefit.[38] Otherwise he remained at the National that summer. In light of subsequent events, it is curious that he took no part in C. W. Taylor's adaptation of *Uncle Tom's Cabin* that opened there on 23 August, but merely appeared as Iago in T. D. Rice's burlesque *Othello*, which, with exquisitely poor judgment, followed it. (One of his lines in this travesty responded to the Moor's demand for his handkerchief with "Blow yah nose on yah sleeve, nigger, and git on wid de show!") It had been over a year since Mrs. Stowe's novel came out in its complete form, after serial publication in *The National Era*, winning hosannas from abolitionists and hisses from southern sympathizers. In its first year the book had sold 305,000 copies, and it would reach the half-million mark by 1857.[39] The delay in adapting it for the stage was less the result of Mrs. Stowe's anti-theatrical sentiments than of an anti-abolitionist or at least conservative feeling within the theatrical profession. Outside of New England, the anti-slavery movement was not especially strong, and the Boweryites in particular, working-class and Irish, had no tenderness toward oppressed blacks.

Taylor's version of the play diverged sharply from the original. Most of the characters were renamed or newly invented; the episodes at St. Clare's plantation were omitted (thus leaving out Eva, Topsy, and Aunt Ophelia), and the eccentric role was invested in a Meg Merrilies type called Crazy Mag of the Glen. This was played by Mrs. W. G. Jones, a character woman of staggering versatility, who was reputed, by the time of her death in 1907, to have studied more lines than any other woman on the American stage.[40] The adaptation ended happily, like most sentimental melodramas, with Uncle Tom's homecoming and the discovery of a hidden parentage. Despite hostile reviews, this "insult to the South"[41] managed to stumble on for eleven nights, enlivened by Rice's minstrel routines and a rope-dancing act, and it was revived off and on throughout the season.

Since the cast of *Uncle Tom* drew upon the strength of the resident company, Fox's absence is all the more remarkable, but he did appear in that year's Christmas pantomime, *The Mystic Lily, or Harlequin and the Lake of Beauty.* In the transformation scene, he became Harlequin to Cony's Clown, chasing through the Highgate Farmyard, Doctor's, Baker's, and Poultry Stores, a Chamber of Horrors, P. T. Barnum's new Clothing Depot, Chatham Square, and the Cavern of the Hag. He was growing familiar with the way the English harlequinade could be adapted to the mores of Manhattan. His miscellany of Irish, character, and farce roles swelled as the bills themselves became more variegated, with horse and dog acts, comic singers, and visiting tragedians. Typically, when Fox took his benefit on April Fool's Day, 1853, as Valentine Verdict in *The Charcoal Burners*, Andy O'Loughlin in *The Irish Princess*, and Consideration Cotton in *The First of April*, he shared billing with the Diavolo Brothers, contortionists and acrobats, the climax of whose act had Master Lorenzo kicking the back of his head with both feet while in the air. "This extraordinary Feat," proclaimed the advertisements, "is thought to be impossible." [42]

The wilful variety of these programs reflects Captain Purdy's desperation in the face of competition more than it does the short attention span of Bowery spectators. Business was falling off badly, as locals and sightseers alike flocked to the Crystal Palace, erected for the first Exposition. He needed a sensational attraction to draw his errant audiences during the hot summer months. Fox suggested a new *Uncle Tom's Cabin* in a version that had been mounted by George Howard in Troy. Stage manager Anderson pooh-poohed the idea, pointing out that the previous *Uncle Tom*, a mediocre play, had exhausted any public interest in such abolitionist claptrap. Captain Purdy, however, let himself be persuaded by his popular comedian. The sequel is the stuff of theatrical legend.

5

Uncle Tom's Cabin
and the Triumph of Sentiment

(1852-54)

George C. Howard's decision to mount his own version of *Uncle Tom's Cabin* was prompted less by abolitionist convictions than by the need for a novel vehicle for little Cordelia. He entrusted the task of adaptation to cousin George Aiken, the company's "juvenile man," who had been acting with him since 1848, and who could be relied upon to tailor the script to the strengths of his colleagues. "Pode" Aiken followed Mrs. Stowe's story closely enough, much more so than Taylor had, but even with a running time of three hours and fifteen minutes, he couldn't bring the plot beyond Little Eva's death.

When the adaptation opened at the Troy Museum on 27 September 1852, Howard was seen as St. Clare, Caddie as Topsy, and Cordelia as Eva, the first time these latter characters had appeared on stage. Aiken, following all-male minstrel tradition and assuming that no woman would black up for Topsy, had turned her into a boy, but Howard insisted on following the original. When the company's soubrette Mrs. Green C. Germon indignantly turned down the part, the manager's wife agreed to assume it. Caddie, with the help of a wig and padding, also doubled Aunt Chloe, and Emily Fox lent her New England twang to Aunt Ophelia. Uncle Tom was played by Greenbury C. Germon, against his better judgement, for he too equated blacking-up with minstrel shows. His wife condescended to take part as Eliza in a less African complexion. The comic role of Deacon Perry had been fitted to the talents of the

Figure 8. Caroline Howard as Topsy on the cover of a song to *Uncle Tom's Cabin,* "I'se so wicked." The legend informs the public that "Little Cordelia Howard has an interest in the sale of this song." (Author's collection)

company's "old man," William J. LeMoyne. The rest of the major roles were apportioned to family members: Phineas Fletcher the rough and ready Kentuckian to Charles K. Fox, slippery Lawyer Marks to Frank Aiken, and the mulatto George Harris to the adapter himself.

The adaptation caused little stir and, after Cordelia took her benefits on October 18 and 25, it was announced that it would be retired for good. This created an artificial interest, which grew steadily, and the play was frequently revived, absorbing incremental lines and speeches from other pieces in the repertory. "It has lived through and survived several of the most exacting days preceding and succeeding the election," reported the local paper, "drawing houses, and since that event has passed off, 'comes out' stronger than ever."[1] The presidential contest had eventuated in the election of another doughface, Franklin Pierce of New Hampshire. His vacillation on the burning issue of slave and free territories would serve to make *Uncle Tom* all the more topical.

The growing popularity of the adaptation led to a four-act sequel entitled *The Death of Uncle Tom, or The Religion of the Lowly,* which brought the story to the denouement invented by Mrs. Stowe. The only cast changes were Charlie Fox's exchanging his frontiersman for the Yankee Gumption Cute who does not appear in the original novel, Frank Aiken's blacking up for Alf Man, and Mrs. Germon's carrying on as the high-yellow gal Cassy. But the sequel made scant sense to anyone who had not seen part 1, and it was only a matter of time until Howard commissioned Aiken to conflate the two into a six-act play, with considerable doubling on the part of the actors. To enliven the eight tableaux and thirty scenes, Howard purloined music from current hits and wrote fresh lyrics to it. His musical director Prof. Barnekoy was adept at weaving plantation melodies and minstrel tunes into the accompaniment.

Howard also cleverly though sincerely played upon the religious affections of his audience, lingering over such moments as Eva reading the Bible to Uncle Tom, the prayerful reception of George and Eliza by the Quakers, Eva's ascension to Heaven as angels flock from the grid to greet her, and her welcome at the pearly gates to Uncle Tom, as he gives up the ghost. Consequently, devout Trojans who had never before set foot in a theatre made an exception for *Uncle Tom,* as Bostonians had for *The Drunkard,*[2] leading the newspapers to comment on the respectability of the audiences.

A few hardshell reactionaries continued to rail, but to no purpose. When the minister of the Baptist Church called a special meeting to reprimand some of his erring flock who had been seen at the show, he discovered that a full two-thirds of his congregation were guilty of this sin.[3] Eventually, most of Troy's thirty thousand inhabitants passed

Figure 9. George C. Howard as St. Clare, a lithographed portrait on the cover to a song he wrote for *Uncle Tom's Cabin,* and dedicated to Cordelia. (Author's collection)

through the Museum to witness the edifying spectacle, many repeating their visit when the two parts were welded into one.[4]

Uncle Tom's Cabin ran for a hundred performances, closing on 1 December, a run equal to a seven-year's run in New York City, if one takes into account the relative populations.[5] There followed a triumphal tour to Albany, where Cordelia effaced memories of her precursor, the little Eva of stout, middle-aged Julie de Marguerites. Whatever the effect of the rest of the play, it was four-year-old Cordelia's Eva that made the strongest impression and constituted the chief attraction, primarily because of its unstudied nature. "She beats all youthful prodigies, *les petites*, etc., that we have ever seen," declared the *Troy Times*.[6]

George L. Fox may have had a free day or two in which to see his family triumph in *Uncle Tom;* unquestionably he heard about its success, and it may have been his brother-in-law who suggested a showing in New York. "Irish" Anderson was not the only member of the National Theatre to be unsure of the outcome; the regular company resented the intrusion of a provincial troupe, especially when they heard that Mrs. Howard and her daughter were earning one hundred dollars a week. Mrs. Jones, who had played Mag of the Glen in the Taylor version for a weekly salary of eighteen dollars, recalled, "I was astonished. I was certain that she would become rich in a very short time. I had never acted with anyone who received so much."[7] More serious objections were that the previous *Uncle Tom* had been a nonsensical near-failure, the protest that never before had a single play filled a whole evening's bill, and the fact that New York was a Democratic stronghold, not least in the Five Points. Such abolitionist propaganda would be hooted off. Anderson refused point blank to stage the piece, and so, for the first time, Laff Fox assumed the mantle of stage manager, although Anderson continued to draw his salary throughout the run.[8]

On 18 July 1853, during the hottest and least propitious part of the season, the Aiken dramatization of *Uncle Tom's Cabin* opened at the National Theatre. The amalgamation of Purdy's company with the Trojan troupe obviated the need for doubling, but even so there were no important cast changes. Howard continued to play St. Clare in "a black broadcloth frock coat, and lavender trousers. This was usually his costume in private life, so he was nearly always *St. Clare*."[9] Germon was again Uncle Tom, but his wife had been replaced as Eliza by Mrs. Jones and as Cassy by Mrs. Bannister. Frank Aiken had already quit Troy to join the touring company of his Uncle Wyatt, and W. J. LeMoyne was producing his own *Uncle Tom* in the provinces. Their roles were assumed by National regulars, with J. W. Lingard, soon to become an important figure in Laff's career, as Deacon Perry. Aunt Ophelia was announced to be played by Mrs. Bradshaw, but after the first three per-

Figure 10. This poster of *Uncle Tom's Cabin* at Purdy's National Theatre shows how negligently the Aiken-Howard version was treated at first. The vignettes, based on book illustrations, had already served to advertise C. W. Taylor's dramatization, and are simply altered to suit the new staging. Note that "Little Cordelia Howard" is cited as the chief attraction. (Courtesy of the New-York Historical Society, New York City)

formances she was replaced by Emily Fox. Charlie Fox still imperson-ated Gumption Cute but ceded the other comic role, Phineas Fletcher, to his brother Laff.

Later in the run, when Lingard replaced Germon as Uncle Tom, Laff doubled Fletcher and Deacon Perry, turning this latter into a remark-able display of comic flair, "an artistic humor I never saw equalled," claimed one veteran playgoer.[10] And of course, Caddie and little Delia clung to their creations of Topsy and Eva, which were a revelation to the actors in the Bowery. Even the dubious Mrs. Jones had to confess

[Mrs. Howard's] performance was not in the least like the *Topsies* of today [1902]. She was very much more refined than they are now, although she put plenty of humor into the role. The most hoydenish thing she did was to scratch one leg with her foot—a piece of business that every *Topsy* I have ever seen since her time invariably does—and it always makes the audience laugh.

Little Cordelia . . . was a born actress. I have never seen anything more natural and beautiful than the way in which she played little *Eva*. And she had required no training for it.[11]

The opening night obviously suffered from nerves and uncertainty. Luckily, a very detailed New York *Times* description of the performances during the first week reveals the play's gradual acceptance by a typical Bowery audience. The galleries and boxes were packed, the third tier with sailors and "short-boys." Although the pit was not so full as in winter, when the boys would crowd in for warmth and shelter, it still held a goodly complement of, so the *Times* said, "ragged, dirty lads . . . newsboys, baggage smashers, candy sellers, young factory-hands, who knew nothing of Church and School, and who come to the Theatre as the only agreeable and cheerful places they can enter of an evening."

The first scene between the mulattoes George Harris, represented with a brick-red face, and Eliza, depicted as a pretty white girl, made no more impression than the usual tender farewell of any lover and mistress. The boys were also left cold by the scene of bargaining between Shelby and the slave-trader; but in the following scene when Eliza comes to Tom's cabin to tell him he is sold, the ragamuffins in the gallery laughed at the high-pitched screech of night-gowned Aunt Chloe (Mrs. Lingard). Chances were that Uncle Tom was also greeted with laughter, since blackface and a "darky" dialect were associated with minstrelsy, and audiences were preconditioned to accept stage negroes as comic figures. As he began to spout religious sentiments, there was a danger that he would be taken as an absurd camp-meeting preacher.

His very first words, however, showed that a good hand had his part. The accent, a broad and gutteral negro accent, but the voice deep and earnest—so earnest that the first laugh at his nigger words, from the pit, died away into deep stillness.

The boys got their chance to laugh when Fox came on stage in the next scene as Phineas Fletcher, "a long-haired, strong, thundering Kentuckian who is drinking hot whiskey . . . This is the old favorite stage character, and quite as much with the Bowery boys as with any rough, swearing, storming fellow with a real soft, good heart at bottom . . . " Fletcher's sympathies with the fleeing Eliza immediately put the audience on the side of the fugitive slaves, and when she and her child sailed across the blue river on a piece of pasteboard ice, with the frustrated slave-catchers shaking their whips from the shore, the boys were "wrought up to the highest pitch" and, at Eliza's escape, "one grand cheer goes up from pit and galleries." [12]

The scene between Fletcher and the nervous Quaker Mr. Wilson convulsed the boys with delight when the Kentuckian spat a quid of 'baccy at a Runaway Slave handbill on the wall; and by the time George Harris entered in disguise, the audience was totally absorbed. Their delight with Fletcher was understandable: his catchphrases "Chaw me up" and "Chaw me into sassage meat"; his stage business with Bowie knives and tobacco; his extravagant similes, such as describing the ice-bound Ohio as "a permiscuous ice-cream shop come to an awful state of friz" were all calculated mirth-raisers. [13]

Sympathy for a runaway mulatto was harder to extract from the case-hardened urchins in the gallery, and yet

Perhaps the actor knows he is uttering real sentiments of these times—for he speaks with an unusual spirit. The caps wave, and the "Heys" sound at almost every sentence, at words which would be hissed down in most public meetings, and would be coldly received in the churches—but which somehow strike some strange chord in the dirty, ragged audience. [14]

Harris's declaration that he will be a freeman or die was met with wild cheering, which doubled in the next episode when the slave-hunter was rolled down the cliff as Harris put up a fight for his freedom.

The entrance of Little Eva added a new, more reflective element to the story, and from that point on the religious sentiments of the tale became more manifest. They were made acceptable to the audience of roughnecks and ragamuffins because they fell from the lips of a child. Cordelia Howard did not correspond to latterday conceptions of Eva: no long blond ringlets, but brown sausage curls; no ethereal physique, but plump, sturdy limbs; no pale, other-worldly face, but, in her own words, a piquant expression. [15] But she represented what Carl Bode calls "the powerful archetypal figure of the self as a child" [16] and therefore was closer to her audience than any sanctimonious adult could be.

Moreover, Eva's goodness was validated by Topsy's mischief, a point of identification for the boys. Topsy's respect for Eva was projected on to them.

Topsy is her foil—wilder and more tangle-haired and moping and grinning than in the original, and with a touch—showing an artist's hand—of additional bitterness "'cos she's a nigger!" She seems as the play goes on the very Parish of our Society. In the scene Eva asks her "Don't you love anybody Topsy?" and she says she "never had no father or mother" and Eva finally throws her arms about her and says "Poor child, I love you. I love you because you haven't any father or mother or friends, because you've been a poor abused child," I saw several ragged cuffs going up almost unconsciously to dirty eyes where tears had not often been.[17]

It should be remembered that none of the Howards or Foxes had ever been farther south than Baltimore, and their portrayal of plantation manners would hardly have satisfied a native of Dixie. Caroline's Topsy has been described by Julie de Marguerites as "a minstrel wench, thoroughly Northern" to whom she preferred the "*bona fide* little nigger" of Julia Drake Chapman.[18] But for a Bowery audience, the impersonation was familiar enough, not alienatingly exotic, to engage them. Howard's St. Clare, however, was viewed as a mere walking gentleman, though even he got a rousing hand when he rebuked Aunt Ophelia for her arm's length Christianity.

The audience at the National was "hooked" as never before. When Tom remonstrated with his master about his drinking, those rum-swigging seamen and rude mechanicals hearkened "in the deepest stillness, almost solemnity." Eva's deathbed and her valedictory "I'm going there, to the spirits bright, Tom" were met with a long silence, the boys not daring to applaud. Instead of the parody of piety the reporter had feared, the scene exuded "grand truths of immortality and religion . . . uttered to ears unaccustomed." He was struck by the play's ennobling of blacks and speculated that henceforth United States officers would get little help from Bowery boys in their pursuit of fugitive slaves.

We came expecting the usual 'blood-and-murder' acting of the National, and curious to see how such a piece would be managed there, and how the 'boys' would receive it. Most of the pit audience had, probably, never seen the book or any good book. They could not be got to listen to a sermon. They could not be moved by it if they did. These low theatres are usually the places where coarseness and lewdness are bred, and where the better thoughts are only expressed to be parodied. It seems strange that, in such a place, the piety and talent of a New England woman should be uttering grand religious sentiments and the truest feelings of humanity, in tones which could not be heard, to the very dregs of the outcasts of our city. Some writers have said that 'to arouse one true feeling of generosity and pity is better for man's soul than to study a whole system of moral philosophy.' In that view, perhaps, no better sermon was ever preached to the boys of the Bowery, than this acting of *Uncle Tom's Cabin*.[19]

The Howards and the Foxes introduced their own recipe for entertainment mingled with edification to the appetite of New York and found that they pleased its taste.

As word spread and the public flocked to the theatre, Captain Purdy was compelled to accommodate the crowds. Two weeks into the run, he moved his orchestra to the wings and replaced the eight rows of benches in the pit, some sixty by twenty feet, with three hundred cushioned armchairs to be rented at the handsome sum of 50¢. (When *Uncle Tom* opened, the usual prices were 6 1/2¢ for the pit or parquette as it was elegantly named, 25¢ for the dress circle, and 12 1/2¢ for both galleries.) The cost can best be reckoned when one is aware that the highest wage earned by a skilled craftsman was eleven dollars a week.[20] Four months later, the parquette seats were going for 75¢, the first gallery for 50¢, and the "gods" for 25¢, which prices were maintained to the end of the run.[21] These extraordinary rates by no means discouraged audiences, despite the enervating heat wave that killed two hundred and twenty New Yorkers in early August. Still the public crammed the National to the rafters.

The National was also the first theatre in New York to provide separate accommodation for blacks. On 15 August, Purdy opened a "neat and comfortable parquette" for blacks at twenty-five cents, the front seats reserved for "females accompanied by males, and no female admitted unless with company."[22] The rival Bowery Theatre held off in this respect until 1860 when it penned off a section of its topmost gallery at thirty-five cents a seat.

With the regular season approaching in September, Howard had to return to his managerial duties in Troy. He was replaced by a young and newly-landed English actor, J. B. Howe, who was favorably impressed by Purdy, his manners mellowed by prosperity. "It was a treat to meet such a man. His very face was the reflex of an honest heart, and his Pickwickian form emblazoned with diamonds and heavy jewellery, bespoke ostentatious success which gives encouragement to rising aspirants."[23] Although Howard had taken his mother-in-law and brother-in-law Charles back with him, he had left Caddie and Delia to collect their weekly hundred dollars as the hits of the show.

"One might suppose that a play might be done to death," remarked *The Spirit of the Times,* "but it seems that Uncle Tom is now beginning to live."[24] Word spread westward, and staid citizens who had never before ventured into a sordid hole like the National now sought it out. (An 1854 guide counselled visitors to the Five Points to saturate their handkerchiefs in camphor to alleviate the stench.) Women and children would not enter the Bowery after dark, so Purdy resorted to a revolutionary device. He instituted Wednesday and Saturday matinees (which only Barnum's Museum had used hitherto), and later, a third matinee, compelling the cast to perform the six-act drama nine times a week. However, the strain may have been less than rehearsing three new plays every other day. Saturday matinees were particularly radical, since any weekend performance was taken to be Sabbath-breaking. The Boston

Museum had won a modicum of religious sanction by remaining closed on Saturdays.

In addition to the extended run, the full evening's entertainment, and the matinees, *Uncle Tom's Cabin* effected other innovations. The Second and Third Avenue horse railroad's stock went up, for the new stage-lines that ran through Chatham Street were busy transporting this new influx of decorous Gothamites to and fro. Purdy began to adopt the coloration of his new audience and had himself portrayed in a lobby painting with a Bible in one hand, Mrs. Stowe's novel in the other. The walls were plastered with Biblical texts. He instituted a series of Sunday night religious meetings in the theatre, led by the ministers of the Stanton-Street Baptist Church, and the Bowery Theatre was forced to follow suit. [25]

The amplified performance schedule told most on Cordelia who received private tutoring whenever she was offstage. Eventually her mother found a way to substitute a double for her in "The Apotheosis of Little Eva," which took place nightly at half past ten. [26] The child's services were called into play again in December when Purdy considered varying the fare with another dramatization by Charles W. Taylor, *Katy the Hot Corn Girl*, which coincided with the serial publication of Solon Robinson's *Hot Corn: Life Scenes in New York Illustrated*, appearing in the New York *Tribune*. It had the assets of timeliness and local interest, since the scene was set in the Five Points. G. L. Fox as Corney Joe was the spittin' image of the boys in the gallery, and Cordelia as an abused and barefoot waif excited as much pathos as she had as Eva, a role she continued to play every night and at the twice-weekly matinees. (*Katy* was a Monday, Tuesday, Thursday, and Friday matinee feature.)

Purdy decided to plow back some of the considerable profits of *Uncle Tom* into a remounting of the production. The refurbished version boasted two thousand dollars worth of new scenery, including "a grand panoramic view of the Ohio and Mississippi rivers" [27] to vie with the one at Barnum's Museum, which enabled an enactment of Eva's falling from the steamer deck into the water. As the play drew towards its two hundredth performance, "moist eyes and refined feelings" still responded to it in undiminished numbers. Competition from the Bowery Theatre's and Barnum's *Uncle Tom*s could in no way tarnish its success.

The year 1854 brought with it one of the hardest and most formidable winters New York had known, creating widespread unemployment and distress. By early February, the city was struck by a snowstorm and cold wave that drove the temperature down to negative ten degrees, and the price of flour reached an eighteen-year high. [28] And still people clamored to see the National's *Uncle Tom*.

Whatever may be the prejudices, political or otherwise, for or against the 'colored bredern' of this country, the feelings provoked by the representation of *Uncle Tom's Cabin* do us credit. It had demonstrated that our benevolence and humanity are wholly irrespective and independent of any sectional sentiment or predilection, and will be exhibited and exercised whenever excited, be the subject good or bad.[29]

Thus the pro-slavery *Spirit of the Times* congratulated itself, suggesting that *Uncle Tom*'s appeal was based on a fundamental core of humaneness. The fact was that most Democrats could not conceive of equal rights for blacks and therefore would not credit the sincerity of the abolitionists. They regarded abolitionism as a fanatical incursion of morality upon secular freedom.[30] Consequently, the message of *Uncle Tom* was acceptable to most New Yorkers only if taken as a generalized appeal to the emotions.

But sectionalism also helped keep the play on the boards. The passage of the Kansas-Nebraska bill, which gave the South what it wanted by repealing the Missouri Compromise and admitting slavery into the new territories, infuriated even the mildly anti-slavery elements in the North. New Yorkers demonstrated by organizing theatre parties to *Uncle Tom's Cabin*. *The Spirit of the Times* was bemused by this development:

The performance of this drama had made converts to the abolition doctrine many persons we have no doubt, who have never examined the subject, and know nothing of its merits. Well represented sufferings and wrongs, whether fabulous or not, create sympathy, and that sentiment grows into advocacy. We have nothing to do here with the matter politically, but we can perceive what the drama may do to foster or eradicate passions or prejudices of high or low degree.[31]

Purdy continued to feature "moral" dramas at his matinees, which invariably displayed Cordelia, her mother, and her uncle Laff in the cast. The child had already received a silver salver and cup and a basket of flowers as tall as herself at the hundredth performance.[32] She took a benefit on 13 May, at which time the *Cabin* was temporarily boarded up. May was moving month in New York, when audiences became erratic. Moreover, the Ravels had returned to Niblo's Garden, and Purdy may have felt that fresh attractions were called for to rival these perennial favorites. By the time he declared a breathing spell, *Uncle Tom's Cabin* had achieved the record-breaking run of 325 consecutive performances, and Purdy had pocketed thirty thousand dollars.

6

The Chatham Street Theatre

(1854-58)

Even before *Uncle Tom's Cabin*, Purdy's management had been commended for the "steady perseverance, tact, and liberality" that made the National "one of the most prosperous theatres in the city."[1] Throughout the run of *Uncle Tom*, Purdy warranted such praise, for he regularly re-invested his profits in advertising and improvements to secure the pre-eminence of his phenomenal hit. The hundredth performance had been celebrated by a Grand Jubilee Festival complete with brass band and fireworks. His portrait in the lobby was now flanked by one of Mrs. Stowe. He wooed the godly by asserting that "the Manager has taken every precaution that no disorderly person be admitted to the Theatre during the performance of this great production."[2]

This last assurance related to a newspaper war that had capitalized on the reputation of the National's regular patrons. The pro-slavery New York *Observer*, furious at the play's success, excoriated the National as a "rendezvous for prostitution," and the play as "the means of enticing hundreds of innocent souls within its halls and on the road to ruin." The *Tribune* and the *Sunday Atlas* leapt to the theatre's defense, attesting the respectability of the audiences they had observed and the total absence of soiled doves. This controversy attracted west-siders to see for themselves whether the gallery was packed with harlots.[3]

Expenses kept pace with profits, and when *Uncle Tom* was retired and Mrs. and Miss Howard joined their family in Troy to take a cut-down version of the play on tour, Purdy, basically cautious and unimaginative in matters of repertory, fell back into his rut. The death of little Eva gave way to Cony and his wonderful dogs, and with them the old prices and the old blood-and-thunder melodramas. At first, nothing changed at the box-office, and *The Spirit of the Times* could congratulate the National on "doing as well as it ever did in the days of *Uncle Tom's Cabin* and the moral drama dodge"[4]—a remark that indicates how much a fluke *Uncle Tom* had been. Declining receipts soon prompted a revival of the Tom show with a lesser cast; the indefatigable Mrs. W. G. Jones was promoted to Topsy. But it failed to draw. In the fall of 1854, the house hack Charles W. Taylor carpentered a stage version of another current novel, *Fashion and Famine* by Mrs. Anne S. Stephens, which offered Laff the part of Jacob Strong. Very quickly the National bill's touted nothing but revivals of melodramas, burlesques, and equestrian comedy, with Fox starring in his own *Mazeppa*. By November, the house was leased out to a circus until the annual Christmas pantomime, *The Golden Axe*, could be mounted. It was popular but not so popular as the Ravels who had capered nimbly at Niblo's all year with gorgeous new scenery and astounding tricks in their latest hit, *Asphodel or The Magic Pen*.

What had happened to Purdy's business acumen? It had been an unpropitious season for commerce in general, for money grew tight in the uncertain political climate. But Purdy's improvidence was of his own making; having won over new audiences who could be lured to the National only by the unassailable moral tone of *Uncle Tom* and Cordelia's ingenuousness, he failed to hold them with a series of similar offerings. His new public was soon disgusted with the blood-bucket standards and stopped coming. Purdy thought money better spent on advertising and scenery than on commissioning playwrights, and by early 1855, he was virtually bankrupt.[5]

During these doldrums, Laff Fox became the man of the hour. His comic abilities were proficient at making bricks with no straw and, nominally or not, he was the star of the company, which now included cousin George Aiken as an ally. The result was that melodrama, in which Fox never played more than an incidental role, began to fade from its prominence in the bills, and its place was usurped by farces, extravaganzas, and pantomimes. Moral drama made an occasional foray for topical reasons, as when *The Bottle*, based on Cruikshank's engravings, was staged in conjunction with the 1856 prohibition law forbidding the sale of "domestically produced" intoxicants in stores, boarding houses, and places of amusement.[6] But the public paid far more attention to burlesque *fééries* like *The Romance of the Nose*, "a new and original Musical, Aerial, Floral and Conchological Fairy Extravaganza."[7]

By the start of the fall season, the National's repertory was topheavy with direct imitations of the Ravels. *The Green Monster* with Fox as the White Knight, *The Magic Barrel*, *The Magic Pills*, and *The Golden Axe* held sway in the staging of a Monsieur Schmidt, and, if the advertising is to be believed, much money had been lavished on them.[8] The star of the company was given out to be Annie Hathaway, but the success of these pantos and burlesques was abetted by a newcomer, Fanny Herring.

Fanny Herring had, like Laff, spent her childhood in an atmosphere of grease-paint and orange-peel. Born in London in 1832, the daughter of a comedian and a soubrette, both Jews, she came to New York at the age of ten, where her mother, already a star at the Old Bowery, put her on stage in *The Bottle*. On her first entrance, the child sprawled and the bottle of whiskey and loaf of bread she was carrying rolled down the raked floor to the footlights. When she rushed to pick them up, she forgot her lines. "Bow, bow," whispered her experienced mother, but the little girl, disguised as a boy, curtseyed instead. The urchins in the pit roared with laughter, and someone in the gallery shouted, "Turn a somersault, little one, and it will be all right."

Orphaned at fourteen, Fanny got a job as a ballet-girl at four dollars a week at the Chatham Street Theatre, while Charles Burke was its stage manager. She opened as the lead in *The Yellow Dwarf* when the actress playing the Fairy Queen fell ill. When Purdy took over as manager, Fanny was promoted to general utility woman at double her previous salary, but she could not brook "Irish" Anderson's malicious tongue and his dictatorial insistence that she dress elegantly for her roles on her weekly pittance. (Actors customarily provided their own costumes.) Fanny Herring had left the company before Fox joined it, and for the next few years played in many theatres in New York, Rochester, and New Orleans. At last, in 1855, she returned to Chatham Street, aware that her nemesis Anderson had been effaced by Fox. There she opened in a colleen role in *Wealth and Worth*, counterbalancing one of Fox's Hibernian characters. They hit it off immediately and were frequently teamed over the next few years.[9]

Fanny Herring had a glass eye but, except for a slight cast in her gaze, it did not spoil her sultry good looks. Besides, she was a past mistress of makeup.[10] She became a great favorite of the Bowery boys: "I could sing, dance a hornpipe or grand pas seul, fight a broadsword combat, enact pantomime characters, and play anything from Lady Macbeth to Sally Scraggs in farce or burlesque."[11] She was particularly adept in breeches roles, making a name for herself as The Boy Scout,

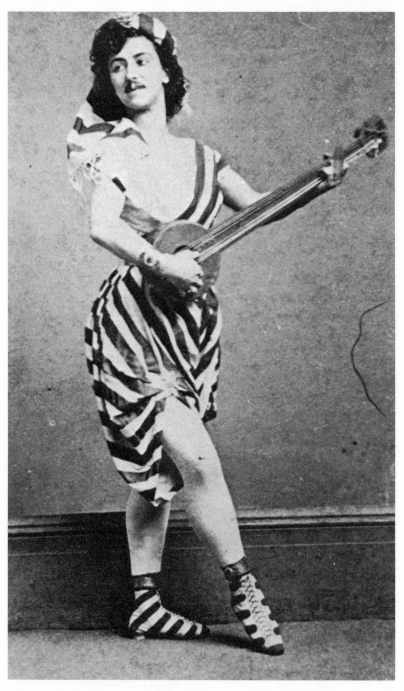

Figure 11. Fanny Herring, probably in the role of Hamet, the Arab Boy in the pantomimic melodrama *The French Spy.* Photograph by C. D. Fredricks, New York. (Author's Collection)

Jack Sheppard, and The Young Mexican, patterns of pluck and intrepidity. In alluding to the intimacy between the comedian and his stage partner, J. B. Howe, the English actor who had replaced Howard as St. Clare, described her as "a little lady who used to pass most of her time in the centre of the dress circle during the day, and at night disported in fleshings and short trunks, fighting half-a-dozen gladiators on the stage with an iron sword and a tin shield, and exclaiming, 'Once more I stand erect, in the God-like attitude of freedom and *man*.'" [12]

Almost from the start of their collaboration, she and Fox were linked romantically. Laff's shadowy wife had retired from stage life as soon as they arrived in New York. Laff hoped to train their daughter, Emily, born in Providence in 1847, to be a facsimile of her cousin Cordelia. Mrs. Fox was rumored to be weak in health, whereas Fanny Herring was strong and strapping. The obvious inferences were drawn.

By this time, "Funny Fox," as he was known, was such a favorite with the gallery gods that he could scarcely walk out the stage door into the Roosevelt Street alley without being pursued by a mob of adoring ragamuffins. He flailed his cane at them to no avail and had to stroll home toward Division and Allen Streets, trailed by this noisy retinue. The procession would be interrupted only if a couple of his followers got into a fight over whether his name was "George Washington Lafayette" or "George Washington Leroy." The result was, illogically, that Fox dropped the *W* from his panoply of initials. [13] Theatrical gossip ran that Fox had become Purdy's partner, and the intense pallor of his face seemed to testify to a new load of responsibilities. It was his influence that enabled him to recruit his brother Charles Kemble in 1857, as a prime ally in the overthrow of melodrama by pantomime.

Poor Charlie had had his own romantic difficulties since the run of *Uncle Tom's Cabin.* He had fallen in love with Kate Denin, half of a sister act that had made its reputation at the Chatham St. Theatre. In 1845, she and Susan Denin had played Paul and Justin in *The Wandering Boys,* in which their stepfather, John Winan (the actor whose illness was supposed to have made Fox's advent possible), sang "The Newsboy's Song."

> *Oh, I'se a newsboy, sassy and free,*
> *A selling my papers daily;*
> *The banks may bust, they're nothing to me,*
> *Nor the coppers I handles daily.*
> *Oh, I sells the extra, the Herald a-n-d the S-u-n,*

and so on. This doggerel, interlarded with recitations by the girls, drove the newsboys in the audience delirious with delight.

How and when Kate Denin met Charles K. Fox remains unknown,

but at all events they were married in the greenroom of the Troy Museum on 3 March 1854. At eleven the next morning she entrained for New York City, with the understanding that the bridegroom would meet her within the next two days. For some unexplained reason, he failed to show up or even to send word—perhaps the wedding night had been a disaster. Coolly, the jilted bride embarked on a steamer for San Francisco three days later, to join her sister for a theatrical engagement. Later on, she secured a legal release from Charlie Fox and married the alcoholic Irish comedian Samuel Ryan. But on another cross-country jaunt, Kate Denin carried off John Wilson, the actor-husband of the Boston Museum's favorite character woman Mrs. Vincent. Kate and John became inseparable, even unto his deathbed, but these irregular carryings-on made her name unsavory to the public and the press for much of her career.[14]

Despite this disastrous honeymoon, Charles Fox soon got back on the horse, so to speak. Two years after this contretemps, he married Mary Hewins. Her love of the stage had been so strong that she ran away to join a circus at the age of twelve and later made her professional theatrical debut at the Troy Museum. She had met Charlie while on the road sometime in the early 1850s, and after their marriage they travelled together, Mary dancing and playing Irishmen with the traditional shillalegh and knee-breeches. She was a valuable addition to Laff Fox's company, for when he later took over the Bowery Theatre, she would become a female C. W. Taylor, a play-doctor ready to turn her hand to anything from nautical drama to scenarios for performing dogs. Mary Hewins was also one of the few women the Fox brothers married of whom her in-laws, the Howards, approved.[15]

As Fox's influence over Purdy increased, the amount of money spent on pantomime increased as well. The prominent dailies, the *Times*, the *Tribune*, the *Herald*, and the *Sun* disdained to cover Bowery entertainments, except when an anomaly like *Uncle Tom* claimed their attention. Only *The Spirit of the Times*, primarily a sporting sheet, regularly noticed its offerings, if only cursorily, and so the first report that Purdy was back on his financial feet appears there. The event was the opening of *Herne the Humbug*, starring Fox in the title role, a burlesque of W. H. Ainsworth's *Herne the Hunter* which had been dramatized at several theatres. "The hits are palpable and the fun abundant, and receipts all that Manager Purdy can desire," recorded the *Spirit*. "Mr. G. L. Fox is particularly happy as the Humbug Huntsman."[16] Another newspaper stated

The 'National' is the favorite resort of the masses, and has probably as critical an audience as many of the more pretentious theatres. The prices of admission are very small; the house is clean and handsome, and the nightly bill displays quantity as well as quality not to be slighted . . . [*Herne the Humbug's*] attraction is so great that hundreds are nightly unable to gain admission to see it. The management is deserving of success, and we are glad to say, it has it.[17]

This was probably puffery paid for by the lessee since *Herne* lasted no more than a fortnight.

The next noteworthy burlesque was *A-Lad-In* which the press claimed "won't let a lad-in front of the house ten minutes after the doors open." Charlie Fox, freed from his Trojan commitments, appeared in it; but most of the praise went to the gorgeous scenery and costumes. "The outlay for the piece has been more than considerable but it will pay itself back with interest."[18] This was a lesson Fox heeded very closely.

Despite another torrid summer, business continued strong in the well-ventilated National, with praise for the pantomimes *The Red Gnome* and *The Golden Axe* in particular.[19] Something of a family reunion took place in September, when Fox and Purdy put on Taylor's adaptation of Mrs. Stowe's latest novel, *Dred, A Tale of the Dismal Swamp*, in the hope of recreating their earlier sensation. The cast included George and Caroline Howard, Frank Aiken, Emily Fox, Laff, Fanny Herring, and, most memorably, little Cordelia in her first blackface role as Tom Tit, the mischievous slave boy. She was the only player to transcend tepid reviews; the *Tribune* rated Howard a foppish milquetoast, his wife devoid of grace and vivacity, and cousin Frank mistaken in his belief that he was making an impression.[20] Unlike its precursor, this play founded its abolitionist argument more on political and economic grounds than emotional ones, and it failed to make a similar impact on Bowery audiences.[21] For all that, it ran a decent five weeks, and the management took advantage of the Howards's presence to revive *Uncle Tom* for Saturday matinees. The chief attraction of this period was Laff's first essay as Master Bobby in *The Schoolmaster*, a farce copied from the Ravels; his impersonation of a gangling, naughty schoolboy would be refined over time into a classic.

When the Howards left for Europe in October, the National, as usual, reverted to Ravelations, *Asphodel* being "nightly received with unbounded applause."[22] The Ravels themselves were still at Niblo's Garden, entrancing the public with *Esmeralda, or The Hunchback of Notre Dame*, the most lavish romantic ballet yet seen in the United States. But Fox and Purdy knew that, before Christmas, the Ravels were to leave New York on a national tour. Consequently, on 29 November, the newspapers announced:

Mr. Purdy has in preparation a new, gorgeous, and immensely extensive pantomime just received from Paris, with models, plots, and a portion of machinery, and translated expressly for this theatre, by Mons. Perett, entitled "Planche, or the Lively Fairies."[23]

"The long-looked for, the wonderful, the gorgeous, brilliantly grand and immensely extensive" *Planche* opened three days before Christmas to take full advantage of the holiday. Monsieur Pereth (not Perett) of London (not Paris) had sent over models of the original scenery, which was amplified with other trickwork by William Crane, the National's machinist, who patented his inventions. All the tricks and transformations had been directed by Fox, with a number of his own additions. "Several thousand dollars have been expended in the preparation of this stupendous Pantomime, and neither pains, expense nor care been spared" in preparing scenery, costumes, and original music, all under Fox's supervision.[24]

Never before had the National invested so heavily in the staging and advertising of a pantomime, but it paid off. The play became a real moneyspinner for the theatre and drew immense houses with standing-room only, unlucky latecomers losing their seats and having to cling to the doors. The gadgetry went off without a hitch. "The spectators spend the evening here in admiration of the scenery, or in laughing and wondering at the extraordinary tricks, transformations &c. in the piece. Some of the tricks are rather 'broad,' rather indelicate, but they were heartily laughed at by the masculines, while the ladies tittered behind their fans."[25] This bawdy latitude suited the taste of the locals, but such indelicacy kept away family audiences, to whom newspapers could not recommend the show. Fox would have to learn to tone down his coarseness if he was to become big-time.

No one quarrels with success, and Purdy added his usual Wednesday matinee, allowing *Planche* to run into March. The only variety in the bill meantime was provided by burlesques and afterpieces. Fox and Annie Hathaway appeared as Medea and Jason respectively in *Medea and My-Deary*, a parody of Mathilde Heron's classical revival. The legitimate star was assaulted anew for her Camille with *Clam-Eel*, with Fox in the title part and Fanny Herring betrousered as Armand. Brother Charles was conspicuous in many of these pieces, including the old panto *The Magic Barrel*, which "keeps the audience in a continuous roar of laughter."[26] Laff Fox was such a local celebrity by now that when Crane the machinist took his benefit, the afterpiece was a *drame à clef* called *Who Pinn'd Fox's Coat Tail?*[27]

Purdy followed his pantomimic success with another winner, the three-act drama *Life in Brooklyn*, with Laff as Jerry Vandevere and Charlie as George Timerton. This kind of panoramic mirror of familiar city life, portraying a cross-section of society set against recognizable locales, was immensely popular at the time. Such urban dramas were direct descendants of Pierce Egan's *Life in London* (1821), which had enjoyed many stage adaptations, including an American sequel by

John Brougham, *Life in New York; or, Tom and Jerry on a Visit* (1856). They coincided with the consolidation of urban centers themselves and seemed to reconcile the spectator to this burgeoning environment by reproducing it in miniaturized form on stage. The multiple facets of metropolitan existence, depicted as realistically as possible, automatically took on a romantic aura by being framed within a proscenium.

Life in Brooklyn featured gentlemen, garroters, farmers, mechanics, and firemen, with scenery faithfully replicating the sights of the town. "Everything went off with the utmost satisfaction amid roars of laughter and shouts of applause," reported *The Spirit of the Times*.[28] Once again the house was so crowded that benches had to be set up in the boxes.

Purdy, who had been suffering from inflammation of the lungs, returned to his post in May to spend much of his profits on a thorough renovation and redecoration of the theatre, with new upholstery and a new drop curtain to herald the next spectacular drama, Taylor's *Cleopatra or, The Battle of Actium*. In this echo of classical tragedy, Fox's acting was noted as "particularly good."

The drama is exceedingly interesting, and spiced with much humor, which that sly old (or rather young) *Fox* dispenses to the delectation of his audience; nor does he hesitate about adding to or altering the text, when he knows he can thereby 'bring down the house.'[29]

Three years later, when Fox revived the play, he would be criticized for gagging,[30] but by then critics were taking him more seriously.

The remainder of the season saw another return of the Howards and a rash of those Irish parts in which Fox had made his reputation. On 13 July, *The Irishman in Baghdad, a Musical Romance* featured Fox as Terence Kilrooney, Fanny Herring as his daughter Norah, Charlie as Boubikir Mussin the grand vizier, George Aiken as King of the Genii, and Frank Aiken as the Caliph. Most of the scripts performed at the National never attained the dignity of print and exist, if at all, in prompter's copies and written sides. Asa Cushman's prompt-copy of this play survives to reveal the kind of entertainment that regaled Bowery audiences in the mid-1850s.

The two-act piece takes place in Baghdad, which the author apparently believed to be in Turkey. Terence Kilrooney, separated from his daughter Norah, has accidentally saved the Sultan's life and been ennobled. His first entrance is in sumptuous Turkish costume, a sight gag in itself, but when asked to kowtow to the Sultan, Terence replies with all the family pride of the stage Irishman:

Och sure it's the glory o' St. Patrick myself does honor to! Tare and 'ouns! I'm a descindint o' the Kings o' Munster—the Mac Murroughs—the O'Brians—the

Delaneys—and the Donohues, it's a better use I have for this head o'mine than clapping it under a stool, mind dat once't.

One can be sure that each of these clans met with a rousing cheer from their namesakes in the galleries.

When asked about his home town, Terence explains that it produces "Fist fights,—mealy patatys—bog whiskey—sturrip tail cows—buttermilk—pretty feminines—and thumping big babies." Himself he describes as a leveller and a turner: "I level the grass, and turn it into hay." And his tag to the scene, as the Sultan exits, is "Long life to your honor—I pray you niver die in childbed."

Meanwhile Norah, a role which gave Fanny Herring a chance to wear Oriental pajamas and boy's clothes, is languishing in the harem. She is soon reunited with her father, but the two of them get embroiled in a virtually incomprehensible plot involving a magic mirror obtained from the King of the Genii by the evil vizier. Before the act ends, Terence gets a chance to review the squadron of janissaries under his charge. His monologue scarcely hints at the fun Fox must have had with his Islamic Mulligan Guard.

Och, mother o'Moses! It's a great man I am! The men rule the women—the Sultan rules the men—and I rule the Sultan! Terence ye divil, you're born to good luck! Whoop!—attention, centre division—drop all alongside, while I stand in the middle. (*men advance*) now heads up, and toes out—that gentleman's Turban's a little out o'line there—mind orders now—(*Man Sneezes*) who was dat? who was dat coughed through his nose? Bad manners to the likes o'ye—but I'll cut the next nose off that dares to cough—now, I'm goin' to march ye to the Guard house—then, ye may break ranks, and go to the Divil. Follow me, I'll lead the way. (*Exeunt L.*)

In the second act, Terence's part is somewhat subordinated to that of Norah, who enters disguised as a page. Dialogue between her and Guina the old nurse discloses that the magic mirror can reveal whether a woman is chaste. Such a situation could easily have been trimmed with equivocal remarks, and Norah's claim that she is virtuous because she comes from Ireland is a patent claptrap. There is a drinking scene between Terence and Boubikir—the brothers Fox in a double-act—that may owe something to Mozart's *Abduction from the Seraglio*, and the next time we see the Irishman he is in drag or, as he puts it, "woman's machinery." "What have you made a lady of me for?" he protests. "Is it my innocence ye're goin' to take advantage of, bad manners to ye?" The finale takes place in a great Hall of Statues where everything is set right and the Sultan weds Norah.[31]

On the page, the fooling is thin, but the script is merely a skeleton to be fleshed out by gaudy scenery, the illusive charms of gaslight, and the expert clowning and singing of the cast. By this time, Fox's name alone was enough to secure a full house at the National; announcing that Fox would play a large part in an upcoming production, the *Spirit of the Times* concluded "*Nuff sed.*"[32] Throughout the summer heat, the house was crowded.

In August, Fox played Higginbotham in *Fast Young Men of New York and Brooklyn*, a three-hour exploitation of local color, in which he was judged "all fun and few can refrain from laughing whenever he 'gives the signal.'"[33] Legend has it that when he played Farmer Van de Wercken in a similar play, he based his characterization on a well-known eccentric whose peculiarities and pet phrase "Come boys, let's go to work and take a drink" were hit off so well that the farmer's wife boxed her husband's ears during a performance.[34]

During the gymnasium scene in *Fast Young Men*, the acrobatics of the Denier Brothers were featured. This may signal the first appearance in Fox's career of Tony Denier, who was to be his close associate, rival, and heir in years to come. The Deniers and several other circus acts also appeared in Fox's extravagant pantomimic chinoiserie, *The Magic Hands*, at the end of August. He understood that the more feats of physical skill he could interpolate into the comedy, the more closely his efforts would resemble the Ravels. The fun was variegated with the Deniers on a double trapeze, Adelaide Price in a Scottish dance, and S. Weed performing an Ethiopian (read minstrel) jig. At the old price of fifty cents in the orchestra and twenty-five cents in the dress circle, it convulsed audiences with laughter throughout the fall season, and proved to be solid competition for the Ravels, who had returned to Niblo's with their usual standbys.[35]

Fox's success is all the more astonishing, since these performances ran parallel to the great riot that broke out between the street gangs the "Dead Rabbits" and the "Bowery Boys." After it had raged for two days, the state militia had to be called in to suppress it. This could hardly have rendered the National alluring to respectable patrons. Then, on 13 October, New York banks announced that they were suspending specie payment. This panic triggered the depression that had been predicted since August.[36] The National managed to take the minds of the public off these dire events and diverged from pantomime in November with the topical *Revolt in India*, which enjoyed a decent run. The horrors of the Sepoy mutiny were painted in lurid colors, "softened somewhat by the laughable acting of Fox, and his comical *phiz.*"[37]

As Christmas loomed ahead, pantomime once more was made the order of the day. The Ravels had been playing *Boreas, or The Spirit of the Air* at Niblo's; Fox concocted his own version, stealing partly from the French troupe, and partly from an English panto called *Aurilla, the*

North Wind; or, Spirit of the Air. It meant to outdo all the National's previous efforts in this direction and cost a lordly three thousand dollars.
Much of this was spent on opulent scenery by J. R. Smith and the
strenuous gymnastics of the Carlo Family, with father Felix in the role of
Boreas. "Mr. G. L. Fox has a character which keeps the audience in a
roar of laughter when he is on the stage—and he has much to do in the
piece."[38] So great was the audience's enthusiasm that Purdy kept it running well into the middle of January 1858.[39]

Throughout the rest of the season, Fox was seen in his customary
diversity of roles, from Flimsy Bogus in *Life of the Mormons at Salt
Lake* to the infant Furibond in *The Invisible Prince*.[40] But by the summer of 1858, he was no longer on Purdy's salary list. That August, in
partnership with James W. Lingard, he took over the management of the
Bowery Theatre. Lingard, two years older than Fox, was a Londoner,
who had been apprenticed to an architect at fourteen, but after eight
years of acting in the English provinces and capital, came to New York
in 1848. After stints at the Baltimore Museum and Philadelphia's Chestnut Street Theatre, Lingard moved to the National in 1852 to play
Uncle Tom in the Taylor version at a moment's notice.[41] He and his wife
had stayed on to act with Fox in the Aiken *Uncle Tom* and to be ser-
viceable if mediocre performers in Purdy's company.

Why Fox decided to go into management on his own is obvious. Re-
alizing his indispensable position as stage manager and comic star, he
expected greater fame and fortune by controlling his own playhouse.
His native ambition was probably fanned into a flame by greenroom
hangers-on. Some rumors ran that Fox and Purdy had quarrelled;[42] possibly Fox's grandiose ideas ran counter to the manager's conservatism.
But whatever the cause of the defection, the National was dealt a fatal
blow when Fox, "the greatest favorite ever seen there,"[43] left it. Without the talents and ideas of his prime mover, Purdy, who had been able
to weather the panic of 1857 thanks only to the popularity of his star,
slid steadily toward bankruptcy. He revived many of Fox's vehicles with
George A. Beane in the comic roles and managed to muddle through
till 21 March 1859. Then, physically ailing and financially depleted,
he gave up the reins to his treasurer Thomas C. Steers, who promoted
George Aiken to stage manager. The theatre succumbed by summer's
end, and, after many vicissitudes, in 1862 the National Theatre in
Chatham Street was turned into a store. That same year Purdy died at
his home in Brooklyn, expiring with his beloved playhouse.[44]

Tracing the ups and downs of the National's seasons during the tenure of Purdy and Fox reveals how the latter gradually rose to prominence and how he altered the repertory to suit his own particular abilities. When he first came to Chatham Street, a hick from down east, he

was relegated to comic relief in a bill that preponderated with gory melo-drama and jerry-built farces. Over time, burlesque and pantomime came to the fore, and money was spent to lure audiences with clam-orous advertising and lavish decor. How much of this evolution was willed and how much intuitive cannot be determined, but by the time Fox left to run the Bowery Theatre, his was a name to conjure with, and he was fixed in his ideas of what constituted a proper repertory for a popular theatre.

7

The Old Bowery and the New

(1858-60)

"The New York audiences," Olive Logan assured her readers in 1870, "are for the most part, extremely sedate, decorous, and, save at the Bowery, seem devoid of the decidedly plebeian element."[1] Her one exception had been notorious for over half-a-century. The same year that Fox and Lingard took on the management of the Old Bowery, Edward Eddy explained to German-born actor Charles Pope his reasons for getting the theatre off his hands. Pope, in his imperfect English, recorded them in his diary: "He says it is a hole. The neighborhood is in the hands of half grown men. Thieves and *'dead rabids.'*"[2]

Although the National and the Bowery enjoyed similar types of audiences and styles of repertory, until *Uncle Tom* had made the former's fortune the Bowery had been the better-known, better-reported playhouse. It had been rebuilt four times before Fox and Lingard rented it, most recently in 1845. The building held three thousand persons, with the usual hard benches in the pit, an exclusively stag preserve, and four semi-circular galleries.[3] As at the National, the pit was headquarters for newsboys who were, if possible, more obstreperous here than at the Chatham St. house. On walking down the few steps from sidewalk level, they would remove their coats and sit on them, partly to cushion the hard seats, partly to prevent those garments from being stolen.[4] Then they would shove their caps back on to their necks, to suit the newsboy fashion of combing their hair over their eyes. The male occupants of the boxes also retained their hats and stolidly chewed tobacco. Whereas the foreign contingent at the National had been chiefly Jews who ran old clothes businesses and pawnshops, the Bowery's Europeans were German artisans and storekeepers, recent emigrants, who filled the boxes and lower balconies.

At the back of the house, below the box tier, was a lunch counter, refreshing playgoers with pickled pigs' feet, peanuts, sandwiches, pickles, sarsaparilla, ginger pop, soda water, and fruit. The boys were chiefly tempted by bolivars, a kind of molasses cake, and Washington pie, a slab two inches thick composed of stale pies and gingerbread ground up and rebaked. Apples, oranges, peanuts, and candy were also hawked in the aisles.[5] The munching of these comestibles and the tossing of shells and bones on the floor provided a crunchy accompaniment to any performance, and if the boys did not like what they saw, the fruit and nuts served as missiles to drive performers into the wings.

The audience supplied a virtual antiphony to anything that went on on stage. A favorite actor would be treated on his entrance with three cheers, a less favored one with hisses, catcalls, rotten eggs, and wadded-up peanut bags. If the hapless actor remained in this state of disgrace for any length of time, the management would rescind his contract, for the Bowery audience was all-powerful and ruled through this spontaneous *vox populi*. One commentator compared it to the Restoration wits, whose praise or damnation could make or ruin a play. The slightest hitch, like the clumsy working of a trapdoor hinge or an unorthodox costume on a demon, could determine the balance of favor.[6]

What they preferred was a flamboyant melodrama, sodden with gore and frantic with mayhem, physical action, and thrills; in short, they shared the tastes of most modern film audiences.[7] The tragic hero was expected to rescue the damsel in distress from an impregnable castle, carry her down a forty-foot ladder, hold her with one arm while annihilating half a score of pursuers by picking up one by the heels and knocking out the brains of the rest with this human bludgeon, spring on his horse, and make good his escape with the damsel in tow, "amid a tempest of bullets, Congreve rockets, Greek fire and bomb-shells."[8] The louder the rant, the better, and if the hero were an outlaw, a glamorous highwayman like Dick Turpin, or a teen-aged jail-breaker like Jack Sheppard, success was assured.

Admission prices were relatively low, fifty cents for the orchestra, seventy-five for the balcony, the most select part of the house, five and seven dollars for boxes, and twelve and a half cents (known as a shilling) for the upper gallery and pit. Anyone who wished to be admitted to the pit before the house opened could do so by paying an extra three cents, a custom that led occupants of the gallery to yell in stentorian

Figure 12. "The Shoe Shine Brigade, New York City." This half of a stereopticon slide photographed by E. & H. T. Anthony Co. captures Fox's juvenile audience standing before a poster of him at the Old Bowery in *The Duke's What Is It?* a parody of the melodrama *The Duke's Motto*, advertised further down the wall as an offering at Niblo's Garden. The date is 1862 and the location probably the area near City Hall Park where walls were set aside for theatrical advertisement. (Courtesy of the Lightfoot Collection, Greenport, N. Y.)

tones to lucky comrades below, "Hey, Johnny, how did yer git the extry pennies to git in de pit wid?" Any delays in raising the curtain were met with the irrepressible unison cry of "Hist da rag!" The top gallery was occasionally the scene of minor riots, arguments over the merits of an actor that would terminate in the threat of one disputant to chuck the other into the pit. These menaces would be greeted with the traditional shout, "Naw, don't do dat. Kill a fiddler wid'im."

In the Bowery Theatre's earlier days, a row of iron spikes had extended across the stage before the footlights and halfway up the proscenium arch to prevent just such an audience participation. A policeman was stationed at the front of the pit with a rattan cane to stifle shouts of "Hi! hi!" or any extraordinary rumpus, but some thought he more than contributed his own share to the general uproar.

Bowery audiences got their money's worth, for the doors opened at seven, the curtain went up at a quarter to eight, and the performance seldom ended before midnight, to accommodate a bill of four or five plays. The management arranged for its non-local patrons to travel via "the Dry Dock stages at the door of the theatre as late as half-past twelve o'clock, also with the Spring Street line of stages running through Hudson Street and Tenth Avenue to Thirty-second Street." [9] The history of public transportation and that of public amusements are closely bound together.

Fox had played at the Bowery on 15 December 1854 at a benefit for Mrs. T. D. Yeomans, [10] and he was well aware of the legacy of noise, rowdyism, and bloodcurdling histrionics that he and Lingard were inheriting. For the season they ran it, they prescribed the mixture as before, with swashbuckling tragedies and Fox-fangled pantomimes as their staples. They were careful to engage a company studded with local favorites; Fanny Herring and other leading members of the National troupe were, as the French say, "debauched" to the neighboring house. J. B. Howe, the English *jeune premier* who had replaced George Howard, was wooed by Lingard with an offer of thirty dollars a week and the chance to write a riproaring sensation drama for the Bowery's opening. [11] He accepted, but was disappointed to find that the new lessees reopened the Bowery on 7 August 1858 with a mixed bill of *Macbeth*, songs and dance, Fox and Fanny Herring in *Sketches in India* (presumably a cut down version of the Sepoy mutiny drama), and the pantomime *The Schoolmaster*, with Fox cutting capers as a naughty scholar.

An attempt was made to keep the offerings topical. The laying of the transoceanic telegraph prompted *John Bull and Brother Jonathan on the Atlantic Cable*, with Fox himself as the allegorical Yankee and Fanny as Young Sam, "a specimen of juvenile America." [12] Serial novels running in New York newspapers were dramatized hot off the press, and, to glorify Ireland, the plays of Dion Boucicault began to appear with some frequency, usually with the playwright's authorization. The Howard family lent customary support by descending *en masse* from Troy to treat the public to its well-worn versions of *Uncle Tom* and *Dred.* The Trojan enterprise had finally foundered and the Howards had to take to the road to earn their back salaries. Charles Kemble Fox, who had left the National to return to Troy, now definitively rejoined brother Laff in Manhattan.

Fox continued to emphasize topicality and local color with *New York and Brooklyn, or The Poor Sewing Girl,* which featured "The Conflagration of the Crystal Palace, the Fireman's Torchlight Procession— Band of Music, Engine, Hose Carriages, &c.; Reception of the Philadelphia Hose Company; Crook's Dining Saloon, Bowery; Brandreth House, Broadway; City Hall, Brooklyn, by moonlight; Pier No. 1, North River."[13] Engine-chasing audience members must have thrilled to the shock of recognition. Although the house dramatist invested with churning out spectacular crimes and exciting denouements weekly was Harry Seymour, Fox was thought to have had the lion's share in writing *Our English Cousin,* a takeoff of Laura Keene's hit *Our American Cousin.* Besides appearing in the unusual (for him) role of the Hon. Augustus Fitzberry Cecil, Fox flattered spectators with a scene of the skating pond in Central Park, in imitation of the drama *Central Park* playing at Wallack's. Fox could be secure in his plagiarisms from first-class houses for, at this period, the two audiences never commingled, and it was unlikely that anyone but a fugitive reporter would be in a position to compare the painted ice of the rival theatres.

During the course of this undistinguished season, something occurred that casts light on Fox's hitherto obscure personality. J. B. Howe had joined the Bowery company ignorant of how long Fox and Lingard intended to manage the theatre. He had only a verbal agreement with them that a fortnight's notice on either side could cancel their agreement. His disappointment at not having a play produced was assuaged by several juicy roles, including the lead in *Glendower, or The North Sea Rover* which ran for eleven weeks. But thereafter his parts paled to drab romantic heroes, unsympathetic to the Bowery public, and he decided to return to the National.

Desperate Captain Purdy had offered Howe a salary of fifty dollars a week to be leading man and stage manager, provided he would let himself be billed as Purdy's co-lessee. Purdy's reasoning was that Howe had won such popularity at the Bowery that his name alone would "attract the boys down here."

I accepted his terms [Howe recollected] and gave in my notice to Fox and Lingard, when I was immediately assailed with the grossest abuse, and even threatened to have my head punched. I reasoned with them that it was equally my duty to look after myself as it was for them to get the best material available for their purpose, and that had I not suited them they were equally at liberty to get rid of me, as there was no contract which bound us together.

But my reasoning was all in vain, and from that moment to the time I left the theatre [sometime in November], I had nothing but the most ungracious and outrageous treatment from them for fourteen days that any actor could be subjected to; for on my last night they both waited at the foot of the dressing-room stairs and threatened to kick me from the stage door.[14]

This episode reveals that, whatever Fox's popularity with his public, he was beginning to develop a reputation for unpleasantness with his associates. His manner had never been polished or urbane; his brother-in-law's gentility had never rubbed off on him. His spotty education, ambulant adolescence, and generally saturnine temperament combined to make him a formidably antipathetic figure on first acquaintance. J. J. McCloskey, a later member of his Bowery company, went so far as to say that "the first impression of him was, as a rule, repellent."[15] It took the ten years he stayed with Fox for McCloskey to perceive the good qualities deeply imbedded beneath this crude exterior.

McCloskey had come in contact with Fox when the comedian and his partner Lingard began to recruit for a newer venture. The proprietors of the Bowery had raised the rent when they saw the popularity of the new management,[16] and in turn the managers decided to open a theatre of their own. They wanted a troupe that, beyond being classified into lines of business, the usual stock company arrangement, would be outstanding in its versatility, each member capable of playing a host of different roles, as Fox did himself. McCloskey, then at the Broadway Theatre, was alternating Dick Turpin in *Rookwood,* a role requiring horsemanship and melodramatic acting, with a light comedy part. Fox attended a matinee and afterwards offered to engage McCloskey, "but his repellent manner made me waver, until the inducement of higher pay overcame my personal dislike."[17] Higher but not high, for McCloskey also recalled it as "small remuneration" for three or four different plays a night with a daily change of program. An actor's handbook of the period cites Bowery salaries as "from $6 to $20 and $25 a week."[18]

Whatever the inducements, Fox put together a strong working company that displayed the desired virtuosity. In addition to himself and his brother, there were McCloskey; Joseph E. Nagle; John Nunan; Asa Cushman, the former prompter at the National; Kate Fisher, who succeeded to Fanny Herring's roles for a while; Fanny herself; the experienced Mrs. W. G. Jones, who was lured from the Old Bowery in mid-season; and later, George C. Boniface, Welsh Edwards, William Stanton, and Maurice Pike. This host was being raised for an ambitious enterprise, for Fox and Lingard, no doubt buoyed up by the rich receipts of their Bowery season, were about to open a brand-new playhouse, untainted by any forerunner's failures and unvandalized by rambunctious audiences.

During the summer of 1859, Fox instituted a series of outdoor festivals and balloon ascensions in Jones's Wood, conducted on so large a scale that they failed to put any money in the entrepreneur's pocket. This was typical of Fox's projects, on which he would unstintingly lavish huge sums unmindful of whether or not they could recoup his investment. A like prodigality was evident in the theatre Fox and Lingard audaciously called the New Bowery.

The New Bowery was located a block above its namesake, on the west side of the Bowery between Canal and Hester Streets, the latest comer in a city glutted with playhouses. The handsome edifice seated twenty-five hundred persons in a pit seventy-two feet deep by ninety feet wide, and another two hundred in the three tiers of boxes. The stage was eighty-five feet deep and fifty feet wide at the proscenium, and was flanked by dressing-rooms, scene shops, and greenrooms, with plenty of space to admit any spectacular effect required. The exterior of the building, a great improvement over the wooden ramshackle façade it replaced, was an imitation of the Old Bowery on a grander scale, with a handsome portico of iron Corinthian columns twenty-five feet wide. The scenery had been purchased from the Broadway Theatre and was repainted by the Smith brothers, with a special curtain and act drop by Hillyard. The interior facilities boasted the latest improvement in lighting, ventilation, and white and gold embellishments, with a fresco ceiling by Guidicini.

All these amenities ran into money and it was reputed that Fox and Lingard had already paid $150,000 for the building even before improvements were added. Nevertheless they clung to their old prices and retained their old audience. On opening night, 5 September 1859, the spectators who thronged the new house to see *The Orange Girl of Venice* and *The Four Lovers* were the proletarian habitués, still kept in order by the sergeant-at-arms with the rattan cane, but cheering "when the patriotic youth triumphed over the aristocratic scoundrel, revenged a parent's murder, and freed his country at the same time." The *Herald*, covering the opening as a news event, reported that "the b'hoys were in their glory, and the juvenile worshippers of their drama enjoyed their peanuts, boos and peculiar calls and whistles to the top of their bent."[19]

Besides the new ambience, there was nothing very novel or au-

Figure 13. G. L. Fox as Salem Scudder in *The Octoroon.* An unattributed lithograph based on a photograph. (Courtesy of the Harvard Theatre Collection)

dacious about the fare Fox served. He perpetuated the Bowery system of several plays to a bill, a mélange of thrillers, patriotic spectacles, and ribtickling farces, with spectacular pantos and burlesques to season the blend every so often. The Howards returned on an almost seasonal basis to blow the dust off *Uncle Tom*, even after Cordelia retired at the advanced age of thirteen in 1861. At one of her benefits, the three-act version of *Oliver Twist* in which she had been promoted from Dick to the title role, Uncle Laff could be seen as the Artful Dodger, Uncle Charlie as Mr. Bumble, and mother and father as Nancy and Monks. Fanny Herring, gaining in popularity daily, played the breeches roles she practiced well into old age and introduced a Protean vehicle, *Fast Women of the Modern Time, or Life in the City and Suburbs*, allowing her to play seven characters of either sex.

Occasionally, under pressure from visiting stars, the management would attempt a more intellectually strenuous bill. *The Corsican Brothers* and *Faust*, despite their spectacular elements, failed to arouse interest during J. A. J. Neafie's guest appearance, but the current hit *The Octoroon*, Dion Boucicault's melodrama of slave auctions and exploding steamboats, proved to be a huge success. It also embroiled Fox and Lingard in a legal action that showed them to be in the pursuit of the main chance irrespective of author's rights.

Boucicault had originally produced *The Octoroon* at the Winter Garden, but, having disagreed over salary with the managers, William Stuart and Thomas C. Fields, cancelled performances. The Irish dramatist had taken out a copyright on the play and withdrawn his prompt-script from the Winter Garden, but the wily Stuart, in anticipation of this move, had had it copied. The managers recast the play, but as soon as the lawsuit Boucicault had instigated looked like being settled in his favor, they astutely sold their tenuous rights to *The Octoroon* to Fox and Lingard for two hundred dollars, throwing in the scenery for a trifle more. Stuart and Fields closed their Winter Garden production, leaving Boucicault's lawsuit dangling in mid-air.

Fox and Lingard audaciously advertised their *Octoroon* as the same production as the Winter Garden's, with "a cast embracing all the available talent of the original cast and the entire company," and staged "in the same excellent manner as at the Winter Garden."[20] Fox essayed Joe Jefferson's role of Salem Scudder, the philosophical Yankee, and made a personal success of it.

Enraged at this turn of events, Boucicault gave his imprimatur to another production at the Old Bowery, which rapidly failed, and then directed his legal artillery at the New Bowery's management, charging them with outright piracy. Fox and Lingard, in their defence, took the tack that the play itself was a plagiarism and that therefore Boucicault had no rights to it as an original work. Even Jefferson was called to testify that the broad plot outlines came from Mayne Reid's novel *The Quadroon*. But since originality was not at issue legally, that line of defence had to be abandoned. As the case dragged its weary length through the courts, Fox was emboldened to try a touring company with himself and several of his troupe, and *The Octoroon* got as far as the National Theatre in Boston in February 1860 before it returned to New York. As usual with Fox's financial ventures, this tour earned him prestige but no money. Eventually, after two years of litigation, the case was settled in October 1862 in favor of the plaintiff. Boucicault received a judgement of five hundred dollars against Fox and Lingard.[21]

Meanwhile the box-office flourished. Two Thanksgiving Day performances in 1859 had together grossed fifteen hundred dollars which, considering the cheap admission, spelled packed houses. The theatre was "enjoying the full tide of success."[22] To the advantage of Fox and Lingard, the Old Bowery was collapsing. George C. Boniface, who had succeeded to the lesseeship in their wake, quit in mid-season to join the acting company at the New Bowery.

But then the Old Bowery showed unexpected signs of life and jolted the rival managers into a semblance of concern. This happened, briefly, when George Wood reopened the senior house in September 1860 with an excellent troupe. Fox and Lingard responded with an uncharacteristic display of Shakespearean tragedy: Edward Eddy in *Antony and Cleopatra*, *Richard III*, and *Hamlet*, with Fanny Herring changing from tights to draperies to play Ophelia; along with *Werner* and other fustian vehicles beloved of barnstormers. *The Spirit of the Times* commented wryly:

The New Bowery, somewhat startled by the vigorous management of the old, instead of depending upon its own resources, calls to its assistance seventh rate stars, whose only ability consists in shaking the rafters of the building with their rant. Unless they pursue a more sensible policy, they cannot well stand before the progressive enterprise of George Wood. They may draw houses for a while, but they gain no permanent advantage.[23]

Perhaps Fox and Lingard heeded the press, for, with Eddy's departure, they reverted to melodrama and pantomime, and as Wood proved over the long haul to be the latest in a line of lessees incapable of making the Old Bowery a paying proposition, they regained the upper hand. Wood was succeeded by Spalding and Rogers who introduced circus shows, against which the New Bowery fought back with a series of equestrian presentations, including the ever-popular *Mazeppa*, the fifth act of *Richard III* on horseback, and *The Cataract of the Ganges*, featuring Nathan's stud of twenty steeds. And, on the principle that bigger is better, the horses were succeeded by Nathan's wonderful elephants in *Bluebeard*.[24] These distractions aside, the bills were not dissimilar to the usual Fox and Lingard offerings.

By 1861, pantomime was once again edging out the other genres at the New Bowery. Billing his company as the G. L. Fox Troupe of American Pantomimists, Fox regaled audiences with Ravel clones such as *Asphodel* and *Raoul*, along with standard English panto with nursery tale preludes and slapstick harlequinades, such as *Mother Goose and the Golden Egg* and *Harlequin Jack, the Giant Killer*. In the latter, Fox assumed the role of Clown and his brother Charles that of Pantaloon. It was a team that would become famous.

When they first played these parts individually is unclear. Under Purdy, Fox had usually played Harlequin to the Clowns of Cony and Blanchard, and, although his face was celebrated for its mobility, his body was lankier and less muscled than was usual in the clown *emploi*. One legend has it that when Purdy staged *Mazulme the Night Owl*, a Frenchman was cast as Clown and Fox as Harlequin, because Fox was a good dancer who could take high leaps through the flats and do pratfalls. The Frenchman quit in a huff following a quarrel and Fox succeeded to his role.[25] He was certainly billed at the National on 7 January 1856 as Maclou in *Mazulme*, a part usually played by one of the Ravels, but Fox was not normally noted for his acrobatics. Another, even less credible account, alleged to come from the comedian himself, says that the two Frenchmen engaged to play Clown and Pantaloon at the Old Bowery were found "suicided" in their beds and so the Fox brothers volunteered for their roles.[26]

In any case, by this period, the Fox brothers had improved their own pantomimic skills to such a pitch that they could easily rival the Ravels in all but acrobatics. The Bowery demand for horseplay was honored. All but the rough outlines of a Ravel barber-shop sketch would disappear in Fox's translation with its whitewash brushes and buckets of lather, and cleavers stropped in place of razors.[27] Fox was never averse to a bit of *double entendre* if it got a laugh, a characteristic that would tar his reputation when he moved to Broadway. It was his fondness for coarse material, along with the unwashed nature of his audiences, that continued to keep his name out of the papers until his successes were too great to be ignored. However funny his performances, families could not safely be recommended to venture their children or their fastidiousness into the Bowery.

This may explain why the best description we have of a Fox pantomime of this vintage comes from an Englishwoman, Emilie Cowell. Her husband, Samuel Houghton Cowell, was a well-known comic singer, born in the United States, who had risen to fame in the London music

halls with such song-and-patter numbers as *Villikins and his Dinah,*
Billee Barlow, and *The Ratcatcher's Daughter.* He had embarked on a
concert tour of the States and had the misfortune to coincide with the
outbreak of the Civil War; the consequence for him was financial
disaster.

When Cowell was not himself performing, he and his wife would attend local theatres. And so, on 28 March 1861, they came to the New
Bowery and beheld *The Liberty Boys of 1786,* a stock scream of the
eagle, republican propaganda featuring one Yankee putting four red-
coats to rout. The Cowells were not amused, but of the Ravel-inspired
panto, *Raoul,* that followed, Mrs. Cowell records in her diary:

The Pantomime was very pleasing. The manager Mr. Fox was "Conraci" or
clown after the style of the Ravels, and was exceedingly quaint, and humorous, though scarcely ever smiling, and not once indulging in speech. This
style of pantomime is more satisfactory to grown persons, but I doubt its being
so amusing to children as the broad fun of the English Clown and Pantaloon.
Mr. Fox was dressed in pink and white striped vest and drawers, with variegated stockings, and white face, and his own brown hair (or wig of that color).
Everything was seriously done, though the cause of merriment. A scene in
prison, where the rats squeak and frighten "Clown and Pantaloon"—and at
last come on, and run away with the bedclothes, etc., was very neat. Conraci
after decorating the portrait of a lady with beard and whiskers, takes a telescope to view it through. A little black boy bears it on his shoulder and
obstructs the view by his cap, etc. At last Conraci is satisfied, crossing one
foot over the other, leans on the telescope, which *collapses,* and makes him
fall. All the tricks, though simple, were neat. One with a box or tea chest
which moves about the stage—rises to monumental height, sinks into the
ground—is opened and encloses "Pantaloon" (Excuse the name—very foolish.
"'Don Something' much more proper" as Flora F. would say.) Pantaloon is en-
closed, box shrinks, Pantaloon is taken out, jammed to half his height, thrown
in again, and restored to his own proportions. Indeed we were sorry when it
was over.[28]

This praise from a British professional pinpoints a number of striking
features in Fox's performance. There is the silence and seriousness with
which the absurdities are conducted, possibly a legacy from the laconic
down-easterners Fox had played in his time. It may derive more directly, however, from his own taciturn nature, but it was a characteristically American way of playing comedy, later honed to a fine edge by
Buster Keaton.[29] Unlike Grimaldi's antics, Fox's boisterousness was
tempered by sobriety of execution.

Then there is the familiar delinquency of defacing a female image
with a moustache, a piece of mischief congenial to every newsboy in
the house. Bowery children were old before their time, street-wise in

modern parlance. No wonder Mrs. Cowell could not conceive of the style amusing parlor-bred Victorian juveniles. Fox's rascality was sly and homegrown, never so extravagant as to lose the correlative of everyday life, even in surrealistic pieces of business worthy of Deburau. One of Fox's favorite *lazzi* at the Bowery was to be shot out of a gun, flatten against a wall, and be peeled off like a strip of tape.[30] Fox also exemplified the observation of Champfleury, the French author of pantomimes, that "English and American actors have a precious quality the best performers in Paris lack entirely: continuity of gesture. They wish to be understood at all costs, exaggerate the movement and hold it."[31] It was a quality of exceptional value to unsophisticated audiences.

A month before Mrs. Cowell testified to the excellence of Fox's *vis comica*, another pantomime, *Harlequin Jack, the Giant Killer*, had been withdrawn, because of what the bills referred to as a bereavement in his family. His twelve-year-old daughter Emily had died on 12 February, an only child whom he had hoped to groom into a star like Cordelia Howard. However grieved he must have been, six days later he was back on stage as Ralpho a blacksmith's apprentice, afterwards Clown, teasing his brother Charles as Hudibras a blacksmith, afterwards Pantaloon. The only reflection we have of his state of mind is *Bereavement*, composed by John Mahon, which carols the ethereality of a brown-haired child who trips along "dew-clad" lawns with fairy playmates. In the final verse

> *An angel, soaring through the air,*
> *Beheld that fair young blossom;*
> *And [b]are it in her bosom:*
> *She paus'd a moment in her flight,*
> *As if entranc'd with wonder;*
> *Then darting down from realms of light,*
> *Bore her sister angel "yonder."*
> *Ah! too fair for earth was she,*
> *So all earthly ties were riven;*
> *And now, 'mid seraph minstrelsy,*
> *She sings her strains in heaven.*[32]

If this is only a footling example of the graveyard school of poetry rife in nineteenth-century America, with a sidelong glance at Little Eva's angel-borne demise, it still betokens Fox's growing place in the imagination of New Yorkers. Ordinarily, topical songs were dedicated to politicians, musicians, or soldiers. Fox's private grief had been made a public matter, but it was rapidly to be swallowed up in a greater calamity, the War between the States.

8

Lieutenant Fox Goes to War

(1860-63)

New York City, beyond its aberrant attraction to *Uncle Tom's Cabin*, was scarcely anti-slavery; however, on the eve of the Great Rebellion, the fever of approaching conflict made it enthusiastically pro-Union. The overheated patriotism of the time was reflected in the main-pieces at the New Bowery. No sooner had war been officially declared on 12 April 1861 than *The Liberty Boys of '76* was revived, to be closely followed by *The Stars and Stripes, or The Patriot's Dream* and *The Traitor's Doom, or The Fate of Secession.* An advertisement on 22 April announced that the co-manager had himself trooped to the colors: "G. L. Fox, being a member of the 8th Regiment, will leave for the seat of war, during the ensuing week."[1]

Fox was another victim of the war fever that swept over the city. Democrats and Republicans shared the opinion that the nation had to be saved from imminent peril, and from every shop, dwelling, church, theatre, office, and lamppost, Old Glory dangled.[2] As early as December 1860, the New York State Legislature had offered its services to President Lincoln, and Commodore Vanderbilt donated his steamships for government service. When Lincoln called for volunteers, Massachusetts was the most active state in providing them. Back in Boston, brother James left his law practice to serve in the Thirteenth Massachusetts Volunteers where he saw active duty during the perilous Virginia

campaigns of 1861–62.[3] But New York came second only to the Bay
State in the number of voluntary warriors.

These early regiments, raised during the frothing excitement of those
first days, were enlisted for only three months, with the assurance that
they would be delivered back home at that end of that term. No one
thought the war would last any longer or considered the possibilities of
privation, discomfort, mutilation, or death. "It was to be a picnic on a
grand scale, with brass buttons, tinsel, silk banners and music to enliven it, and the fun to be hallowed by its patriotic purpose. The adven-
turous and frolicsome were attracted while the apparently temporary
needs of the country did not demand any sacrifice from the steady and
thoughtful men, who had other responsibilities on them."[4]

Fox's regiment was the Eighth State Militia Infantry, not to be confused with the Eighth Regiment Infantry or "German Rifles," well-
trained German and Austro-Hungarian marksmen whose performance
at the First Battle of Bull Run was one of the few things the Union had
to be proud of on that occasion. On the contrary, Fox's was an amateurish
troop, known as "The Washington Greys," and composed chiefly of mechanics, workingmen, and theatricals, with families to provide for and
little money to spare. Their joining up for three months away from home
was clear testimony to their disinterested enthusiasm. Spontaneous patriotism was strong amid mercurial theatre people who fancied themselves in uniform. Thomas Hanlon-Lees, the English acrobat who had
popularized calisthenics in the United States, was rumored to have
been offered the command of a gymnast corps of fifteen hundred men,
to be equipped by the government, but his father told him to stay out of
a conflict that was opposed by his home government.[5]

The nine hundred volunteers of Fox's regiment gathered in Sixteenth
and Seventeenth streets on 23 April 1861 to be transported to the defence of Washington City, which, it was feared, the Rebels would try to
capture at any moment. Fox, elected a second lieutenant in Company E
(all officers served at the pleasure of their subordinates),[6] waited with
his comrades in the sun-baked street, laden with rucksack, rifle, and
full kit, as they got their first taste of army red-tape. There had been
a mix-up in orders regarding the guns; the Greys were to leave the
howitzers and take the six-pounders, but the government had to be tele-
graphed for permission to move the necessary horses and harnesses. It
was four o'clock before they began to march.

A large contingent of friends and family walked ahead of the procession, including the G. L. Fox Guard, a club of some hundred members who performed parade drills in vacant lots around the Bowery and
deemed themselves a local militia. "All along the line, on Broadway,
down to Canal Street, the windows of the various stores and the side-

walks, were crowded with ladies and children, all desirous of seeing the departure ... many of them with well-tried hearts were comforting each other with an indefinite variety of patriotic sentiments."[7] Fox's own face, according to an eye-witness, bore a solemn and miserable expression—whether this was his usual comic deadpan or a growing awareness of what he had got himself into is unclear. But this Knight of the Rueful Countenance was greeted with the loudest ovation along the way, for everyone in the crowd seemed to know him. The cheer was kept up as far as Pier No. 36, North River, where eleven hundred men crowded abroad the steamship *Alabama*. The crowds on the adjacent piers were immense and bolstered the spirits of the men, who shouted back and fired their revolvers as the boat pulled away at about seven o'clock.

The inconveniences, if not the horrors, of war were soon in evidence. There was nowhere to sleep on the overcrowded steamer, and the overheated cabins were insufferable; most of the men were landlubbers who began to pale as wind and water rose. "George L. Fox lay on the forward hatch a picture of abject misery. I can see that elongated woebegone countenance of his as he lay there. His contributions to Neptune were liberal. With what dejection and tragic air he offered money to any one who would throw him overboard."[8]

Fox and his fellows, minus a hundred men dropped off at Baltimore, disembarked two days later at Washington City. They had been preceded by several other New York regiments, including the colorful Fire Zouaves, a cohort of Bowery rowdies, engine chasers, and hooligans, incongruously headed by the gallant young Captain Ellsworth, a friend of the President. They were later joined by New York's Irish and Italian regiments. But these displaced Gothamites, fired up for battle, found the nation's capital a dismal anticlimax, with its muddy, unpaved streets, ramshackle buildings and unfinished Capitol, which one volunteer declared "hardly worth defending, except for the éclat of the thing."[9] Accustomed to the constant activity and nightlife of Manhattan, they were bewildered by the rural lethargy and somnolence of Washington.

None of these men had any military training, and three months were insufficient to turn them into soldiers. Their discipline was only as sound as their officers, whom they themselves selected from among their friends. Although most of the New England regiments conducted themselves decently, the New Yorkers went berserk with boredom, drinking themselves into whooping and hollering fits. This caused the formation of a provost guard to patrol the town, the imposition of a nine-thirty military curfew, and the closure of dramshops at the same early hour. It was thought that Fox's regiment the Eighth, the Fire Zouaves,

Figure 14. G. L. Fox in his lieutenant's uniform, 1862. The beard was grown during the First Bull Run episode. (Courtesy Theatre Arts Library, the Harry Ransom Humanities Research Center, the University of Texas at Austin)

and the Garibaldi Guard were the worst offenders, and when the troops were paid in June, there was no restraining them. "Fire Zouaves raced up and down the Avenue, brandishing pistols and exchanging their red caps for the hats they snatched from the heads of the passers-by. Boys from New York and New Jersey went on the rampage and broke up bars and restaurants."[10]

Fox probably did not participate in these sprees, for he did not drink. (None of the Fox-Howard clan did; how else could they make the public believe in the sincerity of *The Drunkard* and *Ten Nights in a Barroom*, which they were playing at the New Bowery while Uncle Laff was at war?) Instead, he may have gorged himself on the tainted pastry and candy sold by the numberless sutlers infesting the camps, or fallen ill from the nauseating effluvia that arose from the gutters, since the untried soldiers had set the tents too close together, seldom dug latrines and failed to provide drainage. No doubt a great sigh of relief was uttered by both the military and the citizenry when these regiments were finally sent into battle.

Meanwhile, the New York newspapers were lauding Fox's example to malingerers and stay-at-homes, the so-called "Cocktail Guard." The *Tribune* indicated that

several gallant young fellows of the profession—whose loyalty has never been doubted—are proving their faith by their works. Among the earliest to leave for the "Theatre of War" was G. L. Fox, manager of the Bowery Theatre, and an actor of renown in broad comedy and farce—not exactly the "line of business" leading to the stern experiences of the battle field ... Actors out of employment, especially those who are anxious to "set themselves right" with the stars and stripes, are informed that the Theater of War is open for the season, Uncle Sam, Lessee; Abraham Lincoln, Manager; Winfield Scott, Stage Manager; and that excellent positions in the company will be secured by those who make early applications. The next representation will probably come off near Manassas; rehearsal has already been called. One day of action is worth a whole season of noisy profession.[11]

Actors were indeed unemployed, in large numbers; many Northern performers broke off Southern engagements and hastened above the Mason-Dixon line as soon as Fort Sumter had been fired upon. J. B. Howe had almost been lynched by a Southern audience that recognized him as a veteran of *Uncle Tom's Cabin*. Moreover, there was competition from parades and news bulletins. Audiences who could be cajoled into the theatre lingered for half an hour, started yawning and, by the play's end, a third to a half of the house would be in a saloon next door discussing the war or marching in step with a volunteer regiment heading down Broadway.

A number of managers, for both patriotic and fiscal reasons, staged benefits for the families of soldiers gone to war. These included Laura Keene, Lester Wallack, Nixon, and Fox and Lingard, but, commented *The Spirit of the Times*, "we believe none of them turned out particularly remunerative."[12] To exploit public sentiment and fill the New Bowery, Lingard had his partner write letters home to the boys in the pit and gallery, to be read from the stage, "a novel, but clever dodge."[13] Harry Seymour's *The Battle of Boonville and New Union Tableaux*, produced on 1 July, attempted to capitalize on current events,[14] but the box-office receipts remained disappointing to the end of the season.

The *Tribune* had joked that actors who joined up would soon appear on stage at Manassas, and, indeed, the Eighth New York did take part in the first major engagement of the conflict. The New York *Clipper* stated in Fox's obituary notice, "Upon the eve of the Battle of Bull Run the battery attached to [the regiment] conceived that its three months' time was up, and, spite of Captain Varian, recrossed the Potomac. The infantry remained, and, with a few exceptions among its officers, did its duty in that momentous fight."[15] Fox was not one of the exceptions.

The first Battle of Bull Run is a setpiece in every history of the Civil War. Historians have expatiated repeatedly on the cocky inexperience of the Union forces, the civilians trooping along as if on a picnic, the unexpected severity of the Rebel attack, and the humiliating, disordered rout and retreat back to the capital. The Eighth New York Regiment, attached to Porter's First Brigade of McDowell's Army of Northeastern Virginia, advanced to Manassas on 16 July. It was stationed with Fourteenth New York on the far right, with Colonel Hunter at their head. They suffered intensively in the hottest part of the battle, but maintained an unbroken front and later received the personal thanks of General Morgan.[16] Eventually, however, even they were ordered back and merged with the hordes of beaten and terrified men slogging their way to safety.

The proud regiments that had sallied forth to battle returned in the pouring rain, a rabble, their bright blue uniforms drenched and smoke-blackened, their equipment and outer garments tossed away to lighten their load. Fox, whose face had so often been covered with the clown white of French chalks, staggered back to Washington smeared with the black cosmetic of gunpowder. When, after their forty-five mile trek, the soldiers arrived in the capital they were supposed to defend, they dropped on to doorsteps and curbstones, collapsed in gutters, exhausted and famished. Sandwiches and coffee were doled out by solicitous ladies, while elegant carriages were sent across the Potomac to collect the wounded.[17]

The casualties of the Eighth Militia included eight enlisted men dead, seventeen men and four officers wounded and nine men captured or missing. Fox was not one of these.[18] The Regiment was mustered out at the end of its term of service on 2 August and returned to New York, where, despite the defeat, it was met with the same enthusiasm that had seen it off. But this surface excitement soon wore off, as the ex-soldiers told their tales. One New York civilian reported to his brother:

There is now a great deal of crimination and recrimination among the officers and men. The officers charge the defeat upon the men and the men in turn charge the defeat upon the officers. Many regiments were charged with cowardice. The Fire Zouaves, the Fourteenth and Eighth Regiments of this State and the Fourteenth Regiment of Brooklyn upon their return a few days ago had a terrible fight among themselves.

Recruiting or re-enlisting is now uphill work. Bounties of from $30 to $50 are offered and but few are willing to go. None would go if employment could be had.[19]

Lieutenant Fox's glory, however, was undimmed by this sordid aftermath. When he made an early return to New York on 26 July, the streets filled with crowds to applaud him as they would have in the theatre, for he had shown himself "a brave and patriotic soldier."[20] Newsboys covered the awnings at the ferry and shouted, "Where's Old Fox? We want to see Fox." A policeman inquired of the actor, "Is Fox in this regiment?" and, disguised by a newly-grown beard and moustache, the comedian could safely respond, "Yes, back there, somewhere." His regiment presented him with a banner "in appreciation of G. L. Fox's Gallant Conduct at the Battle of Bull Run."[21]

The very day after his return, "the people's favorite" appeared on stage in a couple of his choicest parts and was heartily welcomed.[22] He brought out a drama called *Bull Run, or The Sacking of Fairfax Court House*, in which he played Rolf Ironsides, and his brother Charles a character denominated Lieutenant G. L. Fox. Fairfax Courthouse was the site of the first casualty of the war, when Colonel Ellsworth of the Fire Zouaves was shot down, an event depicted in the play. Fox had probably not been on the spot and was simply exercising poetic license.[23]

Such timely novelties were few. The tried-and-true melodramas were once more trotted out, and the routine was broken only in late October when the New Bowery underwent extensive renovation. The pit was replaced by a handsome "parquette," and the Bowery boys relegated to the gallery because "the demands of upper twenty-five-cent-dom could no longer be resisted."[24] This move indicates not only economic necessity, but an attempt to add tone and attract a new clientele. Further managerial ambition was evinced when Fox and Lingard rented the mammoth Academy of Music in December to introduce the Hanlon-Lees Brothers in their remarkable acrobatic act "Zampillaerostation," followed by the Fox Pantomime Troupe in *Les Quatre Amants* (known simply in the Bowery as *The Four Lovers*) and *L'Oger*.[25] The west-side audiences were much taken by the English acrobats who, for the first time, showed them a trapeze switch in midair, but Fox's contribution was nothing new to those brought up on the Ravels. The *Tribune* even referred to *L'Oger* as "one of Ravel's pantomimes," adding "the imitation of their style not being very successful"[26] The usually sympathetic *Spirit of the Times* reported that "the audience paid little attention" to it.[27]

Fox and his company returned to standard frontier thrillers at the New Bowery. The only noteworthy appearances he made were in the in-joke *Fox Worried by Boniface*, a reference to the rivalry between the two Bowery Theatres; the fairy panto *Cherry and Fair Star*, which he had first seen as a child at the Boston Museum; and a successful burlesque of Boucicault's *Colleen Bawn*, then playing at Niblo's—*The Co-Lean Born*, with Fanny Herring as Myles-na-Coppaleen and Fox as the hapless Eily. One can only imagine his floundering and shrieking in the drowning scene. Yet another war drama was mounted in February 1862 with *The Capture of Fort Donelson*, which featured Irish regiments.[28]

Slack business left the partners plenty of time in which to quarrel. On 22 March 1862, Fox and Lingard dissolved their partnership by mutual consent. The reasons for this divorce went unstated but, most likely, had to do with the repertorial policy. Fox, as usual, was the more ambitious, anxious to branch out into multiple enterprises and accrue more prestige, even when, as with his balloon ascensions, out-of-state tours, and Academy of Music venture, the financial gain was nil. Lingard bought out Fox's share in the New Bowery, on condition that the comedian pledge himself not to appear on the East Side and thus ruin Lingard's business.[29] So, for the rest of the season, Fox was to be at James Wallack the elder's old theatre, the Lyceum, far to the west, on the corner of Broadway and Broome Streets.

For years the Lyceum had been one of the most prestigious theatres in the city, noted for its high-toned English plays. When Broome Street started to deteriorate, Wallack moved to Thirteenth Street.[30] Fox reopened the house on 21 April 1862 as G. L. Fox's Olympic Theatre, the first time his name had appeared over the portals of a playhouse. The solo manager raised his admission prices as well: private boxes ran three to five dollars, with single seats in them a dollar each; orchestra seats cost fifty cents; box and parquet admission were twenty-five cents; and benches in the amphitheatre were twelve cents. The very nomenclature—the avoidance of "pit" and "gallery"—suggests his hope of attracting a more refined and well-heeled public.[31] He had skimmed the cream, including Fanny Herring, off the New Bowery company, and used it to sauce what Odell has called "ancient preserves from the Bowery shelves."[32]

A sample of Fox's account books reveals not only the routine repertory but the slender takings. Fox had not managed to win a west-side audience during his brief tenure at the Olympic.

Monday April 28, 1862
    The Angel of Midnight
    The Co-Lean Born $157.51
Tuesday April 29th
    The Angel of Midnight
    The Co-Lean Born $110.16
Wednesday April 30th
    Jessie, or the Return of the Wanderer
    The Co-Lean Born $107.27
Thursday May 1st
    Perfection
    The Co-Lean Born
    The Schoolmaster $ 74.30
Friday May 2nd
    The French Spy
    The Co-Lean Born $107.30
Saturday May 3rd
    New Orleans, the Crescent City
    Ours
    Valentine and Orson $161.86
                          $718.84

The third week showed no improvement, with a disheartening total of $579.11.[33] One conclusion that can be drawn from this tabulation is that the neighborhood audiences were not enough to sustain repeated performances of the same plays, and that it took a novelty like *New Orleans* or *Ours* on a weekend night to awake interest. Fox must have felt out of his element and unsure of the local taste, and so, at the risk of a lawsuit, he retreated to familiar ground. Despite his promise to Lingard, he moved his company to the Old Bowery Theatre, to commence a long and prosperous career there as manager and performer.

After a thorough renovation inside and out, Fox's Bowery Theatre, as it was now called (for he had become an addict to frontal glory) opened on 17 May with a company that included Fanny Herring, C. K. Fox, J. J. Prior, Mary Mitchell (sister of Maggie), and Rachel Denvil. The star's name at the top of the playbill was spelled out in a garland of little foxes, but he himself did not appear on stage for the first month and a half. Since the new manager would normally have applied his talents to make his venture a success, this absence was probably due to his pledge to Lingard. Or he may have been recalled to his regiment. Although his three months's stint was officially over, the Eighth Regiment saw active duty at this period. On 26 May it marched off, 895 strong, not to return until November. Yet Fox was certainly in New York by 2 August, when he finally made a Bowery stage appearance.

The number of burlesque and supernatural extravaganzas that loaded the bills clearly reflects Fox's busy hand in the stage management. Even without his presence before the footlights, the first week's receipts were a material advance over the Olympic's: $1216.11.[34] This heartening total dwindled and then stabilized, and Fox, leaving the bulk of his company to entertain summer visitors, went off to Boston with a few performers, including brother Charlie.[35] The billing "Fox's Ravel Troupe" can be seen as backsliding, since he had earlier called such a touring company "Fox's American Pantomime Troupe." Presumably the lure of the Ravel name was a greater draw than patriotism.

Box-office takings remained respectable, averaging about $250 a night, although on occasion they soared over $350 (usually on weekends or whenever a generous sampling of Fanny Herring's specialties were on offer) or dipped below a hundred (2 July saw a derisible $88.22). This situation changed definitively for the better when Fox decided to return to the Bowery stage. His season debut on 2 August in *The Schoolmaster* and *The Wizard Skiff* garnered the second largest single house of the month, $342.45, topped only by the overcharged bill of August 30, which offered Boweryites *The Cabin Boy, The Evil Eye, The Female Horse-Thief* and *The Spirit of Jack Sheppard.* Fox's August appearances were booster shots to the box-office.

With the Fall season, he became a regular on stage, opening on 15 September in a mixed bill that earned $404.92, a munificent sum, and nothing that week played to less than $268. The second week featured a topical piece, *How to Avoid Drafting,* and the third tipped the financial scales at $384.13 when Fox revived the pantomime *Mother Goose and the Golden Egg.*[36]

Lingard did not take this competition lying down. No sooner had Fox announced his return to the stage than the newspapers called it a "most flagrant breach of conduct and scandalous violation of his agreement with his old friend and partner." Lingard went to law, and won an injunction preventing Fox from performing; but somehow the matter was settled out of court, for, by the end of September, the comedian was constantly on the boards.[37] At year's end, the same newspapers were praising him as one of the strongest managers and cleverest actors in the city, someone who had "increased the sale of peanuts (which have gone up lately) twenty percent."[38]

His own playbills proudly proclaimed "TRIUMPHANT SUCCESS OF MR. G. L. FOX, The American Comedian and Pantomimist"[39] and his "beautiful comic pantomimes," and he never quailed before fresh challenges. In *The Quicksands, or Life at the Devil's Gap*, he had great fun as Digweed Mutton, a ploughboy, afterwards a showman, "the proprietory of Mutton's original Theatre of Arts, the cheapest place of amusement in the world—price only a penny."[40] As the White Knight in *The Red Gnome and the White Warrior* and Orson the Wild Man in *Valentine and Orson*, he was brilliant at devising tricks to tickle the audience's funnybone. Another favorite line was comic frontiersmen, whom he enriched with fruity humor. Moreover, he was adept at mingling serious emotions with comicality. He would uncover a vein of fun in the most serious roles and, conversely, when he died as Jacques Strop, after an hour's worth of mirth, he was startling in his reality.[41]

The average weekly take at the Bowery stayed steady between sixteen and seventeen hundred dollars, and even when Fox experimented in February 1863 by allowing Joseph Proctor, a popular Bowery tragedian, to play six weeks of Shakespeare, receipts remained high, especially on Mondays, which seems to have been one of the favorite nights for theatregoing in the Bowery, perhaps because the long entertainmentless Sunday made locals itchy. The critics found Proctor bombastic, turgid, dull, even atrocious, but they had to admit he pleased Fox's audience.[42]

Made confident by the steady cash flow, Fox played his hunches, and pantomime once more began to dominate the bill in a way never before seen outside Niblo's Garden. *Mother Goose* had been rapidly followed by *Raoul, The Magic Barrel, The Castle of the Seven Passions, The Magic Pills, The Red Gnome*, and *Little Red Riding Hood*. Burlesque also put in an appearance with *Jack Cade, Camille with the Cracked Heart*, and *Macbeth*, but these were revivals used as curtain-raisers or afterpieces. Pantomime prevailed, enhanced by Fox's brainstorms. He displayed the first advertising curtain in New York and used the full depth of the Bowery stage to present Sherwood Forest in a new *Robin Hood*.[43]

These successful innovations paved the way for a major breakthrough. Remembering Purdy's profits following a lavish expenditure on Christmas pantos, Fox poured a goodly portion of his own well-gotten gains into *Jack and the Beanstalk*, which opened on 5 January 1863. His advertising boasted

In this splendid and novel scene will be exhibited a chef d'oeuvre of artistic and mechanical skill, surpassing all that has hitherto been attempted, even in this establishment so celebrated for extraordinary illusions and effects. The combination of inventing genius and proficiency, employed in this production will, it is confidently asserted, challenge comparison with the most bold and successful experiment in any theatre in the world.[44]

These vainglorious words were backed by exceptional scenic effects, including huge crystallized leaves that rose up through the stage and ascended by degrees into the flies.[45]

Barnum's Palestinian giant Colonel Goshen had appeared in New York casts from 1859 on, and had recently played the villain in *Jack the Giant Killer* at the Melodeon. Fox leapt at the idea and hired Barnum's Belgian colossus Monsieur Bihin to impersonate the giant Swallowallup. (In earlier Bowery pantos, giants had been cast from meaty bare-knuckle pugilists.)[46] Fox, of course, played Happy-Go-Lucky, later Clown, and C. K Fox was Uppercrust, later Pantaloon, with George Davenport and Louisa Browne as Harlequin and Columbine. A topical addition to the cast was Jackson Haines, the champion roller-skater (and inventor of several ice-skating techniques), who was to become a regular in Fox pantomimes. Skating was in the news, for James Plimpton of Massachusetts had just patented a "walking skate" with two parallel bars of wheels on rubber springs that enabled skaters to change direction with all four wheels on the ground.[47] Audiences who enjoyed Haines's tricks could try to duplicate them on the New York sidewalks.

The pantomime, sandwiched as usual between "mellers" and chauvinist shrieks, had a remarkable run, playing three separate stints at the Bowery alone in 1863: 5 January to 14 February, 6 April to 23 April, and 28 September to 17 October. This was unheard of at a theatre whose audience had a short attention span and a hungry maw ever open for novelty. Pantomimes had long been audience-pleasers but never so enthusiastically received as this one. Previously only a freak occurrence like *Uncle Tom's Cabin*, owing to its moral earnestness, contemporaneity, and child prodigies, had engaged audiences for so long. And *Uncle Tom* had drawn on the Broadway public.

Pantomime, on the other hand, was a spectacle of comedy and music, thin in plot and characterization, devoid of sentiment, significant dialogue, or even desperate situations in which anything was at stake. Each brief but eye-catching scene was rapidly effaced by the next, so that the public had no chance to get impatient. The quantity of action in *Jack* is hinted at by a surviving property list which, amid its specifications for exploding newspapers and rats popping out of puddings, insists on <u>Rosin! Rosin! Rosin!</u>, to keep the performers from slipping.[48] In short, it was the perfect wartime entertainment, capable of diverting the audience's mind from the seemingly endless bloodshed of the conflict now in its third year. *Jack and the Beanstalk* confirmed Fox's faith in the value of pantomime as a mainpiece, ornamented with special attractions. It also blinded him to the fact that plowing his profits back into these shows might leave him with little capital of his own.

Fox's association with the horrors of war had not yet ended. Although no contemporary mentions it, he may have been called up for the Battle of Gettysburg; this can be deduced from the fact that he took a benefit on 12 June but did not appear in *The Battle of Bunker Hill*, a play that required the full strength of the company, five days later. On that day the Eighth Militia left New York for Pennsylvania, 650 strong. Moreover, at this time, George C. Howard took over as acting manager of the Bowery.

Three hundred and fifty men of the Eighth bivouacked a mile from Harrisburg, and spent six days in a holding action that made Lee's foraging expedition a failure. Those wretched soldiers, having suffered more fatigue than any other regiment, had to undergo a 270 mile march in rain and mud, and when they arrived back in New York, exhausted and disheartened, they were confronted with the smoke-blackened ruins of the Draft Riots. Protesting the Conscription Act, Irish mobs from the Five Points and Mulberry Bend had terrorized the city, burned the Second Avenue Armory, the Provost-Marshal's Office, and the Colored Orphan Asylum, lynched blacks, killed policemen, and fired and looted homes. The Eighth Regiment found a New York that resembled the worst battlefield of its experience.[49]

Fox had returned by 22 June and ended his season on 6 July, less than a week before the Riots. The theatre reopened on 6 August, the Thanksgiving day observed for Gettysburg. Fox, now promoted to Major, maintained his interest in his regiment and continued to drill his own Fox Guard near the theatre. Unfortunately, whenever his troops were on parade, the Bowery urchins would follow up and down the sidewalks, hooting and hollering. Eventually he gave up the drill to avoid this mockery.[50] For the rest of his life he marched in Decoration Day parades in full kit, and not for publicity purposes. And he it was who supplied the Armory with curtains. In turn, the Eighth New York notified his family that, when he died, they should like to give him a military funeral.[51]

Fox's military career, like so many individual involvements in the Civil War, may seem pointless and inglorious, but it had the advantage of certifying his credibility as a participant in the real world, a figure who could be viable not just in "make-believe," but in actuality. Even so, at the same time that his war record was enhancing his popularity, he retreated, with his audiences, more and more into the fantasy-land of pantomime, where violence had no dire effects.

9

The Triumph of Pantomime

(1863-66)

The phenomenal success of *Jack and the Beanstalk* had been enhanced by the addition to Fox's company of Tony Denier, "one of the best pantomimists on the stage," as he was dubbed by the poster that had announced his first appearance at the New Bowery some years before.[1] Antoine Denier had been born in Brooklyn in 1839, the son of a French lawyer, allegedly of aristocratic descent, who had taken refuge in America after the 1830 Revolution. When his mother, an English lady, remarried, Tony took a dislike to his overly severe stepfather and, at the age of fifteen, ran off to join the circus—in this case, Sands and Nathan's in Philadelphia, a one-ring show. There he was apprenticed as a tanbark acrobat, set to learn leaping and tumbling. When he gained a little experience, he performed under the billing "Young America" and "Youngest Clown." A missed trick on a trapeze or, according to another source, a fall from a horse dislocated his hip. For a time he joined the Ravels under an assumed name and studied pantomime under their expert tutelage.

Tony Denier scraped up an acquaintance with Christian "Papa" Lehman, the Ravels's property man, and discovered the secrets of their transformations and mechanical surprises. In later years, he claimed that the Ravels had presented him with copies of their pantomimes. What is certain is that, gifted with mechanical ingenuity, he took copies of their tricks. When at last he left their company, he toured the West and the South with indifferent success, and formed his own troupe in 1855, playing Clown in his personal versions of such popular pantomimes as *The House That Jack Built, Mother Goose, Wee Willie Winkie, Old Dame Trot and Her Comical Cat, The Magic Hands,* and *Jack Sheppard.* Outside the big cities, however, the American public was not interested in fairy pantos, and his company failed. Denier sailed for London and played a successful engagement as Clown in a run of 145 consecutive nights at the Theatre Royal, Manchester. On a brief return to the States in 1861, he married an opera-dancer from the Academy of Music, Emma Auriol, niece of the famous clown of that name. She now travelled with her husband as his Columbine.

Returning to New York in 1862 with a great reputation, Denier was engaged by James Nixon, an old circus man, for Cremorne Gardens on Fourteenth Street, where he made a tremendous hit in *The Spirit of the Flood.* At season's end, he and his brother John, an aerialist and rope-dancer, appeared together at a number of theatres, including Lingard's New Bowery, for four successful months. Following another sojourn out west, Denier appeared at Barnum's Museum in early summer 1863, and was then hired by Fox for a year at the Old Bowery, where he became a favorite of the patrons of that house.[2]

Under Fox's management, Denier was allowed to play Clown only when the role's requirements went beyond Fox's physical capacities, as with the zany on stilts in *The Hunchback of Lambythe.* Still, Denier's participation in Bowery pantos was extensive, ranging from Swallow-allup the giant in *Jack and the Beanstalk* on M. Bihin's withdrawal to Harlequin in *The House that Jack Built.* He was a godsend, for Fox knew pantomime only from watching it and training himself on the job. Denier, with his checkered background in French and English pantomimes, his close familiarity with the Ravels's methods, and his trunk full of scripts, could extend Fox's repertory and amplify the trickwork of the spectacles.

Tony Denier always claimed that he would go on for Fox in costume and makeup on opening night, while the comedian sat in the house and watched. "People used to ask when Fox appeared the second night what was the matter with the old man," Denier would chuckle. "He's not as good as last night." The mime first put this story abroad during Fox's lifetime,[3] simply saying that he had gone on unannounced for the actor-manager on several occasions. This seems likely since Fox's physical stamina was not always up to strenuous acrobatics. Only after the clown's death in 1877, however, did Denier make his assertion about opening nights. The allegation is improbable since at the Bowery Fox's presence in the audience would have been spotted at once.[4]

The House That Jack Built, the pantomime for January 1864, was

Figure 15. Tony Denier on tour as Humpty Dumpty in the early 1870s, with a portrait of himself as Clown, and medals allegedly from foreign governments. A photograph by Houseworth of San Francisco. (Author's collection)

intended to match the success of *Jack and the Beanstalk*, which it did and more. *The Beanstalk* had grown for two weeks and five nights on its initial run; *The House* kept a-building for six weeks. One of its features was a horde of children, costumed as gnomes in hooded green jackets, who constructed the house for Jack before the audience's eyes.[5] This was one of Denier's homegrown devices, and he may have received a special fee for exhibiting it at the Bowery.

Another resource of house drama was Fox's sister-in-law Mary Hewins, whose capacity for literary work was astounding; it was said that she could turn out a play a week. Her specialty seems to have been canine drama, a popular standby. *Vamp the Fireman's Dog* and *The Rag Woman and Her Dogs* are from her pen; she updated the outmoded *Forest of Bondy*; and she stitched together the composite *Jack Sheppard and His Dogs* (one of whom was named Lafayette in homage to the manager). Another type of play popular with Bowery audiences, and which dated back to Guilbert de Pixérécourt and the origins of melodrama, was the "idiot" piece, such as *Lendormie, The Idiot Boy*, and *The Dumb Boy of Manchester*, in which the lead, invariably a put-upon and tongue-tied imbecile, entrusted with the secret of the plot and portrayed by Fanny Herring in ragged trousers, unmasked the villain's turpitude by means of elaborate mime.

If these were tried-and-true genres, 1863 introduced a novelty to outvie their popularity. The "Pepper's Ghost" illusion, whereby a reflection of an actor was cast on a sheet of glass between stage and audience, had been brought to America by Harry Watkins, who had so disliked Fox as a comrade in Purdy's company. In a fustian ghost drama called *True to the Last*, Watkins had made the audience thrill to the mirrored apparitions of a phantom, a murdered miser with a slashed throat, and a lady wraith, all moving to spooky pizzicato music. Ghost fever assailed the New York stage. Every manager wanted to jump on the hearse, and Fox was no exception. He dusted off a shopworn melo, refurbished it to provide for spectral appearances, and retitled it *The Ghost of Altenburg, or The Mystic Harp*. It settled in for a remarkably long run. *The Spirit of the Times* refused to be terrified, however:

The very first tableau of the play in question presents "the illusion," and the dismal person of the piece says to us in the language of the playbill, "Behold my murderer!" In the second tableau (the play is all tableaux) the shadow flits upon the scene, and the "husband" registers before Heaven a solemn oath, ha! ha! In the third tableau, the dreadful spectre appears, and the double-dyed villain is requested to "prepare for his doom." The fourth tableau brings on a real, reliable "skeleton," and "the death-fetch at last." Things become very uncomfortable now for the double dyed villain. The "death-fetch" has, so to speak, "fetched" him at last. In the fifth tableau our senses were further harrowed by the appearance of "the phantom," immediately after which, the impassioned advertisement writer ... puts in the query, "do our senses wander?" We fully expect to be asked, at the conclusion of the next tableau, "are you a miserable idiot?" but the advertisement writer is so kind as to let us off with "can this be reality?" which we take to be a conundrum and vainly endeavor to find an answer for it.[6]

Altenburgh's phantom was rapidly effaced by *The Mistletoe Bough or The Bride and the Ghost; Midnight, or the Ghost of the Ferry; Susan Hopley, or The Ghost of the Manor House; The Ancestress, or The Ghost of Destiny* (a version of Grillparzer's *Die Ahnfrau?*); and *Giles Scroggins' Ghost*, as the season stalked to its close.

The only explanation for this host of messengers from the grave, beyond the technical innovation of the mirrored illusion, is the American public's changing attitude to death. Before the Civil War, with high infant mortality and low life-expectancy, deaths in the household were familiar, even cherished events. The dear departed were commemorated with post-mortem photographs, samplers, mourning jewelry, and rings of hair, and the embroidery and deathbed verse that Mark Twain attributes to Emmeline Grangerford in *Huckleberry Finn:* weeping willows, funerary urns, and an inscription "O Art Thou Gone Yes Thou Art Gone Alas." The ballad composed on the death of Fox's daughter was not untypical.

But the Civil War, with its immense casualty figures enumerating the slaughter of the best and the brightest, not the frailest and the feeblest, confronted America with a quantity of mortality it could not easily absorb. The result was traumatic, a withdrawal from the cosy memorabilia of the 1840s and 1850s to an obsession with the physical facts of death: decomposition and dissolution. The deathbed of Little Eva, in the bosom of her family, with her escort of seraphs, was replaced in the popular imagination by the blood-sodden battlefield and the ambulant embalming tent. Spirit mediums did a thriving business with bereft kinfolk. No wonder ghosts haunted the New York stage in the last years of the Rebellion, to a degree that a columnist could satirize the week's bill as:

Wallack's

Ghost

New Bowery

Ghost

Old Bowery

Ghost

Bryant's Minstrels

Colored Ghost[7]

When the season was over, Tony Denier moved from the Bowery to Barnum's Museum. Barnum had boggled at paying the price demanded by Donato, a celebrated one-legged dancer, and swore he would make his own jigging amputee. Denier, a jack of all trades, filled the bill. In his absence, Fox reverted to such standard pantos as *The Red Gnome, The Golden Axe, Little Red Riding Hood,* and *Mother Goose.* But now the rest of the city was sitting up and taking notice. The *Tribune,* which rarely deigned to notice the Bowery, cited Fox's talent for pantomine and condescended, "One may find a good deal of entertainment at the Old Bowery, whether observing the audience, or in following the serious course of several plays presented."[8] Another notice of this period, more puff than objective opinion, informed that public that

Mr. G. L. FOX is still the "bright particular star" at this house and his brightness cannot be dimmed, we think; at least, the public seem determined that it shall not be, and by their large attendance nightly, give gratifying evidence of the esteem in which he is held. He appears every evening in two characters, and is equally at home in drama, comedy and pantomine; in fact, in the last-named style of entertainment, we doubt if he can be excelled, either as author or actor. He is supported by a very excellent company, and the pieces are produced here with commendable care and great liberality.[9]

Praise such as this began to draw Broadway audiences, at least at holidays. The "new and gorgeous pantomime" for January 1865 was one of Denier's, *Old Dame Trot and Her Comical Cat,* with Fox as Sappy Saponaceous, afterwards Clown, and C. K. Fox as Antiquated Solderwell, afterwards Pantaloon; the Harlequin and Columbine were foreign pupils of the Ravels, Baptistine and Mlle Martinetti. J. J. McCloskey assumed the title role, a traditional dame part, and Master Timothy crept about in her cat's skin. This effort was rewarded with a record-breaking eight-week run.[10]

The surrender of Lee at Appomatox was celebrated with a revival of *Uncle Tom's Cabin,* with Fox himself as Phineas Fletcher and Deacon Perry, his sister as Topsy, Charlie as Lawyer Marks, and little Emma Chapman replacing Cordelia as Eva. But the run of this play was interrupted by Lincoln's death, when all theatres closed. After its resumption a week later, *Uncle Tom* ran respectably into May.

Throughout the 1865/66 season, Fox spent less time on stage than usual and devoted more attention behind the scenes to the preparation of his special attractions, the holiday pantomimes. *Sinbad the Sailor* was the successful Thanksgiving offering, but the best was yet to come. On February 19, 1866, *Jack and Gill Went Up the Hill,* a spectacle in eleven scenes and "illuminated tableaux," outdid all its predecessors and packed the Bowery Theatre to the rafters for what was to be an unprecedented run of nine weeks, twice extended, with a five week revival the following year.

"An immense pantomime," "a perfect triumph," crowed *The Spirit of the Times;* "a lucky hit" granted the more sedate *Daily Tribune.*[11] In the tradition of *Uncle Tom, Jack and Gill* was kept alive not by Bowery habitués but by "a better class of spectators than was wont to throng to 'Old Drury,'" which prompted the *Tribune* to hope that Fox would thereby be stimulated to improve the quality of Bowery amusements in general.[12] One member of the company recalled that "night after night, dozens of carriages lined the curb in front of the 'Old Bowery,' carrying members of the then 'Four Hundred' to witness [Fox's] wonderful mimicry."[13] "Thousands of people" were prevented from seeing the show, owing to a horse-car strike, another reason to extend the run.[14] After a final performance on 27 April, it was reported that "in a pecuniary sense, I think it was by far the most profitable play of the season."[15]

What factors determined the astounding success of a pantomime that, at first blush, would seem in no way dissimilar to its precursors? The answer must be Fox himself. The souvenir program bore his name as author, and the advertising listed him as inventor and stage director as well.[16] The style and flavor owed little either to the Ravels or Tony Denier, but was largely American in inspiration, flavor, and wit. *The Spirit of the Times*, while admitting that *Jack and Gill* was "to a certain extent, founded on the French models—this is inevitable," continued, "but though in its construction it has a foreign smack, in the acting it is thoroughly American. The Clown of Mr. Fox is neither English in broad, ungainly, stupid heaviness, nor French in pure trickery and sporting gymnastics, but, while partaking somewhat of the characteristics of the two, it has still a peculiarly American humor of its own."[17]

Back in January 1858, when Fox was still working for Purdy at the National, Laura Keene, New York's most respectable manageress, noted for her Anglophilia, had imported an English pantomime for Christmas. This *Harlequin Blue Beard* made a weak stab at translating its English tone into New Yorkese; the comic scenes displayed the Battery and Governor's Island, a view of Broadway, a chamber in the St. Nicholas Hotel, the exterior of Fredrick's photographic studio and Babcock's fruit-store, and a corridor in the Tombs, the whole concluding with an allegorical tableau dedicated to the American Genius. Nevertheless, one reviewer concluded, that genius had not been busily employed in the pantomime: "in these stirring times there is ample *matériel* for 'hits,' social, political, and personal, which has not been made available."[18] Fox seems to have acted on this tip; he was the first to treat pantomime, not as an imported luxury item, but as an indigenous form, capable of commenting on the lives of his audience.

The plot of *Jack and Gill* was of the simplest: Little Jack Horner is courting Mary whose little lamb belongs to a flock held sacred by the Sun Spirit. The Sea King offers some opposition, but the lovers are eventually wedded. Despite the supernatural framework and the pastoral subject, the action took place in New York. The cast included conventional Olde Englyshe rustics such as Wheaten, Oatcake, and Barleycorn, but they were abetted by Grits, a wholly indigenous husbandman, and the American twang could be heard in such local types as P. O Bummer, a beggar; Freedman Bureau Bill, a black boy; Levy Stickemall, a merchant offering "two segars for five cents"; the Irishman Mike O'Rafferty; a Yankee peddler; and Madame Anybody, a shoplifter.[19] Fox's clown itself rejoiced in the Appelachian appelation "Jackdaw Jaculation."

A large sum had been spent on spectacle, with special calcium lights and illuminated scenery. The pantomime opened with a Grand Tableau of "The Frozen Regions" near the North Pole, site of a contest between King Icicle Icy, Grand Ruler of the Frozen Waters, and Luminous the Sun Spirit, where three illuminated pictures were unfolded. These visions were only vaguely connected with one another. The first, which displayed Sir John Franklin and Doctor Kane the explorers, had some topical significance, since the American Captain Hall had for three years been trying to trace the perished remnants of Franklin's party in the Arctic wastes. This tableau became more relevant during the 1867 revival, after America had annexed Seward's Folly. Vision two presented Washington Crossing the Delaware (because of the ice floes?), and vision three "Our Country's Glory, General Grant!" (Later in the run, William Penn and General Meade were also honored in these visions.) By beginning rather than closing with a patriotic tableau, Fox secured the audience's approbation at once and cleared the stage for more important matters, the buffoonery.

The scene shifted, not to an English farm, but to "Foxborough, near Valentine Plantation," disclosing C. K. Fox as Mistress Jurisprudence Gill. The knockabout started with Fox in the lumber business, and a balloon ascension rapidly triggered the transformations heralding the harlequinade. At a time when English pantomimes were curtailing the harlequinade to a few cursory scenes stitched loosely to an opening spectacle amplified with songs, processions, and dances, Fox made the briefest of introductions before plunging directly into Bowery pantomime's *raison d'être*, physical comedy.

Fox's harlequinade was played out in a series of familiar locales, in-

Figure 16. Fox attacked by the turkey in *Jack & Gill*, an illustration to the souvenir booklet accompanying the production. The description reads "Mammoth Turkey on a Bend." (Author's collection)

cluding a tobacco and wine store featuring Jim Crow; a hotel dining room with a peripatetic turkey who turned the tables on the diners by attacking them with a carving knife; and a dry goods and variety store. Clown disguised himself as an Italian organ-grinder, complete with monkey. Slapstick was the order of the day as characters fell into bread-dough, crashed through walls, were tumbled up in Murphy beds, and got boiled in hot water. The Irish contingent of the audience was bound to be gratified by a scene in which the English got the worst in a neighborhood donnybrook.

Another element in the panto's success was advertising. Newspaper coverage had been remarkably widespread, and G. C. Howard, now acting manager of the Bowery, composed a plot synopsis, available in a booklet lavishly illustrated with woodcut cartoons. It served as both souvenir and handbill. These strategies and the show's astonishing success had not gone unnoticed by another master of publicity. At the end of the season, the call came from Broadway: P. T. Barnum wanted Fox to revive *Jack and Gill* at his Museum.

10

Barnum's and Beyond

(1866-67)

Barnum's American Museum, like the New England enterprises of his good friend Moses Kimball, had opened with a miscellany of attractions, including, in the words of the Prince of Humbugs himself, "educated dogs, industrious fleas, automatons, jugglers, ventriloquists, living statuary, tableaux, gipsies, dwarfs, rope-dancers, live 'Yankees,' pantomime, instrumental music, singing and dance," not to mention panoramas, dioramas, puppets and such industrial marvels as knitting machines. Barnum sought to draw crowds by mingling instruction with amusement, edification with patriotism, and morality with merriment.

The theatrical aspect of Barnum's Museum had never been noted for originality or sophistication. At first, he had stuck closely to homiletic dramas like *The Drunkard*, hoping thereby to reassure audiences made nervous by the proximity of playacting to educational displays. He was careful to call his theatre a "lecture room" and supported his exaggerated moral claims with the occasional scriptural dramas meant "to catch the quiet country people—the simple New Hampshire farmers, the Connecticut pedlars, and the Boston persuasionists, who have the old puritanical horror of the ordinary theatrical performance."[1]

Then the great showman began to imitate the hits at other playhouses. When *Uncle Tom's Cabin* at the National ran away with the public, Barnum was first in the field to erect his own *Cabin*, albeit with a happy ending. That he himself considered drama merely a hook on which to dangle other bait is clear from his practice of interpolating a midget performing statuary poses between the acts of the fugitive slave play *Dred*. If the Ravels were playing to capacity crowds at Niblo's Garden, Barnum confected his own fairy pantomimes with Ravel surrogates such as Tony Denier.[2]

Henry James when a boy saw *Uncle Tom* both at the National and at Barnum's, and judged that, at the latter, whatever odious comparisons might be made about the acting, "the rocking of the ice-floes on the Ohio ... had here less of the audible creak of carpentry, emulated a trifle more, to my perception, the real water of Mr. Crummles's pump."[3] This technical expertise resided in the museum's chief machinist Charles Burns and its set designer George Heilge, who were capable of matching and even bettering the Pepper's Ghost illusion. They could easily supply the proto-naturalistic efforts needed for local color drama ("an interior of a New York iron foundry, with the machinery in full operation," in *The Workmen of New York, or The Curse of Intemperance*), and the spectacular trickwork of a fairy pantomime.

It was during the preparations for a matinee of that Ravel perennial *The Green Monster*, with C. K. Fox and Emma Denier in the cast, that Barnum's Museum had burnt down in 1865. But it was soon reconstructed on Broadway between Spring and Prince Streets, ready to welcome G. L. Fox.[4] The transference of *Jack and Gill* to Barnum's entailed certain changes; the Bowery boasted one of the largest stages in New York, whereas the Museum's platform was of lecture-hall proportions. At the former theatre, the scenery, costumes, and properties had been specially commissioned; at Barnum's they were entirely re-executed by the house staff. The Bowery Columbine had been Mlle Martinetti; at Barnum's she was replaced by the American Kate Pennoyer. Indeed, of the original cast, only the Fox brothers and Master Timothy, the Harlequin, who had already appeared in the Museum *Green Monster*, remained. The sole noteworthy name among the new performers was George Topack, as the black boy Freedman Bureau Bill. He was to become Fox's dresser and remain with him to the end of his career.[5]

This time Fox's move to Broadway was far more successful than the ill-advised three weeks at the Olympic had been, for Barnum was a shrewder hand at publicity and an older-established firm than Fox. He kept his prices low (thirty cents for adults and fifteen for children under ten) and his organs of puffery at full steam, heralding Fox as a "brilliant and talented ... great American artist."[6] This fanfare lent Fox more prestige than his own trumpetings could have. The revival also reactivated interest in the pantomime through fresh, more circumstantial reviews. The *Tribune* was ecstatic and saved its carping for the halting meter of the rhymed dialogue in the opening tableau: it praised the sce-

Figure 17. "The Lecture Room," a euphemism for "theatre," at Barnum's American Museum. A wood engraving that appeared in *Gleason's Pictorial*, 29 January 1853. (Courtesy Harvard Theatre Collection)

nery, acting, and unflagging fun, complimenting the audiences on being "wise enough to go and see it."

Mr. Fox's pantomime acting, by the way, shows that he at least appreciates the force of the saying, "he enters with all his heart into the work, and he keeps the stage alive with his merriment." His part is *Jack Daw*, and his province in the pantomime is to stimulate all manner of mischief, and set everybody by the ears; and his province is duly fulfilled ... In some respects the present is better than the former presentation ... and should be seen by all lovers of mirth.[7]

That *Jack and Gill* was primarily a medley of knockabout is clear from a surviving scenario. Near the very beginning, Widow Gill, the dame role played by Charlie, no sooner enters than she is hit in the face with a cabbage meant for someone else, and falls down. In her indignation she blames Jack Daw (Fox). She then orders him to pick up a log.

Dame tells him to hurry, he says he will fly, and commences to walk about as slow as a snail—Dame gives him a blow from her stick on his back—he takes no notice of it whatever, but still continues on his way, this vexes the old woman and she keeps on belabouring him on his back, harder and harder each time, at last she makes one powerful blow, Jack dodges it and old woman falls—... Jack who has log on shoulder ... runs against her, knocks her down—old woman gets up knocks down again—gets up once more and she is knocked way to front of stage C. Jack falling with log at same time on top of her. Jack gets up, laughs—leaving log on top of old woman—old woman motions to take log off of her, Jack tries to do it and lets log fall again—this two or three times at last old woman gets up. Tells him to take log away. He says he can't lift it up—wants old woman to put her foot on one end so he can get it up, she does so—When he gets log up perpendicular, he lets go to spit on his hands, which causes log to fall and knock old woman down.[8]

This business ricochets into a collision with a man carrying a basket of eggs, an attack with a rolling pin, and a ball game played with stolen dumplings. The hapless old Dame is pelted with flour and dough, and the rest of the rural opening continues this comedy of assault until the appearance of the supernatural characters. It is fun of the most homegrown and physical variety, an almost mechanical choreography of slap and counter-slap, uncontaminated by plot or even elaborate machinery, but raised to the nth power by Fox's wide array of human expressions. Unlike a Ravel routine in which a boulder would squash a character flat only to have him inflated to life by a bellows, these antics were devoid of the fantastic. The appeal would seem to lie in their naked but inconsequential aggression, which left their victims ready to spring back into action, no matter how dire the attack.

Significantly, the decades in which Fox had developed as a performer and cultivated his particular audience were those which have been characterized as the period of greatest urban violence America has ever experienced. Mob uprisings, quite distinct from the personal outbursts associated with rural areas and the frontier, were a frequent feature of city life. Fox's childhood had seen the 1834 burning of the Charlestown Convent in a Boston where smaller riots were often regarded as "sporting events," such as the outbreak that followed a meeting of Boston fire companies and their critics at the National Theatre two years earlier. Nativist and abolitionist riots in major cities throughout the 1830s, 1840s, and 1850s had culminated but not ended in the Draft Riots of 1863. New York theatre had even generated its own outrage with the Astor Place Riot of 1849. It was as if the anxieties of the modern melting-pot regularly bubbled to the surface and overflowed into mass demonstrations of hostility.

After the war, the nature of this violence changed without disappearing; the physical deterioration of cities, the influx of immigrants who did not share a language or tradition, and the sophistication of crime maintained urban disorder. Middle-class households were made profoundly uneasy by this phenomenon, and the uneasiness was to become pervasive in the 1870s.[9] The excessive bodily harm of the pantomime may have acted as a pressure valve by neutralizing the effect of the all too familiar and feared violence. Through the mayhem of Fox's clowning, Barnum's housed a purified form of the standard Bowery b'hoy *modus operandi*, one which leached the assault on the individual of its natural effects, and thus rendered it laughable, purging the audience of its anxieties, at least temporarily.

For a respectable mamma, an excursion to the Bowery, especially in the evening, would have been a redoubtable adventure, not lightly undertaken, but a visit to Barnum's, especially at a matinee, was commonplace. As a result, new audiences who had not dared to see *Jack and Gill* in its original habitat flocked to the Broadway revival, even braving the cholera epidemic that had emptied out other places of amusement.[10] Three weeks may have been long enough to exhaust this new public, however, for Barnum replaced *Jack and Gill* with *The Magic Barrel*, *The Schoolmaster*, and other farcical warhorses of the Fox brothers.[11]

Two hours of laughter are given to the present frequenters of Barnum's Museum. "The Golden Axe" and "The Frisky Cobbler" are the pantomimes now presented daily and nightly. We have seen them better acted; but we judged that every good natured spectator will delight in Mr. G. L. Fox's exuberance of the mischief and vivacity [*sic*] the inspiring quality of the performance—and will care as little as we do to criticize the shortcomings of the other performers. These pantomimes afford many opportunities for fun and mischief making, and Mr. Fox improves them all. Description of pieces so thoroughly familiar to persons who have seen the Ravels—and who hasn't—would be wasteful and ridiculous excess ... Mr. Fox's personations are a great delight to childhood, as we have often noted. Whatever he does is sure to amuse the little ones, and they, happily, are not critical. His introduction of a living pig into the present entertainment is received with great glee on the part of the children. We ought to hint, however, that Mr. Fox owes it to his peculiar audience as well as to himself to avoid even the slightest indelicacy in his pantomimes.[12]

This critique is a revelation; evidently, Fox had not fully acclimated himself to his new public. His greatest fans at Barnum's were children, but they were not the streetwise bootblacks and newsvendors who paid down hard-earned pennies to cheer the horseplay. These were spic-and-span, middle-class youngsters, escorted to the show by their parents and nurses as a treat. However much they might appreciate the live pig and even the "indelicacy," it was their grownup chaperones whom Fox had to take into account. As children themselves, they had been taken to the more refined diversions of the Ravels, and comparisons were only natural. Although the critics were patronizingly indulgent, Fox on Broadway was chided for his east-side manners.

The day after he left Barnum's, 1 September, Fox began his regular winter season back at the Old Bowery and, an apt pupil of the master of humbug, now peppered his press releases with vivid adjectives and high-sounding epithets, billing himself as "the popular and versatile comedian" and promising "a company of fifty," "the full Corps Dramatics" [*sic*].[13] Without altering his usual repertory, he maintained his spell over his audiences: "a word from Fox would still a tumult, and at his command the shrill strains of the 'Bowery pit' instantly cease."[14] The denizens of the pit had in fact been banished to the galleries along with such old-fashioned crudities as the policeman and his rattan. The boys were losing some of their boisterousness, but

one thing, thank heaven, they have not lost, and that is, the loud ringing, hearty laugh which seems to be peculiar to the east side. Such tumultuous haw-hawing in a Broadway House would be very likely to cause the ejection of the offender as a lunatic; but over the way, Fox (the Bowery boys' idol) makes a face or cuts a dido, the shouting is enough to shake the walls of Jericho.[15]

His quickness at improvisation was also a valuable resource. On one occasion, as he made an entrance, his hat caught on a gas fixture, and it and his wig came off together. Without turning back, Fox coolly took a hat off one actor's head, snatched the wig from another and proceeded to speak his lines as if the denuding had been part of the role's legitimate business.[16]

Although the management of Fox and Howard was all that could be wished, the building itself had begun to deteriorate. The winding staircase that led the sixty feet from pit to gallery was uncarpeted and dilapidated and stank of urine. The gallery, poorly ventilated and shoved up near the roof, reeked of gas fumes and hot breath. Many of the benches and all of the aisles had been worn down by the shuffling of boyish feet, and chunks of plaster fell through broken portions of the low ceiling.[17] Fox had no opportunity to renovate the house, however, for shortly after a November revival of *Jack and Gill*, the Old Bowery was put up for sale to satisfy a mortgage held by its former owner, Thomas Hamblin. That pending mortgage was what had prevented the lessees from attempting any earlier improvements. Because the site was considered an excellent commercial property, rumors ran that the playhouse would be demolished.[18] Fox was on the lookout for a new theatre once the season was over.

There was no possibility of moving back to the New Bowery, for on 18 December it burned to the ground. J. W. Lingard, who had been losing money steadily throughout his term of management, was now totally ruined and his wife reduced to letting rooms.[19] Lingard's improvidence had been notorious, for he was a free-spending roisterer and hard drinker, but the fire was an unforeseen calamity. Letting bygones be bygones, Fox arranged two benefits for his former partner, recruiting such Bowery veterans as Fanny Herring, Kate Newton, J. J. Prior, and George Boniface, along with a drum corps from the Eighth New York

Regiment. Lingard was then enrolled as an actor in the Old Bowery company.

These friendly actions were to little avail; failure had set its stamp on Lingard. In 1867 he bought Wood's Theatre to open it as a music hall, and when that enterprise foundered, he transformed it to "Lingard's" dramatic theatre, starring Fanny Herring. The receipts barely paid the gas bill, and the playhouse closed. With another, unrelated Fox, Lingard operated a billiard and bar-room on Broadway, but his partner absconded with the capital. By fall 1868, he was employed as a New York tax collector and the following year kept a saloon on Eighth Street. His wife had thrown him out. In 1870, when G. L. Fox was at the height of his fame, earning a purported twenty thousand dollars a year, James Lingard jumped off a ferryboat into the North River and drowned. His former partner did not serve as a pallbearer nor did he contribute to a fund for Mrs. Lingard's welfare.[20] Fox's charity went only so far.

Jack and Gill visited the Arch Street Theatre in Philadelphia in January 1867 to combat a pirated version called *The Sea King's Vow* at the American Theatre. It was thought that to exhibit the original would be more effective than to start a lawsuit, since it had been American theatrical practice from time immemorial to purloin plays, change the titles and characters's names, and produce them as original works. Courts were not anxious to establish copyright precedents in the theatre. Fox, whose own hands were not clean in this regard, hereby initiated a custom of touring his pantos that would become standard operating procedure in the years to come. The very fact that his work was thought worth stealing indicates a new prominence.[21]

After the comedian returned to the Bowery Theatre (as it was now called, since, with its rival in ashes, there was no need to distinguish it as "Fox's"), Fanny Herring made her departure to join Lingard on 16 March. She received a gold medal from the front-of-house staff.[22] This exit marked the end of a close association between her and Fox on stage and, possibly, in the bedroom. The New York *Clipper* hinted at an intimate relationship between the two Bowery stars in a jingle:

> *The Foxes, to the Bowery Boys,*
> *Continue, like some preachers,*
> *To prove that in their very art*
> *They're very (H)erring creatures.*[23]

Such was the gossip among the professionals, and an 1868 article, referring to Fox's current exemplary conduct, explained it by saying, "His personal relations with Miss Fanny Herring have been, we believe, dissolved."[24]

Fanny Herring's dashing beauty had animated her Bowery roles, and there was even a story that she once replaced Fox in a pantomime. According to the anecdote, the comedian fell ill one night and she declared herself capable of taking his part in a panto in his costume and makeup, for she had long regaled the company with her imitations of him. But before the performance started, word got out that "the Herring" and not "the Fox" was the beast in question. Some Bowery boys went out to a delicatessen, purchased a dozen kippered herrings, known locally as "blind robins," and poked out an eye on each. When Clown leaped on stage, she was immediately bombarded with one-eyed herrings, driving her into the wings.[25] After Lingard's failure, Fanny Herring went on a starring tour, became a fixture in the newly emerging style of burlesque, and made her last major appearance playing the evergreen Jack Sheppard in 1891. Having invested shrewdly in real estate, she was able to retire in comfort and died at Simsbury, Connecticut, in 1906.

The new pantomime was rehearsed without her, and tickets for the premiere, April Fool's night, had to be secured a week in advance, for it signalled the end of the Fox regime at the Bowery.[26] This was the opening night recalled by Cordelia Howard, when a bit of decaying plasterwork fell into the upper gallery, causing a cry of "Fire!" With the New Bowery's holocaust fresh in the audience's mind, a panic was imminent.

In one instant the stage was black with people. What a frightful sight an excited mob is! We were in a private box, and my father sprang up on the railing, gesticulating, waving his tall hat in one hand and holding on to the box curtains with the other, crying out to the crowd to keep calm, while both my uncles were on the stage doing the same thing. Finally, after some terrible moments, things quieted down, people returned to their seats, except those who had fled through the stage door, and three enthusiastic cheers were given for George L. Fox. Fortunately, no one was hurt, but the next day a poor shabby-looking young fellow came to the box-office, saying he had lost his overcoat in the confusion, and would they buy him another? My father, who was business manager for my uncle, gave him a sufficient sum to buy a new coat. Next day the box-office was flooded with applications for coats lost that night.[27]

This contretemps failed to mar the success of *Little Boy Blue and Hush-a-Bye Baby, or Patty and her Pitcher*, which featured G. L. Fox as Disturbance Discomfiture alias Hush-a-Bye, "a rising young gardener," and C. K. Fox as Ungrateful Ingratitude, "supposed to be a Farmer, but hard to tell."[28] Among the professional types in the case were Unrelenting Birch, the Schoolmaster, Lardandpaste, a waffleman, and Tobias Mainspring, a watchmaker. This time the hostile power was no less a personage than Mephistopheles, aided by Spiderion and Reptile, who opened the panto in Hell, reminding one critic, by way of contrast, of the prelude to Goethe's *Faust*. Another was bored by the stock couplets bandied about by the Genius of Harmony and the Genius of Evil. The script's author, that seasoned Bowery workhorse C. W. Taylor, had evidently plagiarized an English extravaganza called *La Tarantula*.

But these were the only sour notes in a chorus of praise. Once the harlequinade got under way, no one spoke of dullness or piracy. All the tricks were thought amusing, especially "the transformation of a tucket [tuffet? bucket?] into a distorted head, with immense frilled body and legs, which walk off with human ease," and "the eccentric life that is infused into the pictures and models in the painter's studio."[29] The show ended with a spectacular tableau of a revolving wheel of fire and a picturesque arrangement of attractive young ladies.

Fox's pantomimes had always used little boys as extras, no doubt to engage the sympathies of their counterparts in the gallery, and *Little Boy Blue* was no exception. The property list, compiled by the stage manager Ferdinand Hofele, required four boys with musical instruments to come over a bridge and play in scene 3, two small boys to play marbles in scene 4, twelve boys to hold a blanket and two others to carry props in scene 7, all the boys for a game in scene 10, and six boys for trick chairs and a quick change in scene 12.[30] Thus, a crazy-mirror reflection of the public's reality would be cast back from the stage, enhancing the bond between performers and audience.

Clown was even more criminal than usual in this panto, shoving policemen into ovens, robbing and boozing at every opportunity, and squashing flat a wooden baby. Summary justice was meted out in the final scene when demons dragged him *à la* Don Giovanni to a fiery fate, but that was hardly enough to efface the impact of his amorality on the minds of the enthusiastic youths in the gallery. Fox's pantomimic talents were highly commended. "He is an actor of real and peculiar humor," granted the *Tribune*. "He is a careful artist, too. You may see in the workings of his countenance a complete index to the workings of his mind. He keeps his audience in a continual good humor."[31] This is one of the earliest mentions in print of Fox's exceptionally mobile face. Not an acrobat like Denier and the Ravels, he relied on his physiognomy for laughs.

The movement of an eye or change in the muscles of the face was sufficient to send his audience into a roar of laughter ... His expression was accomplished with an ease that completely concealed the art by which it was achieved.[32]

There were still complaints of vulgarity. Without going into embarrassing detail, the squeamish *Tribune* objected to a trick involving a stomach pump. And Fox's originality remained at issue with some, for

the *Times*, which lauded him as the finest performer in the show, qualified its praise, saying that he "has long imitated the clever despatch
and humor, which made Gabriel Ravel famous."[33] But the same reviewer admitted that if *Little Boy Blue* did not come up to the scintillat-
ing standard of *Jack and Gill*, it was because audiences now expected a
great deal from pantomime. This was a significant perception. The previous year the *Clipper* had dismissed the pantomime at Barnum's by
remarking, "now that the dramatic season is over, this sort of entertainment, combined with a variety of curiosities, helps to fill out the dull
season."[34] Pantomime had hitherto been viewed as a reliable if peripheral makeweight, in default of more worthy diversions. Fox made it the
crucial lynchpin in a theatre's season.

Little Boy Blue tooted his horn until 14 May, with the usual benefits,
and so Fox's tenancy of the Old Bowery came to an end. When he had
dissolved partnership with Lingard five years before, he had made no
money to speak of, but in his single-handed management of the Old
Bowery, he should have earned some fifty thousand dollars. Instead, he
left it with a mere profit of two thousand. This discrepancy was not due
to expenses entailed by the lavish pantomimes but, according to one
familiar with the theatre, "there was a combination not specially to
fleece him, but to fleece anyone who could be fleeced; and a Bowery
faro bank used to be opened in midday to win Fox's money, there not
being time enough to win it all at night."[35] Fox himself did not gamble,
but his box-office attendants and bookkeepers did, and even the presence of an in-law as business manager could not keep the receipts from
flowing into the pockets of others. The theatre had been sold at auction
for $106,000 on 23 April. A few days later, at one of the benefit perfor-
mances, Fox discovered that he was not the prosperous lessee he had
imagined but a relatively poor man. The ruin of the management was
a tradition at the Bowery; it would be Fox's fate whenever he played
manager.

Luckily, he was in demand as an actor. One of the few letters in his
hand is to Augustin Daly, turning down an offer of work because of a
previous engagement at the Arch Street in Philadelphia in June.[36]
Thereafter, *Little Boy Blue* spent the summer months at Barnum's sharing the bill with General Tom Thumb and a giant seal.[37] Some new tricks
were added, but when it had outworn its attraction, it was replaced by
Mother Goose and Her Golden Egg, a patchwork of earlier pantos, and
the season concluded dismally with similar jerrybuilt pieces.

Yet, even at Barnum's with its frequent matinees and lethargic summer tourists, "Mr. Fox was in excellent humor, as the white-faced clown
who is the very spirit of mischief and drollery."[38] Perhaps he was glad to
be relieved of managerial responsibilities. And there too he teamed up

again with Tony Denier. One young audience member could, in old age, still vividly recall the hit they made.

Denier was supposed to kill Fox in a duel, to avenge a fancied insult, and then endeavor to conceal the body in an empty barrel. Try as he would, he was unable to hide the feet of the "corpse" so they could not be seen. Much perplexed, he laboriously contrived to lay the body of Fox across the mouth of the barrel, and turning his back, went into a deep study as to his next move. Fox then suddenly "jack-knifed" into the barrel, completely hiding himself.

Then began on the part of Denier a search for the body. Each time he backed up to the barrel, Fox reached out and grabbed him from behind, much to his consternation and fright and the amusement of the audience. The act ended in Fox rolling the barrel off the stage and Denier showing remorse for his deed by crying into a large handkerchief, from which a deluge of tears would fall from a big sponge which was concealed in the cloth.[39]

I would suggest that it was Denier with his acrobatic training who did the jack-knives and Fox with his mobile expressions who reacted.

It was also while appearing at Barnum's that Fox was seen by John Oxenford, dramatic critic of the London *Times,* who pronounced him "the Grimaldi of America."[40] The justice of the title deserves examination. One admirer of Fox believed that, had the chronology been reversed, Grimaldi might have been described as the Fox of England.[41] Another, when a boy, had seen Grimaldi and recalled that "the G was saturnine, F is mellow, like its note in music. G was not so unctuous. He was more mobile in the face, but not so irresistibly comic as Fox is when he strikes an attitude, or lets his brow go up and his jaws come down, as if struck by opposite currents of electricity."[42]

More important, Grimaldi was renowned for his catchphrases and comic songs; Fox, following the principle of the French Pierrot, seldom spoke. Without the gymnastic expertise of the Ravels, Fox was more a comic actor than an agile clown. His absurdity resided especially in his wide range of facial expressions, from a Fanny Brice smirk of smugness to a Stan Laurel grimace of tears. His costume was that of the Joey, elaborately spangled satin, ornate with frills, but his makeup was that of Pierrot, the white face and egg-bald pate, with touches of color only in the outlined lips and three apostrophes between the eyebrows. This *tabula rasa* was the best surface for the face-making that delineated his character.

And it was the character of Clown, behaving like a flour-smeared Bowery boy, feisty, greedy, pugnacious, bullying, and showing off, yet cowardly and expedient, that enlivened the pantos, distinguishing them from the elegant and less earthbound mimes of the Ravels. Some historians, taking a leap of faith from Fox's early career in New England, claim that he turned Clown into a Yankee,[43] but this cannot be demonstrated. Fox had played hundreds of roles without making a specialty of Yankees, which were, in fact, the *emploi* of his brother James. Moreover, the Yankee character was defined by his pithy and aphoristic speech, his phlegmatic temper, and his native cunning and common-sense. He was poker-faced, seldom revealing emotion beneath the laconism. But Fox's Clown was not only mute, he was manic, sensual, volatile, brutal, and enterprising, exhibiting all his feelings on his countenance. Fox turned Clown not into a Yankee but into a New Yorker.

American audiences had learned from the Ravels to expect skilled mime from a panto clown, in contrast to a circus clown like Dan Rice who pattered away volubly, mangling Shakespearean quotations. Fox's ingenuity, which ensured his popularity, was in amalgamating French dumbshow with the English pantomime structure to create an original species of entertainment that incorporated a crucial quantum of social reality. It was paradoxical that at this time in England, the burlesque opening sequence with its rhymed couplets, fairy-tale plot, variety acts, and display of stockinetted legs was expanding to fill the evening, leaving the harlequinade as a vestigial tail. Fox's pantomimes relegated the burlesque to a brief prologue and devoted their energies to the mute shenanigans of the protracted harlequinade. While English pantomimes played, at most, for three months, starting at Christmas, Fox made his style so popular that his pantomime played year after year, in every season.

11

The Rise of Humpty Dumpty

(1867)

With his makeup removed and his costume exchanged for street-clothes, Fox was not a striking figure. Of average height and wiry build, with brown hair, slightly protuberant pale eyes that looked quizzically at the world, and a thin-lipped but flexible mouth, he had no prominent feature other than the long slender nose that protruded from this narrow face like a duck's bill. His teeth, poorly tended over the years, were few and far between, and so black that they were barely distinguishable from the intermittent gaps. Towards the end of his career, it was rumored that he had had his teeth extracted to increase the mobility of his features and make greater play with the white clown-face surrounding the black hole of a mouth. In fact, he was wont to remove his one hundred dollar pair of "store-teeth" and give them to the prompter to hold, before going on as a clown.

Fox was that anomaly in his profession, an abstainer. His only stimulant was a spoonful of gin in a glass of lemonade with a cracker soaked in it. In compensation, he was a stalwart trencherman and tucked away great quantities of food, and although he had begun as a moderate smoker, by the end of his career, he puffed away whole jars of Cavendish. Nor was he a fashion plate. His clothes were usually rumpled and apparently off the racks of the Chatham street second-hand shops; but his linen was always immaculate, and his necktie held in place by a jewel set in an onyx fox-head.

Figure 18. Fox in civilian life as a respectable Victorian gentleman posed against the rustic gate of an anonymous photographer's studio in New York. (Author's collection)

Slow of speech and sluggish of movement, in everyday life he hardly seemed capable of acting the clown. His most salient characteristic continued to be his taciturnity, which led him, on occasion, to be taken for a clergyman. Once, before a benefit performance at the Academy of Music, Fox went to a Bowery barber for a twenty-five cent shave, and plumped himself in the chair with the laconic caveat, "Now then, lively. No bay rum, no shampooing, no invigorator, no dye, no talk, shave!"[1] Notwithstanding his dour exterior and unprepossessing manner Fox had gained among actors a reputation for managerial honesty, owing perhaps to his financial naiveté. He was excellent at casting, never jealous, and extremely charitable, a first-rate study who never stinted his energies on stage. Most important, he always paid his debts faithfully.[2]

Such was the individual who, on departing the Bowery where he had been a favorite star for seventeen years, making and losing a fortune in the process, had two thousand dollars to his name. He left Barnum's Museum on 9 September 1867 and, the same day, accepted a post as stage manager at the Olympic Theatre at $125 a week. His old friend James E. Hayes, a set designer, had just taken it over as nominal lessee from gruff but dependable John Duff, his and Augustin Daly's father-in-law. This was not the same Olympic where Fox had first braved west-side audiences in 1862. Originally known as "The Varieties," this play-house stood at 622 Broadway, on the east side above Houston Street. It had been run by Laura Keene under her own name for seven years, and when she left, it passed through the hands of a number of female lessees. As Mrs. John Wood's Olympic, it had been managed by Leonard Grover, and when he was ousted following litigation, it devolved upon Hayes.

In addition to hiring Fox, Hayes appointed Clifton W. Tayleure as his business-manager. Tayleure was a canny and imaginative man of the theatre, who had written the very first dramatization of *East Lynne* for Lucille Western in 1862. Although he had served as a Confederate offi-cer, his military past was forgiven and forgotten, for he proved to be an invaluable ally in promoting Fox's coming successes. Under his guidance, the house was entirely renovated, repainted, recarpeted, re-upholstered, and a new stage laid down.[3]

The first production to come under Fox's direction was *Rip van Winkle*, Joseph Jefferson's bread-and-butter piece. A Howard family tradition has it that Jefferson was jealous of Fox and never mentioned him.[4] Certainly, his name makes no appearance in Jefferson's autobiog-raphy. Perhaps the actor may have resented Fox's effacement of his half-brother Charles Burke at the National. However, Jefferson's term at the Olympic was only seven weeks, and the two comedians had only one serious chance to interfere with one another.

The major production of the season opened on 28 October: "Shakespeare's Fairy Operatic Spectacle," *A Midsummer Night's Dream*, "magnificently presented and embellished with costumes, armors, jewels &c., expressly imported from Paris."[5] This revival was Tayleure's inspiration and strongly opposed by the lessee Hayes, but his father-in-law, the theatre's owner Duff, approved the choice, and his word was law. Hayes was so chagrined by the subsequent success that he stayed away from the theatre for two weeks.[6]

Fox was billed as both stage manager and Bottom, headlining the program in tandem with Fannie Stockton as Oberon in true burlesque tradition. The production was significant primarily as the first American mounting of the play since William Burton and W. P. Davidge had performed rival Bottoms in 1854, when it enjoyed the longest run of the comedy to that time. This was also Fox's first Shakespearean role of any magnitude and it was unveiled to a Broadway audience. During rehearsals, he refrained from making any points or revealing any outstanding qualities, which caused Jefferson to bewail the certainty of his failure.

According to William Winter, it was Jefferson who actually supervised the production, having brought William Telbin's splendid panorama of Fairyland from London the preceding summer. His sister Cornelia played Titania.[7] With the exception of Fox and Davidge (who agreed to step down to the role of Quince), the cast was not a strong one, the poetry was slighted, and the strongest impression was made by the scenery. Critics disagreed on the merits of this *Dream*; but they all concurred that Fox as the metamorphosed weaver was hilariously funny. The *Tribune* referred to his "positive excellence" and "careful thought and study, and a profound sense of humor, not to mention the rare skill in characterization and the apt portraiture of extravagant and bombastic emotion which betoken a true artist in farce and burlesque."[8] The scene in which Bottom tries to play all the parts was singled out for commendation. His lion's roar was especially spirited.[9] The *Times*, which considered the play of Pyramus and Thisbe the redeeming feature of an "unreal" evening, ambiguously complimented Fox on being "effectively comic ... without hampering himself with any particular conception of the part."[10] When he died athletically as Pyramus, the audience, both on stage and in the house, applauded furiously, so that Fox rose, took a bow and proceeded to die all over again.[11]

In some quarters, however, there was a snobbish complaint that Bowery values had been imposed on Shakespearean comedy. Fox's humor, sniffed the *Herald*, was "marred by a coarseness that smacked of the east-side. With more experience in a Broadway theatre, we think

Mr. Fox will become an acceptable comedian."[12] Even more censoriously, the *Clipper* grieved

Mr Fox is a favorite with the galleries, as was proved on making his appearance. Unfortunately, the galleries can make more noise than all the rest of the house, as was the case on Monday evening. Mr Fox is one of those actors, who, knowing that they are favorites with an audience, are apt to take too many liberties, and gag throughout the entire performance. Portions of Fox's Bottom were good, while other portions were directly the reverse.[13]

Curate's egg appraisals of this sort never deter audiences, although Fox may have heeded them when he returned to Bottom six years later.

This *Dream* was, despite critical demurs, one of the few Shakespearean comedies played in New York in those years to turn a profit. Even at the stiff tariff of $1.50 for orchestra seats and fifty cents for "family circle" and children's admission, the Olympic receipts for September to December exceeded those of every theatre in New York but one by at least thirty thousand dollars.[14] The production also gave Clifton Tayleure a chance to display his publicity skills; the high granite curbstones being installed along Broadway were stenciled in yellow paint, "Have you seen Fox's Bottom?"[15]

The run ended on 1 February, when Fox was presented with a laurel wreath entwined with the Union's red, white, and blue, in honor of his hundredth performance in the part.[16] He was promoted from Bowery celebrity, acceptable only in monkey-shines and farce, to uptown artiste, on a par with Laura Keene, the Wallacks, and Edwin Booth. From now on, his every theatrical move would be vetted and criticized. With fame came the need to outshine previous efforts, so Fox returned to what he knew best. While Maggie Mitchell was charming the Olympic audience, Fox diligently prepared a pantomime that was to excel anything he had done before.

New York had grown considerably since Fox's arrival eighteen years earlier, its population now hovering around a million. A wealthy city, known for its commercial acumen, it still presented an appalling physical appearance. There were no bridges or adequate transport, the buildings were ramshackle, and the squares untended. Defective sewage disposal and filthy streets, rotten wharves laden with produce, all contributed to an exceptionally high death toll.[17] Despite a new Metropolitan Police Force named by the State Legislature in 1857, crime of all sorts was rampant; burglaries, robberies, and murders burgeoned so much that concerned citizens debated forming themselves into vigilante committees.[18]

Much of the crime was committed, not by pickpockets or garrotters, but by elected officials, for this was the halcyon age of corruption in

American politics. William Marcy Tweed, once a member of a Five Points engine company, ruled every aspect of the city's operations, his tentacles of graft and patronage twisting from City Hall and the law courts down to street sweeping and ditch digging. A millionaire by 1867, Tweed controlled the State Legislature from his seven-room suite in the Albany Hotel, and was an associate of James Fisk and Jay Gould in their plundering of the Erie Railroad. The concerned New Yorker waxed indignant at the blatant malfeasance, but was powerless. George Templeton Strong wrote futilely in his diary, "To be a citizen of New York is a disgrace. The New Yorker belongs to a community worse governed by lower and baser blackguard scum than any city in Western Christendom."[19] Tweed himself cynically rationalized his *modus operandi* by pointing to the composite nature of New York's populace: "This population is too hopelessly split up into races and factions to govern it under universal suffrage, except by the bribery of patronage, or corruption."[20]

This public divided against itself sought in the theatre nothing but amusement, the hearty laugh or the urgent tug at the heart-strings, escape from the pressing problems of everyday life. The greater influx of playgoers did not mean an increase in audience literacy; at least forty-three thousand New Yorkers over the age of ten could not read at all, sixty-two thousand more could not write, and a larger group was unable to read or write in English.[21] In the early 1860s, the only drama with any literary pretensions had been imported from England. A London premiere was the necessary cachet to win favor with Broadway audiences, a situation not unfamiliar today. The Civil War, rather than inspiring original plays founded on the American experience, had compelled the theatre to take the spectator's mind off grim military bulletins and the political crisis, and distract him with situations more easily digested and dismissed.

After the war, there was a rapid psychological recovery in public opinion, a resilience due partly to economic expansion, and partly to a traditional American avoidance of retrospection. Audiences were not in the market for tragedy, and their taste for comedy was debased by the insipid fare provided by the British, originally French, vaudevilles emasculated by concessions to the Lord Chamberlain's Office and further denatured by adaptation to naive and prudish American sensibilities. As managers in quest of the almighty dollar built vaster houses, the possibility of nuanced acting and intimate situations grew more remote.[22] These cavernous theatres best housed sight and sound with little sense, escapism decked out in lavish trimmings. It is no coincidence that the three most successful and influential stage productions in New York in the late 1860s were the musical extravaganza *The*

Black Crook at Niblo's Garden, the burlesques of Lydia Thompson and her British Blondes, and, outvying them in endurance and popularity, George L. Fox's *Humpty Dumpty.*

Before *Humpty Dumpty,* no pantomime had ever had a full evening to itself, even at the Old Bowery.[23] Fox had, however, made it a main course on the menu of New York entertainment. In late 1867, it was announced that pantomime would be the chief attraction at Butler's American Theatre. The following January, Tony Pastor, who had taken over the Old Bowery, presented *There Was an Old Woman Who Lived in a Shoe,* which contained one regrettable innovation; instead of staging the transformation of the characters into their harlequinade *personae* before the eyes of the audiences, Pastor had them replaced by other actors who played Clown, Pantaloon, Harlequin, and Columbine.[24] It was a step in the wrong direction, indicating a loss of expertise and tradition in American exponents of the form.

Fox entered the lists late, but he swept all before him. Tony Denier claimed that he provided a scenario called *Tom, Tom the Piper's Son,* but Fox thought the title too long for the billboards. When Denier came up with *Humpty Dumpty,* Fox cried jubilantly, "That's it! That's it!"[25] Such was Denier's story, spread in later life when he was in the poorhouse. On the other hand, the clown Bob Fraser claimed that Fox found a tattered volume of nursery rhymes in a bookstall and got the idea of the show opening with an egg on a wall, falling to disclose the clown.[26] But the image of Fox haunting bookstalls is rather improbable.

The truth, as usual, is more pedestrian. The author of this, the first American pantomime in two acts, was the ever-inventive Clifton Tayleure. While the copy was at the printer's, the critic William Winter, the artist Sol Eytinge, Tayleure and proprietor Duff each contributed a possible title; Tayleure's was *Humpty Dumpty.* It was also the ingenious business manager who recommended adding a ballet and hiring Rita Sangalli to star in it. Fox stubbornly opposed these innovations; he was afraid that the length of the panto and the interpolation of elaborate dance would ruin his fun and kill the show. He could not have been more mistaken.[27]

When *Humpty Dumpty* opened at the Olympic on 10 March 1867, it made a contribution to American mythology. A few old inhabitants opined that it was not a patch on its half-dozen precursors at the Bowery, for the Olympic's stage was narrow and did not allow for the hyperactive effects the downtown theatre had housed.[28] But *Humpty Dumpty* was the culmination of all that had led to the sophistication or, rather, the naturalization of pantomime in the United States. A popular entertainment, hitherto regarded as low and auxiliary no matter how funny, gained social, artistic, and commercial respectability. It was no longer filler for a torpid summer or a child-pleasing holiday; there were no seasons to *Humpty Dumpty*. It ran on and on, breaking the record set by *The Black Crook* and garnering $1,406,000 in its first version. Whenever Fox or his managers needed a box-office draw, it was revived with alterations, until Fox had chalked up an exhausting 1,168 appearances in the title role in New York City alone.[29]

The opening night did not presage such a hit, and wiseacres were betting it wouldn't run sixty nights.[30] The opening had, in fact, been postponed by a day because of mechanical hitches, and the play was under-rehearsed, causing the premiere to suffer stage waits and blunders in the tricks and transformations. It also ran too long. The protracted delay before the curtain went up gave the critics a chance to note the vociferous presence of an element that had migrated westward to hail its favorite comedian in its favorite genre.

Long before the curtain rose the busy notes of preparation, the clatter of tongues and pounding of hammers could be heard issuing from behind the scenes, and this but served to raise the expectation of the unwashed, unterrified gods of the gallery who gave vent to the high wrought state of their feelings in shrill whistles, catcalls, and cries of "Ha! ha! hi! hi!" which served to beguile the time and evidently amuse the more refined and aristocratic of the audiences in the boxes and parquette.[31]

The critics were unanimous in pointing out that these catcalls and sarcastic laughs were often heard in the Bowery, but seldom in a leading Broadway theatre,[32] and at least one journalist thought the disgraceful rowdyism deserved "a vigorous application of the much-abused but salutary police-clubs which Mr. Fox humorously satirizes."[33] When the curtain finally rose at eight-thirty, the response was tumultuous, but the boys gradually quieted down as their interest was captivated by the action.

In its *Ur*-form, *Humpty Dumpty* was pure New York. Tayleure had written the prologue as well, but gave out that it had been penned by no less a personage than the mayor of the city, "Elegant" A. Oakey Hall. Hall, a henchman of the Tweed Ring, a would-be actor and author of a *féerie* plagiarized from Planché that had been produced at the Olympic in 1864, was one of the city's most conspicuous celebrities. The saying ran that "New York is now governed by Oakey Hall, Tammany Hall, and Alcohol,"[34] and his alleged participation suggested a piquant merger of Tweed's venality with Clown's amorality.

Hall had actually contributed a single couplet:

> *But Boston knows a fate that's harder—*
> *She knows the loss of the Line Cunarder,*

a reference to the withdrawal of Cunard ocean service between Boston and England.[35] The entire prologue was larded with similar topical allusions, greeted by the audience with knowing laughter. In a rocky pass, Romance (Mrs. C. Edmonds) sits bemoaning her unemployment during the popular reign of Burlesque (Alice Harrison), a situation patently obvious from the attendance records of Manhattan theatres. Burlesque in turn taunts Romance for being "Beadle-dime stuff." They decide to compromise on a new style of presentation.

ROMANCE. Suppose a rather foreign subject we import.
BURLESQUE. It would take too long, and our time's too short.
NEW JERSEY (E. T. Sinclair) (*outside*). Consarn your all fired picter! Hold on there a spell.

(*as he speaks the last words, he enters, backing in from 1.E.L.*)

BURLESQUE. Who can this be, all dressed up in kersey?
JERSEY. Who be I? I be, you be darned, I be New Jersey.
. . . .
BURLESQUE. New Jersey? New Jersey? I never heard of it—no never!
JERSEY. Never heard of New Jersey?—that's clever.
    Perhaps you've heard of Jersey lightning?
BURLESQUE. No!
JERSEY. Well, I swow, I never—
ROMANCE. Some undiscovered country—
JERSEY. No! That's the place where people flock,
    Anxious to buy Erie Railroad stock.[36]

This was an especially timely sally, since the papers were full of the stratagem of wily old Daniel Drew; when the New York courts prohibited the issuance of any more Erie Company stocks and bonds, he simply moved the company's office to Jersey City and bribed the New Jersey legislature to legitimize the watered stock issue.[37]

After more backchat about early closing and cranberry bogs, Romance gets a brainstorm:

ROMANCE. Hold! with his ideas he may give us aid.
BURLESQUE. Yes, if for them he is well paid.
    A new idea in Jersey—that's funny.
    They've only one idea—that's making money.[38]

The appealing parochiality of this opening concluded with the orchestra playing "Independence Day Has Come" and an old-fashioned Yankee dance, which developed into a parody of the can-can, itself a welcome novelty. There then followed a New Year's offering to Young America, in which the four continents marched on, with Alaska and St. Thomas, the latest annexations to the Union, present as babes-in-arms.

Seward's Folly sang of its parentage, "His-name-is-Hunky-Billy-I-adore-him / He-sewer-ed me as did his pa afore him."[39]

Topicality, novelty, patriotism: a sure-fire well-tested preliminary to the mélange of ballet and slapstick that was to follow. The entrance of Fox as Humpty Dumpty and C. K. Fox as Avaricious Fearfulness in a two-wheeled cart drawn by a white jackass was met with a deafening ovation from the gallery, a demonstration of gratitude for the past decade of amusement. Entering with a donkey had become something of a trademark for Fox, who at the Bowery had kept the beast stabled at the rear of the theatre. Poor Irishwomen from Mott Street would beg to be allowed to pass their children under the animal's belly three times to cure the whooping cough, "on account of the blissed cross on the craychur's back."[40]

A great deal of money had been spent to make *Humpty Dumpty* as gorgeous as *The Black Crook*, and the ballet alone cost $943 a week.[41] Carrie Augusta Moore, the "skatorial Queen," glided over a frozen pond with great skill, considering the number of trapdoors that had been let into the stage. Frank Lacy the Harlequin was a British import. The music was a blend of Offenbach's *Grande Duchesse de Gérolstein* and popular music-hall tunes. The breathtaking scenery culminated in "The Dell of Ferns," a finale that was a masterpiece of the Victorian machinist's craft: pendant drops of pearls and diamonds glittered from the wing-and-border pieces, a giant shamrock opened to reveal attendant fays, spangled caryatids and pyramids of fairies in silver skirts ascended to the flies, each item in the tableau slowly unfolding and lighting up until the stage dazzled with gas-lit splendor. The effect was received with a shout of approbation.[42]

Glamor aside, the key to success was the play's local color and the inspiriting presence of Fox. The familiarity of the locales provided much of the fun, one scene taking place in a German billiard saloon, complete with beer and pretzels and "performing fowls" in a cage; in the next, Wild's Candy and Walstein's Optician Stores on Broadway were recognizable backdrops for the rough-and-tumble. A view of the Olympic Theatre by night bestowed a sense of participation on the audience. The new courthouse in City Hall Park raised a laugh for its unfinished state and the enormous billboard announcing that it would open in 1960. This was a telling shaft at municipal corruption; work had begun on the Court House six years earlier and more money was required annually to complete it, at such Pentagonal prices as $41,190.95 for brooms. It was estimated that its cost quadrupled that of the Houses of Parliament, and that almost eleven million dollars had been stolen during its construction.[43] Thus was the English harlequinade assimilated to the *mores* of Boss Tweed's New York.

The violence of the slapstick was extreme, involving pistols, hot flat-irons, billy-clubs, snowballs, and any handy missile. This too corresponded to the brutality and criminality of New York, and also to the mobility that had long been taken to be a prime characteristic of Americans. Lady Emmeline Stuart-Wortley had said if you ask a Yankee how he is, he replies, "moving, Sir." Historically, geographical mobility had determined social mobility and an impatience with the slow paths of evolution. This love of movement was reflected in popular entertainment. Of Humpty's knockabout, one clown recollected that "as played by Fox, it was art of the most convincing kind. It was all action—action—action."[44] Gravity and grace were both sacrificed to rapid and continuous movement.

In eighteenth century London, John Rich had refined the *lazzo* of Harlequin gradually hatching from an egg, each chip of the shell and each awakening to the outside world a revelation of mimic skill. Fox Americanized this routine by speeding it up and making it violent; instead of inciting wonder, his discovery on the wall in a huge shell and the subsequent smash-up prompted one gross belly-laugh.

The classic sequence utilized bricks from this wall. A brick fight had been featured in an eighteenth century panto, *Harlequin Sorcerer*,[45] but Fox made it his own. The Fop, a Gothamite equivalent of the Dandy in Regency pantomime, comes on singing:

> *My Jane, my Jane, my dearest Jane,*
> *Oh, never, never look so shy.*

As he says "shy" HUMPTY fires a stuffed brick from the wall and hits him bang on the head. FOP stops singing, runs down to the foot lights, takes off his hat, and feels his head with his hand—looks at his hand—don't see any blood—shakes his fist, and expresses "he will sing it or die"—goes down in front of cottage and commences again—

> *"Oh, let me like a soldier fall."*

As he says "fall," HUMPTY throws a second stuffed brick, which hits him in the head, and he does a sort of half-forward somersault, and lands sitting. He gets up quick, looks toward pig-pen, sees HUMPTY laughing, and shakes his fist at him. HUMPTY fires third stuffed brick. FOP dodges it and runs off 5 E.L., just as OLD ONE TWO [C. K. Fox as Pantaloon] comes out of cottage and catches brick in the face, which knocks him down flat on his back in front of cottage. HUMPTY laughs, and ONE TWO gets up apparently stunned—picks up brick, looks at it, rubs his head, studies a moment, puts finger aside his nose, and walks with a circling motion, the brick in his hand, to front of the pig-pen and looks behind it, supposing some one to be there hiding, when HUMPTY takes all the bricks and lets them fall on ONE TWO, who falls flat on his face from the weight of the bricks—he gets up, takes three bricks, and circles around stage cautiously to R. corner. HUMPTY jumps down, takes three bricks and follows very cautiously—when ONE TWO gets to extreme R. he turns quickly and meets HUMPTY face to face. They both stand still in a picture, each with a brick raised to throw. (*Music chord.*) HUMPTY makes three big steps backward to L. corner—ONE TWO follows, but makes big steps forward in time with HUMPTY—at the end of third step picture as before. Repeat back to first position. HUMPTY fires bricks at ONE TWO who dodges—ONE TWO fires bricks at HUMPTY, who dodges in turn. This is repeated until each has thrown three bricks, when HUMPTY hits ONE TWO with a fourth brick in the head.[46]

Witnesses of this scene vividly recalled the accelerating pace of the choreography, until the air was thick with brickbats, a favored Bowery weapon and one familiar as the breadwinner of Irish hodcarriers. Members of the audience were moved to call out, at the height of battle, "Who threw that last?" This ballet of assault entered the folklore of American comedy, and was gradually transmuted into poetry by George Herriman in the sado-masochistic courtship of Ignatz Mouse by Krazy Kat. Just as Fox's bald and leering physiognomy recurs in the grinning inanity of the Yellow Kid, so his epic war of projectiles lived again in the antics of the Keystone comedies and the mayhem of the animated cartoon.

The Tammany pol George Washington Plunkett said of Tweed, "He Seen His Opportunitys and He Took them."[47] The same could be said of Fox's Clown. To the vast glee of the audience, Humpty Dumpty kicked over the donkey shay, stole live pigs, toppled vegetable stalls and market carts, pilfered foodstuffs, kidnapped babies, burned the Pantaloon with a red-hot poker in true Grimaldi tradition, and was carried out by a gigantic bed bug when he retired for the night. A little boy who gorged on candy "swelled wisibly" before the public's eyes. But even in its outrageous exaggeration, the pantomime was grounded in the common stock of audience experience. When Fox disguised himself as one of New York's finest and indiscriminately beat characters about the head with a night-stick, he was a brazen but recognizable portrait of police brutality. When he encountered a blazing tenement and vandalized the furniture tossed out of window or turned the hose on the bystanders, he was living out every fire-wagon-chasing urchin's dream.

However much this exuberance delighted the paying customers, it was too much for some of the critics to take. The *Times* saw Humpty Dumpty as "the picture of hundreds of young mischievous youths who are daily suffered to wander about too little guarded for their years and their propensities."[48] *The Spirit of the Times* was especially censorious and reprimanded the actors for poor diction, the dancers for insignificance in contrast to Niblo's ballet, Fox for vulgarity, and the whole show as a "farrago of nonsense," "a medley of concert-saloon, minstrel-hall, and country circus attraction."

Figure 19. Humpty Dumpty in stolen policeman's garb admonishes Old One-Two: the Fox brothers in *Humpty Dumpty* as portrayed by Thomas Nast. (Courtesy Harvard Theatre Collection)

Boys in a barn, with a donkey, a pig and a few farm utensils at command, would devise just such a performance in incident and action, lacking only in finish of appointments ... there is nothing to amuse or please save the ludicrous facial expression of the author, manager and clown.[49]

The Spirit may have been motivated by pique, since Fox, having defected to Broadway, no longer chose to advertise in a sporting journal.

It resumed its attack a month later, no doubt chagrined that this "meaningless and silly" gallimaufry was still playing,

> as crowded and vulgar as ever. That Mr. Fox can insult the audiences as he does, and not be hissed and hooted off the stage, is proof that long-suffering hath made us patient. It is unfortunate that Mr. Fox should mar a very enjoyable and funny performance by pointless obscenity. It is also a strange fact that people will sit quietly and look at the pantomimic indecencies of the stage, but if the slightest insinuation is clothed with language, there is a howl of holy horror.[50]

It is an interesting point, borne out by the more stringent censorship applied to films when sound came in, but one would also like to know more about the "obscenity." Then too, the critic fell into the common fallacy that shows are produced for the discriminating few. His rearguard action in condemning *Humpty Dumpty* could not stem the tide that flowed to the box-office.

The second night was packed, despite a torrential rainstorm, and by the fourth week of the run the ticket-brokers were under siege. Certain cast changes were needed. Master Timothy, a veteran of Fox pantos, quit after the third night, weakened by pneumonia, and died in April at the age of eighteen. Frank Lacy injured a back muscle during a leap and had to be replaced as Harlequin by Mr. Wallace. Ada Laurent stood in for Emily Rigl as Columbine, a change for the better, and Gabriel Ravel's niece joined the company.[51]

By the end of March, it was clear that New York was hosting something extraordinary, and theatrical chroniclers announced that never had any play in the city, not even *The Black Crook*, met with such success. The average weekly take came to seventeen hundred dollars and often surpassed that. The Standing Room Only sign stood permanently beside the box-office. A Saturday matinee during a snowstorm was just as congested as any other performance, packed, significantly, with ladies. "Manager Tayleure may congratulate himself on having a theatre that is not only doing the best business in town, but is the fashionable place of amusement of the city, his patrons being those who used to visit Wallacks before it commenced playing such a class of pieces as it has the present season"[52] This epoch-making statement reveals that pantomime was at last respectable and to be preferred to sensation drama spiced with adulteries.

Despite rebuke, the Fox brothers kept on gagging, no doubt to keep the show fresh. *Humpty Dumpty* was now divided by an intermission to prevent attention from flagging, and its tricks and transformations moved like clockwork. New comic situations were added: a tooth-drawing in which the aching molar was attached to a bullet fired from a gun; Clown's theft of a trombone from a napping black minstrel; and a quack doctor's spiel, lifted from *L'Elisir d'amore*.[53] Lord Dundreary, the asinine peer of *Our American Cousin*, was inserted into a ballet, probably in imitation of a similar routine in *Dundreary in a Fix*, seen at the Theatre Comique in January.[54] The best of the addenda was a Grimaldi-like "trick of construction," in which Fox rigged out a little steamer: he set a vegetable crate in the river, put in its prow a kettle heated by a lamp, added a boot leg on top of that, then took two wheels from an old-fashioned spinning wheel and stuck them on either side. He made his exit, propelled by a stage wagon, under a full head of steam, with a butcher's cleaver for a rudder. Shortly a miniature was glimpsed in the distance. It exploded sending two dummies of Humpty and Old One-Two into the air.[55] This made a sardonic comment on the safety record of the local steamship lines.

In the summer of 1868 Tony Denier secured the rights to produce *Humpty Dumpty* outside New York and, with C. K. Fox as Old One-Two, introduced the rest of America to the joy of brick fights. By the end of the July he had to protest imitators in such patent ripoffs as *Humpy-Dumpy* and *Dumpty-Humpty*.[56] While the pantomime gained new life in the provinces, business slackened somewhat in Manhattan, despite a drop curtain by Lewis added on the 111th night of the show, a new burlesque opening, again attributed to Mayor Hall, and a lightning Zouave drill and bayonet combat.[57] But the management was not fazed by this falling-off, for *Humpty Dumpty* had the lightest running expenses of any play in the city. The cost of the ballet had been increased to five hundred dollars a night, but that was still half of what the dances cost in *The Black Crook* and *The White Fawn*. Fox made $175 a week, and rental of the theatre came to only $15,000 a year. Meanwhile *Humpty Dumpty* was raking in a net profit of $36,000 in February 1868 alone. Manager Tayleure felt confident enough to relieve the strain on the performers by cancelling the Wednesday matinee.[58]

Much of this success must be attributed to Tayleure, who for *Humpty Dumpty* virtually created the modern press-agent's technique of continuous scatter-gun publicity. Press agents were not a new phenomenon in the New York theatre. When the Bowery opened in 1826, it employed "a very capable man ... at a handsome salary, to 'write up' the merits of the theatre, and such members of the company as the management desired to be advanced."[59] Edwin Forrest was among the earliest stars to recognize the need for strong advertising and hired "Chevalier" Harry Wickoff, who was also responsible for the *réclame* that accompanied Fanny Elssler's American tour.[60] Barnum, of course, was a past master at blowing his own horn, and his stunts were classics in the field.

Tayleure was a worthy successor to these pioneers of puffery. No sooner had *Humpty Dumpty* opened, than all sorts of souvenir programs and pamphlets were distributed; twenty-five thousand copies of a doggerel rendition of the plot showered down upon the public. The verses were by Mark Vale, a pseudonym of William Winter, and the woodcuts by *Harper's Weekly*'s celebrated caricaturist Thomas Nast, who later did delightful full-color illustrations for two children's picture-books based on *Humpty Dumpty*.[61]

The pantomime had opened during the impeachment proceedings against Andrew Johnson, and during the summer the Republican Convention prepared to draft General Grant as its presidential candidate. This was conveyed by a surprise curtain painted by Nast, showing two pedestals, one bearing the words "Republican Nominee, Chicago, May 20th," and topped by a uniformed Grant, the other "Democratic Nominee, New York, July 4th," left unoccupied, with a caption reading, "Match Him!" underneath. This curtain was suddenly revealed to the delegates when Grant was announced as their unanimous choice. "Match Him!" posters, poems, and songs mushroomed.[62] Tayleure immediately plastered all the hoardings, brick stacks, and fences in Manhattan with a comical one-sheet lithograph offering Fox's Humpty on the empty pedestal and the word "Matched" at the top of the sheet. (It became outdated as soon as the Democrats selected Horatio Seymour as their candidate.)

Tayleure pioneered full-color posters, which daily grew "more Oriental in splendor of imagination and glowing warmth of color." The regular updating of the burlesque prologue attributed to Mayor Hall was meant to lure his constituents to catch the latest puns and topical jokes. On the pantomime's hundredth birthday, the front of the Olympic was illuminated and the manager offered a banquet to the cast.[63]

The Olympic Theatre also boasted certain architectural improvements. A small but powerful sun lamp in the center of the dome lit the house, allowing the other lights to be extinguished and reducing the heat from the side lights. Over the sun lamp small holes were bored to dissipate its heat, with peripheral ventilation admitting a current of fresh air. These, abetted by rotating fans suspended from the galleries, made the Olympic the coolest theatre in the city.[64]

Such allurements and amenities brought in out-of-towners by the score, and it was noted that "the pantomime, in days past, was not particularly in vogue among our amusement-seekers, either town or country bred; but the inimitable vagaries of George L. Fox have of late made it a specialty, and now our country cousins consider that a trip to the metropolis is incomplete unless it has afforded them an opportunity to see *Humpty Dumpty*."[65] Visitors were informed that:

Figure 20. G. L. Fox as Humpty Dumpty pays court to a dressmaker's dummy, while a bemused Old One-Two, played by C. K. Fox, wonders at the folly. A drawing by Thomas Nast. (Courtesy Harvard Theatre Collection)

At the Olympic Theatre, you might have a rare chance
To gaze upon those funny things, the Foxes and the bare dance.[66]

Humpty Dumpty had become one of the sights of New York, the first *production* to intrigue an extra-theatrical public of curiosity-seekers. In this respect, it is the direct ancestor of such long-running shows as *Oh! Calcutta!* and *A Chorus Line*.

The phenomenal achievement of *Humpty Dumpty* can be attributed to its disciplined staging, its strong and dedicated cast, its charming ballets, its low expenses, and the extensive advertising campaign that made Fox and Humpty household words.[67] But ultimately its success over its competitors was due to Fox himself, whose salary had been raised to $175 in recognition of his contribution. Fox's indispensability became clear the following year when rivals failed miserably to match his record. Audiences who delighted in *Humpty Dumpty* had little interest in the how or why of the performance: that the pig stretched the width of the stage was rubber, that the bricks were paper boxes, that the trick pump was worked from the side-scenes by a string, that the clothes which vanished through windows were controlled by black threads, that the candle which grew and shrank as Humpty tried to read a newspaper by it was a wooden shaft pushed through the table-leg. They were kept in their suspension of joyous disbelief by the legibility of Fox's heart upon his face.[68] One old timer recalled

I can see Fox now—stealing a policeman's coat, canting the cap over one eye and strutting with swinging club, as a guardian of the peace. Again shooting a little firecracker, with a loud noise and his comical puzzlement when a great big one proves only a sizzler ... The wonder of the performance was not in the things he did, but the changing comicality of his chalk-whitened visage—his taking the audience into his confidence as to some profound secret, or some novel stunt he was about to do, and the wry twisting of his mobile features, while he endeavors to recover his balance when he fails ... None of [his tricks] amused half as much as a slight look of dismay on his chalked countenance.[69]

His stare of injured innocence, accompanied by a sly wink, evoked shouts of laughter. "A miracle of fine acting" it was called. "He could animatedly say more with his hand than a dozen ordinary actors could with their tongues."[70] "What vitality, what inexhaustible comic force animated that frame and that face, certainly among the most wildly hilarious of modern times," wrote the historian G. C. D. Odell. "Old men have informed me that Fox was incontestably the funniest entertainer they ever saw."[71] For *Humpty Dumpty*, there was no fall in sight.

12

A Hard Act to Follow

(1868-70)

As the summer run of *Humpty Dumpty* turned into the autumn run, George Fox heard that his wife was dying. Throughout their married life, she had been an invalid, and for a number of years they had been estranged. She lived in New Haven, but, although their marriage was virtually null, the clown rushed to her bedside—or more exactly, to the house where she lay, for her friends and family would not let him near her. Even after her death on 30 September 1868, he told his associates in New York as tears streamed down his face, he was not allowed to view her body. The most he could exact from Caroline Gould's attendants was the privilege of defraying the funeral expenses.

Widowhood did not suit Fox, who was living a very economical life in Defau Row off Bleecker Street, where he kept his team and carriage. Once *Humpty Dumpty* resumed its performances, on 18 October he married Mattie Temple, a ballet girl who was playing Alaska in the opening tableau, and rapidly fathered a daughter, christened Georgiana Lafayette. Years later, Mattie confessed that rumors of Fox's fortune had played some part in the match.[1]

Around this time brother Charles was also in marital transition. He separated from Mary Hewins, who remarried twice, the second time to Stephen Fiske, manager of Daly's Fifth Avenue Theatre and dramatic critic for *The Spirit of the Times*. As Mary Fiske, she adopted the pseudonym "The Giddy Gusher," and still on good terms with the Howards, wrote a theatrical gossip column.[2] Charles Kemble Fox solaced himself almost as quickly as Laff had by marrying his Columbine, the divorced Lydia Dulaney. The Howards did not approve of either remarriage; they never countenanced Mattie Fox, and Charlie's third alliance went unrecorded in their otherwise compendious family records.[3] The Howards would not imperil their hard-won respectability by embracing a ballet girl or a pantomimist whose divorce may not have been entirely legal, and they resented the way in which Laff had so abruptly curtailed his three-week period of mourning. These marriages thus had the unfortunate effect of severing the New York Foxes from the good advice and temperate influence of their New England relations.

Meanwhile, Fox had got in hot water over a sight-gag. The newest routine in the revised *Humpty Dumpty* exploited a lawsuit that Augustin Daly had instituted against Dion Boucicault over the railway scene in the Irishman's *After Dark*. This scene as introduced in Daly's *Under the Gaslight* has become a *locus classicus* of melodrama; the hero, or in this case the comic man Snorkey, is tied to the railway tracks by the villain as the train bears down upon him. The heroine, locked up in a signalman's shed, finally manages to break down the door with an axe and untie the victim, just as the express hurtles across the stage. "And these are the women who ain't to have the vote!" exclaims the relieved comic. A similar scene had been inserted into Boucicault's *After Dark* in London, and when that play came to America, Daly was furious. As the legal proceedings dragged on, Fox announced a burlesque railway scene that was unveiled in January 1869 and so charmed the public that it was encored. *After Sunset*, as the skit was called, had Clown bound to the tracks, while a diminutive choo-choo, making enough noise for twenty locomotives, steamed between Old One-Two's legs.[4]

Daly was not amused, and proceeded to sue the managers of the Olympic for what he termed a violation of his rights. He managed to secure an injunction, and, in response, Fox altered the scene and paid Daly a fee.[5] It showed a certain insouciance on Fox's part to have staged such a parody in a theatre owned by Daly's father-in-law, but he could scarcely have expected Daly to be so touchy as to object to satire that constituted excellent publicity for the original.

Other changes resulted in a complete overhaul, and on 25 January *The Second Volume (Bound to Please) of Humpty Dumpty*, "arranged and compiled from traditional facts, dilapidated scraps, memory and imagination by the Great Purveyor of Pantomimic Humor George L. Fox, under whose able authorship this Sensational and Brilliant Performance will be turned over, leaf by leaf" opened its covers.[6] Thomas Nast contributed fresh caricatures, and the new prologue was set in

Figure 21. Charles Kemble Fox. A photograph by Charles D. Fredricks, New York. (Author's Collection)

Vulcan's stithy. One fresh episode parodied well-known New York actors, with Fox as Sothern's Lord Dundreary and Charlie as Burton's Captain Cuttle.[7] But the emphasis was placed on the company's balletic strength, for the Olympic had absorbed the coryphées from Niblo's much praised but now disbanded troupe. The dances—a cutdown version of *La Sylphide*, a Scandinavian polka, a costume ballet, and a supplemental grand finale—were arranged by David Costa, New York's leading choreographer, whose wife took charge of the costumes. The finale, which cost several thousand dollars and featured ornamental papier-mâché work, was considered of such importance that the program warned, "H. D. without wishing to be intrusive (which is not one of his small vices) ventures upon a mere suggestion to his generous friends. Please keep your seat until the Curtain falls upon

The Gorgeous Fairy Scene."[8]

These concessions to dance and spectacle no doubt helped to counter the animadversions of the original reviews on the seediness of the Olympic's *corps de ballet*. But this turn toward non-slapstick attractions hinted that the pantomime had started on its decline. When a mattress failed to be in place and the Harlequin, Frank Lacy, injured his knee in a leap, his role was split in two, with the acrobatic bounding meted out to another performer, thus following the ill-advised precedent set by Tony Pastor. Fox's comedy was far from eclipsed, however. Other freshly introduced routines included a fall into the water during a fishing scene, a travelling keyhole, a troop of miniature Humpties put through a military drill, and an artist's studio full of living statues who puzzled Clown by returning to their petrified state whenever he turned around. This routine would later be elaborated by the Hanlon-Lees and the Byrne Brothers.[9]

One further change was the departure of C. W. Tayleure to become press agent for James "Prince Erie" Fisk's new opera house. His function at the Olympic was assumed by Dan Simonds or Symons, who had been Joe Jefferson's agent but lacked Tayleure's ingenuity.[10] Thus Fox lost another important ally in the currying of his career.

Tayleure, for instance, had no part in devising this revision and *Humpty Dumpty* looked as if it might be wearing out its welcome as summer approached. A drastic but superficial move was tried. *Humpty Dumpty* closed on 15 May 1869, after a sixty-two week run, and a mere three days later was succeeded by *Hiccory Diccory Dock*. This had first been advertised as *Little Red Riding Hood, or, Harlequin Jack and the Beanstalk*, at which time Fox was applauded for announcing that "with a sincere feeling of very great pride he is enabled to state the fact that foreign nations have not been resorted to for this new production, the immense resources of the Olympic having precluded the necessity of importing aid of any description for the satisfactory completion of his new American pantomimes." This was a chauvinist shot at Wood's Museum, which had engaged three English companies to stage a panto, and at Wallack's, which was desperately considering a similar entertainment for the summer season. The *Tribune* had rather shamelessly reported that the Wood's Museum enterprise was the first time English pantomime had been offered to the public. *The Spirit of the Times* rebuked its fellow journal for this counterfeit claim and cheered, "Bravo, Fox! Your platform needs no worn-out British timber to make it trustworthy and substantial."[11]

The Americanism of Fox's enterprise charmed audiences and critics alike. The highest praise one chronicler could bestow on *Humpty Dumpty* had been that "its humor, its business, its contrivances were thoroughly American. There was nothing foreign in anything he did."[12] But *Hiccory Diccory Dock* belied patriotic expectations. Got up during the day while the company was performing *Humpty* at night, it was a hodge-podge of several nursery stories including "Jack and the Beanstalk," "Jack Spratt," and "Little Red Riding Hood," conflating episodes from several earlier Bowery pantos. The scene was now set in a non-localized fairyland, and the American touch was retained only in an "Ice Cream Saloon and Grocery Store" (later altered to an Ice Cream Saloon and Ladies Seminary). Humpty's barroom was even given the British appelation "public house." On the whole, it was a reversion to a nondescript style.

The haste with which *Hiccory* had been cobbled together was obvious on opening night, with interminable stage waits, the omission of scenes whose machinery was not yet perfected, and even the dropping of the curtain in the middle of some scenes to cover defective trickwork. Pantomimes are miscellaneous by nature, but *Hiccory* struck most of the critics as too patchy a confection by far. The ninth scene took place in a courtroom and parodied the efforts of Henry Bergh on behalf of mistreated animals. There was some topicality to this; Bergh had founded the A.S.P.C.A. in 1866, the same year the New York Legislature had passed an animal welfare act. The gaunt reformer was often in the news for expostulating with brutal draymen and even with Barnum for feeding his python live rabbits.[13] Fox's trial scene introduced a live bear whose owner had been arrested for putting a ring in the beast's snout. During the proceedings, Fox uncharacteristically made a malapropistic harangue in the burnt cork manner, but critics pointed out that he was no rival to James Unsworth, the minstrel who had invented the stump speech. The scene was deemed a bore and soon cut out of the show.

Most of the complaints focussed on Fox's talking. In an attempt to show his versatility, he not only co-opted minstrel material but padded out his dialogue altogether. "Less talk" was the burden of the reviews:

Jack's sale of the castle, for instance, would be equally effective in dumb show, and far less trite than it is in speech . . .

Mr. Fox is still the best pantomime player on the stage. He does not beat the air and roll heels over head, and palm off physical activity and general rumpus as acting. He acts with face and gesture, letting the spectator see the workings of his mind, and follow him step by step from the conception of a piece of mischief to its execution. His humor is real and his invention and energy never flag ... His mirth was the soul of the piece.[14]

The trick of construction in this panto was a velocipede made from a grindstone. It was supposed to fly but failed to do so on opening night. This was another timely stroke; velocipedes had become so fashionable that a riding-school for them had opened that year, and one newspaper explained that "all the skating ponds will be metamorphosed into velocipedariums and velocipede rinks."[15] Hence the switch from the usual trick figure-skaters to bike-riders. This episode was found less wearisome than Walter Neville and a chorus of two singing G. C. Howard's patriotic ditty *Our Nation*, during which the ballet company represented the states of the Union, and a conclusion in which a "lady with dishevelled air, and a general looseness and carelessness about her mien, appears as Cuba."[16] Audiences must have tired of the manifest destiny approach, for this was badly received and also cut.

The consensus was that, despite gorgeous scenery and Fox's comedy, the show was tedious and threadbare, a catchpenny aimed at summer tourists.[17] *The Spirit of the Times* ended its wholly unfavorable notice with the caution, "What the managers do not seem to see is that to repeat a success of this kind it is requisite that the copy should at all points outdo the original." However, there was a grudging admission from the *Clipper* of 22 May 1869, "American clowns take the lead, so if we are to be surfeited with this style of entertainment let us have it of the home manufacture."[18]

Fox must not have heeded these critiques, for, despite his claims of native Americanism, a week later, in the midst of a heat wave, he introduced the Kiralfys to the public. Two brothers, Imre and Bolossy, heading a troupe of eight European dancers, had been brought to the United States by Samuel Colville, who sold their contract to John Duff, the owner of the Olympic.[19] Probably Duff had pushed their employment, and Fox gave them considerable leeway to make their impression in *Hiccory*, with a Magyar csardas in act 1 and a "Sailors Ashore" number in act 2, as the courtroom scene and Neville's song went the way of all flops. The Kiralfys, billed as the "Dancers of the Age," were an instant hit, and the pantomime so condensed that it ended by 10:15.[20] The Hungarian paprika unquestionably saved the show and kept it running longer than it might, but it was another divagation from the panto's farcical origins in the direction of variety and musical comedy.

Fox, now esteemed as "the Talma of pantomime,"[21] continued to be favorably compared with the English clowns imported to raise the receipts of Broadway houses. It is ironic that when pantomime had begun to be regularly performed in New York in the 1850s, the critics had insisted that only English performers had the knack and knew the style. Now such clowns were deemed far inferior to Fox, the native interpreter. Copy-cat attempts to rival the Olympic pantomimes proved

Figure 22. The Kiralfys in their high-kicking Csardas in the revised version of *Humpty Dumpty.* A wood engraving from the *Sporting Times and Theatrical News.* (Courtesy Harvard Theatre Collection)

failures at other houses. Wallack's, in particular, formerly the most prestigious theatre in the city, had had recourse to a *Mother Hubbard,* which was castigated for its weak burlesque opening and rickety comedy. It collapsed in short space. Triumphantly the *Clipper* reported that

G. L. FOX the American clown, remains master of the situation, having, in spite of all opposition in the way of clowns—who have been brought across the water for the purpose of showing what English pantomime was—come out victorious and not only compelled all others to close up, but with quite a loss of money. Excepting the Lydia Thompson Troupe—and their early success was due to the free exhibition of legs—not one of the imported pantomimes or burlesque troupes had met with encouragement.[22]

The *Sporting Times* went even further in venturing that "he has no superior either in Europe or America. It is true that he does not leap as well as some of them, and it is not necessary that any one supposed to be a clumsy, half-witted, stumbling fellow should do so; but in facial expression and dry humor, he excels."[23] The reverse of the coin was that the critics expected a top performance every night, and as C. K. Fox told the Kiralfys, it was taking a serious toll on the clown's physical stamina.[24]

The run of *Hiccory Diccory Dock* was decent, if anticlimactic. Sixteen weeks brought it to a closing night on 4 September, leaving Fox distressed that he had been unable to surpass or even match the success of *Humpty Dumpty*. The run had been uneventful; bruised Frank Lacy finally left and C. Winter Ravel (actually Charles Winther Lehman, a former apprentice to the Ravels) was promoted from Sprite to Harlequin, in which role the critics did not like him. Another alliance between pantomime dynasties occurred on 1 August, when John Denier married C. K. Fox's daughter Jenny at Laff's home.[25] Almost mechanically the Olympic followed *Hiccory* with a revival of *Uncle Tom's Cabin*, marking the return of Caroline Howard as Topsy. Fox doubled the roles of Deacon Perry and, for the first time, slippery Lawyer Marks, "a part for which he is capitally suited," and was greeted by a huge ovation on his fourth act entrance.[26]

Thereupon followed a tour, chiefly in one-night stands, of *Humpty* and *Hiccory*, during the holiday season: Newark, Brooklyn, Boston, Providence, Newport, Hartford, Trenton, Baltimore, Washington, Pittsburgh, Cincinnati, and Lexington. The success of this venture confirmed Fox in his decision to repeat it annually. That the success was due to his participation is suggested by the failure of Tony Denier's *Humpty Dumpty* troupe in Boston the previous summer.[27]

During Fox's absence from New York, the Bowery Theatre, now under the management of W. B. Freligh, bid fair to carry on his tradition. That March, the Bowery had had a runaway success with *The Seven Dwarfs, or Harlequin in the World of Wonders*, a pantomime that borrowed heavily from Fox's model and was for the down-market public what *Humpty* had been for the up. It featured sumptuous scenery and magical effects and transformations, and it played to standing room.[28] Joseph C. Foster's script copied the French *féérie* more than the English panto, setting the action in a mythical Oriental kingdom during its lengthy opening sequence. Once the harliquinade began, however, it moved to the Liverpool docks. No attempt to Americanize the action had been made, except for a tableau called "America the Home of the Oppressed," in which Columbia lorded it over a banquet table, as villainous-looking Irishmen stood on pedestals marked "Patriot," a rather stupid attack on immigration policy if meant for the Five Points neighborhood.[29] To capitalize on this hit, in January 1870 the Bowery offered *Buck, Buck, How Many Horns?* with such local scenes as a Lunch House and Saloon in the Bowery. It also staged a transformation scene based on Watteau's "The Flight of Neptune and the Bathing Naiad," which would have been too risqué for Broadway and was probably meant to rival the leggy attractions of burlesque.[30]

Whether or not Fox regarded his old stamping-ground as serious competition, he made a curious choice on his return to the Olympic that January: the four-act melodrama *The Writing on the Wall*, featuring "George L. Fox's Model Farm," a hack job of no special merit. "The Model Farm" was an extended sight gag, with live chickens and a pig in a pen, pigeons perched on a small dovecote and model farmers in recumbent postures. Fox himself played Fergusson Trotter, a gentleman from London who sets up the farm to procure himself a well-deserved rest. His entrance on stage was greeted by one of the most prolonged bursts of applause that any New York actor had received for years. Audiences were as eager to enjoy Fox in legitimate drama as in pantomime, and his performance met their expectations. His love scene with Lotty Smithers had the house in an uproar.[31]

For the next few weeks, Fox plowed familiar furrows, in tried-and-true roles such as Paul Pry, Tobias Shortcut, and Jacques Strop. His only new creation was Aminabad Sleek, the Methodistical busybody in *The Serious Family*; the part had been one of the veteran comedian William Burton's warhorses and Fox mistakenly dressed and made up for it in imitation of Burton. The comparison was not to his advantage. Reviewers preferred him in the farcical afterpieces in which he exploited every comic opportunity, despite a weak supporting cast.[32] Clearly, he was husbanding his strength for a major effort. What Fox had up his sleeve was *Hamlet*.

13

Hamlet *and the*
Triumph of Travesty

(1870-71)

Edwin Booth, generally accounted to be the greatest Hamlet of his generation, had just reappeared as the melancholy Dane. The lavish revival at his own theatre on Sixth Avenue and Twenty-third Street had opened in January 1870 to critical accolades. This peerless performance, which would eventually be seen by over one hundred thousand spectators, was about to receive competition from the Franco-English actor Charles Fechter, who had caused a sensation in London with his blond, Alsatian-accented Hamlet. Fechter arrived in New York with the announcement that he would shortly appear as the Prince of Denmark.

With *Hamlet* in the air, it is not surprising that Fox decided to capitalize on the publicity. An old hand at Shakespearean travesty, he recommended to the managers of the Olympic that a burlesque *Hamlet*, staged to fill an evening, would be an excellent drawing-card. The idea itself was stale; John Poole's *Hamlet Travestie* had been the first such piece played in New York, and old inhabitants could remember the important production at Mitchell's Olympic in 1840. Another notable burlesque had been the *Hamlet* of 1857, with John Brougham as an Irish prince, Burton as the Ghost, and ponderous Mark Smith as Ophelia.[1] Such send-ups were standard fare as after-pieces, concert recitals, and minstrel sketches. Fox's originality lay in the scope of the project: an entire evening devoted to a burlesque which would follow the play faithfully with the central performance offered seriously.

The script, in pun-riddled couplets, was by Thomas Cooper De Leon, former Confederate soldier and editor of the Mobile *Register,* and, oddly enough, it incorporated whole chunks of unadapted Shakespeare. It had already been performed in Alabama with "signal success," but the producers announced in extra-space advertisements that Fox had written the play, driven to the classics by the demands of his fans.[2] Laurence Hutton's unreliable recollection of De Leon's concoction is often quoted: "an improvement on the general run of burlesques of its generation: it did not depend upon limelights or upon anatomical display, and it did not harrow up the young blood of its auditors by its horrible play upon unoffending words ... it never sank into imbecility or indelicacy."[3] Hutton's memory, however, was defective. The burlesque *Hamlet* exhibited plenty of female legs and its punning was mindlessly logorrhetic. What lent it class was Fox in the lead.

The audience on the rainy opening night of 14 February was first treated to a magnificent procession of courtiers, followed by the King, Queen, Polonius, Rosencrantz and Guildenstern, four Italian boys with harps, and the ladies of the ballet, amazons in short skirts who carried red cotton umbrellas—not unlike a minstrel walkaround, in fact. As the harpists strummed soft music, Fox (listed in the playbill as "Hamlet [HD]" which could be an abbreviation of either Hamlet the Dane or Humpty Dumpty) entered in suit of deepest woe and visage of equal melancholy. The audience roared for there, before them, was their favorite clown almost a double for Booth, in tunic, cross-gartered tights and, most of all, chestnut wig and somber countenance. Poker-faced, without the slightest glimmer of a smile, and affecting a lugubrious *basso profundo,* Fox was all the more ludicrous. At no point did he give a hint that he thought anything was funny.

The first scene ended with music from *Fra Diavolo* and, in the second, a female Laertes and Ophelia, who was played by the popular burlesque actress Belle Howitt, sang a duet of Thomas Moore's "You'll Remember Me," during which Ophelia turned away from her partner in true prima donna fashion, leaving Laertes to sing his affectionate farewell to her backside. Polonius offered his advice, "Look Out for Number One," and his daughter sang and danced a minstrel tune, "The Girl with the Golden Switch," which was encored, no doubt because male necks in the parquet stretched to catch a glimpse of the golden gaiters she displayed in her frolic.

Scene 3 gave Fox his first chance for protracted comedy. Marcellus and Bernardo, played by the Queen Sisters, Fanny and Laura, pranced on to the ramparts with long spears and intoned "Beautiful Night," whereupon Hamlet stalked in slowly and cautiously. Again the audience roared, for to his Booth-like garb Fox had added Arctic overshoes, red mittens, and a sealskin cap with earflaps, to protect him from the shrewd and nipping air. Critics had referred to the "winteriness" of Booth's performance: Fox's took it literally. Offstage an unseen chorus sang "Johnny Fill Up the Bowl," which Hamlet followed by "I am a Native Here," as he pulled blue woollen stockings over his galoshes and shivered at a tiny fire.

The Ghost (Mrs. Edward Wright) then strode forth, in a green tarlatan and clutching a huge demijohn of poison in her right hand. At this sight, Hamlet shrieked, pulled a mirth-raising grimace of horror, and fled behind a battlement. Peering round it, he watched the Ghost warming her hands at his fire. Hamlet threw off his fur garments and drew his sword, a four-foot stick of wood topped by a black umbrella that opened to a breadth of nine inches. Once he had discovered the Ghost's cordiality, Hamlet joined it at the fire for a passage of topical chitchat, the Ghost giggling and gossiping and the Prince earnestly professing disbelief. When cockcrow failed to stir the Ghost from the comfortable fire, even at several reprises, at last a huge rooster crossed the stage, tapped the phantom on the shoulder and crowed in its ear, as it pointed to the exit. In the following scene, at the Ghost's injunction to swear, Hamlet uttered some mild profanity, while Marcellus and a female Horatio were pounded on the back with the demijohn.

One of the current hit songs in New York was the Gendarmes' Duet in Offenbach's *Geneviève de Brabant*, so Rosencrantz and Guildenstern, who appeared in the next scene, wore the gendarmes' tricorner hats and chain-mail. Hamlet re-entered reading *The Police Gazette*, followed by the Players, with quondam Bowery prompter Asa Cushman in drag as the Actress. The First Actor, with an Irish accent, recited a verse condensation of *Othello*, which was succeeded by what many thought to be the finest moment in the burlesque, Hamlet's interview with Ophelia, when Fox chased her into a corner and bade her, in sepulchral tones, "Get thee to a brewery." He was called before the curtain numerous times for this sally.

His advice to the Players was exceptionally well-delivered, and the play-within-a-play kept the audience screaming with laughter. Shadowgraphs had become popular in minstrel shows and variety houses. Consequently, the "Mousetrap" was set up as a shadow pantomime against a large transparency; the silhouettes culminated with "a gigantic fiend who pours a demi-john of poison into the sleeper's ear, after having inserted a large funnel in the auricular orifice."[4] The King's consternation and Hamlet's triumph brought down the curtain in a sudden lunatic chorus of "Shoo-fly."

The second act opened with Hamlet inviting Rosencrantz and Guildenstern, not to play a pipe, but to smoke a pipe with him. The bass viol player stood up in the orchestra pit and beautifully sang "The Heart Bowed Down" as the King on stage "lip-synched" with sheet music in hand. The closet scene with Hamlet, his mother, and deceased father ended in the domestic trio dancing a can-can, just as the subsequent mad scene of Ophelia closed with a *pas de deux* for Laertes and Claudius.

The graveyard scene began solemnly with another Queen Sister, Julia, in a short skirt, singing quietly—so as to make no noise in a cemetery—"Five O'Clock in the Morning," a song which became as popular as "After the Ball" later in the century. Hamlet's apostrophe to Yorick's skull, patently that of a horse, was another comic triumph, particularly when the clown grimaced with disgust as he gingerly smelled this relic of mortality. His squeamishness did not, however, prevent him from dancing a double-shuffle on the newly dug grave. On Ophelia's interment, the gravedigger feelingly sang "Why Do I Weap for Thee?" Osric, Hamlet, and Horatio tripped it in the next scene, and the duel was fought with wooden swords. After the entire cast had been killed off, a jump-up resurrection occurred, ending in a song-and-dance reprise of "Shoo Fly."[5]

Two and a half hours of this kind of fun may seem excessive, but the opening night ran smoothly and the audience was won over to the inordinately lengthy burlesque. A long run was predicted. *The Spirit of the Times* opined that "a graveyard is hardly susceptible of humorous treatment,"[6] but most critics agreed that *Hamlet*'s success "proves that the public's appreciation of burlesque is not conditional upon the fact that it should be spoken or sung by young ladies with bottles of aureated tincture in one hand and riding-whips for editors who affend [*sic*] them in the other [a reference to Lydia Thompson]."[7] The success was attributed first to the popularity of Booth's Hamlet, then to the precision with which appropriate moments for travesty had been found, and finally to the harmony of the ensemble. "Mr. Fox," praised the *Tribune*, "knows the secret of the art of true burlesque. He is perfectly earnest. He preserves repose. He uses quiet humor. His voice is warm with suppressed drollery."[8]

The attribution to Booth of some of the success is intriguing. The Bowery stage manager F. W. Hofele once said that Fox was ambitious to play tragedy,[9] but this may simply be the cliché of the clown wanting to enact Hamlet. This clown did know Booth well. He had begun his stage career playing with the tragedian's father in Boston; Fox and Booth had both made debuts at the National Theatre in 1850, occasionally appearing on the same bill though in different plays; and the comedian had already parodied the actor's style in *The Coarse-Haired Brothers*. They were similar in build and stature, though not in face, and Fox was

Figure 23. Fox as Hamlet, contemplating the grave of Yorick. A photograph by Gurney, New York. (Author's Collection)

capable of imitating Booth's somber, soulful stare easily, since he shared the same taciturn nature. Occasionally, Fox tossed in a touch of Fechter for accent and expression, as well as a cavernous echo of Studley, the ranting Bowery histrion whose style was familiar. But essentially it was Booth's earnestness, velvety voice, and brooding sadness that Fox best captured.

The comic actor Nat Goodwin later claimed that no one but another Booth could imitate the original.

No one could recognize a straight imitation of him—it would be—too *different*. As for burlesquing him—what's there to hang a caricature on? His art's rounded like a bell. He has no rough knobs sticking out for pegs ... You cannot be funny by exaggerating something that is not in the first place a little overdone by the one you burlesque ... Mr. Booth stresses his vowels ... He says altar, as if it were spelled a-l-t-a-r—which it is—and he does not pronounce it altur (like the rest of us) ... He's right! and the fool who tries to be funny over the correct English pronunciations of Edwin Booth just shows himself up.[10]

Fox did not make that mistake. Aside from a basic external similarity in costume and makeup, what he sought to imitate was Booths' inward melancholy, which became the more laughable given the bathetic context. But it is probably too strong to say, as one modern writer has, that Fox was drawing on unwitting elements of sorrow and madness, unconscious memories of the elder Booth's aberrations, when he decided to play Hamlet in the Boothian manner. The incongruity of his poker-face and the nonsense of minstrel walkarounds and buck-and-wings had been a regular feature of his earlier work; only the starkness of *Hamlet* put it in relief.[11] Here he perfected the deadpan that would later characterize Buster Keaton (who played Hamlet in his film *Three Ages*). "Truth to nature, it might be said, is mainly characteristic of Mr. Booth's performance," allowed the New York *Sun*. "Truth to goodnature of Mr. Fox's."[12]

Booth himself was aware of the likeness and keenly appreciated its comedy. He took his family to see it several times and laughed himself to tears, saying, "He looks just like me." His wife, during the "Words, words, words" scene, had to turn to the tragedian and ask, "Are you here, or is that you on stage?" According to a superannuated doorman, Booth sat in one box on opening night, John McCullough in another, E. L. Davenport in a third, and Lawrence Barrett in a fourth, composing a constellation of Hamlets. Barrett, himself an epigone of Booth, was said to have been especially enthusiastic and declared that Fox could probably give one of the best straight performances of the part. Booth congratulated Fox warmly, declaring his Hamlet "to have such beauty of understanding in its humor that it was a very great Dane in-

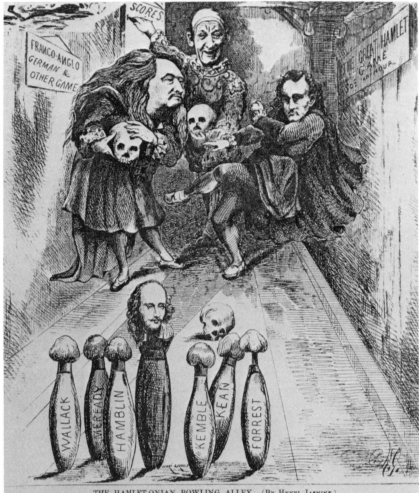

THE HAMLETONIAN BOWLING ALLEY. (By Henri Jasmine.)

Fechter—*I very much fear zat I no make one hit, or zat I knock down ze Shakspeare wiz mine French skull.*
Booth—*Ah! there's a hit with the skull my father gave me!*
Fox—*By my daddy's ghost, bully! Now, Fechter, go for 'em, if you have to roll in the "gutter."*

Figure 24. "The Hamletonian Bowling Alley," a caricature by Henri Jasmine, showing Charles Fechter, left, Fox, center, and Edwin Booth, right, competing for the great Hamlet prize. Fechter: "I very much fear zat I no make one hit, or zat I knock down ze Shakespeare wiz mine French skull." Booth: "Ah! there's a hit with the skull my father gave me!" Fox: "By my daddy's ghost, bully! Now, Fechter, go for 'em, if you have to roll in the 'gutter.'" (Courtesy Harvard Theatre Collection)

deed."[13] He left to the Players' Club, which he had founded, two poly-chrome wooden statuettes of Fox as Hamlet and as Humpty Dumpty, which may have been gifts from the comedian. Of these figures, prob-ably sculpted by Jonathan Scott Hartley, president of the Arts Students League, the Hamlet is still to be viewed at the Players'.

Although the advertisements boasted that fifty-three thousand per-sons had seen the travesty by its fourth week and reporters insisted that evening and matinee performances alike were crammed,[14] *Hamlet* was not a huge popular success. The average weekly gross was $5165,[15] indicating that the theatre was playing only to about 50 per cent capac-ity. After nine weeks and seventy-two performances it closed on 16 April. A parody of this sort requires a close acquaintance with the original, and neither Booth nor Shakespeare was as accessible to the ordinary spectator as were slapstick and spectacle. Moreover, audi-ences were unaccustomed to a full evening of burlesque and felt the need for greater diversity. Fox's Hamlet was caviare to the general.

Unfortunately, he made the mistake of planning a sequel and sched-uled a burlesque of *Macbeth* to take *Hamlet*'s place. De Leon's *Hamlet* script had not been wholly original (the line "Take him for half-and-half" was a particularly hoary chestnut), but it had the advantage of tight construction and literary taste behind it. Fox concocted the *Macbeth* script himself, according to the publicity, although he dis-claimed authorship after the reviews appeared.[16] In all likelihood it was patched together from as many gags as Fox could recall from the Fox-Howard burlesque of the Scottish play with whatever the Olympic staff could provide.

As the "Thane of Chowder," Fox assumed the same grave mien he had for Hamlet. In the dagger scene he gasped, "By Heavens, what is that before me? It is a dagger—made of wood and almost full of bloot!" (a Dutch comic's pronunciation). This was the first hit of the evening. Other successes were the banquet scene wherein Banquo, with his eye bunged up, stalked coolly in, smoking a cheroot; the sleepwalking scene in which "Mrs. Macbeth" appeared with a pail and scrub-brush to wash out the damned spot; and the advent of Birnam Wood an-nounced by a messenger with the news that a cord of wood has been left at the door. The battle scene, like the *Macbeth* burlesque at the Odeon a generation earlier, ended in a boxing match in which Macduff laid on until "enough said," and with a hilariously protracted death during which Fox vanished through a trap to reappear just as the crown was being placed on Malcolm's head. The curtain closed on a tableau of jigging. The full score of the legitimate *Macbeth* (i.e., the witches's choruses) was sung, and Fox laid on Caledonian atmosphere with yards of tartan and plenty of pipers. The Queen Sisters were still featured, and C. K. Fox played Macduff, a role in which he was said to be too genuinely Shakespearean to achieve the mock-heroic.[17]

The 18 April opening was sparsely attended, and the critics, striving to be enthusiastic, could not conceal their disappointment. They noted that the original tragedy was of an unrelieved grimness less apt for travesty than *Hamlet* and that the Olympic script was too uneven. More serious was the accusation of auto-plagiarism, the same complaint that had followed the sequel to *Humpty Dumpty*. As *The Spirit of the Times* explained, "Travesty of this sort must leap from one extreme to the other of possibilities and not trudge the beaten track. The quality of the business was new in 'Hamlet,' but it is not new in 'Macbeth.'"[18] This did not prevent the sincerest form of flattery; Tony Pastor, who had already run a *Hamlet the Second* while Fox's was on, with a setting in Congress, a Dutch King, an Irish gravedigger, and a pumpkin for skull, put on a short-lived *Macbeth* as well.[19]

Some sort of stopgap was needed to keep the Olympic filled in the summer months, so Alice Oates's Comedy company was jobbed in. Fox appeared with her in two benefit performances of *Swiss Swains* a week after *Macbeth* closed.[20] Perhaps he had been discomfited on hearing of his former partner Lingard's suicide, for he dropped out of sight until 22 August, when a "newly organized comic opera company" presented *Le Petit Faust*, a hackneyed adaptation by H. B. Farnie of Hervé's original, with Mrs. Oates as Mephistopheles and Fox in the dame role of Martha. The whole enterprise was trashy, saved only by Fox's "artistically drawn picture of an ancient spinster who apes the manners of sweet sixteen ... the only mirth of the evening, his gags possessed real wit and were opportunely introduced."[21] "Nothing," the *Tribune* cooed, "could be neater than his method, and the mood that underlies his method is that of keenest sympathy with comic situations and amplest knowledge of human nature."[22] As usual, Fox was superior to his material, and, in this case, saved his strength for a spectacular autumn pantomime.

Wee Willie Winkie, which played to a full house on its 5 October premiere, was the same mixture as before, indeed somewhat diluted by a closer adherence to the French *féérie* and the claims of variety and spectacle. Brother Charlie was not on hand, for he was touring with Tony Denier and his wooden-headed acrobatic puppets in C. K.'s own panto *3 Blind Mice or Harlequin Tell-Tale Tit*.[23] In his absence, George Beane assumed the Pantaloon function. Fox was now clown under the name Wee Willie Winkie, man of all work to Old Grain the Miller, and, in deference to adversaries of the leg show, the heroine Blondette, played by Fanny Beane, was billed as "flaxen-haired, though not a Blonde." The action was laid in a generic French fairyland, and not until the second act did such American tokens as Red Indians, a dollar store and pawnbroker's with a billiard table, and an Irish laundry make their appearance. Even then, the final scenes took place in China, a Gothic cellarage and Hell itself.

Fox's first entrance was, as usual, greeted with long and sincere applause "that testified to his deeply rooted popularity."[24] The critics were fulsome in their praise of his skills as "the best pantomimic clown of the French school now upon the stage in either hemisphere." By now, he had shaken off all traces of Bowery coarseness, and his performances were lauded as "remarkably chaste and free from even suggestive vulgarity."[25] This was all the more astonishing in view of the finicky standards that prevailed. The previous year Edward Lauri in *Little Boy Blue* at Wallack's had been scolded for scratching himself while playing a monkey.[26]

Familiar routines included a chopped tree rising again, a stretchable horse, mayhem in a kitchen and a blacksmith's shop, and a battle royal with barrel staves.[27] But certain significant and unwonted comments show that an important evolution was taking place. The real hit of the show was not Fox, but eleven-year-old Jennie Yeamans, a Victorian Shirley Temple, hailed as "the most promising prodigy that has appeared since the debut of the Bateman children." She sang and drummed and played a policeman, while her mother Annie did an Irish act she would later perfect with Harrigan and Hart. There was also a preadolescent drum corps commanded by a youth got up to resemble Jim Fisk. This emphasis on children was reflected in the audience, for, as the *Clipper* remarked, "the true aim of pantomime is, we hold, to amuse the youthful mind."[28] Times had changed since Mrs. Cowell noted the adult appeal of the Bowery pantos.

The critics also began to boggle at the irrelevant variety acts, especially a prestidigitator named Professor Maximilian who performed a genuine vanishing act shortly after the show opened. This, complained the *Tribune* "is pantomime freighted with many sorts of extraneous attractions."[29] Later in the run, a comment was made suggestive of the first signs of Fox's mental troubles: "now that his mind is not confused by watching the business details of the pantomime, [he] has become funnier than ever."[30] Had he evinced traces of derangement or merely preoccupation on opening night?

At first *Wee Willie Winkie* proved to be so popular, despite the rival excitement of the November elections, that the house was filled well into the holiday season, stimulating the usual competition. The Kiralfys mounted a *Humpty Dumpty Jr.* at Wood's Museum, casting six- and eight-year-olds in the major roles. The Theatre Comique countered with *Hanky Panky or The Lively Quaker and the Genii of the Enchanted*

Comique. Its acrobatic clown, Charles Abbott, who performed a complicated ladder dance, was judged "as holding a position if not equalling George L. Fox, certainly close to him in artistic merit."[31] To freshen its appeal, *Wee Willie Winkie* kept adding variety material, but by early 1871, business had fallen off badly. When John H. Selwyn of the Boston Theatre took over the stage management of the Olympic on 28 January, he suggested that it was time for a change. Fox's pantomime closed on 4 February, after 132 performances, nowhere near the record set by *Humpty Dumpty.*[32]

Fox must have been desperate for inspiration. Hustled back and forth between pantomime and burlesque for so long, he seemed incapable of breaking the pattern. He looked again to Booth; on 9 January, the tragedian had presented a splendidly mounted revival of Bulwer Lytton's *Richelieu* at his own theatre. Fox, in true copycat fashion, then announced *The Richelieu of the Period* (an allusion to Lydia Thompson's "Girl of the Period"), with "all the Cardinal Virtues of the Duc de Richelieu."[33] James Schonberg and Thomas B. De Walden, a prolific ex-army chaplain, who tailored plays to order, were entrusted with script responsibilities, perhaps to avoid the charges of literary ineptitude that had been levelled at *Macbeth.* It was a clear case of theatrical opportunism; Fox had no particular point to make in burlesquing Bulwer Lytton, but simply hoped to cash in on the topicality of Booth's production.

Topicality, therefore, was the order of the day. The famous sword speech alluded to Bull Run and the Black Horse Cavalry. One famous quotation was altered to read "in the hands of newspaper men, the pen is mightier than the sword." At the close of act 1, when Richelieu feigned death, Fox as "G. L. Armand Jean des Etats Unis," Lillie Eldridge as Julie de Mortemar and Ada Harland as De Mauprat sang an arrangement of the popular tune "Put Me in My Little Bed," which brought down the house. In the celebrated Curse of Rome scene (pronounced "the cuss of rum" by Fox), the "awful circle of Tammany" was chalked on the floor by the infant phenomenon Jenny Yeamans (as François), while the clown-cardinal proclaimed to Julie's persecutors: "I draw the Magic Circle of Tammany Hall—set but a hoof within that bound and on thy head—aye, though it wore a crown—I launch the Erie injunction." Referring to a proposed elevated train, the prelate informed François that "On the bright Lexington Avenue, which fate has marked for a railroad, there is no such word as fail."[34] All the characters made their exits to current hit songs, including grim Brother Joseph, played by Pantaloon George Beane, who had great fun with the music-hall catchphrase "Not for Joe."[35]

The scanty audience that attended on the bitterly cold opening night

Figure 25. A misspelled poster for *Richelieu of the Period,* showing Fox invoking the "Cuss of Rum." (Courtesy The Billy Rose Theatre Collection, The New York Public Library at Lincoln Center, Astor, Lenox and Tilden Foundations)

of 6 February appreciated the lavishness of scenery and costumes that might well have adorned a straight production of *Richelieu:* "it was a pity to see so much money expended upon such a weak affair as it is. There are so few points to laugh at that it is useless to mention them."[36] A similar criticism was directed at Fox himself; funny though he was, and so admirably like Booth in manner and appearance as to be a "formidable rival … it is a pity that such an admirable comedian should be so long hidden under a clown's face or obscured by wretched burlesques."[37]

When Booth, who again richly enjoyed the clown's lampoon, closed his *Richelieu* after forty-eight performances, the *raison d'être* for Fox's vanished. It was suggested that he remodel his acting to introduce some of the idiosyncrasies of Edwin Forrest, since that tragedian had also revived the play.[38] But Fox too stopped after forty-eight performances, on 28 March.

To some degree, he had miscalculated his public. Speaking of the "tangible spirit of anarchy" that is a primary dynamic of American humor, a writer on minstrelsy has considered that "the American common man, on whose behalf this nation's democratic philosophy was ostensibly developed, has persistently expressed in a kind of comic nihilism his essential distrust of the goals toward which the American dream has directed him."[39] In the mid-nineteenth century, this was often expressed in a playful animosity toward the European cultural traditions Americans wanted to repudiate or supersede. Burlesque launched a no-holds-barred attack on the sacred cows of old world civilization, often in the name of democracy.

Shakespeare might seem a natural target. On the one hand, he represented a symbolic bond with English civilization, and was thus fair game for farcical parody that sought to debase him to the lowest common denominator. This was especially true when polished English stars strove to outshine more exuberant native players. But on the other hand, Shakespeare had long been an integral part of American popular culture, easily absorbed into democratically miscellaneous entertainments. When Fox was first making a name for himself, Shakespeare was readily accepted as a vigorous medium for declamation, well suited to the boisterous life of the young republic. Parodic allusions were welcomed by a populace conversant with the original lines.

By the 1860s, however, a cultural division was taking effect. The audience for ranting Edwin Forrest and that for reflective Edwin Booth had become two distinct entities. As society sought gentility, Shakespeare was beginning to be classed as "high culture," to be set apart from melodramas, hornpipes, and horseplay. The middle-class New York public, sharply distinguished from immigrant spectators who lacked a Shakespearean background, plumed itself on refinement, and welcomed European sophistication in the production of the classics. Blank verse drama was a touchstone for highbrows, and Fox's reduction of Shakespeare and Bulwer Lytton to absurdity ran counter to Broadway's prevailing ambitions.[40]

Richelieu was to be Fox's last burlesque of any magnitude, and also the last production wholly conceived by and for him. From this time on, although he retained his fame and popularity, his influence and autonomy as a theatrical creator became considerably reduced. In the past, Fox's innovations had occurred within a basic framework provided by someone else, as with Tayleure's two-act *Humpty Dumpty* and De Leon's travesty *Hamlet*. Now, cast on his own devices, no longer a manager aided by a talented staff, Fox would have to showcase his gifts in less suitable vehicles.

14

*Humpty's Return
and the Triumph of Variety*

(1871-73)

The Olympic Theatre was in parlous straits. Audiences continued to dwindle, in sharp contrast to the throngs that had swelled the house during the heyday of *Humpty Dumpty*. As New York's middle-class population moved farther uptown, the theatre's location was growing unfashionable: 624 Broadway was too far south to appeal when the leading playhouses were now bounded by Union and Madison squares. Twenty-five cents was still cheap admission to the gallery, but the boys who filled it often got round the charge by slipping unwary ticket-takers ten cents or mere metal slugs instead.

The Olympic's proprietor, bluff James Duff, had spent a great deal of money buying the decree of foreclosure that had cancelled the owner-ship of the theatre's builder Trimble, but, as might have been expected in the inefficient and corrupt courts of the day, final judgement had never been entered. Once Fox's successes had turned the Olympic into a valuable property, Trimble's creditors, aroused to their opportunity by a shyster lawyer, were allowed to put in their bills, and Duff had to lay out his profits making good Trimble's deficits. The builder's heirs also claimed to retain ownership, and a messy lawsuit wound up with Duff having to pay the Trimble family $400,000.[1]

Augustin Daly hoped to bail out his father-in-law by writing an origi-nal frontier drama, *Horizon*, in which Agnes Ethel, on loan from Daly's Theatre, would, as the delicate heroine, keep a tribe of hostile Indians

Figure 26. The façade of the Olympic Theatre, c. 1875. Half of a stereopticon slide by an unknown photographer. (Author's Collection)

at bay with her expert marksmanship. It was the first play at the Olympic in four years that had not been written as a vehicle for Fox, although he got star billing alongside Miss Ethel. Instead of the customary frontiersman, Daly provided him with the role of a corrupt lobbyist, the Hon. Sundown Rowse, who, in one historian's words, was "destined to become the forerunner of such notables as Bardwell Slote, Colonel Sellers, and Silas K. Woolcott—yes, and even of Senator Claghorn"[2] Rowse is described in the playbill as "a distinguished member of the *Third House* at Washington, owning a slice of every Territory, and bound for the Far West to survey his new Congressional land grant, which lies just this side of the horizon."[3] The character was representative of an era when politics were dirtier than ever, and the very word "politician" was synonymous with grafter. Rowse was intended, however, not as the lead, but as comic relief.

Horizon, which opened on 21 March 1871, did succeed, but Fox was only one of many attractions, including beautiful scenic effects, a plethora of incident and a host of amusing characters. His passages with little Jennie Yeamans as Notah the papoose who trailed him wherever he went made a great hit. Fox was also memorable in his scenes with the excellent actor Charles Wheatleigh as the Indian chief Wannemucka, who wanted whatever he set his eyes on. When Rowse took out his watch, the Chief asserted, "Wannamucka want," and Fox's face assumed a memorable expression when he gravely replied, "Well, Wannamucka can't have."[4] Fox excited much laughter, reported the *Spirit of the Times*, "for which he is not to blame, since he cannot help it," but the *Times* complained that the part was not well enough defined to give Fox scope for his talent.[5]

When Agnes Ethel returned to Daly's fold, Fox's top billing went unchallenged, and *Horizon* ran through 6 May, thus "carrying the Olympic through more than seven months with only three plays—an excellent record."[6] After a dark week and a half, the theatre reopened with a refurbished version of that Bowery favorite *Jack Sheppard*, written and directed by the acting manager John Selwyn. It was an odd choice, an old-fashioned romantic melodrama out of keeping with the more sophisticated plays of adultery and marital imbroglios that kept New York theatres filled. In the Bowery in the 1850s, its fustian sentiments and Fanny Herring's vitality had been appropriate. On Broadway in the 1870s, it gave off a musty odor, which even the charms of British blonde Ada Harland in the title role could not dispel. In recounting the plot, one reviewer expatiated on the absurdities for which an urbane public was supposed to suspend its disbelief:

During the early scenes of the play the chief characters are a prey to a wild thirst for infants, and a varied succession of men and women rush violently on the stage, seize the nearest available baby, and rush frantically away with it only to be succeeded by other pedomaniacs who bring forward additional infants, which are subject to similar seizures ... In the succeeding acts, the mania for infants gives way to a passion for miniatures, which are worn or stolen by most of the *dramatis personae*.[7]

Fox, in the relatively colorless role of the carpenter Owen Wood, was cited for his broad, genuine, and quaint humor,[8] but that was hardly enough to salvage an ill-advised enterprise. After three weeks, *Jack Sheppard* retired on 3 June. Lucille Western moved into the house with her sempiternal *East Lynne*, and the last of Fox to be seen that summer was at a benefit for the family of the recently deceased Olympic press agent Dan Symons; the clown appeared in a series of farces with his alleged rival Joe Jefferson.[9]

That same summer, C. K. Fox and Tony Denier brought their troupe of wooden acrobats off the road and into Wood's Museum to mount a *Humpty Dumpty*. "How is this, Charlie?" asked one columnist, "when brother George is so soon to re-reproduce it at the Olympic?"[10] (Denier and C. K. were nevertheless praised for being "singularly free from coarseness and vulgarity.")[11] This was the earliest intimation that Fox and the Olympic management had fallen back yet again on the proven crowd-pleasing of that old favorite. Advance publicity promised that this would be an "unsurpassed edition," embellished with untold expenditure on European variety artistes.[12]

Such a boast reveals the radical transformation *Humpty Dumpty* was to undergo. The foreign performers were of such importance to the new concept that the opening was postponed several days, until the steamer bringing them over had docked.[13] The Kiralfys had been sent to Europe to recruit and returned with Tyrolean singers from St. Petersburg, cyclists from England, ballerinas from Egypt, France, and Italy, and some eccentric comedians from Belgium.[14] When *Humpty Dumpty* opened on 31 August, it was immediately apparent that pantomime had evolved into a new form. As usual, there was an allegorical opening, followed by the pastoral story and the metamorphosis of the characters who then romped through three scenes of comedy. But the second act was devoted exclusively to the incidental attractions, and the plot line and pantomime business were not resumed until the supplemental third act.

In other words, for a third or more of the evening, Fox was off-stage, *primus inter pares* in the galaxy of vaudeville acts. These included a grand ballet; the Martens family of Tyrolean vocalists, who made a stunning success with a cat duet; a performer on the "invisible wire"; the Belgian Zig-Zags or Human Insects, grotesques in the style of the Clodoche dancers; two-and-one-half-year old Little Venus and four-and-

one-half-year old Young Adonis, bicyclists; the ever popular Jennie
Yeamans singing character songs; and the Kiralfy troupe, whose stars,
Imre, Bolossy, Haniola, and Emilie, also personated dual Harlequins
and Columbines in the panto. The bulk of the newspaper criticism was
devoted to describing these virtuosi, and Fox, somewhat taken for
granted, was awarded a generalized meed of praise.[15]

On opening night, when he and brother Charles, now reinstated as
Pantaloon, made their first entrance in the traditional donkey cart, the
applause was long and loud, and Fox seemed in the best of spirits in his
congenial and familiar ambience. He seemed to enjoy the fun as much
as any of the audience. What had once been seen as animal spirits was
now exalted by middle-brow critics to a loftier plane. He was said to
have "elevated the business of *Clown* to what might be called an art."[16]
"If pantomime is not art," the *Clipper* demurred, "G. L. Fox has raised
it to that close approach thereto, that it would be difficult to distinguish
the dividing line." In any case, "he is one of the best clowns of the
French school, now upon our stage ... he produces his effects naturally
and apparently without exertion. In other words, the art is so concealed
that it would seem that none was used."[17]

"The new 'Humpty Dumpty' bears about as much resemblance to its
preceding namesake as does a modern six-in-hand at Jerome Park to an
old-fashioned stage coach," noted the *Herald*.[18] This was meant as a
compliment, but it expressed the shift in interest the pantomime had
undergone. The interruption of the harlequinade was, to all intents and
purposes, an autonomous variety bill and decreased the coherence and
narrative value of the panto. It denatured the show's identity by en-
abling the managers to vary the acts at will. *Humpty Dumpty* was barely
three weeks old when a number of new features were added, and by
25 October the Martens Family, whose Cat Duo had been encored to the
echo, were receiving star billing with Fox. A troupe of trained dogs who
performed creditably as buffo vocalists and a bevy of children known as
the Seven Little Men of the Mountain came in around Christmas-time,
along with a Clodoche quadrille for the Zig-Zags.[19] If this was intended
to win repeat business, it also allowed spectators to come for the second
act alone, as they would for a weekly change at a variety house.

"Pantomime," declared the *Herald*, "is fast decaying," and it noted
that the vaudeville segment "has won such general approbation [as] to
be the great attraction of the entertainment."[20] In the process, whatever
topicality or relevance to current events the pantomime had possessed
was lost. It is significant that the *Clipper* cited as *Humpty*'s most loyal
audiences the children, untouched by "the corruptions of the Ring,
stolen vouchers or other discreditable acts of politicians."[21]

For if Humpty himself was slipping from prominence, so was his real-life counterpart Boss Tweed, now heavily assailed by adverse publicity, subpoenas, and grand jury indictments. Journalists had long perceived a relation between Tweed's career and crime drama; when his charter had passed the Assembly at Albany, the *Herald* reported, "the gallery audience cleared out as quickly as if the drop of the Bowery Theatre had fallen upon the last scene of *Jack Sheppard*."[22] Political cartoonists quickly followed up the resemblance between Tweed's peculations and the pantomime clown's mischief. After all, the Boss's chief press opponent was German-born caricaturist Thomas Nast, whose cross-hatched cartoons got the message across even to the illiterate, and Nast had been part of *Humpty Dumpty*'s publicity campaigns from the beginning. One Nast drawing in *Harper's Weekly* for 14 January 1871 had portrayed Tweed as Humpty and his associate Peter "Brains" Sweeney as Old One-Two rifling the public treasury and handing it out to the poor as part of a "new Christmas pantomime at the Tammany Hall." The caption read, "Let's blind them with this, and then take some more," a reference to the Boss's distribution of fifty thousand dollars for relief in his own ward just before the State Senate election.[23] The image was too powerful not to be copied by others. Bellew in *Harper's Weekly* in 1872, when Tweed was feebly menaced with prosecution, showed Oakey Hall as Old One-Two and Judge Barnard as Harlequin wielding a writ of *habeas corpus* to spring the clown-costumed Tweed from a box marked TOMBS.[24] Since Fox's Humpty was a byword for greed and amorality, these pictorial references were acute visual shorthand.

The revived *Humpty Dumpty* led to one of the few letters of Fox that has survived, which sheds light on his character at this time. A Mr. Thomas Kean, who had bought tickets for the Thanksgiving Day matinee, found the house to be oversold, with no available seats except those with obstructed view. Receiving no answers to letters sent directly to Fox, the indignant customer had had recourse to the columns of the *Herald*. His open complaint evoked this reply:

Olympic Theatre, New York
Dec. 16, 1871

To the Editor of the Herald:

I notice in to-day's *Herald* a communication from a party by the name of "Thomas Kean, of the savings bank near to hand," accusing me of failing to furnish him with free passes to witness my performance of "Humpty Dumpty." According to his own statements the only ground on which he rested this bold claim was that he bought admission tickets, and had found, on entering the house, that nothing was left for his accommodation but a backseat. I plead guilty to this charge; and further, I acknowledge that I did fail to enter into correspondence with the gentleman from the savings bank "near to hand." While I would willingly pay \$2 or more to be guaranteed immunity from the annoyance of receiving his letters I decidedly object to "seeing" him in order that he may see me. My line of business, it appears, is too near that of Mr. Kean, and two of a kind never can agree, you know. The Olympic is my bank for savings; Mr. Kean has his in Chambers Street, "near to hand." Let him stick to it, and I will stick to the Olympic. I do not complain of this Kean's as an isolated, but aggravated case. He, however, being the only of my epistolary tormentors who has gotten himself into print, I have found him altogether too sharp a blade—too keen, indeed—to run loose. I am not willing that he shall thus publicly "cut and come again." I propose to be as blunt in my expressions as he is sharp in his tricks. I claim that I filled my contract with him; that he received all the facilities that he purchased at the box office. If all who came late and are obliged to take back seats in the Olympic nightly are to demand as a right free passes the day after, what is to become of me? There is a great error which many people act on, and notably this Kean man of the savings bank "close to hand." They confound my character on the stage with my character off. They evidently think that because I am called a good clown I must of necessity be a great fool. Now, I assure you most earnestly this is a mistake. I am not half so simple as I appear. Indeed, mine is an intricate nature; I admire financial complexities and am even sordid enough to regard "Humpty Dumpty" exclusively from "a two dollar point of view." And, moreover, let me say, however willing I may be to play for the public, I have a constitutional aversion to allowing anyone to "play on" me. Assuring you once more than I have a separate individuality, and that I have financial ideas as economical as those of the gentleman from the savings bank "near to hand," I beg in conclusion that you record me in your esteemed journal. Yours truly,

Humpty Dumpty Fox
"Not such a fool as he looks."[25]

This is a remarkably unpleasant letter and reveals Fox in the worst light. The ham-fisted sarcasm, the ponderous repetition of his correspondent's phrases and the punning on his name, the refusal to accept that the customer is always right bespeak the Fox whom so many colleagues found roughhewn and crude. The protests of acuity and assertion of financial acumen are overdone, and all the more dismaying for being so wide of the mark. His wife was later to declare that "he had less idea of business than a child,"[26] and in any case a stage favorite has no business proclaiming to the world that he amuses it only for the money. The letter exudes a whiff of paranoia that may announce the madness to come.

Fox's lack of financial shrewdness was apparent in his dealings with Duff, who regularly prevailed upon his sense of magnanimity to wheedle him into bad bargains. Mattie Fox had managed to save four thousand dollars of her husband's salary (he was said to be making twenty thousand dollars a year), but he made her hand it over so that he could buy from Duff a piece of land in Westchester County, the deeds to which she could never find after Fox's death. Duff also convinced the comedian to buy at a very high price a small, narrow brick house at 177 Carlton Avenue in Brooklyn. The cost was charged against his salary, and Fox never knew whether or not he had worked off the price. In fact, he never received the deed until Mrs. Fox set to work to obtain it. The house was to be their home until his demise, but then the title proved to be flawed, preventing his widow from mortgaging it.

The acrimonious open letter did not hurt the two dollar sales. By 30 December, the managers toted up 483 performances of *Humpty Dumpty*, with gross receipts for the first sixteen and a half weeks at $148,387. The average receipts in September had been $1300 a night. This seems princely at first sight, but when the higher running costs of the pantomime are figured in, this gross is all the more evidence that Fox was not an astute businessman.[27]

To celebrate the New Year, *Humpty Dumpty* was officially reconstructed, with a new burlesque prologue cut down to two characters, Lulu Prior as the Sun Spirit and George Beane as the Ice King. Henry Willio the Sprite who had dropped out of the cast and been jailed for breach of contract was back while his appeal was pending. New acts included Monsieur Robere and Mlle Emma, who walked upside-down on the ceiling, and the Carroll family in Irish songs and clog dances. There were new specialties by the Martens, Zig Zags, and Kiralfys.[28] The Hungarians led the ballet in a Warrior Dance, which was an important innovation in theatrical choreography:

> The performers of the Legions of the Sun Spirit had during the performances of the [sunbeam] ballet been ranged around the stage, the males bearing large shields at the back, and the ladies carrying lances on either side. The males at the back now fixed their shields together over their heads—upon which they rested—making a circular platform. The ladies on either side now stuck their lances into the stage at equidistant points, and taking shields attached them to the handles of the lances at various heights forming a staircase on either side leading to the circular platform. Four ladies of the ballet quickly ascending these stairways, grouped themselves in picturesque attitudes around the platform, while the remaining portion of the ballet disported themselves in graceful evolutions around it. This platform was moved with a circular motion down the stage and back to its original position. Long wreaths of flowers were now held by one end of the ladies upon the platform, while the other ends, held by the corps de ballet as they moved through the mazes of the dance, presented a kaleidoscopic picture of much beauty. At the termination

of this dance the ladies tripped lightly from the platform down the staircases, and each performer seizing his particular spear or shield with one motion, the picture faded and the performers were beheld in their original positions.[29]

Such precise geometrical configurations, foretastes of Busby Berkeley and June Taylor, must have made the ordinary pantomime antics seem amateurish.

But Fox had a new trick as well. In act 3, he came on with a gas-filled cloth elephant, so light that it would assume a grotesque position every time Clown touched it. It was tossed in the air, made to stand on its head, turn a somersault, and perform a series of lifelike and hilarious motions, not unlike the huge globe that Charlie Chaplin later juggled in *The Great Dictator.* At the end of the act, it was switched for another trick elephant that swallowed the Sprite, now played by Imre Kiralfy, for Willio had won his suit and left the cast.[30]

The "improvements" and alterations never ended. February saw a shivering chorus in a snow scene "imported from Russia," the Kiralfy Brothers dancing gracefully in the air suspended from ropes, the Three Wilson Brothers performing gymnastics on the horizontal bars, the Martens in a Savoyard scena, and Fox on skates, cutting ludicrous capers in the snow, side by side with real skatorial artists, Kynock and Smith. April brought more refurbishments, freshly painted scenery, yet another burlesque opening, and some new business for Humpty. Borrowing from his *Hamlet* burlesque, he introduced hilarious magic shadows. In the closing scene, instead of the usual transformation, a marble tableau set in the Hall of Scenes filled up the entire stage from the second groove to the back wall. The upstage area, wings and a series of raised platforms were covered with maroon cloth; on the platforms were large figures of horses painted to resemble marble, with live actors on their backs, while other living statues posed around the stage in the glare of calcium lights. They were arranged to represent the Rape of the Sabines. The immobility and lighting produced an illusion of marble statuary that much impressed the audiences. But one wonders what such a classical and static finale was doing in a popular and dynamic form like the pantomime that Fox had made all "action, action, action."[31]

By the time *Humpty Dumpty* closed on 11 June, rumor had it that the Olympic was going to be turned into a variety theatre. Given the changes made in the pantomime, it already had been. At the final evening performance, the pantomime had been preceded by a farce called *The Lottery Ticket,* in which Fox played Wormwood. When it was over and before he had put on his clown makeup, he stepped before the wildly applauding audience and addressed it.

Figure 27. The trick elephant in *Humpty Dumpty* swallowing a Kiralfy as Imp, as Fox gloats and the corps de ballet panics. A wood engraving from the *Sporting Times and Theatrical News.* (Courtesy Harvard Theatre Collection)

Ladies and gentlemen—I am almost ashamed to come out before you in habiliments like these, and as I am not used to public speaking except when I commit it to memory, I hope you will excuse me from making any lengthy remarks on this occasion. But you must see that I return you my sincere and heartfelt thanks—as they all say—everybody knows that's said, and I hope I am right there. I have been in New York just twenty-one years, and I always boast of it. I was quite a youngster when I first came here, and I am an old "rooster" now. But, ladies and gentlemen, I always strive to do my best. Neither sickness nor anything else keeps me away. For twenty-one years have I been in New York, and I have never missed a night for sickness or anything else. And there are a great many here that know that, and my heart is so full that they must speak for me.[32]

After the show went down, a banquet in the theatre lasted well into the wee hours. The management, counting the performances of *Humpty Dumpty* from the first at the Olympic on 10 March 1868 and adding the Bowery appearances for good measure, proclaimed that Fox had performed it a total of 1,001 times. It was a record-breaking figure and very useful for publicity.

Throughout the latest run of the pantomime, Fox's star seemed to be in the ascendant, and it was suggested that he and his brother should go to poor benighted England where panto came only at Christmas, to "show them what kind of pantomimists America can produce."[33] John Oxenford, the London critic who had pronounced Fox the greatest clown since Grimaldi, was said to be trying fruitlessly to induce him to cross the Atlantic.[34] Gossip put it about that Fox had been offered a fabulous salary by Ben Webster and Dion Boucicault to take *Humpty* to London at season's end; though this was an advertising canard to spur attendance, the rumor caught on, with the additional statement that he would remain abroad for several years.[35] One writer, comparing English and American pantomimes, averred that

George Fox *ought* to have a fortune before him in a trip to England ... For his style is different from his English brethren. It is indescribably, but palpably so. In no Clown in England is there the same mirth-provoking powers as in Fox ... One very great difference I noted that while the American clown only utters an occasional word, De Forrest kept up a continual flood of patter.[36]

This was why Fox was said to be of the French school.

Rumor to the contrary, by late May, Fox renounced Europe to go on an American tour of *Humpty Dumpty* with his brother Charles. "Managers have been in such a hurry to negotiate with the wily pair, that it puts us very much in mind of a fox chase," joked the *Clipper*.[37] Tony Denier was playing the authorized touring version of *Humpty* in San Francisco by this time, but pirate companies calling themselves "Fox's Humpty Dumpty" were warned to desist by Fox himself.[38] He personally appeared in the gruelling and extensive tour from early October 1872 to early February 1873, in an itinerary that took in Brooklyn, Syracuse, Buffalo, Columbus, Dayton, Springfield, Toledo, Detroit, Milwaukee, Chicago, St. Louis, Memphis, New Orleans, Selma, Montgomery, and Norfolk. The longest stop-over was two weeks in New Orleans. Most of the stays were for one, two, three, or at the most four performances. It is difficult to conceive of the energy and stamina needed for such a trek, particularly in a pantomime that travelled with heavy scenery and spectacular effects and required special vitality in performance. Fortunately, it paid off; the few days in Albany alone garnered six thousand dollars.[39]

With Fox out of New York, the Lauri Family offered "Five Minutes with Humpty Dumpty" in *Round the Clock* at the Grand Opera House, a play in which Fox would later appear himself. The Christmas season must have seemed desolate without him, but the slack was taken up by *Humpty Dumpty in the Bowery* at Tony Pastor's, with Robert Butler as Clown, and *Ding Dong Bell, Pussy in the Well; or, Fairy Bo-Peep and*

Harlequin Now-a-Days at the Theatre Comique, starring George H. Adams, a newly imported English clown. But Fox had clearly spoiled the public for the English tradition; the imported clown's "habit of talking and anticipating the incidents of the pantomime we think detracts from the enjoyment of the spectators."[40] Fox was generous to his competitor, however, and after seeing him, declared, "Mr. Adams, you are the nearest to it," and presented him with the first costume he had worn as Humpty. Adams kept it as a treasured souvenir until his death in 1935.[41]

Once more the rumor surfaced, very circumstantially this time, that Fox had been engaged to act at Covent Garden, London, in *Jack the Giant Killer*,[42] but once more the offer failed to materialize. Instead, a fourth edition of *Humpty Dumpty* was announced to open for a limited engagement on 17 February 1873. And so it did, with the Fox brothers and C. Winter Ravel, who had played Harlequin during their tours. The Martens, Adonis and Venus, the skaters Kynock and Smith, and the gymnastic Wilson brothers returned to pad out the bill, this time assisted by ten Bedouins. The critics, who had run out of things to say, granted that Fox's performances "have now reached so high a degree of perfection that the art by which he produces his effects is entirely concealed,"[43] a formula which covered the reviewer's inability to analyze. The usual alterations were carried on throughout the run, with a fifth and full-scale reconstruction in April, to introduce William and Harry Jee, champion hat-spinners of the world and players on the musical rocks; the prodigy violinist Americus; a Russian quartet; and the celebrated danseuse Mlle Morlacchi in the Bee Dance. Traces of the Bowery were hard to find in Mme Charlotte V. Winterburn who sang contralto ballads, but the German billiard saloon and Washington crossing the Delaware resurfaced from the very first edition.[44] By means of this chopping and changing, and despite only fair attendance, *Humpty Dumpty* managed to rack up another hundred or so performances before it closed on 7 June.

Just before the run ended, on 7 May, James E. Hayes died. Hayes, the lessee and manager of the Olympic, had in the old days been scene painter and partner in Fox's earliest pantomimes there. His passing meant that Fox no longer had a friend at the court of proprietor James Duff, no one to look after his interests when he himself was not in charge. He might have begun to feel merely a cog in the machine, a cipher in the roster of variety acts that now constituted an American pantomime. He had reached the crest of his success; the rest would be downhill.

15

Augustin Daly at the Helm

(1873-74)

The machinations of the recently murdered Jim Fisk and his associates Gould and Drew, along with the tactics of smaller fry in the pool of peculators, had brought the national economy to its knees. Much United States capital was tied up in railroad building, which in turn prompted overinvestment in the iron industry and overproduction in the wheat-growing areas throughout which the new rails ran. A drop in grain prices, combined with massive indebtedness to European financiers, the stasis of invested capital, and the stock jobbings of shrewd crooks like Fisk, Gould, and Co. combined to precipitate a crash. On 18 September 1873, the banking house of Jay Cooke of Philadelphia failed and declared itself bankrupt. This collapse of a pillar of the financial community initiated the Panic of 1873, which caused the loss of over two billion dollars. For the next five years, the United States would be at the lowest economic ebb in its history.[1]

Eighteen seventy-three had not begun as a good year for Augustin Daly either. On New Year's Day, while Fox was being serenaded at his Brooklyn home by the Olympic's orchestra, Daly's little Fifth Avenue Theatre was burning down, and his stock company had to be sent on the road until a new venue could be fitted up at Broadway and Twenty-eighth Street in the former St. James Theatre.[2] With the death of James Hayes, neither Daly nor his father-in-law Duff wanted anything more to do with the Olympic; it was a losing proposition trying to lure the public to an increasingly unfashionable neighborhood while striving to pay off the builder's debts. Instead, they acquired the late Fisk's Grand Opera House, a great handsome barn on the corner of the Eighth Avenue and Twenty-Third Street, to present a season of popular plays at low prices.

Fox, still under contract to Duff, was farmed out to Daly at a straight salary that, according to varying reports, was either $400 or $750 a week.[3] The offer was not munificent, considering Fox's drawing power, and he was allowed no part in the management of the theatre. But he accepted. It was believed that at this time the clown was worth $80,000, and he could afford to be compliant. Shortly, he would have nothing.[4]

The previous spring an announcement had suggested that Fox was intending to renounce pantomime and act in eccentric and low comedy at the Grand Opera House; in other words, give up what he did best and go for a more legitimate status.[5] The forecast was borne out by the Opera House's first offering, a sumptuous revival of *A Midsummer Night's Dream* in a four-act version more elaborate than that of 1867. Once more Fox played Bottom and was so warmly greeted on his entrance that, denuded of Humpty Dumpty's white makeup, his face was seen to mantle with a blush. For the most part, the reviews were generous in praising his "rare artistic skill" and "keen appreciation of the humor." Despite his wildly absurd countenance and attire, he preserved his imperturbable gravity throughout, and in the Pyramus and Thisbe interlude died so successfully that his death was encored some three or four times. This gave him the opportunity to burlesque the antehumous convulsions of several well-known tragedians. It was highly entertaining, but, as the *Times* commented, "Mr. Fox is not a great comedian, for we are not aware that he has ever elaborated a character." Apparently, when contrasted with the nuanced portrayals of Joseph Jefferson as Rip or William Burton as Toodles, Fox was simply funny, not illuminating. He lacked "a rich, round mellow humor, exuberant and copious," said the *Tribune*. It might be good enough for the children who enjoyed pantomime, but not for adults who savored the fruitiness of Shakespearean comedy.[6]

Fox's insignificance to the company at the Opera House became clearer as the repertory unfolded. Economic conditions caused the *Dream* to evaporate after a mere twenty-one performances. It was followed by *The Wandering Jew*, a convoluted melodrama forged from Eugène Sue's *roman-feuilleton* by Leopold Lewis, author of *The Bells*. Daly, a foe of the star system, secreted Fox in the tiny role of Goliath the strongman and muffled his expressive face in an "Assyrian beard." The clown had virtually nothing to do, although he somehow managed to sneak in a few laughs, "a grateful and not unneeded flavor of humor."[7]

Daly had hoped for a four week's run at least, but the half-filled house on opening night forecast poor business, and the *Jew* came to a halt after fourteen performances. As if in desperation, the manager announced a "thrilling, romantic and sensationally spectacular"[8] realistic drama called *Haunted Houses or London and the Bush* by H. J. Byron. Fox was cast in the uncharacteristic role of Moss Morris, a Jewish old clothes dealer and fence, but made a surprisingly strong impression. His makeup and cockney dialect were cited as wonderfully authentic: "he infused the character with pungent humor, which became infectious to the audience, and he apparently enjoyed the fun he created quite as much as his auditors."[9] Despite Fox's efforts, the play failed to draw and Daly was compelled to close it after eleven nights. The Maretzek Opera Company came in as a stopgap until he could regroup his forces.

The company was sent touring to Providence and Albany until Daly could reopen the Grand Opera House with a revival of *Under the Gaslight* on 21 October. Ticket prices had been halved, and Fox was playing Bermudas, a ballad-monger who aspires to be a prize fighter (and who appears in but one scene), but neither inducement could keep the play running more than five nights, in the wake of the Panic.[10] Aware at last that traditional melodrama had no appeal and that something novel was indispensable, Daly filled the breach with a hodgepodge of music and drama called *Round the Clock*, probably an elaborated version of the entertainment the Lauri Family had appeared in the previous Christmas.

Using a time-honored device that goes back at least as far as Pierce Egan's *Life in London*, Daly presented scenes of New York life at various hours of the day. One of the cleverer gimmicks was to double-cast Fox as Gadigott a lawyer and as himself. Thus, Fox as lawyer, slumming at Harry Hill's dive at Houston and Crosby Streets, is so well disguised in an old brown coat and dilapidated hat of uncertain color that, as he remarks, "his own mother wouldn't know him." Gadigott and his party leave the Bowery and head north via Crosby Street, where they reach the stage door of the Olympic. "What's going on inside?" they ask the doorman. "Humpty Dumpty" is the reply. Fox gets permission to take his party in, and, as they enter, the scene shifts to the stage of the Olympic, with stagehands changing the scenery. When the stage manager is assured that everything is set, he gives the signal, up goes the curtain to reveal another audience watching the pantomime. Fox enters as Clown and renders choice bits from his classic performance. It was a wonderful trick of proto-Pirandellian stage magic, and, as one critic remarked half-sarcastically, "it would be difficult for anyone to act himself more naturally."[11] Cleverness, however, was not enough to combat the Panic, and the *Clock* stopped two weeks later.

The interpolation of Humpty Dumpty may have been a desperate measure, but it inspired Daly to invigorate his flagging receipts with pantomime. While preparing the panto, he threw in a revival of his "thrilling and sensational local drama of New York life and steamboat perils." *A Flash of Lightning* was limited to a two-week run during rehearsals of a more prodigious effort. Fox played Sam Pidge, a clerk on the steamboat "Daniel Doo," and made a comical impression, especially with improvised wise-cracks, but he too was husbanding his powers for the big push.[12]

Humpty Dumpty Abroad was not ready to open on the announced date of 24 November, and it had to be postponed till the following night. Although Fox was credited with authorship on the program, Daly had adapted it from a French *féérie*, so that the structure clove more closely to traditional pantomime format than had the three-act *Humpty* at the Olympic the previous year.[13] The *Herald* was delighted by the return to tradition.

It is as nearly a play as it is possible to make a trick and show piece. The special attractions are included in the action of the piece and not, as has been customary with theatres which included variety business in their performances, in an act by themselves. We have frequently complained of the system of stopping the play for acrobats, ventriloquists, jugglers and the like, and we were pleased to see that wherever they are used in this piece they help rather than retard the action.[14]

Nevertheless, Fox was still overshadowed by guest turns, in the *Clipper*'s words, "too much obscured by the variety performances and other surroundings. The people rush to the Opera-house with the belief that they are about to see Fox at his best, and to be thoroughly amused during the evening by his artistic performance; but they find that during the first two acts, as a clown, he is but seldom seen, and in the final act the pantomimic portion is too brief."[15]

As a fairy story, the plot offered little opportunity for American interpolations, and significantly, on the playbill one scene in the harlequinade was listed as "Street in Aniplace." Docilion, the son of the magician Oldstile, presents Humpty Dumpty with a watch, which, if wound every day, will exercise magic powers. The Fairy Badtempter tries to make Humpty forget to wind it, while Docilion works to protect him; such is the kernel of the plot. On receiving the watch, Humpty changed from peasant garb to a suit of white satin, not unlike that worn

Figure 28. The (G. L.) Fox chase. A lithograph by Thomas, c. 1869, showing Fox, heralded by his brother Charlie as Pantaloon, outstripping all other entertainments in New York. These include Booth as Hamlet, a rival Clown and Pantaloon, burnt-cork minstrels, the soprano Adelaide Phillips, the equestrian James Robinson, British blondes, Irish comics, Brother Jonathan and John Bull, mystery dramas, the Hanlon acrobats, Lord Dundreary, Mme Azella the Parisian trapezist, Harry Gurr the "man-fish," various pantomimic characters, the eccentric Clodoche dancers, Bourgoin and Gabel as the Two Gendarmes in *Geneviève de Brabant*, and miscellaneous ballet dancers, velocipedists, stilt-walkers, and even a terminal Humpty Dumpty. (Courtesy Harvard Theatre Collection)

by Yankee characters in extravaganzas, and married a princess. This summoned up the Palace of Instruments in the Isle of Harmony, with a ballet featuring the Rigl sisters, chorus girls dressed as mandolins (Daly's *corps* was by no means first-rate), and an acrobatic exhibition by Karl Lind. During all this, Fox was seated quietly upstage as a mere spectator.

Then the transformations took place, and act 1 ended with a tableau of the hours. In act 2 Humpty and Pantaloon arrived in China via balloon; they fell into the river and were pulled out, Humpty on the back of a fish, Pantaloon inside a leviathan. But comedy speedily made way for another ballet, the Fête of Pekin, after which Fox had scant time for more tricks before variety supervened. Pyramidal groupings of the Jackley troupe of acrobats, a panorama of the North Pole and Italy, another ballet, and the Tyrolean airs of the ever-popular Martens Family regaled the audience. Humpty and Old One-Two got a chance to fight some brigands, before being transported to the Bay of New York for an yacht race; again all they did was watch.

The last act opened in a painter's studio in New York, where, to no one's surprise, the Martens revived their celebrated Cat Duet. Some topicality was provided by an elevated train that ran off its track and turned into a house as it fell; but Fox was effaced by more acrobatics. Three scenes of pantomime in which Fox appeared to best advantage followed and partially dispelled the audience's disappointment, for the tricks worked well. The final transformation took place in what the program called the Realm of the Hours, but astute observers noted that it had already been seen as the Realm of the Seasons.[16]

"Never since the war has theatrical business in this city evoked so little interest or proved so unprofitable as this season," the *Herald* reported around Christmas time.[17] But *Humpty Dumpty Abroad* had begun by playing to standing room only and business continued strong through the holidays, attesting more to Fox's enduring popularity than to the basic merits of the show. When the master machinist left in mid-December to work at the new Fifth-Avenue Theater, the tricks began to go awry, and inclement weather spoiled business on a few nights. Still, Daly claimed that before 4 January 1874, two hundred thousand "delighted people" had seen it.[18] If true, it would mean that 4,545 persons had attended each of the forty-four performances, although the house held only 1,883.

The customary alterations were made for the New Year, with C. Winter Ravel replacing Lind as Harlequin, and the Jackleys ousted by the familiar Wilson Brothers. A "California Quartette" and King Sabro, the Japanese gymnast who ascended a rope from stage to gallery, were added. Indeed, fresh acts were brought in almost daily, but with Lent staring it in the face, the management closed *Humpty Dumpty Abroad* after a comparatively brief run of seventy-nine performances. Despite the publicity, Fox believed that Daly had simply broken even on his venture into pantomime.[19]

What followed was dismally lackluster and showed how far Daly had been reduced to scraping the bottom of the theatrical barrel. Although he touted *A Round of Pleasure* as "a pleasant and untainted TEN MINUTES WITH EVERY KNOWN AMUSEMENT[, a] constant succes-

Figure 29. Humpty Dumpty in all his glory. The ground color of the costume was white, and the fox's head in the medallion embroidered on the front acted as a trademark. Photograph by J. Gurney and Son, New York. (Courtesy Theatre Arts Library, the Harry Ransom Humanities Research Center, the University of Texas at Austin)

sion of novelties and specialties,"[20] it was a sorry patchwork of tried-and-true sketches and olios. Fox had been enjoined to stitch this crazy quilt together, and so he scoured the files of the Bowery Theatre, coming up with *The Spitfire*, renamed for the occasion *Jack Harkaway at Sea* (*Jack Harkaway* melos were very popular in variety theatres); *The School in an Uproar*, renamed *Humpty Dumpty at School*; and *The Lottery Ticket*, renamed *2450*. His performances, honed by years of repetition, were much appreciated. His Tobias Shortcut "clearly established his claim as being a first-class comedian ... [it] fairly brimmed with unctuous humor and kept his auditors in the best of spirits." The school sketch was excellently cast, with C. K. Fox as the schoolmaster, Winter Ravel as the dancing master, and Emily Rigl as the maid-of-all-work. "It is a long time since we have seen so much cause for merriment condensed into such a brief space of time."[21] For once, sheer fun in the old rambunctious style eclipsed "production values" and variety acts.

Daly's entrepreneurship also gave Fox one last chance at Shakespearean burlesque. The manager organized a charity benefit at the Grand Opera House and concluded the entertainment with the fifth act of *Richard III*, to star Fox as Gloster and the English pantomimist Frederick Vokes as Richmond. The very announcement drew a huge audience, which waited patiently throughout a host of acts for their favorite to appear. *Richard III* was played, not in burlesque couplets, but as Shakespeare (and Colley Cibber) had written it. But whenever Fox attempted to speak, his steel visor would crash down until finally, in vexation, he reversed his helmet and wore it back to front, revealing himself made up as Booth in the part. At every step he took, his greaves shook loose and kicked knee high. In the sword fight between the Yorkist champion and the Lancastrian, the athletic Vokes sprang about with leaps and acrobatic tricks, while Fox moved in his Humpty Dumpty shuffle. It was a one-time-only masterpiece of comedy, and, as a lucky spectator gloated, "until we have another Fox and another Vokes we cannot expect to see again such exquisite fooling."[22]

The Grand Opera House was to see no such fooling in any event. Daly realized that, under prevailing conditions, he could not manage a number of theatres adequately; it was not enough to be what he called a "janitor manager," unlocking the doors for independent companies and closing them again when they departed. He decided to shut down the Broadway Theatre (at 728 Broadway and Waverly Place) and negotiated with an agent of the owner, the department store magnate A. T. Stewart, to relinquish the remaining year of the eighteen thousand dollar lease. Stewart's agent agreed with alacrity to take back the playhouse with its improvements and to accept endorsed notes for the rent in arrears. Daly then proceeded to concentrate his attention on the Opera House, expecting to feature Fox in pantomime and spectacle that would show a profit. At this juncture, Fox quit.[23]

Although the usual rumors had circulated that Fox was unhappy under Daly's management,[24] the abruptness of his departure was inexplicable, until the news spread that the clown was shortly to form a new combination at the very Broadway Theatre that Daly had just abandoned. No wonder the negotiations with Stewart's agent had gone so smoothly. The newspapers were soon announcing that the Broadway would reopen on 6 April, under Fox's management, supported by his brother Charles Kemble Fox and with George H. Tyler as business manager.[25]

Fox's defection was the *coup de grâce* to the Grand Opera House. Daly, who had sunk $120,000 into it, including $15,000 as premium on the lease and the cost of improvements, was heartily sick of the place. The owners, the Erie Railway Company, which had inherited it from Fisk, allowed him to get out of the rest of his lease by giving up the scenery and properties and presenting endorsed notes for the rent due. And so it came to pass.[26] Fox's enterprise, on the other hand, did not meet so neat a conclusion, for the clown had come under the influence of the Machiavellian George H. Tyler.

Tyler had managed the Olympic in partnership with John Duff, Daly's father-in-law. During a dispute over some policy or other, Tyler began to incubate the plan of prying Fox loose from those two and managing the clown to his own advantage. The disaffected Tyler began to "consort together" with the saturnine clown, and convinced Fox that he had been slaving away for Duff all these years; he was now making a pitiful salary of four hundred dollars a week while Duff and Daly lived in the lap of luxury off the clown's peonage. Tyler also pointed out Daly's exploitation of "hamfatters," inexpensive, mediocre variety acts spliced into the pantomime to Fox's detriment. These seeds of disgruntlement fell upon the fertile soil of Fox's delusions of financial shrewdness. He was soon ready to break his contract, once another theatre had been secured. Aware that the only available vacant playhouse was the Broadway, where Daly was lessee, Tyler went clandestinely to Stewart to inquire about tenancy. His inquiries coincided with Daly's attempt to unload the white elephant. The two managers's schemes dovetailed and so, unbeknownst to Daly, Tyler took over the Broadway. Fox then cancelled the open-ended contract he had had with Duff.[27]

Fox himself was probably unaware of Tyler's stratagems, although his name was immediately incorporated into the masthead of the theatre. A shadowy figure named S. A. Swalm was announced as the Broadway's backer and proprietor.[28] The theatre's treasurer, who was to be a contributing factor in the disintegration of Fox's fortunes, was L. Sutton, and the conductor F. Strebinger was wooed away from the Olympic. The company that Fox enlisted for his first production was strong; old colleagues like Winter Ravel, his dresser George Topack, Ida Yearance who had starred in *Humpty Dumpty Abroad*, and brother Charlie were to appear. Even a Sophie Ravel was there to add the lustre of her family's name to the role of Mrs. Sowerby Creamly, a school-marm. Spending Fox's money lavishly, Tyler had the Broadway entirely cleaned and repainted, with a new drop-curtain, and the Parisian boxes at the rear of the parquet were removed to enlarge the lobby.[29] The hopeful proclamation of Fox's new enterprise read:

GEORGE L. FOX ANNOUNCES WITH PLEASURE
and perhaps pardonable pride, that he has secured for a term of years, the admirably located BROADWAY THEATRE, 728–730 Broadway, which will be christened
G. L. Fox's
BROADWAY THEATRE
and opened under his personal management, assisted by MR. GEO. H. TYLER, last Acting Manager of the Olympic Theatre, for the presentation of a series of entertainments in which himself and brother, CHAS. K. FOX, known to everybody as "Old One-Two-Three," will jointly endeavor to afford amusement, assisted by well known faces in the business and artistic circle of the profession. The
GRAND OPENING
will take place
EASTER MONDAY, April 6
And full particulars will be forthcoming as to the attractions to be presented by HUMPTY DUMPTY AT HOME in his own theatre.
GEORGE L. FOX

The public's obedient servant
HUMPTY DUMPTY   witnesses
OLD ONE TWO
New York, March 7 1874[30]

It was a brave beginning which was to have a disastrous conclusion.

16

Humpty Dumpty Has a Great Fall

(1874-75)

There was a superstition in the acting profession that theatres built in or out of the ruins of a church never succeed. The Broadway had been converted from the Unitarian Church of the Messiah in 1865 and retained the reputation of a "hoodoo" house. John Brougham, parodying Moore's melodies, sang, "You may paint, you may fresco the house as you will / But the scent of the church lingers about it still."[1] The redecoration that Fox and Tyler had invested in to remove the taint of failure had cost so much that it prompted a rumor that Fox had won twenty thousand dollars in the Kentucky lottery. Unfortunately, the costs all came out of the clown's own pocket and were lavished on property that would in time revert to the millionaire A. T. Stewart.[2]

Nor was any expense spared on advertising. Besides the daily newspaper blitz, the theatre's curbside billboards were illuminated with new lamps whose glass globes bore the name G. L. Fox and the picture of a fox. A life-size wooden effigy of Humpty Dumpty, which had once stood in the lobby of the Olympic, now guarded the entrance to the Broadway, and the clown's photograph was plastered all over the façade of the building. After all, Fox was the sole reason for Tyler's maneuver, the only justification for taking over the theatre. But those in the know were already predicting that Fox might end up "Schwalmed," and those he had left at the Grand Opera House were reputed to be singing,

> *Grand Opera House has lost its fox,*
> *But just knows where to find him—*
>   *Only let him alone to go and roam,*
>   *And pretty soon George will come home,*
> *With treasury tales behind him!*[3]

The 6 April opening night of the aptly named *Humpty Dumpty at Home* saw the house crammed to bursting; according to the publicity, hundreds had been turned away. This was a demonstration of personal loyalty to Fox, since his admirers knew that he shared in the profits and losses of the undertaking. Most New Yorkers had seen at least one *Humpty Dumpty* by now, and the attraction did not lie in the novelty of the production. Essentially, Fox returned to the original version produced at the Olympic in 1868, but, perhaps at the instigation of his associates, perhaps in accordance with his own taste, he interlarded it with the now customary vaudeville routines. The tripartite structure of pantomime-variety-pantomime was retained. What, one wonders, would the old-time Bowery boy have made of Georgie Dean Spaulding, who played "Fisher's Hornpipe" on a harp with one hand, and "Yankee Doodle" with the other, while singing "Tramp, Tramp" "in so artistic a manner that the ear could distinguish either [*sic*] of the airs"?[4] Acrobats, dog acts, bell-ringers, the alcoholic Professor O'Reardon with his Tumbleronicon of musical water-glasses, and the like abounded.[5]

Fox and brother Charlie received the customary ovation on their donkey-cart entrance, and reviewers refrained from describing their tricks, assuming that the reader was well apprised of Fox's comic genius by that time. A new prologue contained local allusions, and the most up-to-date of the gags concerned "Tom Collins," "a mysterious individual at the present time much inquired after in all circles of society in the metropolis."[6] The reference helps date the arrival of that mixed drink in the barroom repertory. "Humpty Dumpty at his own theatre" was the opening tableau. Another fresh routine was "HER-CULES, KING OF CLUBS," in which the clown gave his own version of living statuary, a send-up of the pretentious *tableaux vivants* that had concluded the entertainment at the Olympic. He and C. K. even resuscitated the old Bowery presentation of Macaire and Jacques Strop in *Les Deux fugitifs*. Why not? asked one journalist; after all, "the boys like Fox, and there are men whose theatrical boyhood expanded on the east side with Fox."[7] He was beginning to turn into a period piece, a repository of nostalgia.

Although the first week drew well, by May business had dropped off badly, an average house described merely as "fair," and on 13 May, the "last week but one," notice of closing was posted.[8] Then, abruptly, the advertising ceased, even before the pantomime closed three days later. The reasons for this strange proceeding leaked to the press over the next few weeks, revealing an ugly state of affairs back stage.[9]

As an employee of Daly, Fox had received four hundred dollars a week, which, at Tyler's urging, he found beggarly; but under his present contract, the clown was to receive only two hundred dollars a week until an apportionment at the year's end would bestow one third of the net profits on him. A week after *Humpty Dumpty at Home* opened, the proprietor and alleged backer Swalm came to Fox with a tale of pecuniary woe and a note for five thousand dollars to be repaid the following week. Fox, who had once signed himself "not such a fool as he looks," accepted the promissory note and handed over the cash. The following week saw no repayment of the debt nor, for that matter, any money to pay the first two weeks' salaries of the company. Swalm was observed "fancying" around town, squiring ladies of easy virtue. He showed up at the theatre only to collect the receipts, which mounted in time to eight or nine thousand unaccounted-for dollars. Fox, no longer able to ignore the swindle, pressed Swalm to redeem the note, and when the backer reneged, the clown refused to make further stage appearances.[10]

Swalm, angered that the goose had stopped laying golden eggs, as nominal proprietor of the Broadway secured an injunction against any further appearances by Fox in New York City.[11] Unable to afford an appeal and, in any case, stymied by the continuing bad theatrical business in the metropolis, Fox had no choice but to take the pantomime on the road. For aid in this enterprise, he foolishly relied on another untrustworthy partner, George Tyler. The travelling arrangements were that Tyler would manage the company for a hundred dollars a week and a small share of the profits. All the stage paraphernalia, properties, scenery, and costumes of the *Humpty Dumpty* troupe were to remain in Fox's ownership. But before they started out, Sutton, the Broadway's treasurer (some say Latham, treasurer of the Olympic) obtained a judgment against Fox for two hundred dollars. Tyler persuaded the clown to make over the show property to him to escape sheriff's execution on the pantomime equipment. Fox signed a paper to effect the transfer, or so Tyler always claimed (Mrs. Fox was later to deny vehemently than any such paper had been signed), but he never bothered to effect the retransfer. Fox was thus held in semi-slavery to pay off a two hundred dollar note.

So ended the only engagement Fox ever had that lost money. As for the Broadway Theatre, it passed through sixteen different managements in five years, with long intervals of darkness. Eventually, Harrigan and

Hart, whose ethnic Irish comedy had supplanted Fox's pantomimes as the most popular fare of the day, built their handsome "New Theatre Comique" on its site.[12]

Fox's tour was to be the most exhausting and wide-ranging of his career. Dropping the now inappropriate *At Home* from the title, he somehow managed to pay off the company and open *Humpty Dumpty* in Brooklyn before heading north through New England, westward from Canada through the Ohio Valley, and then south, zigzagging across the Mississippi Valley to New Orleans; the last leg moved slowly up the East Coast and back to New York. Most of their stops were one- or two-night stands, with slightly longer stays in the larger cities. All in all, Fox played more than four hundred performances in one hundred and fifty separate engagements in twenty-six states or territories over the course of fourteen months (30 May 1874 to 22 Aug 1875), with a week's respite before resuming on 6 September 1875.[13] The tour finally ended on 16 October.

Financially, the tour accomplished what it had set out to do. Fox's name was now a household word, and his clown-face and exploits appeared in children's books, toy theatres, trade cards, pamphlets advertising baking powder, and all sorts of mercantile detritus. There was even a Humpty Dumpty cigar with his cunning leer featured on the label. Moreover, *Humpty Dumpty* had already been seen in the provinces as played by Denier and other, less legitimate imitators, which stimulated an interest in the original. Although Fox's troupe was slightly seedy and not up to the standard of the best travelling panto companies, and the play was abridged to allow room for specialty acts, the clown's reputation was enough to create advance sellout and tremendous business in most cities. He was wise enough not to outstay his welcome in any one place.

But the toll such a schedule took on his stamina and vitality was tremendous. Ideally, a performer should spend the day resting before a strenuous evening of horseplay and knockabout. On tour, however, the time spent off-stage was passed in seeing that the scenery and properties were properly packed, shipped, and unpacked, in giving interviews and making public appearances, and in catching shuteye on noisy, grimy, overheated railway cars. New performers were constantly being worked in and new supernumeraries rehearsed, and alterations made when accidents occurred—as when Louise Boshell was lamed slightly in a fall from a tight-wire in Savannah in December.[14] The company, which included old friends like Annie Yeamans and her talented offspring Jennie, remained faithful. In Milwaukee in October, it presented Fox with a diamond pin in the form of a fox's head with a gold body, covered in diamonds, and a gold ring holding a solitaire diamond

POOR HUMPTY FEARED TO LOSE HIS PRIZE.
SO JUMPED ON TOP TO STOP THE RISE.
WHICH WAS A RECKLESS THING TO DO.
FOR UP WENT HUMPTY DUMPTY TOO.

Figure 30. Humpty Dumpty hoisted on a batch of self-rising dough; a page from an advertising booklet for Gantz's Sea-Foam Baking Powder, 1877, which traces the clown's adventures with their product. (Author's Collection)

in its mouth.[15] Reports of stars' jewelry and lavish gifts were standard press-agent canards, but in this case, the present seems to have been motivated by genuine affection.

In mid-January 1875, Fox had settled into Ford's Opera House in Washington City, where *Humpty Dumpty* was doing the best business of the season. On the night of 16 January, in the middle of act 1, he got a telegram calling him to New York. Charlie, who had left the company a few days earlier, was dying. Some two weeks before he had caught a severe cold in Richmond, but he had paid it no heed, throwing himself into his Pantaloonatic antics as before, while taking medicine for rheumatism, an old complaint. As the ailment worsened, he returned to his house in New York, at the corner of Eighty-third and Lexington, where he was diagnosed as having typhoid fever and ulceration of the bowels. He became unable to take food, and the once vigorous and sinewy comic wasted away to a shadow.

Laff hastily removed his makeup, handed over his costume to his understudy Thomas Chapman, and took the nine o'clock train to Manhattan. There he met his mother and brother James, now a Cambridge alderman, who had travelled down from Boston. Charlie stayed unconscious for six hours and then, at nine o'clock Sunday morning, 17 January, he passed away, leaving his third wife, the former Mrs. Dulaney, and her three children to mourn him. The funeral was to take place the following Saturday; in the meantime Laff had to hurry back to rejoin his company, now heading for Baltimore. There was no time to grieve for the inimitable Old One-Two, partner of his youthful treks with the Little Foxes and companion of his pantomimic escapades. He did manage to attend the funeral, with his wife and daughter and a four-foot-high white floral decoration, its violets spelling out "From the Humpty Dumpty Co." Charlie's remains were interred in the family plot in Mt. Auburn Cemetery, Cambridge.[16] For G. L. Fox, this sudden death was a terrible shock from which he never recovered.

In addition to this domestic bereavement and the ordinary exertions of the tour, Fox had the financial burden on his mind. Box-office receipts did not always cover expenses. When the show was about to open at the Brooklyn Academy of Music on 1 March, the conniving Swalm had a restraining order served on Fox, on the grounds that he was breaking his contract.[17] Mattie Fox, who had joined the company against her husband's will in order to save the cost of another actress, had to pawn her jewelry for four hundred dollars to pay back-salaries before the troupe would agree to resume the tour.

As for Manager Tyler, he too was presented with gems, an elegant cluster pin of nine large diamonds set in gold and enamel, while the company travelled between Taunton and Brockton, Massachusetts, at the end of that month. That this gift was a publicity stunt is suggested by the fact that Tyler was not forthcoming with Fox's salary, nor was Mrs. Fox even on the payroll until they reached Boston in July. There she refused to go on until paid a regular stipend of twenty-five dollars a week.[18] It was not a climate conducive to good work.

The first touring season ended in July 1875, and was purported to be a great success. Fox had managed to play for one year, one month, and two days without missing a performance, if one excludes that third act in Washington. With little more than a week's respite, *Humpty Dumpty in Every Clime*, as it was now retitled, opened for a month's run in his home town at the Boston Museum. Apparently some of the profits had been reinvested in the show, for all the tricks, mechanical effects, scenic illusions, and props were touted as brand new; the polar regions were transformed into Humpty's villa, the villa into a rugged rockbound coast, farm houses into ships, pigeon roosts into flags, robins into sea gulls, dairies into steamships, barrels into rocks, grass into water, frogs into flounders, bridges into light-houses, pumps into yawls, trees into farmers, and farm hands into sailors.[19] So great was the company's popularity in Boston that a Humpty Dumpty club of forty members was founded to indulge in fishing and baseball—one of the troupe's acrobats sprained an ankle at the latter pastime.[20]

As the tour progressed, rumors about Fox's ill health filtered back to New York. It was said that he had had a paralytic stroke in Canada that affected his facial muscles; such an ailment would have been as fatal to his Humpty as paralysis of the legs would be to a dancer.[21] Then word got round that he had suffered further injury in the Freedman Bureau Bill sketch. In that routine, an allusion to the Reconstruction legislation that gave twenty acres and a mule to emancipated slaves, Fox opened the drawers in a "Freedman Bureau" and a number of little black boys popped out. According to report, on one occasion, an extralarge and inexperienced youth emerged too quickly and slammed his head into Fox's nose, straining the optic nerve.[22]

These stories were officially denied in the press, for, somehow or other, Fox and Swalm had resolved their differences, and although the clown gave evidence of a deranged imagination, he was announced to appear as Humpty Dumpty for a limited run of nine weeks at Booth's Theatre, New York, under the management of Jarrett and Palmer. There is obscurity about these arrangements and no information as to who initiated this proposal, how the legal difficulties were settled, or why, other than financial considerations and the joy at being home, the exhausted clown agreed. His old comrade Booth had failed as a manager too, and now his theatre was to shelter another performer working out his debts because of poor business judgment.

Humpty Dumpty in Every Clime opened on schedule on 25 October, and the reviewers did their best to lend support to a tired show and a debilitated star. The performance lacked freshness, except for a new topical prologue set in Hades, "so different from the dreary trash which Oakey Hall was credited with writing."[23] With the Tweed Ring under attack, there was no percentage in praising the ex-mayor. The ingenious Matt Morgan painted one new scene, and the standard tripartite structure prevailed. Among the mediocre variety performers, acrobats, and roller-skaters, including Little Todd, "a surprising infant gymnast, who does things on a candlestick which are more surprising than pleasant,"[24] gentility's voice made itself heard. There was a dulcet tenor who in a musical sketch played an aria from *Il Trovatore* on an oboe. Back in the Bowery he would have been pelted with dead cats; at Booth's thespian palace he was warmly received.

Looking ahead to the United States's hundredth birthday, the show concluded with an elaborate set of tableaux, "The Centennial Celebration."

A painting covering the proscenium opening is first seen, which represents old Father Time seated upon a globe, surrounded with lurid clouds. Above his head appear the figures 1776 and thirteen white stars. As this picture is raised out of the view of the spectators, we see a capital picture of Independence Hall, Philadelphia; and after this is withdrawn, we are presented with a colossal representation of the bell which first pealed forth liberty to our country. On its base are the words "Proclaim liberty," and near these is seen a large crack in the bell. On either side is a group of American flags. This being removed, an excellent copy, colossal size, of a painting representing the signing of the Declaration of Independence is revealed; and that passing from view, shows an animated allegorical tableau occupying the entire stage. In the centre, at the rear of the stage, is a colossal American eagle, and above it in a semicircle are allegorical figures representing our industries—commerce and agriculture. Upon the stage-right, a tableau moves on the stage in which a number of people are seen seated in a houdah, upon the back of an elephant. This is followed by a tableau moving on from the stage-left showing American hunters in the act of capturing a huge bison. Then follows from the right a large marble statue with a sculptor at work upon it, while by his side is poised the living model. This is met from left by a number of small boys clad in Continental uniform, who group themselves effectively as the final curtain descends.[25]

And where was Fox amid all this colossality? Had he finally been submerged beneath the elephants, statuary, and juveniles he had previously manipulated to his own comic advantage?

Judging by the outline in the playbill, his duties were as strenuous as ever, slipping on banana peels, falling into the crevasse opened by an earthquake, knocking his head on a pump. Typical was one new routine involving a moving panorama. Old One-Two, now played by Robert Fraser who had joined the show on tour when C. K. Fox dropped out, sends Humpty to the post-office with a letter. Humpty turns about and marks time as if walking a marathon, while the scenery moves behind him; after a lengthy progress, he reaches his goal or, rather, the mail-slot arrives at him. But just as he is depositing the letter, Harlequin taps the floor with his bat and the post office disappears, to present the same house Humpty started from. This prolonged business was repeated twice more.[26]

The Fox was as funny as ever, but observers noted that he had lost a shade of his vivacity and power of expression, if not his skill. "When detected in his tricks, the look of injured innocence that he assumes, coupled with a sly wink at the audience, is certain to elicit the peals of merry laughter."[27] His opening-night weakness must have been obvious, for later reports assured readers that he had improved in vigor and spirits, with more of the "old-time *chic* and mirth-provoking powers."[28] Business slackened after the first week, except at matinees where children remained Fox's biggest fans.

But his enervation grew increasingly apparent, and he began to show alarming symptoms of erratic behavior. At first, it was thought that the bismuth in his clown-white was affecting his neural centers, bringing on a recurrence of his alleged paralysis, but it soon became obvious that cosmetics were the least of his problems. At the end of the first tableau in the panto, Humpty was to be hoisted in the air on the box of a cab. He could hardly keep his balance and on two occasions fell eight or nine inches, once into the arms of some attendants, and once hurting himself severely. Thereafter he had to be forced to take his place on the beam that elevated him and begged to be spared. Mattie, who was still playing a fairy at the time, tried to intervene, but this only sparked a quarrel with her deranged husband. Fox and Mattie parted on bad terms. She continued to live in the house in Brooklyn, while the clown took up lodgings in the St. Omer Hotel on Sixth Avenue.

At Mattie's request, George C. Howard had come to New York to persuade his brother-in-law to retire, and was appalled at the clown's state of ill health. Howard wrote back to his daughter Cordelia,

St. Omer Hotel
New York Thursday Nov. 11th 1875

My dear Delia
Your Uncle was rather excited last night & got into a rage, sent his wife home & is not going to allow her to play again. Mrs. Tyler plays her part.

November 12th

Your Uncle did strange things on the stage last night. Talked at random. The Doctor says he is much better & that the pressure is removed from his brain, but he is dreadful cross & blowing up George Topack who dresses him. I slept in this hotel with him & at supper he did strange things. Mixed everything together. He talks to me of the past & I can always recall him to himself by referring to it. Direct all letters at present to 'Booth's Theatre.'

. . . .

Tell grandma her eldest born is in a sad condition & yet I do not know whether her presence could alter it. Laf seems better when he is in the theatre. . . What the end will be I cannot tell. He has just gone out to be shaved & I am keeping his breakfast warm for him. Kiss Arthur & Walter for your loving

Father[29]

Mattie's enforced withdrawal owed something to the continuing animosity between her and manager Tyler. Fox was supposed to receive his two hundred dollars a week and share in the profits from Jarrett and Palmer; they gave Tyler five thousand dollars to pay Fox, but the manager turned over only five hundred to Howard to give his brother-in-law. When the demented clown got the money, he lost $150 in Brooklyn, spent $20 in a cigar store, paid $5 for a newspaper and gave away various other sums, in the belief that he was worth sixty million. Tyler, who was supposed to earn only fifty dollars a week and a share if the engagement was successful, was skimming money off the top, and only by dint of industrious application could Mattie Fox squeeze another three hundred dollars out of him.[30]

Delusions of wealth continued to plague Fox. He believed that he owned innumerable diamonds, which he promised to everyone he met. One day he ran into the agent Harry Wall, whom he at first failed to recognize; when he did identify him, he began reminiscing and weeping profusely, offering Wall quantities of diamonds.[31] Bob Fraser the Pantaloon met Fox outside his hotel in the rain in full evening dress. They went to a store where Fox bought about "twenty dollars worth of tooth brushes and tooth powder, although he only had three teeth in his mouth."[32] Jarrett and Palmer were quick to deny the canard that he had broken down on stage and been removed to a hospital, but Fox's increasingly vacant and mechanical performances were symptoms of an irrepressible problem. To those in the know, there was something ghastly about it all, and they blamed the management for making him perform, although the theatre's business manager Tooker announced to all and sundry that Fox would soon be retired.[33]

Behind the scenes, however, Jarrett and Palmer were treating with

Josh Hart, in case Fox did become incapable, for the loan of the clown James Maffitt at a hundred dollars a night. On 13 November Fox insisted on going on in his regimental Civil War uniform. With some difficulty he was coaxed into his clown dress. The next night he secured a piece of chalk and for some time marked several pieces of scenery with "4–11–44" in endless repetition; at first the audience took it to be a gag, but after fifteen minutes he had to be dragged from the stage like a child.[34]

Jarrett and Palmer, who had pleaded with Tyler to allow them to withdraw the deranged comedian, were threatened with suit for breach of contract. They compromised by arranging to have Fox and Thomas Chapman play Clown and Pantaloon in act 1, and Maffitt and Fraser take over in act 3 until 27 December when the run was to end.[35] Since Maffitt was a grotesque clown with a style entirely unlike Fox's, new business had to be introduced to display his specialties, with successful results.[36] Fox was permitted to watch his substitute from a private box and, one observer recollected, "it was a pitiable sight to see the tears roll down the chalk covered cheek of the deposed monarch."[37]

Pity was also felt by the young James T. Powers, later to be the leading comedian of another generation. Powers, who had already seen *Humpty Dumpty* twice at the Olympic, was taken by his uncle to Booth's. Man and boy took refuge in the lobby from a pelting snowstorm, and

as my uncle approached the box office we saw a gentleman pointing to three men who were coming through a doorway in the rear, and we heard him say in an agitated manner, "See there's Fox." What a thrill it gave me! I was looking at the great Fox off the stage and exclaimed, "Uncle it is Fox. I know his face without the powder." My uncle grabbed me by the arm and said, "Hush! Jimmie." Fox was very pale; he was looking toward the ceiling, and with shaking head was mumbling to himself.[38]

Despite the compromise casting, Fox's stage deportment became more and more erratic and unmanageable, and, according to the *Times*, "bordered on indecency."[39] One night he fell down on the stage from weakness and had to be helped up. He accused Harlequin of throwing him down, struck and insulted him, and then, a few moments later, begged his pardon and wept. He would freeze in a posture for moments at a time until led off the stage, and understood nothing of what was said to him as he sat waiting in the wings for his entrance, mumbling to himself. At other times, he would fall to his knees and pray.

On one occasion he refused to leave his dressing room, and Fraser had to go on for him because Maffitt had not yet arrived. When Fox caught sight of the other actor in his costume, he attacked him with a

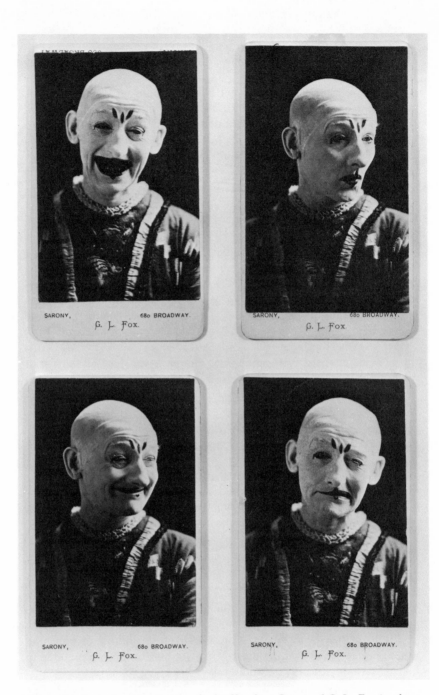

Figure 31. Carte-de-visite photographs by Napoleon Sarony of G. L. Fox in clown makeup, c. 1875. Note how closely the grimaces in the lower set resemble similar faces made by Stan Laurel. (Courtesy Harvard Theatre Collection)

hatchet. The ensuing "slight injuries" prevented Fraser from playing two performances.[40] Fox became convinced that it was his duty to address the audience, so, whenever he opened his mouth to speak off the cuff, his dresser George Topack, garbed as a monkey, would bound on stage and thump him soundly. This worked at first, but as the clown grew used to it, he accepted it as part of the routine. When the monkey hit him, he would pursue it with a howl of rage, while the audience roared with laughter. To what base uses had the Ravels's Jocko come![41]

The managers were continually attacked by the newspapers for letting the clown go on and for denying that anything was wrong. Interested private parties brought in doctors to examine Fox. One medical man opined, "I am afraid Mr. Fox is hopelessly insane. It is undoubtedly the result of softening of the brain, and the disease is becoming worse every day." He suggested that the clown retire and be put to bed, even though no chance of mental recovery was possible. Another, more sanguine physician explained that softening of the brain produced a thick yellow mucus from the mouth, and that Fox's mucus was still white. Yet another doctor expressed the sinister opinion that the clown was being drugged.[42] The medical consensus was that he should be put in a madhouse, and Mrs. Fox consented. Tyler had to tell the relieved Jarrett and Palmer that, after Saturday next, Fox would end his engagement.[43]

They announced a farewell benefit for Fox on 27 November. The program for that week read:

Mr. Fox makes his first personal appeal on Friday Evening of this week, and it may well be anticipated that the response will be an enthusiastic one. The illness this greatest of clowns is suffering under has aroused the sympathies of the entire community, and the knowledge that he is compelled to withdraw from the stage is received with feelings of sincere regret.[44]

During this period, Fox had lucid moments, but whenever anything troublesome was mentioned, especially money, he would relapse into his lethargy and mope. On Thanksgiving Day, after the matinee performance, he went to his hotel and stepped out on a balcony. A company of boys playing soldiers passed by and Fox called for them to halt, and then reviewed them. The boys cheered, a crowd collected, and as the clown grew more frenzied, he went into his hotel room, assembled a pile of boots, hats, brushes, and whatever he could find, and pelted the crowd with them. When a policeman arrived, Fox hit him between the eyes with a pair of boots before he was forced back into the room. The following night he was cheerful and rational, and after performing the first act with considerable élan, was called enthusiastically before the curtain. The clown bowed, flashed a characteristic grin, and, doubling up his arm, said "I wish some doctor would feel my muscle."

Then, slapping his leg, he added, "Not much paralysis here." It was a grisly exhibition.[45]

None of this prevented the theatre from advertising a "production full of merriment" for Fox's farewell benefit and stressing half-price admission for children. On the night of his enforced retirement, 27 November, he was in rather good spirits, but once more attempted to make a speech to the audience, and had to be pushed off by Topack the apeman. "He staggered about the stage, mumbled his lines, and then pelted the audience with stage properties, and fired a volley of bread at the occupants of a private box."[46] Evidently, he was confusing the boundaries of his legendary brick and loaf battles.

Before the first act had ended, George Howard huddled Fox's street clothes over his clown dress with Topack's help, and forced the comedian into a carriage waiting at the stage door. Fox entered it with great reluctance. His wife was not there to meet him, for her very presence increased his mania, and he seemed to blame her for the constraints he was under. It was thought that if he was made aware of his destination, he would be violent. Throughout the ride to the train station, he demanded to return to Booth's Theatre. But finally he was induced to get on board the nine o'clock train for Boston, where he was closeted in a compartment of one of the palace coaches. As he subsided, Fox asked very quietly where he was being taken to; his brother-in-law assured him that he was simply going on a pleasure trip.

On arrival in Boston next morning, Fox was met by a closed carriage, which he entered only under the strongest compulsion. G. C. Howard and James Fox had him driven to Dr. McLean's private asylum in Somerville. Only his closest relatives were allowed to see him, and, although Mattie Fox was expected to come to Boston to authorize his certification, the Fox-Howard clan was not entirely sure she counted as a close relative.[47]

Meanwhile, *Humpty Dumpty in Every Clime* ended at Booth's. Tyler had no intention of losing by his star's misfortune. He prepared to take the show on the road as "The Fox Pantomime Company," exploiting a name that was more newsworthy than ever.[48]

17

Too Cracked to Be Mended

(1875-77)

What precisely is the clinical diagnosis of Fox's insanity? Doctors of his time called it softening of the brain, a blanket term to describe progressive dementia accompanied by paresis. In the nineteenth century, paresis was a common manifestation of the later stages of syphilis, and Fox's delusions and erratic behavior sound very much like the symptoms of the primary stages of syphilitic insanity as described by the textbooks of the time. If this were indeed the root of Fox's madness, it is understandable that his family would put abroad other explanations, and the possibility cannot be ruled out, for Fox, in his younger days, did form some irregular liaisons. The number of American performers of the Victorian age who succumbed to syphilitic insanity is legion; it includes Tony Hart, John McCullough, William Scanlan, Charles Abbott, John Macy, John Gosson, and Samuel Long, the last four all clowns.[1] In the case of Scanlan, he behaved as outrageously on stage as Fox had. But most of these men were admitted in their lifetime to be sufferers from venereal disease and many were alcoholics as well. No hint of either malady was bruited about concerning Fox.

The common attribution of his illness, and one upheld by his family, was made to his clown makeup, although whether the lethal component was bismuth, white lead, or French chalk varied according to the imagination of the speculator. This hypothesis was set forth as late as the fourteenth edition of the *Encyclopædia Britannica* (1929) by Otis

Skinner in his article on makeup. Certain chemically-based cosmetics do have a deleterious effect by closing off the pores or introducing harmful substances subcutaneously; a lifetime of their use may take its toll, but insanity is not the likeliest effect. Fox's colleague Robert Fraser strongly denied the imputation, pointing out that he had worn the same white-face for years without any untoward side effects. Fraser placed the blame for Fox's breakdown on mental overexertion in having to create new gags.[2]

The other extreme explanation was offered by those who thought the Freedman Bureau Bill sketch was the direct cause. Similar accidents may have occurred with some frequency, but by themselves they could not have accounted for the long-term manifestation of Fox's mental aberration.

Fraser's suggestion of overexertion was endorsed in the New York *Clipper*'s obituary of Fox, probably written by the well-informed theatrical agent T. Allston Brown.

It is quite as likely that his brain—lacking adequate nourishment by reason of a physique that despite a frame of more than average size, was manifestly feeble as early as 1855—was weakened by overtaxation at the Chatham Theatre many years ago, and that his non-success in business, together with the death of his brother Charles in January of 1875, preyed upon his mind and developed softening of the brain, just as financial losses, and the fear of dying poor, worried Ben de Bar into mental disease.[3]

However farfetched the *Clipper*'s medical lore, its enumeration of the pressures on Fox is persuasive. It was noticed early that he did not have the physique for a pantomimic clown. The Ravels and their disciples had been trained as acrobats and dancers from childhood, and they tended to live to a hearty old age. Fox came to the trade late in life and with the instincts of a comic actor rather than a mime. His face, not his body, was his instrument of expression. Without the regular calisthenic regimen his exertions required, he could not maintain his fortitude into middle age.

Moreover, the Panic of 1873 had provoked a national psychosis of economic insecurity. Fox, who had never known the meaning of money and spent his high earnings on theatrical improvements as fast as he made them, hedged his increasing penury with delusions of wealth. He could pay five dollars for a newspaper and bestow imaginary diamonds on his friends in memory of the jewels his company had given him in good times and the cash gifts he had doled out to all and sundry when he was flush. Always of a withdrawn and private nature, he was easy prey to paranoia. In the quarrels between his wife and his manager, his manager and his treasurer, his family and his wife, he fluctuated between violence and delusionary aloofness.

Shortly after Fox had been settled in the asylum, a Boston jury *de lunatico inquirendo* was called to determine officially the state of Fox's mental health. The prompter of Booth's Theatre testified that the clown had torn his clothes and interrupted the play to address the audience; Mattie Fox attested that he was "addicted to purchasing articles he didn't need and couldn't pay for"; and Dr. William Hammond, a specialist in diseases of the nervous system and former surgeon general during the Civil War, gave his weighty opinion that Fox was indeed mad. So the jury decided, with Mattie Fox declared her husband's legal executor.

Assuming that she had a half interest in the George L. Fox Pantomime Company, now starring James Maffitt and managed by Tyler, she set off for St. Louis. Before the pantomime company had left New York, a number of creditors, including a Mr. Foos, had presented their bills to Tyler, who told them to see Mrs. Fox in Brooklyn and she would deal with the matter. But Mattie Fox was having trouble scraping together the twenty-five dollars a week needed to keep her husband in the asylum. Together she and Foos went west to beard Tyler.

When they cornered the manager in front of De Bar's Theatre, he pretended to ignore Foos. "I have no business with you, sir, I don't know you." At that, Mattie stepped forward: "Perhaps you don't *know me,* Mr. Tyler?"[4] In a subsequent meeting at a lawyer's office, Tyler produced the paper allegedly signed by Fox in 1874, deeding his manager all interest in the company and sole ownership of properties, wardrobe, and scenery. Mrs. Fox protested that the paper was a forgery and that her husband would never have signed such an instrument. Tyler refused to make a settlement, although he did offer her twenty-five dollars a week in charity. This she angrily refused. Apparently all was not kosher with Tyler's title, for he was sufficiently alarmed by threat of legal action to change the name of the company to the "Tyler & Maffitt Combination."

On her way back to New York, Mattie visited her husband in the asylum, accompanied by his mother and brother. According to her, he was delighted to see her and blamed Tyler for his incarceration. She professed her intention of bringing him her jewelry, now out of pawn, and when she returned to Manhattan, she advertised her plight in the New York *Dramatic News,* whose editor C. A. Byrne became her stalwart champion. She persuaded Latham, the treasurer of the Olympic Theatre, to testify that he had seen Tyler on several occasions urge the clown to sign a document when he was clearly out of his mind.[5]

There is no doubt that Mrs. Fox's financial distress was grave. She was borrowing money from her sister whom she boarded in her Brooklyn home, and the Fox-Howard clan made no contributions to her upkeep. Her sense of mistreatment led her to offend her husband's family with embarrassing publicity. When the article about Tyler's fraud appeared, he wrote an indignant letter from Cincinnati asserting that his conduct to Fox had always been just and fair, and he named G. C. Howard to vouch for his character. This was a daring move if the family had no mind to guarantee his probity. Mrs. Fox nevertheless broadcast her indigence unabashedly:

Brooklyn, January 28, 1876

TO THE EDITOR OF THE DRAMATIC NEWS

SIR:—I trust you will pardon this intrusion, but necessity compels me to take this step, for I am in a very desolate condition.

I would be grateful to you, dear Sir, if you would assist me in getting something to do. I don't care what it will be. I will even do utility. I have no means, whatever, left, for I have tried to let my house and I have not had one to call and see it.

. . . .

Mrs. Geo. L. Fox

177 Carleton Ave., Brooklyn[6]

At her urging and that of Editor Byrne, A. M. Palmer and Josh Hart planned a matinee and evening benefit for Fox at the Brooklyn Academy of Music, for Mattie claimed that without it her husband would have to be transferred to a pauper institution. But this scheme was quashed by Howard and Alderman James Fox, who protested that they were fully capable of paying for their brother's needs.[7]

Fox's absence from the stage did not reduce the attraction of pantomime. When *The Demon Statue* opened at the Eagle Theatre in early January 1876, it won high praise for its polished prologue. "We have," sneered a reviewer, "been in pantomime too much accustomed to the style inaugurated by Fox, to whom an opening was merely a thing of necessity, not a thing of taste."[8] George Adams, the loquacious English clown, was touted as a worthy successor to Fox's mantle. The waning of red-blooded American pantomime and its extended harlequinade had accelerated. In a revival of *Humpty Dumpty* in April, a scene set in front of the Olympic Theatre presented two billboards, one with a likeness of Fox as Clown over the figure 1868, and the other with a portrait of Robert Fraser in the role over the figure 1876. Fraser was another clown in the "French" model, with a quiet, easy manner, a mobile face, and agile movements.[9] He and George Adams bore away the honors in the Clown *emploi* in the next decades.

On the road, Tyler had disastrous luck and closed his road company *Humpty Dumpty* in June. He prudently settled in his home town of Boston.[10] Before he leaves this scene, we must report Tyler's end, for it smacks of poetic justice. For almost a decade, he throve as manager, becoming a successful partner of Henry Abbey and amassing a tidy fortune. On 17 August 1884, the day before he was to participate in a boat race, he attended a club ball at Hull, Massachusetts, where his yacht was docked. While descending a flight of steps leading from the wharf to the water, he was killed instantly by a blow to the back of his skull, and then tossed in the ocean. His assailant was never identified or caught, and no motive was assigned to the murder. But if his behavior to Fox was typical of his business dealings, Tyler must have had plenty of enemies in the profession.[11]

The dramatic gossip columnists made assertions about Fox and refuted them as regular items of interest. He was alleged to be secured in a straitjacket in a padded cell. He was said to be shipped off to Florida, and his relatives were upbraided for not leaving him where he was. When that rumor was quashed, another claimed that he was about to be a guest of John Duff at Long Branch. Mrs. Fox relayed that, according to the family physician Dr. Jelly, the clown was much improved; the opinion of Dr. Brown-Séquard, however, was that he was incurable and gradually expiring. It was significant that two such eminent medicos were concerned with the case. George Frederick Jelly was the youthful superintendent of McLean's Hospital, whose opinions were known to be honest and fearless; Charles Edward Brown-Séquard was an expert on the nervous system, more at home in the laboratory than the consulting room. The former's opinion was therefore more reliable, and readers were relieved to hear that at Long Branch Fox was glad to be in the open air and never wandered far from Duff's house. A week later came the denial that he had ever been in Long Branch. Much of this trivia was fed to the papers by Mattie, hoping to bolster her claims with public sympathy. She circulated stories of the cruelty that had kept her husband on Booth's stage, and insisted that his insane addresses to the audience were attempts to reveal his maltreatment, that he had been moved to an hotel to prevent her from seeing him, which she was permitted to do only on promise of good behavior.[12]

Sensationalism aside, Fox's recovery in the asylum is hard to chart. The present administration of McLean's Hospital adamantly refuses to open its files, even when they are a hundred years old. From its founding in 1821, the asylum had eschewed mechanical constraints and relied on well-screened attendants. It had the reputation of being the most exclusive, as well as most gentle and curative, American hospital for the mentally ill. During Fox's time there, Dr. Jelly had instituted the innovation of female nurses in the men's wards. Still, whatever improvement the clown made can be attributed more to rest than to the bromide of potassium and phosphorus he was supposedly dosed with, which brought on violent reactions.[13] He became pale and thin, grew a beard, and could barely walk and talk. Later he was to complain, "I didn't improve at all in the asylum. I was in a room up five flights of stairs and as it was impossible for me to climb them I stayed in my room most of the time. The food was not what I ought to have had, and I was not comfortable."[14] The loss of strength in his limbs, garbled speech, and infrequent intervals of lucidity notwithstanding, John Duff secured his release from the asylum, presumably at Mattie's insistence, and placed him in the care of New York physicians, presumably Dr. Brown-Séquard among them. By September 1876 Fox was living at home in Brooklyn in a state described as "quiet idiocy."[15]

The description is apt only in part. He was indeed a physical wreck; although he had not gone gray, his left eyelid drooped, the moustache he retained when he shaved off his beard made him seem much older, and his legs moved slowly and with difficulty. None of his friends came to see him, and so by day he sat in his favorite chair, staring in silence at his fingers or ceaselessly tearing up paper. In good weather, he could be seen "wandering over the slopes of Fort Green [Park], with one eye all correct and the other rolling and bobbing from side to side like an apple in a basket."[16] He would recite to children scraps of dimly recollected clownery. At other times, he would volubly lay plans for a resumption of his career, a stupendous production of *Humpty Dumpty in Switzerland* to feature four hundred rare songbirds imported from Europe.

Mattie had found a job at the Park Theatre, and on occasion he would attend a play, seeing more drama from the audience than he ever had before. He returned to Booth's Theatre, the scene of his last stage appearance, for Byron's *Sardanapalus*, which had been converted into a balletic spectacular like *The Black Crook*, but complained, "It's a miserable play. We didn't stay for the second act. The dancing was good, but too long, and the acting was bad." He much preferred the extravaganza *Baba* at Niblo's, with a Ravel in the cast as the Tumbling Sprite. "It has some tip-top transformation scenes—regular pantomime tricks," he approved.[17] He and Mattie were planning to go to the Brooklyn Theatre to see *The Two Orphans* on 5 December, when it burned down with the loss of almost three hundred lives. Luckily, he had felt worse than usual, and they stayed at home. He could never have got out of the burning theatre in his enfeebled condition.[18]

The papers continued to predict his return to the pantomime stage the following season, basing their forecast on Fox's doctor's opinion.

But this was wishful thinking. After four-and-a-half months of this pathetic lethargy, the clown was again attacked by violent paroxysms and stricken with paralysis while walking in the park. In April 1877 he was removed once more to the asylum in Somerville, where he was said to be improving. Mattie refused to accompany him because she claimed it would countenance his desertion of his New York friends (all of whom had already abandoned him), but clearly she resented his removal to Boston and his family.[19] She had again pawned her jewelry and clothing to keep her household fed when Fox was at home; now she tried to mortgage the house and found that the flaw in the title prevented that move.[20]

In July, despite journalist's reports that he would be released in a month, Fox suffered a second paralytic stroke. Nevertheless, John Duff reported that Fox had written that he was recovering and would be able to perform. Spurred by this news and Mattie's pleas, letters began to appear in the editorial columns in October demanding a benefit for the clown. "A Friend to the Stage" wrote to the *Sun*, asking residents of New York "to look back to years gone by, when a talented man appeared before them upon the stage, doing his utmost to make them happy. Now that the gentleman is in embarrassed circumstances, and on his death bed, it would be no more than right for all of us to do our utmost to make him happy."[21] Another appeal in the *Herald* praised him for distilling the "very quintessence of fun out of everything he attempted. The peer, and indeed the superior of any of the once famous Ravel family, who will be his successor?"[22]

This ungrammatical question was more urgent than its asker knew. Mid-September had seen another relapse.[23] Even as his fans in New York were lobbying for a benefit, Fox moved from the asylum to George Howard's house at 826 Main Street, Cambridge. A few doors down lived brother James, Alderman of Ward 4. There, returned to the bosom of the family he had trouped with in his childhood and youth, he went into a slow decline. At 9:30 a.m. on 24 October 1877, after recognizing the friends at his bedside, George L. Fox died peacefully at the age of fifty-two.

Despite the request of the Eighth National Guard to give him a military funeral, modest burial services were held at Howard's home four days later. Very few members of the dramatic profession attended. These included the character actor W. J. LeMoyne, a veteran of the Troy *Uncle Tom*; Thomas Donnelly of New York; the Dutch comedian Gus Williams; the vaudeville team of Schoolcraft and Coes; Napier Lothian, musical director of the Boston Theatre; the dame comedian Neil Burgess up from Philadelphia; and some others. No stars or pantomimic specialists were there; it was the height of the fall season and hard to get away. Fox's body lay in a casket covered with black broadcloth, surrounded by a profusion of flowers, all of which came from the family, except for one large cross from James V. Taylor. As suited so unreligious a man, the service consisted simply of prayer and a brief address. There were no hymns or pallbearers. Fox was buried in the family plot on Ailanthus Path in Mt. Auburn Cemetery, under a stone which read "Alas, Poor Yorick. I knew him, Horatio, a fellow of infinite jest, of most excellent fancy." Sometime later, it was replaced and today he and Charlie rest under identical headstones in the Howard plot, beside George, Caddie, and Delia. Edwin Booth lies not far from them.[24]

Mattie did not attend her husband's funeral and, unreconciled with his family, had to deal single-handedly with her financial distress. Fox had not paid his property taxes and she had to make good the delinquency. She began to let lodgings, reserving only a few rooms in the Brooklyn house for herself and her eight-year-old daughter, living on the twenty-five dollar rent. A reporter who visited her around this time described her as a "slender woman with earnest, straight-forward face, a pair of keen eyes, and a careworn but good-humored expression . . . honest, self-sacrificing." In her upstairs parlor hung three pictures of Fox: as himself, as Richelieu, and as Bottom. Humpty Dumpty had been banished from the premises.[25]

Fox's widow eked out her meager living with the occasional acting role. Less than three months after her husband's death she and her daughter registered with Allen's Dramatic Agency, but of the clown's old friends, only Tony Pastor offered her an engagement, at fifty dollars a week. Apparently, she managed to remain in the profession. There is a sorry whiff of old times in her appearance as Eliza in a Brooklyn production of *Uncle Tom* in 1882, with aging prodigy Jennie Yeamans starred as Eva. In 1885 Mattie Fox was touring in Haverly's *Michael Strogoff* company as Sangaree the gypsy and in Kendall's *Pair of Kids* company. Perhaps she settled in Boston, despite her in-laws, for she died there in 1911. (The Howards did not register her death in their family records.)[26] Her daughter Georgia or Georgiana Lafayette Fox married Joseph L. Slaytor of Albany, Wisconsin, in 1888, but presumably the marriage did not last, for she too went on the stage in Boston in minor roles. In 1890 she could be seen as the maid Jeffreys in *The Stowaway* at the Boston Theatre, and in 1903 she carried on family tradition as Mrs. Yokem the log-cutter's wife in "the beautiful temperance drama," *The Volunteer Organist*, at the Boston Music Hall. In our end is our beginning.[27]

As a member of the Cambridge Committee of Health, Alderman James Fox had been a prime mover in the lowland fill in his riverside ward and was known as a jolly fellow who had built up a successful law practice, becoming an Episcopalian and a Mason in the process. Long cleansed of theatrical taint, he was elected Mayor of Cambridge in 1881 and served four terms, during which time the Harvard Bridge was begun. Urbane, serene, a sympathizer with but not a companion of the poor, he lingered on as a local worthy until his death in Providence in 1900, while on a visit to one of his daughters.[28]

The Wyatt-Fox women were longer lived. The matriarch Emily died at the ripe age of ninety-four in her own home at 22 Putnam Avenue on 5 October 1897. Her granddaughter Cordelia, who had retired from the stage in 1861, finished her education at a girl's school in Cambridge and married a local bookbinder, Edmund Macdonald, in 1871. Her parents continued to tour in *Uncle Tom's Cabin* and other old favorites until shortly before George Howard's death in 1887. Then Caddie Fox-Howard settled down, dying of cancer in Cambridge in 1908. The very last of the Little Foxes troupe to depart this earth was Laff's aunt Julia, his mother's sister and wife to hilarious Uncle George Wyatt; she passed away in New Haven in 1910, nearly a hundred years of age. Little Cordelia, the angel child herself, was close to ninety-four when, in 1941, she finally joined her family in Mt. Auburn Cemetery. With her, there vanished anyone who could recollect the pioneer days of trouping in New England.[29]

Epilogue:
Fox's Legacy

Fox may have died, but Humpty Dumpty did not. He was kept alive primarily by Tony Denier, who produced *Humpty Dumpty* road companies for years. He himself retired from performing, and hired as his Clown the Englishman George H. Adams. Adams, who had trained in circuses and was an acrobat first, a comedian second, had had the audacity, while working with W. W. Cole's Circus and Menagerie in 1874, to be billed as "Grimaldi" Adams. His version of the pantomime was lavish and imposing, heavy on spectacle and specialty acts. In 1881, Adams left Denier's management and went into partnership with the circus showman Adam Forepaugh, to produce an impressively equipped touring version of *Humpty Dumpty*, which was so successful that it bred an even more grandiose and elaborate edition the following year.[1]

Success spawned imitators, and the N.Y. *Clipper* for 2 April 1881 cited, in addition to the Adams enterprise, a *Humpty* managed by Jay Rial, the Tom show producer, playing to full houses in Augusta, Georgia; another starring the gymnastic clown Alfred Miaco in Gilmore, Ohio; yet another playing to fair houses in Boston; Denier's ready to open in New York; and a fifth, produced by Henry Abbey, in Pennsylvania.[2] Pantomimes were played all the year round, claimed one supporter, because "they are interesting to all classes of people," and the Theatre Comique of Boston, under the management of Maffitt and Bartholomew, managed to survive successfully for many years offering pantomime exclusively.³

But it should be apparent that we are not dealing with revivals of Fox's original Olympic Theatre creation, the show that adverse critics had thought boys in a barn might have got up. *Humpty Dumpty* had become the generic term for any large-scale miscellaneous entertainment containing a strong admixture of high-jinks and physical stunts, with Clown, Pantaloon, Harlequin, and Columbine comprising the low-comedy element. It was a string on which all kinds of popular specialties could be hung. The tricks may have been as old as the Ravels, but they were new to a new generation and so they answered well. But the show was no longer organized around the brilliant performance of the star comedian, and, worst of all, it was cluttered with words.

As Cecil Smith has pointed out, words were what had changed English pantomime from harlequinade to burlesque and extravaganza, and a similar transmutation took place in America. The catalytic factor in this conversion was E. E. Rice's phenomenally successful *Evangeline* of 1874, which borrowed the structure of the English burlesque but cleansed it of leggy blondes and sexual innuendo. *Evangeline* had the pantomime's variegated structure, its pastoral opening, its opportunities for song and dance, but not its mute slapstick or its conventionalized *commedia* types. "As a consequence," Smith concludes, "pantomime had no further raison d'être, except as a vehicle for the talents of those who performed it."⁴ And those who performed it became fewer and fewer as the century ended.

Another factor contributing to the decline of pantomime was the combination system: leading stars of the "legitimate" stage toured the country in melodramatic or comic vehicles, and vied for "time" in the chief cities and major theatres, particularly during the holiday season. Clown and Pantaloon were relegated to minor houses and "week stands." Although fit-up companies of *Humpty Dumpty* continued to thrive on the road, no manager succeeded in turning a spectacular Christmas revival of it into a paying proposition. And the American public in the larger cities had become jaded, on the lookout for novelties. One English pantomime author and manager declined to export his shows, claiming that the average American spectator was "a nervous, rather changeful sort of playgoer [who] would tire of our simple pantomime within a month . . . As for your children, bless you! their stage education is too advanced."⁵ Indeed, compared with Fox's satiric and dynamic comedy, English panto remained too parochial and too static to satisfy the American public. When Klaw and Erlanger sponsored a lavish revival of *Humpty Dumpty* at the New Amsterdam Theatre in 1904, with imported English stars along with veterans like W. H. Bartholomew, it lasted only a week before taking to the road.

Silent comedy, therefore, left the realm of musical theatre and found refuge in the more lucrative legitimate drama. The Hanlon-Lees brothers, whom Fox had sponsored in the 1860s when they were merely acrobats, were the most proficient of his unacknowledged imitators. They had become the toast of Paris in the 1870s with macabre pantomimic sketches featuring intricate trickwork and virtually unbelievable acrobatics. When their stunts were sandwiched into a conventional comedy, *Le Voyage en Suisse*, the play became an international hit, and, long before Georges Méliès and Mack Sennett, audiences were enthralled to see characters catapulted out of stage-coaches, walking up walls, drenched with hoses, exploded in train-wrecks, knocked through the middle of pianos. It is noteworthy that the chronicler Jules Claretie, ignoring their British origins, referred to "l'américanisme des frères Hanlon-Lee [*sic*], ces Edison de la pantomime." He viewed their art as a phenomenon cognate with express trains, telegraphs, steamships and Yankee *go ahead*.[6] Fox's hyper-active style of pantomime was thus introduced to Europe and enjoyed a brief but influential vogue.

The Hanlon-Lees took to management and produced the long-lived fairy spectacles *Fantasma* and *Superba*, while their knockabout tradition was maintained by the Byrne Brothers in *Eight Bells*. In all these cases, the stars were the teams of contortionists and gymnasts who performed the feats, not individual funny-men. On the one hand stood the ensemble of actors who had the thankless task of enacting the simple-minded story, on the other the ensemble of stunt-men responsible for evoking laughter through physical mayhem.

In France, the older pantomime of Deburau and the Théâtre des Funambules enjoyed a snob-appeal renaissance at the turn of the century, first in private literary clubs, such as the Cercle funambulesque, founded in 1888, then in such arty and self-conscious efforts as Michel Carré's *L'Enfant prodigue* (1890), which toured to England and America. In this effete exercise, Pierrot, played by a young woman, is turned out of his bourgeois family, goes temporarily to the bad with a courtesan named Phrynette, is disillusioned by her infidelity, and returns to be forgiven by Pierrot *père*. It was all very charming and rather bloodless, but it suited the extreme refinement professed by *fin-de-siècle* audiences in the commercial theatre. There were no belly laughs, only wan smiles of appreciation.[7]

The silent film, however, made belly laughs a stock-in-trade, since by nature it excelled at physical comedy. This rivalry with the stage prompted disparate reactions. In 1912, the manager Robert Grau looked forward to a revival of stage pantomime, asking rhetorically,

"Can it be possible that with the millions of new theatregoers, created by the vogue of the silent drama, as portrayed on the moving picture screen, that an effort to revive the glories of the Fox era would fail of a public response?" Alas, movies were more than a vogue, and after the Great War, the critic Heywood Broun headed an essay, "Films have killed the pantomime."[8] The movie clowns may in some cases have learned their skills on stage, as was the case with Chaplin, Keaton, and Stan Laurel, but just as frequently they sprang full-blown on to the screen. They, and their publicists, admitted no progenitors, no illustrious ancestry—and when high-brow critics did seek to place them in a tradition, they referred loftily to Aristophanes, to the *commedia dell'arte*, possibly to Grimaldi, but never to Fox.

To adopt a term of David Grimsted's, Fox's talent was less integrative—tied to character, plot and unified effort—than disintegrative, the outstanding piece in a welter of elements, providing an artificial cohesion through disruption. Perhaps this destructive tendency derived from his thorny personality, quick to take offense, swift to alienate those persons most necessary to him. This personal aggression turned to art within the fairy-tale framework of the pantomime. The true-to-life ingredient Fox contributed was catalytic to the fantastical solvent. But when pantomime itself began to disintegrate into a loose mixture of individual acts, it left Fox bereft of a context against which to practice his aggression. Too big, too idiosyncratic for the increasingly realistic drama, too dependent on story for the burgeoning variety stage, he lost his orientation. The aggression turned inward and exacerbated his mental imbalance.

With the extinction of the genre in which he excelled, recollection of Fox dimmed and flickered out. At the turn of the century, even long memories tended to be patronizing. William Winter, granting that Fox had "made clowning a fine art," qualified this by adding "his field was not high."[9] He rated a footnote, at best a paragraph, in standard histories. But standard histories seldom quantify the holdings of the popular imagination. For decades, the American image of a clown—circus, pantomime, or musical-comedy—remained that of Fox's bald head, long nose, and ruffled knickerbockers. His best piece of business, the assumption of perfect innocence and docile goodness, was copied again and again, forming part of the basic vocabulary of stage comedy. His intense concentration on the accomplishment of a prank and his lightning transition from hilarity to consternation or from mischief to aimless stupefaction entered the lexicon of comic clichés. That these were mimic, not dialogic, devices meant that their originator went uncredited, but they were his for all that.

What's more, Fox's was the first case to demonstrate that a clown

could occupy as high a position in the esteem of the public as a tragedian. The lesson of Jacksonian democracy was implicit in his mute appeal to all levels of society; the financial and critical success of *Humpty
Dumpty* destroyed, at least for a short time, the artistic hierarchy that
had placed pantomime at the lowest rung. Without the balletic allure of
the Ravels, he took what was earthy and familiar in the American experience and elevated it, through humor, to a super-realism of violent action and contrasting repose.

In essence, two basic strains of comedy have enlivened the American stage. One, exemplified by Fox's rival Joseph Jefferson and his perennial Rip van Winkle, was the low-key, down-home variety. Its favorite exponents were laconic Yankees, down-to-earth farmers, eccentric,
yarn-spinning, but ultimately sensible commentators on the passing
scene. This strain eventuated in the national-hero status of Will Rogers
and, more recently, Bill Cosby. It was a normative kind of comedy, suggesting, after the model of Terence and Molière, an eventual return to
the established patterns and reassuring assumptions of everyday life.

The other strain may be called the anarchic. It launched wild and
nonsensical attacks on public institutions and cultural totems, and was
exemplified by minstrel-show parodies, Shakespearean burlesques, and
circus-ring knockabout. In the hands of the Ravels, it assaulted the
premises of Nature herself, seemingly defying gravity and other physical laws. In our time, this tradition has been gloriously maintained, at
different levels, by the Marx Brothers, the Three Stooges, and the animated cartoon. It is a kind of comedy that questions the world of convention and appearances and undermines our accepted values. Con-
fronting its irreverent literalism and *reductio ad absurdum,* nothing can
be taken for granted.

Fox began his career moving in the safe grooves of normative comedy, and gradually found himself navigating a more original course toward anarchic comedy. His nurture of pantomime and the character of
Humpty Dumpty coincided with a particularly ruthless and aggressive
spirit in America and provided a valuable outlet for national contradic-
tions. Although outwardly American society was trying to project an
image of increased gentility and urbanity, an alignment with European
mores, inwardly it housed crude primal energies that found release in
industrial and territorial expansion. In his best pantomimes, Fox provided a theatrical format for what the Germans call a *Ventilfunktion,* an
escape-valve for these social energies, balancing the subconscious need
for release, action, and violence with the conscious desire for control
and uplift. In his ingenuousness and his enterprise, his assumed innocence and his sly malice, his selfish aggression and his unbridled ap-
petites, Humpty Dumpty was not simply a naturalized Arlecchino. Like

his later Gallic counterpart Ubu, he crystallized in readily apprehensible shape the underlying and often disguised desires and predilections of the world in which he moved.

In this respect, Fox, through his disciples the Hanlon-Lees, repaid his debt to the Ravels by feeding the wellsprings of avant-garde European art. The surrealists, in particular, often looked to "Anglo-Saxon" nonsense as the key to free them from the prison of Cartesian logic. The cinéastes' exaltation of Jerry Lewis is simply the latest in a series of homages to the apparent Dionysianism of American life. At the turn of the century, Paul Margueritte had dedicated his pantomime scenario *Pierrot Mormon* to the Hanlon-Lees. One passage from its nightmarish progress goes like this:

Major Bagstock prepares himself a toddy with neat whisky in which he crushes up, together with a jumble of eggs, a pimento the size of a cucumber. He drinks it hot, without batting an eyelid. Immediately a tiny blue flame appears like a drop on the end of his nose and a practical-minded Yankee dashes to light his cigar at it. One masterly upper-cut followed by a well-planted kick sends him catapulting into the india-rubber hunchback, knocking over Madame Lou, who exhibits as she flounders, the colour of her garters. The rubber-ball-man bounces from the ceiling, flattens out a gentleman like a pancake, and floats through the balcony window to a firework display of broken glass.[10]

This unproduced scenario demonstrates the fascination with transatlantic popular culture that will recur in Cocteau's ballet *Le Boeuf sur le toit* (1920). It exemplifies Zola's comment that the Hanlon-Lees were realists in the way a dream is realistic, never omitting, never forgetting. To a European all this seemed highly exotic, the product of the uncouth mores of a semi-civilized country.

But to a New Yorker who had watched Fox translate the trickwork of the Ravels into the familiar settings of saloons and city streets, all this oneiric rough-and-tumble was plain as piecrust. Even Margueritte's outlandish cocktail simply reiterated the Tom Collins of *Humpty Dumpty*'s last revival under Fox. Fox was realistic all right, not in Zola's special sense, but in the straightforward sense of translating the raw material of the life he knew into hyperbolic theatrical energy. As a comic originator, Fox was of the people, by the people, and for the people. The real triumph of Humpty Dumpty was to have distilled into one striking figure both the disarming innocence and the violent impetuosity of nineteenth-century America.

APPENDIX ONE

FOX-HOWARD GENEALOGY

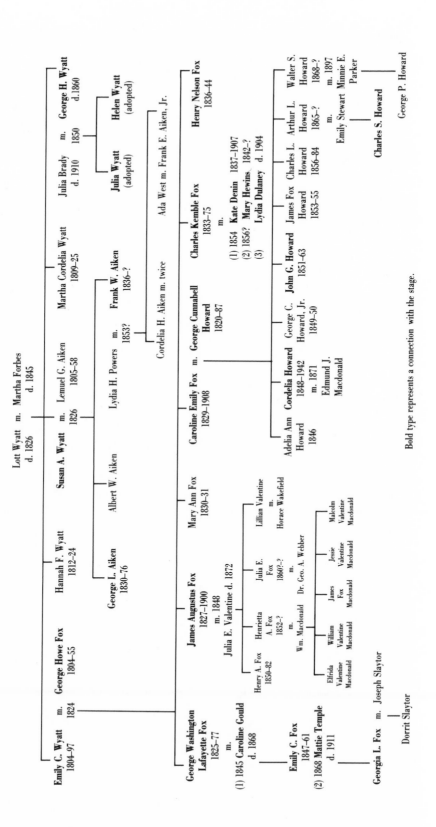

Bold type represents a connection with the stage.

APPENDIX TWO
CIGAR-STORE HUMPTIES

During the run of *Humpty Dumpty* at the Olympic Theatre, a wooden effigy of Fox as clown was set up in the lobby. This may have been the same figure that stood on the sidewalk outside the Broadway Theatre during Fox's last appearances in October and November 1875. That they were identical may be deduced from the fact that the Olympic figure was owned by George H. Tyler, who was Fox's associate manager at the Broadway. When Tyler was murdered in 1884, the figure, known familiarly as George, was sold to William Hardy who set it up outside his cigar store on Church Street, New Haven. Every week it was carefully washed and every year freshly painted. In 1909 the cigar business passed to a Mr. Laske, and when Harvard defeated Yale in a boat race in June 1910, the winning team celebrated its victory by decapitating the inoffensive statue.[1]

In 1956, the Rudolf Frederick Haffenreffer collection of cigar-store Indians and trade signs was auctioned off at the Parke-Bernet Gallery in New York. The collection included a polychromed white pine wood carving that had originally been owned by Dr. A. W. Pendergast. Pendergast and his co-author W. Porter Ware had cited it in their *Cigar Store Figures in American Folk Art* as a "nondescript." Pendergast had sold it to Haffenreffer who made some unskilful repairs to it before the auction, where it was sold, this time to the Abby Aldrich Rockefeller Museum Folk Art Collection, which labelled it simply "Clown."

The museum understood the effigy to have been a shop sign for George W. Childs (1829–94), a Philadelphia philanthropist and publisher of show posters; it stood before his premises in the Ledger Building on the corner of Third and Chestnut Streets in that city. But this information was based solely on the inscription "Geo w. Child" within the oval on the clown's chest, which also held the words "GENEROUSLY GOOD," "5¢" and, in a smaller circle, "J. WERTHEIMER." The folk-art specialist thought the statue might be the work of the carver Joseph Campbell.[3]

When the Rockefeller Collection directed its inquiries to me, I was able to identify the effigy as a portrait of Fox. Not only do the face and costume replicate photographs of him in his *Humpty Dumpty* regalia, but the circle on his chest encloses a fox's head, his personal emblem. The figure was not in good condition. Its toes and the flounces at each

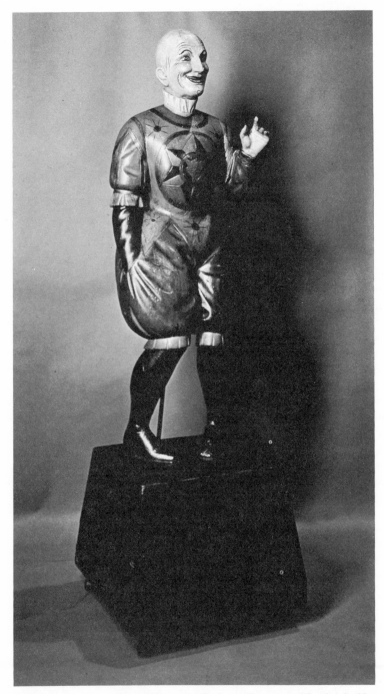

Figure 32. A cigar-store effigy of Fox at the Heritage Plantation of Sandwich, Massachusetts, mislabelled Tom Matthews. (Courtesy Heritage Plantation of Sandwich, Massachusetts Arts and Crafts Museum)

elbow had been broken off and repaired at some later date. Vertical cracks ran down its front. The statue was supported at the back by a small tree limb. More suggestively, the head had been broken off at the neck and repaired. Was this the theatre statue vandalized by Harvard undergraduates, drunk with triumph? If so, how did it get from New Haven to Philadelphia?

Although there is no question that the image is one of Fox as Humpty Dumpty, in all likelihood, it is not the effigy owned by Tyler. For one thing, the clown in his pantomime make-up was a common subject for cigar-store signs. A similar figure is illustrated in Clarence Hornung's *Treasury of American Design* (I, 63, fig. 163) where it is described as a statue of Judy dressed as a clown.

Another, even more vivid figure is on exhibit at the folk art museum of the Heritage Plantation, Sandwich, Massachusetts. It had been purchased from Henry Coger of Ashley Falls, Massachusetts in 1870 and, on the authority of Frederick Fried, identified as Tom Matthews, the English pantomime clown. But this is a misattribution on two counts: the Sandwich statue is an exact portrait of Fox and bears the tell-tale fox's face on his breast; and Matthews never performed in America, where he had no particular reputation. (Tobacconist's figures of clowns are uncommon in England.) Mr. Fried has since concurred with my attribution and believes the statue to be of Fox. The Heritage Plantation, however, despite full testimony to the statue's identity, persists in mislabelling it as "Tom Matthews."[4]

These effigies are clear evidence that the icon of Fox as Humpty Dumpty was stamped deeply on the imagination of the American public through the dissemination of his image in urban centers during his lifetime. But memories quickly faded.

APPENDIX THREE
FOX'S TOURS OF 1874-75

1874

25–26 May	Academy of Music, Brooklyn, N.Y.
30 May	Hartford, Conn.
3–4 June	Worcester, Mass.
8–11 June	Howard Athenaeum, Boston, Mass.
13 July	Springfield, Mass.
14 July	Pittsfield, Mass.
15–16 July	Griswold Opera House, Troy, N.Y.
17–18 July	Albany, N.Y.
22 July	Utica, N.Y.
24–25 July	Corinthian Hall, Rochester, N.Y.
27 July	Lockport, N.Y.
28–30 July	Buffalo, N.Y.
1 August	London, Ont.
3–4 August	Detroit, Mich.
5 August	Lansing, Mich.
6 August	Grand Rapids, Mich.
7 August	Kalamazoo, Mich.
8 August	Jackson, Mich.
13–15 August	Detroit, Mich.
17–22 August	Cleveland, Ohio
24–29 August	Pittsburgh, Pa.
31 August–1 September	Wheeling, West Va.
2 September	Zanesville, Ohio
3–4 September	Columbus, Ohio
5 September	Springfield, Ohio
7–12 September	Louisville, Ky.
19 September	Dayton, Ohio
21 September–3 October	Cincinnati, Ohio
5 October	Toledo, Ohio
9 October	Bay City, Mich.
10 October	Saginaw, Mich.
12 October	Lansing, Mich.
13 October	Jackson, Mich.
14–17 October	Grand Rapids, Mich.
19–21 October	St. Paul, Minn.

23–25 October	Milwaukee, Wis.
26 October	Madison, Wis.
27 October	Janesville, Wis.
28 October	Freeport, Ill.
29 October	Dubuque, Iowa
30 October	Rock Island, Ill.
31 October	Davenport, Iowa
2 November	Burlington, Iowa
3 November	Galesburg, Ill.
4–5 November	Bloomington, Ill.
6–7 November	Springfield, Ill.
9 November	Jacksonville, Ill.
10–11 November	Quincy, Ill.
12 November	Keokuk, Iowa
13–14 November	Peoria, Ill.
16 November	Decatur, Ill.
23–28 November	Memphis, Tenn.
30 November–12 December	New Orleans, La.
14–16 December	Mobile, Ala.
17 December	Montgomery, Ala.
18–19 December	Atlanta, Ga.
21 December	Augusta, Ga.
22–23 December	Savannah, Ga.
24–26 December	Charleston, S.C.
28–29 December	Wilmington, Ga.

1875

2 January	Norfolk, Va.
4–6 January	Petersburg, Va.
7–9 January	Richmond, Va.
11–16 January	Ford's Opera House, Washington, D.C.
18–23 January	Baltimore, Md.
25–26 January	Harrisburg, Pa.
28–29 January	Elmira, N.Y.
1–2 February	Scranton, Pa.
3 February	Port Jervis, N.J.
4 February	Middletown, N.J.
5 February	Paterson, N.J.
6 February	Newark, N.J.
8 February	New Brunswick, N.J.
9 February	Trenton, N.J.
10 February	Easton, Pa.
11 February	Allentown, Pa.

12 February	Reading, Pa.
13 February	Wilmington, Del.
15–27 February	Philadelphia, Pa.
1 March	Brooklyn, N.Y. [restrained by injunction from performing]
3 March	Hartford, Conn.
4–6 March	Providence, R.I.
8 March	Newport, R.I.
9–10 March	New Bedford, Mass.
11 March	Taunton, Mass.
12 March	Brockton, Mass.
13 March	Lynn, Mass.
15 March	Portsmouth, N.H.
16 March	Biddeford, Maine
17–18 March	Lewiston, Maine
19–20 March	Bangor, Maine
22 March	Augusta, Maine
23 March	Gardiner, Maine
24–25 March	Portland, Maine
26 March	Lawrence, Mass.
27 March	Manchester, N.H.
29 March	Lowell, Mass.
30 March	Worcester, Mass.
31 March	Springfield, Mass.
1 April	Pittsfield, Mass.
2–3 April	Albany, N.Y.
6 April	Utica, N.Y.
8 April	Oswego, N.Y.
14 April	Erie, Pa.
16 April	Titusville, Pa.
17 April	Oil City, Pa.
19 April	Meadville, Pa.
20 April	Youngstown, Ohio
21–24 April	Pittsburgh, Pa.
26 April–1 May	Cincinnati, Ohio
3–5 May	Indianapolis, Ind.
6–8 May	Louisville, Ky.
10–15 May	St. Louis, Mo.
17–22 May	Aiken's Opera House, Chicago, Ill.
24–25 May	Milwaukee, Wis.
26 May	LaPorte, Ind.
27 May	Cleveland, Ohio
3–9 June	Grand Opera House, Toronto

14–21 June	De Bar's Opera House, Montreal
26 June	Poughkeepsie, N.Y.

Break in Tour. Eight day respite in New York City.

Resumption of Tour

6 July–14 August	Boston Museum, Boston, Mass.
30 August	Reading, Pa.
31 August	Euclid Opera House, Cleveland, Ohio
2 September	Binghamton, N.Y.
3 September	Elmira, N.Y.
4 September	Hornellsville, N.Y.
5–12 September	Buffalo, N.Y.
14 September	Erie, Pa.
15–16 September	Toledo, Ohio
17–18 September	Detroit, Mich.
23 September	Utica, N.Y.
24 September	Syracuse, N.Y.
27 September	Albany, N.Y.
1–2 October	Springfield, Mass.
4 October	Westfield, Mass.
5 October	Worcester, Mass.
6 October	Hartford, Conn.
7 October	Bridgeport, Conn.
8 October	Waterbury, Conn.
9 October	New Haven, Conn.
11 October	Newport, R.I.
12–14 October	Providence, R.I.
15–16 October	New Bedford, Mass.

Back to New York City to open at Booth's Theatre, 25 October.

NOTES

Abbreviations used in citations

BPL = Boston Public Library.

DAB = *Dictionary of American Biography.*

GPH = George P. Howard papers, Hoblitzelle Theatre Collection, University of Texas at Austin

HTC = Harvard Theatre Collection, Harvard University, Cambridge, Mass.

Lincoln Center = Billy Rose Collection, Lincoln Center Library of the Performing Arts, New York City

Tex = Humanities Research Center, University of Texas at Austin

Introduction
(pp. xiii–xvii)

1. G. C. D. Odell, *Annals of the New York Stage* (New York, 1927), 1:21–22; O. S. Coad and E. Mims, Jr., *The American Stage* (New Haven, 1929).

2. Odell, 2:41, 313.

3. A. Denier, *Denier's Parlor Pantomimes* (New York, c. 1864), series 2, p. 2. The standard works on British pantomime are R. J. Broadbent, *A History of Pantomime* (London, 1901); M. Willson Disher, *Clowns and Pantomimes* (London, 1925); D. Mayer, III, *Harlequin in His Element: The English Pantomime, 1806–1836* (Cambridge, Mass., 1969); and G. Frow, *"Oh, Yes It Is!" A History of Pantomime* (London, 1985).

4. P. Preston, "Pantomimes Ancient and Modern," N.Y. *Clipper,* 8 May 1869, p. 36.

5. L. Wagner, *The Pantomimes and All about Them: Their History, Preparation and Exponents* (London, 1881), pp. 59–60. According to another account, Parsloe had injured his spine on the stormy voyage over and died on the fourth morning of his stay. See E. L. Blanchard, *The Life and Reminiscences of E. L. Blanchard, with notes from the Diary of William Blanchard,* ed. C. Scott and C. Howard (London, 1891), p. 4, note 1.

6. Odell, 3:569.

7. M. H. Winter, *Le Théâtre du merveilleux* (Paris, 1962), p. 143.

8. L. Hutton, *Curiosities of the American Stage* (New York, 1891), pp. 187–88.

9. J. S. G. Hagan, *Records of the New York Stage 1860–1870* (New York, 1877), extra-illustrated volume in HTC, 3:83.

1. On Stage in Boston
(pp. 1–13)

1. M. A. Livermore, *The Story of My Life or The Sunshine and Shadow of Seventy Years* (Hartford, Conn., 1897), ch. 1; M. A. Connolly, *The Boston Schools in the New Republic 1776–1840* (unpub. M.A. thesis, Harvard University, 1963), pp. 245–46,

305. For a demographic study of Boston during this period, see P. R. Knights, *The Plain People of Boston, 1830–1860: A Study in City Growth* (New York, 1971).

2. Livermore, p. 66.

3. W. W. Clapp, "The Drama in Boston," in *The Memorial History of Boston*, ed. J. Winsor (Boston, 1881) 4:361–65; W. W. Clapp, *A Record of the Boston Stage* (Boston, 1853), ch. 1–2.

4. Fox family Bible: GPH, Tex. According to Elizabeth Howard Linzee, the memorable family stories about Emily Wyatt and George Howe Fox were that as a child *she* was sat on a fence and lectured by an Indian to cure her of her fear of redskins, and *he* hid under a bed during the War of 1812.

5. S. A. Drake, ed., *History of Middlesex County, Mass.* (Boston, 1880) 2:224; S. A. Eliot, *A History of Cambridge, Massachusetts* (Cambridge, Mass., 1913), p. 200.

6. G. P. Howard, quoted in W. H. Draper, *George L. Fox, Comedian, in Pantomime and Travesty* (unpub. Ph.D. diss., University of Illinois, 1958), p. 5.

7. C. D. Johnson, "That Guilty Third Tier: Prostitution in Nineteenth-century American Theatres," in *Victorian America*, ed. D. W. Howe (Pittsburgh, 1976), p. 116.

8. O. S. Coad and E. Mims, Jr., *The American Stage* (New Haven, 1929), p. 87.

9. Ibid. See also Clapp, *Record*.

10. R. Stoddard, "Isaiah Rogers's Tremont Theatre, Boston," *Antiques* 105 (1974): 1317–18; M. C. Crawford, *Romantic Days in Old Boston* (Boston, 1910), p. 249; Clapp, "Drama," p. 360.

11. Their names do not appear in any of the bills, but family tradition links them with the Tremont.

12. GPH, Tex.

13. P. Coveney, *The Image of Childhood* (Baltimore, 1967), pp. 37–51; D. T. Miller, *The Birth of Modern America 1820–1850* (New York, 1970), p. 63.

14. Tremont Theatre Account Books, 1839, HTC.

15. T. A. Brown, *A History of the American Stage* (New York, 1870), p. 133, echoed by the DAB.

16. HTC bills.

17. Clapp, *Record*, p. 278.

18. F. A. Kemble, *Journal by Frances Anne Butler* (Philadelphia, 1835) 2:132. This opinion was seconded by T. Power, *Impressions of America: during the Years 1833, 1834 and 1835* (Philadelphia, 1836) 1:81.

19. Kemble, 2:132.

20. Ibid., p. 133.

21. W. S. Howard, *From Slavery to Prohibition: A Dramatic History of the Drama "Uncle Tom's Cabin"* (unpub. typescript, Tex.) p. 5.

22. HTC bills, 4 and 9 Sept. 1843; Tremont Theatre Account Books, HTC. For some reason, Miss Fox is billed on 9 Sept. as "Her First Appearance."

23. C. H. Macdonald, "Memoirs of the Original Little Eva," *Educational Theatre Journal* 8 (Dec. 1956): 269.

24. HTC bills, BPL bills.

25. Macdonald, p. 267; W. S. Howard, p. 6.

26. *Bowen's Picture of Boston*, 3d ed. (Boston, 1838), p. 29; Connolly, p. 193.

27. Drake, pp. 260–61; N. Dearborn, *Boston Notions* (Boston, 1848), p. 172; "The American Grimaldi," N.Y. *Clipper*, 3 Nov. 1877; obituary of James Fox, Cambridge *Chronicle*, 22 Dec. 1900, pp. 17–18.

28. Connolly, pp. 188–89, 193, 208–11; Clapp, *Record*, p. 260.

29. T. Ball, *My Threescore Years and Ten* (Boston, 1892), pp. 19–23.

30. Drake, p. 225.

31. See e.g. New England *Galaxy* 10 (14 Dec. 1827): 531, for full description of pantomime *Faustus.*

32. HTC Scrapbooks, Theatre clippings, Boston and Tremont Theatres 1827–32.

33. Not 16th as Clapp has it, *Records,* p. 299; HTC Scrapbooks.

34. M. H. Winter, *Le Théâtre du merveilleux* (Paris, 1962), pp. 139–43.

35. Quoted in "The Ravel Family," Boston *Courier* 63 (15 Mar. 1858).

36. Ibid.

37. HTC Scrapbooks for Tremont Theatre; Clapp incorrectly gives 12 Nov.

38. HTC Scrapbooks.

39. M. G. Swift, *Belles and Beaux on Their Toes: Dancing Stars in Young America* (Washington, D.C., 1980), pp. 75–77.

40. Macdonald, p. 269.

41. Record book, BPL; Boston City Directory, 1834; G. L. Aiken quoted in GPH, Tex.

42. G. L. Aiken, "Leaves from an Actor's Life," *Saturday Journal,* undated clipping, Tex.

43. A. Corbett, "Boston Theatre 'Mystery House' Only Westerly End of Long Lobby," *Boston Globe,* 8 Mar. 1926.

44. W. T. G. Ball, "The Old Federal Street Theatre," *The Bostonian Society Publications* 8 (1911): 82; Drake, p. 225.

45. HTC bills.

46. J. N. Ireland, *Records of the New York Stage* (New York, 1866–67) 2:173; G. C. D. Odell, *Annals of the New York Stage* (New York, 1928) 4:103–4.

47. L. B. Ellis, *History of New Bedford and Its Vicinity 1602–1892* (Syracuse, N.Y., 1892), p. 719; New Bedford *Mercury,* 10, 17, 23, 31 Mar., 6, 17 Apr. 1836.

2. The Little Foxes
(pp. 14–29)

1. Notes in Townsend Walsh collection, Lincoln Center.

2. See S. Rezneck, "Social History of an American Depression, 1837–1843," *American Historical Review* 40 (July 1935): 662–87; and for the effects on the economy of specific regions, J. R. Sharp, *The Jacksonians versus the Banks: Politics in the States after the Panic of 1837* (New York, 1870); K. Halttunen, *Confidence Men and Painted Women: A Study of Middle-class Culture in America, 1830–1870* (New Haven, 1982), pp. 17–20, describes a national loss of confidence and a new view of the world as uncertain and treacherous as a result of the depression.

3. *Bowen's Picture of Boston,* 3d ed. (Boston, 1838), p. 294.

4. Quoted in *The American Heritage Cookbook and Illustrated History of American Eating and Drinking* (New York, 1964) p. 82.

5. "The American Grimaldi," N.Y. *Clipper,* 3 Nov. 1877; N.Y. *Sun,* 25 Oct. 1877; R. Day, "George Washington Lafayette Fox," DAB, 6:567.

6. J. B. Gough, *Autobiography and Personal Recollections* (Springfield, Mass., 1869), pp. 83–84.

7. BPL bills.

8. M. A. Connolly, *The Boston Schools in the New Republic 1776–1840* (unpub. M.A. thesis, Harvard University, 1963), p. 109; R. B. Nye, *Society and Culture in America, 1830–1860* (New York, 1974), pp. 118, 219–26.

9. Quoted in D. Grimsted, *Melodrama Unveiled: American Theatre Culture 1800–1850* (Chicago, 1968), p. 24.

10. Gough, pp. 83–84.

11. Grimsted, p. 31.

12. GPH, Tex.

13. W. W. Clapp, *A Record of the Boston Stage* (Boston, 1853), p. 473.

14. "Any Type Theater Building Banned by Law Passed 1806," Portland *Evening Express*, 25 June 1977; "Edgar Allan Poe's Mother Made First Theatrical Debut Here," Portland *Sunday Telegram and Sunday Press Herald*, 15 Nov. 1925. Extracts from Waldboro' Maine *Patriot*, Belfast Maine *Journal*, Portland Maine *Advertiser*, in Tex.

15. Church records, Halifax, Nova Scotia, transcription in Tex.

16. Cambridge, Mass. city file 12350.

17. GPH, Tex.

18. C. McGlinchee, *The First Decade of the Boston Museum* (Boston, 1940), p. 73; C. H. Macdonald, "Memoirs of the Original Little Eva," *Educational Theatre Journal* 8 (Dec. 1956): 268.

19. Baltimore *Republican*, 12 Aug. 1839; GPH, Tex.

20. M. E. Hewins, "The Giddy Gusher," N.Y. *Mirror*, 29 Jan. 1887.

21. GPH, Tex.

22. Tremont Theatre Forfait Books 1840–[43], Friday 4 Nov. 1842, Monday 4 Apr. 1843. HTC.

23. Ibid., 26 Jan. 1841.

24. *Bowen's Picture of Boston*, p. 195.

25. Clapp, *Record*, p. 360; W. W. Clapp, "The Drama in Boston," in *The Memorial History of Boston, Including Suffolk County, Massachusetts, 1630–1880*, ed. J. Winsor (Boston, 1881) 4:369; C. D. Johnson, "That Guilty Third Tier: Prostitution in Nineteenth-century American Theatres," in *Victorian America*, ed. D. W. Howe (Pittsburgh, 1976), p. 118.

26. M. C. Crawford, *Romantic Days in Old Boston* (Boston, 1910), p. 249.

27. R. Stoddard, "Isaiah Rogers's Tremont Theatre, Boston," *Antiques* 105 (1974): 1318.

28. G. Carson, "Sylvester Graham," in *The American Heritage Cookbook* (New York, 1964), pp. 173–79.

29. L. Shepherd, ed. *Encyclopedia of Occultism & Parapsychology* (Detroit, 1978) 1:213–14, 2:599, 895–96; L. S. Levy, *Grace Notes in American History* (Norman, Okla., 1967), p. 139; H. W. Haggard, *Devils, Drugs and Doctors* (New York, 1929), pp. 306–11.

30. Levy, pp. 143–46.

31. GPH, Tex.

32. T. A. Brown, *A History of the American Stage* (New York, 1970), p. 6; obituary of "Yankee" Addams, N.Y. *Clipper*, 7 Mar. 1885.

33. GPH, Tex.

34. "New Comic Song entitled 'What Shall We Do for Change' as sung by Master James Fox with unbounded applause, at the Principal Museums in the United States," Tex.

35. H. M. Ordway, "The Drama in Lowell with a Short Sketch of the Life of Perez Fuller," in *Contributions of the Old Residents' Historical Association, Lowell, Mass.* (Lowell, 1883), pp. 246–70; W. M. Leman, *Memories of an Old Actor* (San Francisco, 1886), p. 106.

36. Ordway, p. 273.

37. O. B. Stebbins, "The Oldest Theatre Now in Boston," *The Bostonian* 1:2 (Nov. 1894): 113–17; H. M. Ticknor, "The Passing of the Boston Museum," *The New England Magazine*, n.s. 28:4 (June 1903): 382–83.

38. GPH, Tex.

39. J. R. Towse, *Sixty Years of the Theater* (New York, 1916), p. 9; C. McGlinchee, "The Marvellous in the Pantomime," *Revue d'histoire du théâtre* 15 (Jan.–March 1963): 63–70.

40. G. Vandenhoff, *An Actor's Note-book* (New York, 1860), p. 202.

41. C. H. Holman, Introduction, in T. S. Arthur, *Ten Nights in a Barroom* (New York, 1966), vi–vii; R. L. Taylor, *Vessel of Wrath* (New York, 1966), pp. 285–6.

42. *Biographical Sketch of Ossian T. Dodge* (Boston, 1856); "Long Evening," Worcester *Daily News*, 26 Sept. 1850; I. R. Tyrrel, *Sobering Up: From Temperance to Prohibition in Antebellum America, 1800–1860* (Westport, Conn., 1979), pp. 92–128, 178–79, 196.

43. Levy, pp. 106–12; R. Lane, *Policing the City: Boston 1822–1885* (Cambridge, Mass., 1967), pp. 39–46, 49.

44. Crawford, p. 253; J. B. Clapp, "Boston Museum," Boston *Evening Transcript*, 16 May, 23 May, and 3 July 1903, pp. iv, 24.

45. HTC bills.

46. Taylor, p. 288; preface to *The Drunkard*, quoted in C. Bode, *The Anatomy of American Popular Culture 1840–1861* (Berkeley and Los Angeles, 1959), p. 7. See also M. R. Booth, "The Drunkard's Progress: Nineteenth-century Temperance Drama," *Dalhousie Review* 44 (1964–65): 205–12.

47. Doctor's receipts, GPH, Tex.

48. M. Minnegerode, *The Fabulous Forties 1840–1850* (New York, 1924), pp. 3–5; B. DeVoto, *Mark Twain's America* (Boston, 1967), p. 8.

49. G. L. Aiken, "Leaves from an Actor's Life," *Saturday Journal*, undated clipping, Tex.

3. The Howards and the Foxes
(pp. 30–44)

1. C. Bode, *The Anatomy of American Popular Culture 1840–1861* (Berkeley and Los Angeles, 1959), p. 20; P. R. Knights, *The Plain People of Boston, 1830–1860: A Study in City Growth* (New York, 1971), pp. 33, 120.

2. G. L. Fox's obituary in Cambridge *Chronicle*, 27 Oct. 1877, p. 4, calls her "Constance Gould."

3. HTC bills; GPH, Tex.

4. J. G. Hubbard, "The Late G. L. Fox's First Engagement," N.Y. *Clipper*, 10 Nov. 1877, p. 261. Hubbard is incorrect in assuming Laff's appearance at the Lowell Museum on 17 Feb. 1847 to be his first adult engagement.

5. Quoted in P. Boyer, *Urban Masses and Moral Order in America, 1820–1920* (Cambridge, Mass., 1978), p. 61.

6. J. B. Clapp, "Boston Museum," Boston *Evening Transcript*, 3 July 1903, p. xi. Cf. William Clapp writing in 1853: "We are happy to record that the profession in America, so far as the respectability of its members in private life is concerned, never stood higher; and . . . there never was a period when actors, as a class, were thoroughly respectable. Provident views, and a passion for accumulation, have expelled the erratic and thriftless vice of bygone generations" (W. W. Clapp, *A Record of the Boston Stage* [Boston, 1853], pp. 296–97). Note the characteristically Calvinist equation of morality and wealth.

7. GPH, Tex.

8. W. S. Howard, *From Slavery to Prohibition: A Dramatic History of the Drama "Uncle Tom's Cabin"* (unpub. typescript, Tex), p. 7.

9. GPH, Tex.

10. Editor of the Newport *Mercury, Newport Illustrated in a Series of Pen and Pencil Sketches* (New York, 1854), p. 27; G. B. Smith, "Memories of the Long Ago 1838–1925," *Bulletin of the Newport Historical Society* 56 (Jan. 1926): 10.

11. GPH, Tex.

12. L. B. Ellis, *History of New Bedford and Its Vicinity 1602–1892* (Syracuse, N.Y., 1892), pp. 280, 719. Could I. P. Adams have been a misprint for J. P. "Yankee" Addams?

13. GPH, Tex.

14. O. Macy, *The History of Nantucket*, 2d ed., 1880 (Clifton, Mass., 1972), p. 287; E. K. Godfrey, *The Island of Nantucket: What It Was and What It Is* (Boston, 1882), p. 20; E. A. Stackpole, "The Great Fire of 1846," *Proceedings of the Nantucket Historical Association* 52 (1946): 35–38.

15. GPH, Tex.

16. J. B. Felt, *Annals of Salem*, 2d ed. (Salem, Mass., 1849), 2:44–45.

17. Ibid. There had been an earlier tolerance toward theatre mooted in the Salem *Gazette* for 12 June 1821: "As it is generally allowed that example influences more than precept, it cannot be denied that a well regulated Theatre *may* be more instructive and improving than the lecture room—as in the latter our passions and habits are only described, while in the illusion of the former we witness the punishment of evil, and almost realise the reward of good actions." See P. M. Ryan, "The Old Salem Theatre," *Essex Institute Historical Collections* 98 (Oct. 1962): 287–93.

18. GPH, Tex.

19. G. L. Aiken, "Leaves from an Actor's Life or Recollections of Plays and Players," *Saturday Journal*, undated clipping, Tex.

20. M. Hewins, "The Giddy Gusher," N.Y. *Mirror*, 29 Jan. 1887.

21. C. H. Macdonald, "Memoirs of the Original Little Eva," *Educational Theatre Journal* 8 (Dec. 1956): 269.

22. Ibid., pp. 269–70.

23. Providence *Post*, 6 Jan. 1847. GPH, Tex.

24. Providence *Post*, 1 Feb. 1847. GPH, Tex.

25. Providence *Daily Evening Transcript*, 4 May 1847.

26. Providence *Daily Evening Transcript*, 6 June 1847.

27. C. Blake, *An Historical Account of the Providence Stage* (Providence, R.I., 1868), p. 252.

28. Providence *Daily Evening Transcript*. This is an earlier use of "vaudeville" to suggest a variety performance than the 1862 dates given by the OED.

29. Macdonald, p. 369.

30. *The Iron Chest*, Modern Standard Drama ed., HTC. It is Laff's copy and his role, the comic farmboy Samson Rawbold, is slashed to ribbons.

31. Aiken.

32. S. A. Eliot, *A History of Cambridge, Massachusetts (1630–1913)* (Cambridge, Mass., 1913), p. 200; S. A. Drake, ed. *History of Middlesex County, Massachusetts* (Boston, 1880) 2:224–26; Autograph letter signed from James A. Fox to Gov. J. A. Andrew (29 Mar. 1861), Massachusetts Historical Society. On his mother-in-law's side, James may have married into a branch of the family that produced Lizzie Borden.

33. 30 June 1849; HTC bills.

34. Playbill, Odeon Theatre, Providence, 27, 29 June 1850, Tex.

35. HTC bills; Providence *Morning Mirror* advertisements, 27 and 28 June, 1850. For details about the Providence Museum Company, see D. B. Wilmeth, "Providence Museum Co.," in *American Theatre Companies 1749–1887*, ed. W. B. Durham (Westport, Conn., 1986), pp. 416–26.

36. Playbills, advertisements, GPH, Tex.

37. N. Paine, "The Drama in Worcester," in *History of Worcester County, Mass.,* comp. D. H. Hurd (Philadelphia, 1889) 2:1542–43; E. B. Crane, ed. *History of Worcester County, Massachusetts* (New York and Chicago, 1924) 1:416; P. H. Cook, *History of the Drama in Worcester,* unpub. typescript, Library of American Antiquarian Society.

38. *The Heart of the Commonwealth; or, Worcester As It Is* (Worcester, Mass., 1856), p. 162.

39. GPH data. HTC bills for Providence and Worcester.

40. I. R. Tyrrel, *Sobering Up: From Temperance to Prohibition in Antebellum America, 1800–1860* (Westport, Conn., 1979), pp. 92–124.

41. Worcester *Daily Spy,* 3 Apr. 1851.

42. Worcester *Daily Morning Telegraph,* 5 Apr. 1851.

43. Worcester *Daily Morning Telegraph,* 7 Apr. 1851.

44. Worcester *Palladium,* 9 Apr. 1851.

4. New York Opportunities
(pp. 45–58)

1. Lady E. Stuart-Wortley, *Travels in the United States etc. during 1849 and 1850* (New York, 1851), p. 146.

2. B. Still, *Mirror for Gotham: New York as Seen by Contemporaries from Dutch Days to the Present* (New York, 1956), p. 129; E. K. Spann, *The New Metropolis: New York City 1840–1857* (New York, 1981), pp. 23, 26.

3. Quoted in Still, p. 133.

4. M. C. Henderson, *The City and the Theatre: New York Playhouses from Bowling Green to Times Square* (Clifton, N.J., 1973), p. 93; Still, p. 133.

5. W. F. Barnard, *Forty Years at the Five Points* (New York, 1893), quoting from S. Robinson, *Hot Corn: Life Scenes in New York Illustrated* (New York, 1854); C. Dickens, *American Notes and Pictures from Italy* (London, 1898), p. 104.

6. H. Asbury, *The Gangs of New York: An Informal History of the Underworld* (Garden City, N.Y., 1928), chapters 1 and 2.

7. W. K. Northall, *Before and Behind the Curtain* (New York, 1851), p. 152; O. S. Coad and E. Mims, Jr., *The American Stage* (New Haven, 1929), p. 111; Henderson, pp. 66, 69.

8. "The Declining Days of the Old Chatham," N. Y. *Clipper,* 19 Jan. 1878, p. 341; J. B. Howe, *A Cosmopolitan Actor: His Adventures All Over the World* (London, 1888), p. 67; "Purdy's National Theatre," HTC clippings.

9. *Spirit of the Times,* 21 Dec. 1850, p. 528; 30 Nov. 1850, p. 492; *Figaro! or Corbyn's Chronicle of Amusements* 4 (21 Sept. 1850): 34; 5 (28 Sept. 1850): 47.

10. *Figaro!* 8 (9 Oct. 1850): 94.

11. F. C. Bangs, "Recollections of Players, II," N.Y. *Dramatic Mirror,* 5 Feb. 1898, p. 24; E. F. Edgett, "Charles Burke," DAB, 3:280–91; J. Carboy, "Theatric Reminiscences," in *Records of the New York Stage* (scrapbook c. 1905, HTC); "Charles Burke," N.Y. *Dramatic News,* 26 Nov. 1881.

12. "The Declining Days of the Old Chatham"; F. Herring, "Reminiscences of Fanny Herring," N.Y. *Dramatic Mirror,* 12 July 1902, p. 3.

13. "The Star at the Bowery Theatre," unident. clipping, HTC.

14. "The Great Pantomimist," 1874, unident. clipping, HTC.

15. W. S. Howard, *From Slavery to Prohibition: A Dramatic History of the Drama "Uncle Tom's Cabin"* (unpub. typescript, Tex).

16. "The Declining Days of the Old Chatham"; G. C. D. Odell, *Annals of the New York Stage* (New York, 1931) 6:37; "The Great Pantomimist"; "The American Grimaldi," *N.Y. Clipper*, 3 Nov. 1877; *Porter's Spirit of the Times*, 25 Dec. 1858, p. 552. According to F. C. Wemyss's *Chronology of the American Stage* (1852), p. 168, and Fox's obituary in the N.Y. *Times*, 25 Oct. 1877, he had made his debut at the National in *Demon of the Desert*, but Odell records no such play in his *Annals*.

17. *Spirit of the Times*, 20 Dec. 1851, p. 520.

18. "Barnaby," "Theatrical Reminiscence. G. L. Fox," N.Y. *Herald*, undated clipping, HTC.

19. [G. W. Curtis], "Editor's Easy Chair," *Harper's* 74 (Mar. 1887): 644.

20. E. Crapsey, *The Nether Side of New York; or, The Vice, Crime and Poverty of the Great Metropolis (1872)*, (Montclair, N.J., 1969), pp. 123–24.

21. J. H. Browne, *The Great Metropolis: A Mirror of New York* (Hartford, Conn., 1869), p. 430.

22. *Prompter* 1 (June 1850): 3, quoted in D. Grimsted, *Meldrama Unveiled: American Theatre Culture 1800–1850* (Chicago, 1968), p. 233n. See also G. Lening, *Die Nachtseiten von New York und dessen Verbrecherwelt von der Fünften Avenue bis zu den Five Points* (New York, 1873), pp. 582–86; and J. D. McCabe, Jr., *Lights and Shadows of New York Life* (Philadelphia, 1872), pp. 477–83.

23. Odell, 6:38; T. A. Brown, "Theatre in America," N.Y. *Clipper*, 1889.

24. 8 Feb. 1851, p. 612.

25. N.Y. City Directory, 1851–52.

26. H. Watkins, *One Man in His Time: The Adventures of H. Watkins Strolling Player 1845–1863 from His Journal by Maud and Otis Skinner* (Philadelphia, 1938), p. 105.

27. "Mrs. E. A. Eberle," N.Y. *Dramatic Mirror*, 22 Oct. 1898.

28. 14 Mar. 1853, p. 156.

29. N.Y. *Herald*, 25 Oct. 1877, p. 7.

30. The extant playbill, GPH, neglects to state in which city; C. H. Macdonald, "Memoirs of the Original Little Eva," *Educational Theatre Journal* 8 (Dec. 1956): 270.

31. A. J. Weise, *History of the City of Troy* (Troy, N.Y., 1876), pp. 199–200; I. R. Tyrrel, *Sobering Up: From Temperance to Prohibition in Antebellum America, 1800–1860* (Westport, Conn., 1979), p. 114.

32. R. Hayner, *Troy and Rensselaer County New York: A History* (New York, 1925) 2:691; A. J. Weise, *Troy's One Hundred Years 1789–1889* (Troy, N.Y., 1891), pp. 162, 229.

33. Weise, *Troy's One Hundred Years*, p. 239.

34. *Northern Budget*, 13 Mar. 1852, quoted in A. S. Downer, "Cordelia Howard," in *Notable American Women* (Cambridge, Mass., 1971) 2:224.

35. *Northern Budget*, 26 Mar. 1852.

36. Quoted in Macdonald, p. 271, from Mary Hewins.

37. Playbill, Tex; *The Northern Budget*, 17 Apr. 1852, Tex.

38. Playbill, Tex.

39. C. Bode, *The Anatomy of American Popular Culture 1840–1861* (Berkeley and Los Angeles, 1959), p. 185.

40. T. A. Brown, "The Chatham Theatre," N.Y. *Clipper*, 1889, clipping HTC; Odell, 6:228–29.

41. N.Y. *Herald*, 3 Sept. 1852.

42. Playbills, Tex.

5. Uncle Tom's Cabin *and the Triumph of Sentiment*
(pp. 59–70)

1. *Northern Budget,* 6 Nov. 1852.

2. *Northern Budget,* 19 Oct. 1852.

3. Troy *Daily Times,* 11 Oct. 1852; C. H. Macdonald, "Memoirs of the Original Little Eva," *Educational Theatre Journal* 8 (Dec. 1956): 271.

4. *Northern Budget,* 26 Nov. 1852.

5. H. Birdoff, *The World's Greatest Hit—Uncle Tom's Cabin* (New York, 1947), p. 40–53. Although Birdoff's book is full of interesting material, it is presented in an annoyingly novelized manner and lacks any formal ascription of sources.

6. Quoted in Birdoff, p. 56.

7. "A Pioneer in 'Uncle Tom,'" N.Y. *Sun,* 7 Sept. 1902, p. 596.

8. "The Declining Days of the Old Chatham," N.Y. *Clipper* (29 Jan. 1887), pp. 721–22.

9. "A Pioneer in 'Uncle Tom.'"

10. H. P. Stone, "Memories of Uncle Tom's Cabin," N.Y. *Dramatic Mirror,* 28 Mar. 1901.

11. N.Y. *Times,* 19 July 1853, I, 1.

12. Ibid.

13. G. L. Aiken, *Uncle Tom's Cabin; or, Life among the Lowly* (New York, n.d.), act 1, scene 4.

14. N.Y. *Times,* 19 July 1859.

15. Macdonald, p. 272.

16. C. Bode, *The Anatomy of American Popular Culture 1840–1861* (Berkeley and Los Angeles, 1959), p. 185.

17. N.Y. *Times,* 19 July 1859.

18. "Interview with J. D. Chapman," N.Y. *Dramatic Mirror,* 29 June 1901, p. 15.

19. N.Y. *Times,* 19 July 1859. See also *Spirit of the Times,* 6 Aug. 1853, p. 300, which disapproved of the crudeness and absurdity of the play, but commended the acting and the morality.

20. Bode, p. 35.

21. "Marlowe," "Uncle Tom's Cabin," N.Y. *Dramatic Mirror,* Christmas, 1905, p. vii.

22. G. C. D. Odell, *Annals of the New York Stage* (New York, 1931) 6:238.

23. J. B. Howe, *A Cosmopolitan Actor: His Adventures All Over the World* (London, 1888), p. 67.

24. 10 Sept. 1853, p. 360.

25. N.Y. *Clipper,* 29 Jan. 1887, p. 722; C. Burnham, "Eventful Life of the Chatham Theatre," N.Y. *Sun,* 6 May 1923.

26. N.Y. *Clipper,* 29 Jan. 1887.

27. Birdoff, p. 100.

28. E. K. Spann, *The New Metropolis: New York City 1840–1857* (New York, 1981), p. 309.

29. *Spirit of the Times,* 21 Jan. 1854, p. 588.

30. R. Welter, *The Mind of America 1820–1860* (New York, 1975), pp. 339–40, 352.

31. *Spirit of the Times,* 21 Jan. 1854, p. 588.

32. Macdonald, p. 273.

6. The Chatham Street Theatre
(pp. 71–83)

1. *Spirit of the Times*, 7 Feb. 1852, p. 612.

2. Quoted in H. Birdoff, *The World's Greatest Hit—Uncle Tom's Cabin* (New York, 1947), p. 24.

3. Birdoff, pp. 94–96.

4. 27 May 1854, p. 180.

5. *Spirit of the Times*, 27 Jan. 1855, p. 595; "Recollection," unident. clipping dated Aug. 29, HTC.

6. E. K. Spann, *The New Metropolis: New York City 1840–1857* (New York, 1981), pp. 370–73.

7. *Spirit of the Times*, 21 Apr. 1855, p. 120.

8. *Spirit of the Times*, 22 Sept. 1855, p. 384; G. C. D. Odell, *Annals of the New York Stage* (New York, 1931) 6:464–65.

9. "Reminiscences of Fanny Herring," N.Y. *Dramatic Mirror*, 12 July 1902, p. 3.

10. D. J. Brown, "Footlight Favorites Forty Years Ago: A Stroll Up Broadway," *Valentine's Manual of Old New York*, n.s., 6 (1922): 143; R. E. Sherwood, *Here We Are Again: Recollections of an Old Circus Clown* (Indianapolis, 1926), p. 55.

11. "Reminiscences of Fanny Herring."

12. J. B. Howe, *A Cosmopolitan Actor: His Adventures All Over the World* (London, 1888), p. 74.

13. "The American Grimaldi," N.Y. *Clipper*, 3 Nov. 1877.

14. "Kate Denin," N.Y. *Dramatic Mirror*, 23 July 1910; T. A. Brown, "Kate Denin Wilson," N.Y. *Dramatic Mirror*, 23 Feb. 1907, p. 12; "Huntress," unident. clipping, HTC.

15. Obituary of Mary Hewins Fiske, N.Y. *Clipper*, 9 Feb. 1889, p. 771.

16. 1 Mar. 1856, p. 36.

17. "Purdy's National Theatre," unident. clipping, HTC.

18. *Spirit of the Times*, 31 May 1856, p. 192.

19. *Spirit of the Times*, 28 June 1856; 2 Aug. 1856, p. 300; 16 Aug. 1856.

20. Odell, 6:553.

21. R. L. Cullen, *The Civil War in American Drama before 1900* (Providence, R.I., 1982), p. 13.

22. *Spirit of the Times*, 15 Nov. 1856, p. 480.

23. *Spirit of the Times*, 29 Nov. 1856, p. 504.

24. *Spirit of the Times*, 27 Dec. 1856, p. 552.

25. *Spirit of the Times*, 10 Jan. 1857, p. 76; 17 Jan. 1857, p. 586.

26. *Spirit of the Times*, 7 Mar. 1857, p. 48.

27. Odell, 6:559.

28. 28 Mar. 1857, p. 84. See also G. H. Blayney, "City Life in American Drama, 1825–1860," in *Studies in Honor of John Wilcox* (Detroit, 1958), pp. 99–128; Blayney lists a number of aspects of urban life treated, but does not inquire into the reasons for the popularity of such plays.

29. *Spirit of the Times*, 16 May 1857, p. 168.

30. *Spirit of the Times*, 4 Aug. 1860.

31. *Irishman in Baghdad: A Musical Romance in Two Acts*. Asa Cushman, Prompter, Purdy's National, N.Y. MS. in HTC, Ts 33323.400.

32. *Spirit of the Times*, 27 June 1857, p. 240.

33. *Spirit of the Times*, 15 Aug. 1857, p. 324.

34. "The Great Pantomimist," unident. clipping, HTC.

35. *Spirit of the Times*, 29 Aug. 1857, p. 348; 5 Sept. 1857, p. 360; 12 Sept. 1857, p. 372.

36. Spann, p. 349.

37. *Spirit of the Times*, 12 Dec. 1857, p. 528.

38. *Spirit of the Times*, 7 Nov. 1857, p. 168; 19 Dec. 1857, p. 540.

39. *Spirit of the Times*, 2 Jan. 1858, p. 564; 16 Jan. 1858, p. 588.

40. Odell, 7:44–51.

41. "Our Portrait Gallery," N.Y. *Clipper*, 16 July 1870, p. 114.

42. "Recollection," unident. clipping, HTC.

43. T. A. Brown, "Theatre in America," N.Y. *Clipper*, undated clipping, HTC.

44. T. A. Brown, *A History of the American Stage* (New York, 1870), p. 301.

7. The Old Bowery and the New
(pp. 84–96)

1. O. Logan, *Before the Footlights and Behind the Scenes* (Philadelphia, 1870), p. 385. For a study of the political-aesthetic nexus at the Bowery Theatre before Fox's advent, see B. A. McConachie, "'The Theatre of the Mob': Apocalyptic Melodrama and Preindustrial Riots in Antebellum New York," in *Theatre for Working-Class Audiences in the United States, 1830–1980*, ed. B. A. McConachie and D. Friedman (Westport, Conn., 1985), pp. 19–33.

2. "Charles Pope's Diary," *Educational Theatre Journal* 7:4 (Dec. 1955):332. "Half grown men" is evidently Pope's translation of some word like "adolescents" into the German "Halbwüchsiger" and then back into English.

3. *Spirit of the Times*, 6 May 1858, p. 264.

4. Col. T. W. Knox, in Mrs. H. Campbell, Col. T. W. Knox, and Supt. T. Byrnes, *Darkness and Daylight . . . in New York* (New Haven, 1896), p. 463.

5. D. J. Brown, "Footlight Favorites Forty Years Ago. A Stroll Up Broadway," *Valentine's Manual of Old New York* n.s. 6 (1922):143; H. L. Mencken, *The American Language* (New York, 1923), Supp. 2:163.

6. J. H. Browne, *The Great Metropolis: A Mirror of New York* (Hartford, Conn., 1869), p. 430; Knox, pp. 462–63. See also T. J. Shank, "Theatre for the Majority: Its Influence on a Nineteenth Century American Theatre," *Educational Theatre Journal* 11:3 (Oct. 1959):188–99, for the Bowery Theatre's cultivation of its audience over time.

7. This taste lasted well into the century. Compare this dialogue from Horatio Alger's *Frank Fowler the Cash Boy* (1887):

"I'm going to the Old Bowery to-night, if nothin' happens. There's a stavin' play up now. Seen it?"

"No, what is it?"

"It's 'The Gory Gladiator; or, The Pool of Blood.'"

"Is it one of Shakespeare's plays?" asked Frank, smiling.

"Not much," said the bootblack scornfully. "I seen one of Shakespeare's plays once. He can't begin to write a play like the 'Gory Gladiator.' It's bully."

8. "J. K. P. Doesticks" [Mortimer Thomson], *Doesticks What He Says* (New York, 1855), p. 232.

9. C. Burnham, "New York's Historic Theatres No. 1: The Old Bowery," *Theatre*, Mar. 1918, pp. 160–61; W. Seymour, "G. L. Fox as a Comedian," N.Y. *Herald*, 5 Feb. 1924; J. D. McCabe, Jr., *Lights and Shadows of New York Life* (Philadelphia, 1872),

pp. 473–83; and G. Lening, *Die Nachtseiten von New York und dessen Verbrecherwelt von der Fünften Avenue bis zu den Five Points* (New York, 1873), pp. 585–86.

10. "The American Grimaldi," N.Y. *Clipper*, 3 Nov. 1877.

11. J. B. Howe, *A Cosmopolitan Actor: His Adventures All Over the World* (London, 1888), p. 89.

12. G. C. D. Odell, *Annals of the New York Stage* (New York, 1931) 7:134.

13. Ibid., 7:136.

14. Howe, pp. 89–90.

15. J. J. McCloskey, "The Old Bowery Theatre," N.Y. *Dramatic Mirror*, Christmas, 1896, p. 51.

16. "Our Portrait Gallery. J. W. Lingard. Actor and Manager. His Life, Death and Burial," N.Y. *Clipper*, 16 July 1870, p. 14.

17. McCloskey, p. 51.

18. F. C. Wemyss, "Supplement," to *The Guide to the Stage* by L. T. Rede (New York, 1864), p. 14.

19. N.Y. *Herald*, 16 Sept. 1859; *Spirit of the Times*, 16 July 1859, p. 276; 13 Aug. 1859, p. 324; 3 Sept. 1859, p. 360; T. A. Brown, "The New Bowery Theatre," N.Y. *Clipper*, 20 Dec. 1890, p. 644; A. F. Harlow, *Old Bowery Days* (New York, 1931), p. 273.

20. N.Y. *Times*, 21 Jan. 1860, p. 7; Odell, 8, 241.

21. Boucicault v. Fox *et al.*, The Federal Cases, Book 3, p. 977. See S. Faulkner, "The Octoroon War," *Educational Theatre Journal* 15:1 (Mar. 1863): 33–38.

22. N.Y. *Herald*, 26 Nov. 1859; *Spirit of the Times*, 23 June 1860, p. 256.

23. *Spirit of the Times*, 22 Sept. 1860, p. 48.

24. Odell, 7, 332.

25. "Old Time Stage Favorites," unident. clipping, Lincoln Center; Townsend Walsh notes, Lincoln Center.

26. "Humpty Dumpty Interviewed—What He Said and How He Said It," *Spirit of the Times*, 31 Jan. 1874.

27. H. S. Renton, "Humpty Dupmty [*sic*] and Others," N.Y. *Sun*, 19 Apr. 1929.

28. E. Cowell, *The Cowells in America Being the Diary of Mrs. Sam Cowell . . . 1860–1861*, ed. M. W. Disher (London, 1934), pp. 279–80. Flora F. is of course the garrulous Mrs. Finching in Dickens's *Little Dorrit*.

29. Downplayed delivery and enigmatic expression had long been associated with Yankee comedians like Joshua S. Silsbee. Keaton, curiously, attributed this trait to the English, which suggests that by the turn of the nineteenth century, American comedians had become cruder than their predecessors. "I made a thorough study of how English comedians, whom I consider the most accomplished, attained their results, and gradually I penetrated their secret. It lies simply in the fact that the English comedian is always a little more serious than life itself. On the basis of this knowledge I set myself to the task of remaining completely serious in any situation." Quoted in R. Fülöp-Miller, *The Motion Picture in America: A History in the Making* (New York, 1938), p. 129.

30. "The Great Pantomimist," 1874, unident. clipping, HTC.

31. Translated from Champfleury [Jules Fleury-Husson], *Souvenirs des Funambules* (1859) (Génève, 1971), p. 252.

32. *Bereavement*, Ball, written, composed and dedicated to G. L. Fox by John Mahon, 1861. Tex.

8. *Lieutenant Fox Goes to War*
(pp. 97–109)

1. G. C. D. Odell, *Annals of the New York Stage* (New York, 1936), 8:33.

2. W. J. Tenney, *The Military and Naval History of the Rebellion in the United States*. (New York, 1865), p. 28.

3. F. Moore, ed. *The Rebellion Records: A Diary of American Events*. (New York, 1861–68), 1:21, 62; S. A. Eliot, *A History of Cambridge, Massachusetts (1630–1913)* (Cambridge, Mass., 1913), p. 200.

4. Col. S. W. Burt, *My Memories of the Military History of the State of New York during the War for the Union 1861–65* (Albany, 1902), pp. 39–40.

5. *Mémoires et pantomimes des frères Hanlon-Lees* (Paris, 1880), pp. 72–73.

6. W. E. Horton, *Driftwood of the Stage* (Detroit, 1904), p. 301.

7. N.Y. *Tribune*, 24 Apr. 1861, quoted in Moore, 1:141–42.

8. S. G. Hoytes, "G. L. Fox as Warrior," N.Y. *Sun*, undated clipping, Lincoln Center; N.Y. *Tribune*, 24 Apr. 1861.

9. M. Leech, *Reveille in Washington 1860–1865* (New York, 1941), p. 76.

10. Leech, p. 85.

11. N.Y. *Tribune*, 26 July 1861, p. 3.

12. *Spirit of the Times*, 11 May 1861, p. 144.

13. *Spirit of the Times*, 25 May 1861, p. 192.

14. R. L. Cullen, *The Civil War in American Drama before 1900* (Providence, R.I., 1982), pp. 17–18.

15. "The American Grimaldi," N.Y. *Clipper*, 3 Nov. 1877.

16. F. H. Dyer, comp., *A Compendium of the War of the Rebellion* (Des Moines, 1908), pp. 187, 1408; N.Y. *World*, 23 July 1862, quoted in Moore 1:182; T. S. Townsend, *The Honors of the Empire State in the War of the Rebellion* (New York, 1889), p. 231.

17. Leech, pp. 104–5.

18. F. Phisterer, comp., *New York in the War of the Rebellion 1861 to 1865* (Albany, 1890), p. 288.

19. Benjamin F. Groves to James F. Groves, N.Y., 15 Aug. 1861, in *The War of the Rebellion: A Compilation of the Official Records of the Union and Confederate Armies* (Washington, D.C., 1880), Second Series, 2:636.

20. *Spirit of the Times*, 2 Aug. 1861, p. 352.

21. "George L. Fox at Home," 1877, unident. clipping, Lincoln Center; Townsend Walsh notes, Lincoln Center.

22. G. L. Fox obituary, N.Y. *Times*, 25 Oct. 1877.

23. G. S. Parks, "Old Stage Friends," N.Y. *Tribune*, 8 May 1923.

24. *Spirit of the Times*, 26 Oct. 1861, p. 128.

25. "The American Grimaldi"; N.Y. *Tribune*, 2 Dec. 1861, p. 2.

26. N.Y. *Tribune*, 2 Dec. 1861, p. 1.

27. *Spirit of the Times*, 21 Dec. 1861, p. 256.

28. Cullen, pp. 17–18.

29. G. L. Fox obituary, N.Y. *Times*, 25 Oct. 1877.

30. M. C. Henderson, *The City and the Theatre: New York Playhouses from Bowling Green to Times Square* (Clifton, N.J., 1973), p. 114.

31. N.Y. *Clipper*, 3 Nov. 1877; Olympic Theatre Account Books, Tex.

32. Odell, 7:418.

33. Olympic Theatre Account Books, Tex.

34. Bowery Theatre Account Books 21 Apr. 1862–28 Nov. 1862, HTC.

35. *Spirit of the Times*, 2 Aug. 1862, p. 341.

36. Bowery Theatre Account Books, HTC.

37. *Spirit of the Times*, 20 Sept. 1862, p. 48.

38. *Spirit of the Times*, 8 Nov. 1862, p. 160; 27 Feb. 1862, p. 272.

39. 2 Nov. 1862. Program, Tex.

40. Program, Tex.

41. J. J. McCloskey, "The Old Bowery Theatre," N.Y. *Dramatic Mirror*, Christmas, 1896, p. 51.

42. *Spirit of the Times*, 21 Mar. 1863, p. 48.

43. 27 Oct. 1862 and 15 Dec. 1862, respectively: Odell, 7:490.

44. *Spirit of the Times*, 10 Jan. 1863, p. 16.

45. C. H. Macdonald, "Memoirs of the Original Little Eva," *Educational Theatre Journal* 8 (Dec. 1956): 278.

46. M. E. Folsom, "A Star Pantomimist," N.Y. *Sun*, undated clipping, Lincoln Center.

47. L. S. Levy, *Grace Notes in American History* (Norman, Okla., 1967), p. 173.

48. *Jack and the Beanstalk* property list, McCaddon Collection, Princeton University.

49. Townsend, pp. 231–32; *War of the Rebellion*, Series One, 27, Part 2: 212, 219, 227, 232, 245; H. Asbury, *The Gangs of New York* (Garden City, N.Y., 1928), pp. 118–47; R. Hofstadter and M. Wallace, eds., *American Violence, A Documentary History* (New York, 1971), pp. 211–17.

50. "Barnaby," "Theatrical Reminiscence. G. L. Fox," New York *Herald*, undated clipping, HTC.

51. Macdonald, p. 29; "American Grimaldi"; Townsend Walsh notes. Lincoln Center.

9. The Triumph of Pantomime
(pp. 110–19)

1. Tex.

2. S. Bleecker, "Memoir of the Author," in *Denier's Parlor Pantomimes* (New York, c. 1864), pp. 3–4; "Famed as Clown," Chicago *Chronicle*, 14 July 1904, p. 6; C. W. Collins, "Humpty Dumpty's Old Age," *The Green Room Album*, Oct. 1910, pp. 761–66; "Tony Denier, H.D.," N.Y. *Dramatic Mirror*, 6 Jan. 1906, p. 14; obituary of Emma Denier, N.Y. *Dramatic Mirror*, 17 June 1899, p. 12.

3. N.Y. *Clipper*, 5 Feb. 1876, p. 351.

4. "Now Living in Poorhouse," N.Y. *Journal*, 21 Sept. 1916; H. Renton, "Humpty Dupmty [*sic*] and Others," N.Y. *Sun*, 19 Apr. 1929.

5. C. H. Macdonald, "Memoirs of the Original Little Eva," *Educational Theatre Journal* 8 (Dec. 1956): 278.

6. *Wilkes's Spirit of the Times*, 22 Aug. 1863, p. 400. See also G. Speaight, "Professor Pepper's Ghost," *Revue d'histoire du théâtre* 1 (1963): 48–56; L. Senelick, "Pepper's Ghost Faces the Camera," *History of Photography*, Jan.–Mar. 1983, pp. 69–72.

7. *Spirit of the Times*, 5 Sept. 1863, p. 16. For a discussion of this change, see M. M. McDowell, *American Attitudes Towards Death, 1825–1865* (unpub. Ph.D. diss., Brandeis University, 1977), pp. 410, 413–17; for the earlier period, see C. O. Jackson, ed., *Passing: The Vision of Death in America* (Westport, Conn., 1977).

8. [William Winter?], N.Y. *Tribune*, 21 Oct. 1865, p. 6. For the story of Denier and Donato, see W. J. Lawrence, "Pantomime in the United States," *Theatre*, 1 Feb. 1896,

pp. 85–86. When Donato's agent protested that it had taken the one-legged artiste four years to learn to dance, Barnum replied, "I don't know about that, but I've got a man who can do it in four weeks."

9. Unident. clipping, Tex.

10. G. C. D. Odell, *Annals of the New York Stage* (New York, 1931), 7:656.

11. *Spirit of the Times*, 3 Mar. 1866, p. 16; N.Y. *Daily Tribune*, 26 Feb. 1866, p. 16.

12. N.Y. *Tribune*, 19 Mar. 1866, p. 8.

13. J. J. McCloskey, "The Old Bowery Theatre," N.Y. *Dramatic Mirror*, Christmas, 1896, p. 51.

14. *Spirit of the Times*, 21 Apr. 1866, p. 128.

15. *Spirit of the Times*, 5 May 1866, p. 160.

16. N.Y. *Tribune*, 19 Feb. 1866, p. 3.

17. *Spirit of the Times*, 24 Mar. 1866, p. 64.

18. *Porter's Spirit of the Times*, 2 Jan. 1858, p. 288.

19. G. C. Howard, *Jack & Gill Went Up the Hill* (New York, 1866); scenery list for *Jack & Gill*, McCaddon Collection, Princeton University.

10. Barnum's and Beyond
(pp. 120–31)

1. W. Thornbury, *Criss-Cross Journey* (London, 1873) 1:175, quoted in N. Harris, *Humbug: The Art of P. T. Barnum* (Boston, 1973), pp. 105–7.

2. W. W. Appleton, "The Marvellous Museum of P. T. Barnum," *Revue d'histoire du théâtre* 1 (1963): 59–61; and A. H. Saxon, "P. T. Barnum's American Museum," *Seaport: New York's History Magazine* 20 (Winter 1986/87): 27–33. Barnum himself barely alludes to the theatrical aspect of the museum in his autobiographies; see his *Struggles and Triumphs; or, The Life of P. T. Barnum, written by himself*, ed. G. S. Bryan, 2 vols. (New York, 1927).

3. H. James, *A Small Boy and Others* (New York, 1913), p. 162.

4. N.Y. *Tribune*, 9 July 1866; obituary of Emma Denier, N.Y. *Dramatic Mirror*, 17 June 1899, p. 12.

5. G. C. Howard, *Jack & Gill Went Up the Hill* (New York, 1866), Barnum's American Museum version.

6. N.Y. *Tribune*, 9 July 1866.

7. N.Y. *Tribune*, 16 July 1866, p. 5.

8. Partial MS. of *Jack & Gill* scenario, McCaddon Collection, Princeton University.

9. See R. Hofstadter and M. Wallace, eds., *American Violence, A Documentary History* (New York, 1971), pp. 14–15ff.; R. Lane, *Policing the City: Boston 1822–1885* (Cambridge, Mass., 1967), ch. 1–4; B. A. McConachie, "'The Theatre of the Mob': Apocalyptic Melodrama and Preindustrial Riots in Antebellum New York," in *Theatres for Working-Class Audiences in the United States, 1830–1980*, ed. B. A. McConachie and D. Friedman (Westport, Conn., 1985), pp. 17–46. For the emotional context of urban social control, see P. Boyer, *Urban Masses and Moral Order in America, 1820–1920* (Cambridge, Mass., 1978), pp. 68–70, 123–31. Other worthwhile works include I. J. Sloan, *Our Violent Past* (New York, 1970), and O. Deman's, *America the Violent* (New York, 1970).

10. N.Y. *Times*, 16 July 1866, p. 5.

11. N.Y. *Tribune*, 3 Aug. 1866, p. 5.

12. N.Y. *Tribune*, 24 Aug. 1866, p. 5.

13. N.Y. *Tribune*, 1 Sept. 1866, p. 7.

14. "Barnaby," "Theatrical Reminiscence. G. L. Fox," N.Y. *Herald*, undated clipping, HTC.

15. *Spirit of the Times*, 6 Oct. 1866, p. 96.

16. N.Y. *Mirror*, 6 July 1887.

17. *Spirit of the Times*, 27 Apr. 1867, p. 144.

18. N.Y. *Tribune*, 22 Nov. 1866, p. 7.

19. "Destructive conflagration. The New Bowery Theatre in ruins," unident. clipping, 18 Dec. 1866, HTC; G. C. D. Odell, *Annals of the New York Stage* (New York, 1936) 8:177; "Our Portrait Gallery. James W. Lingard, Actor and Manager. His Life, Death, and Burial," N.Y. *Clipper*, 16 July 1870, p. 114.

20. "Our Portrait Gallery"; T. A. Brown, *A History of the American Stage* (New York, 1870), p. 221.

21. *Spirit of the Times*, 12 Jan. 1867, p. 329; 19 Jan. 1867, p. 332.

22. N.Y. *Tribune*, 11 Mar. 1867; *Spirit of the Times*, 23 Mar. 1867, p. 64.

23. N.Y. *Clipper*, 13 Oct. 1866, p. 214.

24. "Off the Stage, or, In Front of the Footlights," *Sporting Times*, 15 Oct. 1868.

25. R. E. Sherwood, *Here We Are Again: Recollections of an Old Circus Clown* (Indianapolis, 1926), pp. 54–55; he claims it occurred at Tony Pastor's Bowery Theatre, but Fox and Herring never worked together for Pastor.

26. N.Y. *Tribune*, 18 Mar. 1867, p. 64.

27. C. H. Macdonald, "Memoirs of the Original Little Eva," *Educational Theatre Journal* 8 (Dec. 1856): 278–79.

28. Odell, 8:172.

29. N.Y. *Times*, 3 Apr. 1867, p. 5.

30. F. Hofele, *Bowery Theatre Property Books*, HTC.

31. N.Y. *Tribune*, 6 Apr. 1867, p. 4.

32. Unident. clipping, Lincoln Center.

33. N.Y. *Times*, 13 Apr. 1867, p. 5.

34. N.Y. *Clipper*, 28 July 1866, p. 126.

35. "The American Grimaldi," N.Y. *Clipper*, 3 Nov. 1877.

36. G. L. Fox to Augustin Daly, 14 May 1867, ALS in Folger Shakespeare Library, Washington, D.C.

37. N.Y. *Tribune*, 22 July 1867, p. 7.

38. N.Y. *Tribune*, 23 July 1867, p. 4.

39. Sherwood, pp. 52–53. In A. Denier, *Shadow Pantomimes; or, Harlequin in the Shades* (New York, 1868), there is a panto called "The Magic Cask" which seems to be a recording of this routine, and clearly derives from the old "Magic Barrel."

40. T. A. Brown, *A History of the New York Stage from the First Performance in 1732 to 1901* (New York, 1903) 3:117.

41. "The Great Pantomimist," unident. clipping in Townsend Walsh Collection, Lincoln Center.

42. "Joe Jorum," "Our Dramatic Letter," unident. clipping, HTC.

43. E.g., B. Hewitt, *Theatre U.S.A. 1665 to 1957* (New York, 1959), p. 208. For a full study of the stage Yankee, see F. Hodge, *Yankee Theatre: The Image of America on the Stage* (Austin, 1964); for the stage Yankee as a type of the American character, see K. Halttunen, *Confidence Men and Painted Women* (New Haven, 1982), pp. 30–32.

11. The Rise of Humpy Dumpty
(pp. 132–49)

1. H. S. Renton, "More about Fox," N.Y. *Sun*, 2 May 1929; R. Fraser, "Decline of the Stage Clown," N.Y. *Herald*, 22 Sept. 1889; "Humpty Dumpty Interviewed—What He Said, and How He Said It!" *Spirit of the Times*, 31 Jan. 1874; J. Carboy, "Theatric Reminiscences," in *Records of the New York Stage*, c. 1905, HTC; "The American Grimaldi," N.Y. *Clipper*, 3 Nov. 1877; "Off the Stage, or, In Front of the Footlights," *Sporting Times and Theatrical News*, 15 Oct. 1868; "Poor Old Humpty Dumpty," unident. clipping, HTC; "American Pantomime," N.Y. *Mirror*, 18 Feb. 1882, p. 6

2. "The Star at the Broadway Theatre." Unident. clipping, HTC.

3. M. C. Henderson, *The City and the Theatre: New York Playhouses from Bowling Green to Times Square* (Clifton, N.J., 1973), p. 177; "The American Grimaldi"; Olympic Theatre clippings, HTC; "The late Clifton Tayleure," N.Y. *Clipper*, 25 Apr. 1891.

4. W. H. Draper, *George L. Fox, Comedian, in Pantomime and Travesty* (unpub. Ph.D. dissertation, University of Illinois, 1958),p. 77.

5. N.Y. *Tribune*, 24 Oct. 1867, p. 7.

6. "The late Clifton Tayleure."

7. G. C. D. Odell, "'A Midsummer Night's Dream' on the New York Stage," in *Shakespearean Studies by Members of the Department of English and Comparative Literature in Columbia University*, ed. by J. B. Matthews and A. H. Thorndike (New York, 1916), p. 146; "The Great Pantomimist," 1874, unident. clipping in Townsend Walsh Collection, Lincoln Center.

8. N.Y. *Tribune*, 30 Oct. 1867, p. 2.

9. "The Great Pantomimist," 1874, unident. clipping in Townsend Walsh collection, Lincoln Center.

10. N.Y. *Times*, 29 Oct. 1867, p. 2.

11. C. H. Macdonald, "Memoirs of the Original Little Eva," *Educational Theatre Journal* 8 (Dec. 1956): 279.

12. N.Y. *Herald*, 29 Oct. 1867, p. 7.

13. N.Y. *Clipper*, 9 Nov. 1867, p. 246; 7 Dec. 1867, p. 278.

14. N.Y. *Tribune*, 7 Dec. 1867; 13 Jan. 1868, p. 7.

15. Macdonald, p. 279; Draper, p. 79.

16. N.Y. *Tribune*, 6 Feb. 1868, p. 3.

17. M. R. Werner, *Tammany Hall* (Garden City, N.Y., 1928), p. 153.

18. S. J. Mandelbaum, *Boss Tweed's New York* (New York, 1965), p. 47.

19. Quoted in B. Still, *Mirror for Gotham: New York as Seen by Contemporaries from Dutch Days to the Present* (New York, 1956), p. 174. See also Mandelbaum, pp. 7–50. L. Hershkowitz, *Tweed's New York: Another Look* (Garden City, N.Y., 1977) is another useful work.

20. Quoted in D. T. Lynch, *The Wild Seventies* (New York, 1941), p. 53.

21. Mandelbaum, p. 29.

22. O. S. Coad and E. Mims, Jr., *The American Stage* (New Haven, 1929), pp. 212–13.

23. C. Smith, *Musical Comedy in America* (New York, 1950), p. 7.

24. N.Y. *Clipper*, 12 Oct. 1867, p. 214; 4 Jan. 1868, p. 310; 11 Jan. 1868, p. 318.

25. "Now Living in Poorhouse," N.Y. *Journal*, 21 Sept. 1916.

26. "Bob Fraser on the Pantomimic Art," unident. clipping, HTC.

27. "The late Clifton Tayleure."

28. "Barnaby," "Theatrical Reminiscence. G. L. Fox," N.Y. *Herald*, undated clipping, HTC.

29. G. C. D. Odell, *Annals of the New York Stage* (New York, 1938) 10:9; T. A. Brown, *A History of the New York Stage from the First Performance in 1732 to 1901* (New York, 1903) 2:159; N.Y. *Clipper Almanac for 1874*, p. 23.

30. "Fox in Pantomime," N.Y. *Dramatic News*, 30 Oct. 1875, p. 2.

31. N.Y. *Herald*, 11 Mar. 1868, p. 4.

32. N.Y. *Clipper*, 21 Mar. 1868, p. 398.

33. *Spirit of the Times*, 14 Mar. 1868, p. 64.

34. Werner, pp. 118–19.

35. "The late Clifton Tayleure."

36. J. Denier, *Humpty Dumpty, a Pantomime in a Prologue and One Act . . . as originally played by George L. Fox* (New York, c. 1872), pp. 5–6.

37. D. C. Seitz, *The Dreadful Decade . . . 1869–1879* (Indianapolis, 1926), p. 57.

38. J. Denier, pp. 6–7. In an 1872 revival, Jersey's reply "Suppose a modest Congressman you try / who wouldn't come the back-pay grab on the treasur-y," referred to the attempt by the United States Congress to raise its salary retroactively by two years.

39. N.Y. *Tribune*, 11 Mar. 1868, p. 4; notes to *Humpty Dumpty* prologue, McCaddon Collection, Princeton University.

40. Macdonald, p. 278.

41. "The late Clifton Tayleure."

42. N.Y. *Clipper*, 21 Mar. 1868, p. 398.

43. Lynch, p. 89. Souvenir programme for *Humpty Dumpty*, New York 1868, pp. 8–9, HTC.

44. Lady Emmeline, quoted in K. Halttunen, *Confidence Men and Painted Women* (New Haven, 1982), p. 31. The clown quoted is "Bob Fraser on the Pantomimic Art."

45. "Ghostly Pantomimes," *Houseworld Words* 8:8 (1854): 399.

46. J. Denier, p. 17. C. K. Fox's Pantaloon apparently picked up the nickname "Old One-Two" on account of the resiliency with which he received and recovered from blows.

47. Werner, p. 263.

48. N.Y. *Times*, 11 Mar. 1868, p. 4.

49. *Spirit of the Times*, 24 Mar. 1868, p. 64.

50. *Spirit of the Times*, 11 Apr. 1868, p. 128.

51. N.Y. *Clipper*, 4 Apr. 1868, p. 144; N.Y. *Tribune*, 26 Mar. 1868, p. 2; *Spirit of the Times*, 28 Mar. 1868, p. 96; N.Y. *Clipper*, 13 June 1868.

52. N.Y. *Clipper*, 29 Mar. 1868, p. 406.

53. N.Y. *Clipper*, 28 Apr. 1868, p. 18.

54. Odell, *Annals*, 8:354.

55. N.Y. *Clipper*, 27 June 1868, p. 94.

56. N.Y. *Clipper*, 13 June 1868; 25 July 1868, p. 126.

57. Odell, *Annals*, 8:282.

58. N.Y. *Clipper*, 25 July 1868, p. 126; N.Y. *Tribune*, 8 Sept. 1868, p. 5; 3 Apr. 1868, p. 8; *Spirit of the Times*, 28 Nov. 1868, p. 240; "The late Clifton Tayleure."

59. J. Cowell, *Thirty Years Passed Among the Players* (New York, 1844), p. 74.

60. D. Grimsted, *Melodrama Unveiled: American Theatre Culture 1800–1850* (Chicago, 1968), p. 43; for innovation in theatrical press agentry in the later nineteenth century, see J. L. Ford, *Forty-odd Years in the Literary Shop* (New York, 1921), pp. 135–58.

61. Later, Nast made color transparency drawings of Fox as Humpty to be shown within a frame depicting proscenium boxes filled with a fashionable audience; this toy theatre was published by McLoughlin Brothers. P. McPharlin, *The Puppet Theatre in America* (Boston, 1969), p. 315.

62. A. B. Paine, *Thomas Nast: His Period and His Pictures* (New York, 1904), p. 119.

63. *Spirit of the Times*, 11 July 1868, p. 388; 18 July 1868, p. 408; D. Kelley, "Facts about the Olympic," N.Y. *Herald*, 24 Apr. 1923; *Sporting Times and Theatrical News*, 27 Mar. 1869, p. 12.

64. N.Y. *Clipper*, 17 July 1869, p. 119; N.Y. *Tribune*, 29 Apr. 1868, p. 10; *Spirit of the Times*, 11 July 1868, p. 388.

65. *Spirit of the Times*, 22 Aug. 1868, p. 16.

66. N.Y. *Clipper*, 9 May 1868.

67. N.Y. *Clipper*, 7 Nov. 1868, p. 246. For the ballet in *Humpty Dumpty*, see B. Barker, *Ballet or Ballyhoo* (New York, 1984), pp. 71–82.

68. J. J. Jennings, *Theatrical and Circus Life; or, Secrets of the Stage, Greenroom and Sawdust Arena* (New York, 1882), pp. 382–83.

69. H. Renton, "Humpty Dupmty [*sic*] and Others," N.Y. *Sun*, 19 Apr. 1929.

70. "Bob Fraser on the Pantomimic Art."

71. Odell, *Annals*, 9:152–53.

12. A Hard Act to Follow
(pp. 150–58)

1. "Off the Stage, or, In Front of the Footlights," *Sporting Times and Theatrical News*, 15 Oct. 1868; "The American Grimaldi," N.Y. *Clipper*, 3 Nov. 1877; N.Y. *Clipper*, 24 Oct. 1868, p. 230; "Humpty Dumpty's Widow," N.Y. *Dramatic News*, 9 Feb. 1878. The Howards did not bother to record Georgiana's (or in some accounts, Georgia's) birth in their family Bible, which suggests that she may have been conceived out of wedlock. If so, this leads to a whole line of conjecture as to whether Mattie blackmailed Fox into marriage, and may explain their later bad relations.

2. Obituary of Mary Hewins Fiske, N.Y. *Clipper*, 9 Feb. 1889, p. 771.

3. GPH notes, Tex; obituary of Lydia Fox, N.Y. *Dramatic Mirror*, 7 May 1904, p. 19.

4. N.Y. *Clipper*, 26 Dec. 1868, p. 302; 9 Jan. 1869, p. 318; N.Y. *Tribune*, 9 Jan. 1869, p. 7.

5. M. Felheim, *The Theatre of Augustin Daly* (Cambridge, Mass., 1956), p. 58.

6. Program, HTC.

7. N.Y. *Times*, 26 Jan. 1869; L. A. Croghan, *An Abstract of New York Burlesque 1840–1870* (unpub. Ph.D. dissertation, New York University, 1967) 2:221.

8. Program. See B. Barker, *Ballet or Ballyhoo* (New York, 1984), pp. 71–82.

9. *Spirit of the Times*, 27 Feb. 1869, p. 474; *Sporting Times and Theatrical News*, 1869, p. 12.

10. *Spirit of the Times*, 2 Jan. 1869, p. 320.

11. *Spirit of the Times*, 3 Apr. 1869, p. 112; 15 May 1869, p. 208.

12. J. Carboy, "Theatric Reminiscences," in *Records of the New York Stage*, c. 1905, HTC.

13. G. Carson, "The Great Meddler," *American Heritage*, Dec. 1967, pp. 28–33, 94–99.

14. N.Y. *Tribune*, 19 May 1869, p. 5. See also N.Y. *Clipper*, 31 July 1869, p. 134.

15. 1869, quoted in L. S. Levy, *Grace Notes in American History* (Norman, Okla., 1967), p. 272.

16. N.Y. *Clipper*, 29 May 1869.

17. N.Y. *Clipper*, 8 May 1869; N.Y. *Tribune*, 17 May 1869, p. 17; *Spirit of the Times*, 22 May 1869, p. 224; *Sporting Times and Theatrical News*, 15 June 1869, p. 6.

19. Memoirs of Bolossy Kiralfy (unpub. MS. in possession of Kiralfy family). See also Barker, pp. 82–85.

20. N.Y. *Clipper*, 12 June 1869, p. 78.

21. *Stage*, 8 June 1868, p. 2.

22. N.Y. *Clipper*, 10 July 1869, p. 110; 26 June 1869, p. 94; 3 July 1869, p. 102. Cf. *Sporting Times and Theatrical News*, 10 July 1869, p. 6: "That he has no rival as a pantomimist has been fully demonstrated by the public in their patronage of the Olympic Theater in preference to all others, notwithstanding the amount of imported talent that has been engaged at the various theatres in this city."

23. *Sporting Times and Theatrical News*, 23 May 1869, p. 6.

24. Kiralfy memoirs.

25. N.Y. *Clipper*, 14 Aug. 1869, p. 150.

26. N.Y. *Clipper*, 18 Sept. 1869, p. 190.

27. N.Y. *Clipper*, 31 July 1869, p. 134.

28. *Sporting Times and Theatrical News*, 27 Mar. 1869; 3 Apr. 1869, p. 6.

29. J. C. Foster, *The Seven Dwarfs: Grand Spectacular Pantomime at the Bowery Theatre* (New York, 1869).

30. N.Y. *Clipper*, 23 Jan. 1870, p. 334; 29 Jan. 1870, p. 342.

31. N.Y. *Clipper*, 15 Jan. 1870, p. 326.

32. N.Y. *Clipper*, 12 Feb. 1870, p. 358.

13. Hamlet *and the Triumph of Travesty*
(pp. 159–72)

1. L. A. Croghan, *An Abstract of New York Burlesque 1840–1870* (unpub. Ph.D. dissertation, New York University, 1967) 1:17 ff.

2. N.Y. *Daily Tribune*, 14 Feb. 1870, p. 4.

3. L. Hutton, *Curiosities of the American Stage* (New York, 1891), p. 182.

4. *Spirit of the Times*, 19 Feb. 1870, p. 16.

5. Reconstruction of *Hamlet* based on N.Y. *Clipper*, 26 Feb. 1870, p. 374; *Spirit of the Times*, 19 Feb. 1870, p. 16; N.Y. *Times*, 15 Feb. 1870; N.Y. *Daily Tribune*, 14 Feb. 1870, p. 7; N.Y. *Herald*, 15 Feb. 1870; Hutton, *Curiosities*, pp. 182–85; W. E. Horton, *Driftwood of the Stage* (Detroit, 1904), pp. 189–90. See also W. H. Draper, "George L. Fox's burlesque—*Hamlet*," *Quarterly Journal of Speech* 50 (Dec. 1964): pp. 378–84; Y. Shafer, "George L. Fox and the *Hamlet* Travesty," *Theatre Studies* 24/25 (1977–79): pp. 79–94; "Thomas W.," N.Y. *Sun*, 8 Dec. 1912; Croghan, 2:223–302; C. H. Shattuck, *The Hamlet of Edwin Booth* (Urbana, Ill., 1969), pp. 68–69.

6. *Spirit of the Times*, 19 Feb. 1870, p. 11.

7. "Mr. Fox and 'Hamlet'" (26 Feb. 1870), unident. clipping, HTC.

8. N.Y. *Tribune*, 7 Feb. 1871, p. 5.

9. "Thomas W."

10. K. Goodale, *Behind the Scenes with Edwin Booth* (Boston, 1931), p. 175.

11. W. S. Howard, *From Slavery to Prohibition: A Dramatic History of the Drama 'Uncle Tom's Cabin'* (unpub. typescript, Tex), p. 279; Shafer, p. 92.

12. "Olympic Theatre," N.Y. *Sun*, 26 Feb. 1870.

13. E. B. Grossman, *Edwin Booth* (New York, 1895), p. 15; "A Tale of Geo. L. Fox," unident. clipping, Lincoln Center; "A Chat with 'Pop' Wood—the oldest stage-door man in New York," unident. clipping, Lincoln Center; W. Winter, *Other Days* (New York, 1908), p. 217; O. S. Coad and E. Mims, Jr., *The American Stage* (New Haven, 1929), p. 211.

14. N.Y. *Tribune*, 14 Mar. 1870, p. 7; N.Y. *Clipper*, 12 Mar. 1870, p. 90.

15. N.Y. *Times*, 27 Mar. 1870, p. 5.

16. N.Y. *Tribune*, 18 Apr. 1870, p. 7; N.Y. *Times*, 24 Apr. 1870, p. 4.

17. N.Y. *Clipper*, 19 Apr. 1870; 30 Apr. 1870, p. 30; N.Y. *Times*, 19 Apr. 1870, p. 5; N.Y. *Herald*, 19 Apr. 1870.

18. *Spirit of the Times*, 20 Apr. 1870, p. 5; see also N.Y. *Times*, 24 Apr. 1870; N.Y. *Tribune*, 20 Apr. 1870, p. 5; 25 Apr. 1870, p. 7.

19. N.Y. *Herald*, 15 Feb. 1870; see Croghan, 1:200–201.

20. N.Y. *Tribune*, 4 July 1870, p. 7; *Spirit of the Times*, 7 May 1870, p. 192.

21. N.Y. *Clipper*, 3 Sept. 1870, p. 174.

22. N.Y. *Tribune*, 22 Aug. 1870, p. 7; see also N.Y. *Times*, 28 Aug. 1870, p. 5.

23. N.Y. *Clipper*, 30 July 1870, p. 184; 12 Nov. 1870, p. 251.

24. N.Y. *Daily Tribune*, 7 Oct. 1870, p. 5.

25. N.Y. *Clipper*, 15 Oct. 1870, p. 223.

26. N.Y. *Clipper*, 19 June 1869.

27. Playbill, HTC.

28. N.Y. *Clipper*, 15 Oct. 1870, p. 223.

29. N.Y. *Tribune*, 7 Oct. 1870, p. 5.

30. N.Y. *Clipper*, 23 Oct. 1870, p. 230.

31. N.Y. *Clipper*, 15 Nov. 1870, p. 246; 15 Oct. 1870, p. 222; 12 Nov. 1870, p. 254.

32. *Sporting Times and Theatrical News*, 7 Jan. 1871, p. 6; 28 Jan. 1871, p. 6; N.Y. *Tribune*, 30 Jan. 1871, p. 5; G. C. D. Odell, *Annals of the New York Stage* (New York, 1937) 9:20.

33. Playbill, HTC.

34. When Henry Irving revived *Richelieu* at the Lyceum Theatre in 1873, a parody at the London Olympic, *Richelieu Redressed* by Robert Reece, soon followed. It too mocked journalism and politics, with such statements as: "In the great lexicon of Politics, there's no such word as Truth" and "the awful circle of the Daily Press." W. D. Adams, *A Book of Burlesques* (London, 1891), pp. 160–61.

35. N.Y. *Herald*, 6 Feb. 1871, p. 3; 7 Feb. 1871, p. 10; N.Y. *Tribune*, 7 Feb. 1871, p. 5; N.Y. *Clipper*, 18 Feb. 1871, p. 866; *Spirit of the Times*, 4 Mar. 1871, p. 48; Horton, p. 69; L. Hutton, *Talks in a Library* (New York, 1905), p. 68; H. S. Renton, "Humpty Dupmty [*sic*] and Others," N.Y. *Sun*, 19 Apr. 1929.

36. *Sporting Times and Theatrical News*, 26 Feb. 1871, p. 6.

37. N.Y. *Herald*, 7 Feb. 1871, p. 10.

38. N.Y. *Clipper*, 25 Feb. 1871, p. 374.

39. G. D. Engle, *This Grotesque Essence: Plays from the American Minstrel Stage* (Baton Rouge, 1978), pp. xxvii–xxviii.

40. The integration of Shakespeare into American popular culture is persuasively pleaded in L. E. Levine, "William Shakespeare and the American People: A Study in Cultural Transformation," *American Historical Review* 81:1 (Feb. 1984), especially pp. 40–42, 59. The anti-English, anti-highbrow aspect is stressed by C. Johnson in "Burlesques of Shakespeare: The Democratic American's 'Light Artillery,'" *Theatre Survey* 21 (May 1980), pp. 49–62; she follows a line taken by E. S. Dunn in *Shakespeare in America* (New York, 1939), pp. 133–36, who finds the reasons for Shakespeare's prominence "venial, material, snobbish."

14. Humpty's Return and the Triumph of Variety
(pp. 173–84)

1. J. F. Daly, *The Life of Augustin Daly* (New York, 1917), p. 106; T. A. Brown, "The Olympic Theatre," N.Y. *Clipper*, 22 Nov. 1890, p. 580; G. C. D. Odell, *Annals of the New York Stage*, New York, 1937, 9:20; J. T. Powers, *Twinkle Little Star: Sparkling Memories of Seventy Years* (New York, 1939), pp. 50–51.

2. M. Felheim, *The Theatre of Augustin Daly* (Cambridge, Mass., 1956), p. 73, provides a plot summary. The play itself can be found in A. G. Halline, ed., *American Plays* (New York, 1935), and D. B. Wilmeth and R. Cullen, eds., *Plays of Augustin Daly* (Cambridge, 1985).

3. Odell, 9:21, where the character is misspelt "Bose."

4. H. S. Renton, "Humpty Dupmty [*sic*] and Others," N.Y. *Sun*, 19 Apr. 1929.

5. *Spirit of the Times*, 25 Mar. 1871, p. 96; N.Y. *Times*, 25 Mar. 1881, p. 5. See also N.Y. *Tribune*, 22 Mar. 1871, p. 5; 28 Mar. 1871, p. 8; London *Figaro*, 29 Apr. 1871.

6. Odell, 9:22.

7. "Jack Sheppard," *Olympic Theatre*, unident. clipping, HTC.

8. Ibid.; N.Y. *Times*, 16 May 1871, p. 5.

9. Odell, 9:22; N.Y. *Herald*, 18 June 1871, p. 12.

10. *Sporting Times and Theatrical News*, 8 July 1871, p. 6; 17 June 1871, p. 6.

11. Ibid., 23 July 1871, p. 198. See also N.Y. *Clipper*, 17 June 1871, p. 86; 8 July 1871, p. 110.

12. N.Y. *Herald*, 7 July 1871, p. 5; 10 Aug. 1871, p. 8.

13. N.Y. *Herald*, 26 Aug. 1871, p. 2.

14. N.Y. *Clipper*, 8 Feb. 1873, p. 353.

15. N.Y. *Clipper*, 16 Sept. 1871, p. 190; Odell, 9:152.

16. N.Y. *Herald*, 18 June 1871, p. 5.

17. N.Y. *Clipper*, 16 Sept. 1871, p. 190.

18. N.Y. *Herald*, 18 June 1871, p. 5.

19. N.Y. *Clipper*, 23 Dec. 1871, p. 302.

20. N.Y. *Herald*, 25 Oct. 1871, p. 9; 15 Nov. 1871, p. 7; 8 Dec. 1871, p. 5.

21. N.Y. *Clipper*, 30 Sept. 1871, p. 206.

22. M. R. Werner, *Tammany Hall* (Garden City, N.Y., 1928), p. 181.

23. A. B. Paine, *Thomas Nast: His Period and His Pictures* (New York, 1904), p. 158; D. T. Lynch, *The Wild Seventies* (New York, 1941), p. 49; D. C. Seitz, *The Dreadful Decade . . . 1869–1879* (Indianapolis, 1926), p. 165.

24. Lynch, p. 144.

25. N.Y. *Herald*, 17 Dec. 1871, p. 5.

26. "Death of George L. Fox," N.Y. *Times*, 25 Oct. 1877, p. 5.

27. "Humpty Dumpty's Widow," N.Y. *Dramatic News*, 9 Feb. 1878.

28. N.Y. *Herald*, 30 Dec. 1871, p. 6; *Sporting Times and Theatrical News*, 30 Sept. 1871, p. 6; 2 Dec. 1871, p. 14.

29. N.Y. *Clipper*, 30 Jan. 1872, p. 384.

30. Ibid.; *Sporting Times and Theatrical News*, 30 Mar. 1872, pp. 1, 8.

31. N.Y. *Clipper*, 13 Apr. 1872, p. 14.

32. N.Y. *Clipper*, 22 June 1872, p. 94.

33. N.Y. *Clipper*, 9 Dec. 1871, p. 286.

34. "Barnaby," N.Y. *Herald*, 2 Mar. 1878.

35. N.Y. *Clipper*, 27 Jan. 1872, p. 342; 17 Feb. 1872, p. 366; 2 May 1872, p. 282; *Sporting Times and Theatrical News*, 13 Feb. 1872, p. 6.

36. "'The Black Crook,' 'Humpty Dumpty,' and the Christmas Pantomimes," N.Y. *Clipper*, 20 Apr. 1872, p. 20.

37. 29 June 1872, p. 2.

38. N.Y. *Herald*, 15 Feb. 1872, p. 4.

39. H. P. Phelps, *Players of a Century: A Record of the Albany Stage* (Albany, N.Y., 1880), p. 406; N.Y. *Clipper*, 5 Oct. 1872, p. 214; 14 Oct. 1872, p. 230; 26 Oct. 1872, p. 238; 4 Jan. 1873, p. 218; 11 Jan. 1873, p. 327; 8 Feb. 1873, p. 353.

40. N.Y. *Clipper*, 4 Jan. 1873, p. 318.

41. "G. F. [*sic*] Adams dead; famed as clown," N.Y. *Times*, 27 May 1935.

42. N.Y. *Herald*, 22 Nov. 1872, p. 7.

43. N.Y. *Clipper*, 8 Mar. 1873, p. 390.

44. N.Y. *Clipper*, 20 Apr. 1873, p. 30; 3 May 1873, p. 38; 10 May 1873; N.Y. *Herald*, 9 Feb. 1873, p. 4; 7 June 1873, p. 2; Odell, 9:274–75.

15. *Augustin Daly at the Helm*
(pp. 185–94)

1. W. E. Woodward, *A New American History* (New York, 1936), p. 639.

2. M. C. Henderson, *The City and the Theatre: New York Playhouses from Bowling Green to Times Square* (Clifton, N.J., 1973), p. 156.

3. According to I. F. Marcosson, "Sawdust and Gold Dust: The Earnings of the Circus People," *Bookman*, June 1910, Fox made between four and six hundred dollars.

4. *Spirit of the Times*, 31 Jan. 1874, p. 592; 7 Mar. 1874, p. 87; 22 Nov. 1873, p. 355; "The American Grimaldi," N.Y. *Clipper*, 3 Nov. 1877.

5. N.Y. *Clipper*, 17 May 1873.

6. N.Y. *Times*, 20 Aug. 1873, quoted in G. C. D. Odell, "'A Midsummer Night's Dream' on the New York Stage," in *Shakespearean Studies by Members of the Department of English and Comparative Literature in Columbia University*, ed. J. B. Matthews and A. H. Thorndike (New York, 1916), p. 150; N.Y. *Tribune*, 20 Aug. 1873, p. 5; N.Y. *Herald*, 20 Aug. 1873, p. 5; N.Y. *Clipper*, 30 Aug. 1873.

7. *Spirit of the Times*, 13 Sept. 1873, p. 110; N.Y. *Herald*, 10 Sept. 1873, p. 5; N.Y. *Clipper*, 20 Sept. 1873, p. 198. The *Tribune* review, 11 Sept. 1873, p. 2, did not even mention him.

8. N.Y. *Herald*, 22 Sept. 1873, p. 9.

9. N.Y. *Clipper*, 4 Oct. 1873, p. 214. See also N.Y. *Herald*, 24 Sept. 1873, p. 4. The *Tribune* did not bother to review it.

10. N.Y. *Herald*, 12 Oct. 1873, p. 7; 18 Oct. 1873; 25 Oct. 1873, p. 2; N.Y. *Clipper*, 25 Oct. 1873, p. 298.

11. N.Y. *Clipper*, 8 Nov. 1873, p. 254; see also N.Y. *Herald*, 28 Oct. 1873, p. 7.

12. N.Y. *Herald*, 9 Nov. 1873, p. 4; N.Y. *Clipper*, 22 Nov. 1873, p. 270.

13. J. F. Daly, *The Life of Augustin Daly* (New York, 1917), p. 139.

14. N.Y. *Herald*, 26 Nov. 1873, p. 6.

15. N.Y. *Clipper*, 6 Dec. 1873, p. 286.

16. Ibid. See also N.Y. *Herald*, 26 Nov. 1873, p. 6; *Spirit of the Times*, 29 Nov. 1873, p. 376.

17. N.Y. *Herald*, 21 Dec. 1873, p. 9.

18. N.Y. *Clipper*, 13 Dec. 1873, p. 294; N.Y. *Herald*, 4 Jan. 1874, p. 9.

19. N.Y. *Clipper*, 24 Jan. 1874, p. 342; 14 Feb. 1874, p. 366; N.Y. *Herald*, 18 Jan. 1874, p. 8; 19 Jan. 1874, p. 7; 7 Feb. 1874, p. 2; *Spirit of the Times*, 24 Jan. 1874, p. 56; 31 Jan. 1874, p. 592.

20. N.Y. *Herald*, 8 Feb. 1874, p. 4.

21. N.Y. *Clipper*, 21 Feb. 1874, p. 374; 28 Feb. 1874, p. 382; N.Y. *Herald*, 8 Feb. 1874, p. 4; 10 Feb. 1874, p. 7; *Spirit of the Times*, 21 Feb. 1874, p. 38.

22. Daly, p. 139.

23. Ibid., pp. 162–63.

24. *Spirit of the Times*, 22 Nov. 1873, p. 355.

25. N.Y. *Herald*, 7 Mar. 1874, p. 6.

26. Daly, p. 163.

27. *Spirit of the Times*, 7 Mar. 1874, p. 87; Daly, pp. 163–64.

28. N.Y. *Herald*, 14 Mar. 1874, p. 7.

29. N.Y. *Clipper*, 11 Apr. 1874, p. 14.

30. N.Y. *Herald*, 8 Mar. 1874, p. 11.

16. Humpty Dumpty Has a Great Fall
(pp. 195–208)

1. Quoted in M. C. Henderson, *The City and the Theatre: New York Playhouses from Bowling Green to Times Square* (Clifton, N.J., 1973), p. 117.

2. "Joe Jorum," "Our Dramatic Letter," unident. clipping, HTC.

3. N.Y. *Clipper*, 18 Apr. 1872, p. 22; "Joe Jorum."

4. N.Y. *Clipper*, 18 Apr. 1872, p. 22.

5. N.Y. *Tribune*, 7 Apr. 1874, p. 5; N.Y. *Herald*, 7 Apr. 1874, p. 9; *Spirit of the Times*, 11 Apr. 1874, p. 206.

6. N.Y. *Clipper*, 16 May 1874, p. 54.

7. "Joe Jorum"; N.Y. *Clipper*, 7 Mar. 1874, p. 389; 14 Mar. 1874, p. 398.

8. N.Y. *Clipper*, 16 May 1874, p. 54; *Spirit of the Times*, 2 May 1874, p. 270; 9 May 1874, p. 306; N.Y. *Herald*, 13 May 1874, p. 8.

9. N.Y. *Clipper*, 23 May 1874, p. 62.

10. *Spirit of the Times*, 23 May 1874, p. 8; 6 June 1874, p. 41.

11. N.Y. *Herald*, 24 May 1874, p. 7.

12. "Mr. Fox's Legacy," N.Y. *Dramatic News*, 15 Jan. 1876, p. 5; J. F. Daly, *The Life of Augustin Daly* (New York, 1917), p. 162; "George L. Fox Insane," N.Y. *Dramatic News*, 20 Nov. 1875, p. 2.

13. N.Y. *Clipper*, 30 May 1874, p. 70 and following issues. For itinerary, see Appendix Three.

14. N.Y. *Clipper*, 9 Jan. 1875, p. 236.

15. N.Y. *Clipper*, 31 Oct. 1874, p. 245.

16. N.Y. *Clipper*, 23 Jan. 1875, p. 342; 30 Jan. 1875, p. 350.

17. N.Y. *Herald*, 4 Mar. 1875, p. 7.

18. N.Y. *Clipper*, 20 Mar. 1875, p. 407; "Mr. Fox's Legacy."

19. N.Y. *Clipper*, 17 July 1875, pp. 126, 128.

20. N.Y. *Clipper*, 7 Aug. 1875.

21. N.Y. *Dramatic News*, 13 Nov. 1875; N.Y. *Herald*, 4 Oct. 1875, p. 6.

22. "A Favorite Actor's Misfortune," N.Y. *Tribune*, 15 Nov. 1875; "Death of George L. Fox," N.Y. *Times*, 25 Oct. 1877, p. 5.

23. "Fox in Pantomime," N.Y. *Dramatic News*, 30 Oct. 1875, p. 2.

24. *Spirit of the Times*, 6 Nov. 1875, p. 254.

25. N.Y. *Clipper*, 7 Aug. 1875.

26. N.Y. *Times*, quoted in G. Bordman, *American Musical Theatre* (New York, 1978), p. 38.

27. N.Y. *Clipper*, 7 Aug. 1875; "Fox in Pantomime"; *Spirit of the Times*, 6 Nov. 1875, p. 310.

28. N.Y. *Clipper*, 13 Nov. 1875, p. 262; N.Y. *Herald*, 7 Nov. 1875, p. 310.

29. Quoted in W. H. Draper, *George L. Fox, Comedian, in Pantomime and Travesty* (unpub. Ph.D. dissertation, University of Illinois, 1958), p. 149.

30. "Mr. Fox's Legacy"; "Benefit for G. L. Fox," N.Y. *Dramatic News*, 22 Jan. 1876, p. 4; "Humpty Dumpty's Widow," N.Y. *Dramatic News*, 9 Feb. 1878.

31. "George L. Fox Insane."

32. R. Fraser, "Decline of the Stage Clown," N.Y. *Herald*, 22 Sept. 1889.

33. N.Y. *Tribune*, 16 Nov. 1875, p. 5.

34. "G. L. Fox Insane."

35. Ibid.; N.Y. *Herald*, 14 Nov. 1875; 16 Nov. 1875, p. 5.

36. N.Y. *Clipper*, 27 Nov. 1875, p. 278.

37. W. Seymour, "G. L. Fox as a Comedian," N.Y. *Herald*, 5 Feb. 1924.

38. J. T. Powers, *Twinkle Little Star: Sparkling Memories of Seventy Years* (New York, 1939), pp. 50–51. The rest of the story is clearly inaccurate since it refers to a cancelled performance.

39. "Death of George L. Fox," N.Y. *Times*, 25 Oct. 1877.

40. N.Y. *Clipper*, 20 Nov. 1875, p. 270.

41. "George L. Fox Insane"; "Exit 'Humpty Dumpty,'" unident. clipping, Tex; "Decline of the Stage Clown"; "Bob Fraser on the Pantomimic Art," unident. clipping, HTC; "Poor Fox!" N.Y. *Dramatic News*, 2 Sept. 1876, p. 5.

42. "George L. Fox Insane."

43. "Fox in a Madhouse," N.Y. *Dramatic News*, 4 Dec. 1875, p. 4.

44. Program, Booth's Theatre, 27 Nov. 1876, Tex.

45. "Exit 'Humpty Dumpty.'"

46. "George L. Fox at Home," unident. clipping, Lincoln Center; N.Y. *Times*, 26 Nov. 1875, p. 7.

47. W. S. Howard, *From Slavery to Prohibition: A Dramatic History of the Drama 'Uncle Tom's Cabin'* (Unpub. typescript, Tex); "Fox in a Madhouse."

48. N.Y. *Clipper*, 4 Dec. 1875, p. 286.

17. Too Cracked to Be Mended
(pp. 209–17)

1. "Clowns and Clowning," Cincinnati *Gazette*, 3 June 1883.

2. "Bob Fraser on the Pantomimic Art," 1877, unident. clipping, HTC.

3. "The American Grimaldi," N.Y. *Clipper*, 3 Nov. 1877, seconded by "The Life Story of George L. Fox," unident. clipping in the John Denier file, Lincoln Center.

4. N.Y. *Herald*, 22 Dec. 1875.

5. "Mr. Fox's Legacy," N.Y. *Dramatic News*, 15 Jan. 1876, p. 5; "The Case of George L. Fox," N.Y. *Dramatic News*, 22 Jan. 1876, p. 5.

6. N.Y. *Dramatic News*, 5 Feb. 1876, p. 4.

7. Ibid. See also "A Benefit for G. L. Fox," N.Y. *Dramatic News*, 22 Jan. 1876, p. 4.

8. N.Y. *Dramatic News*, 8 Jan. 1876, p. 2.

9. N.Y. *Clipper*, 29 Apr. 1876, p. 38.

10. N.Y. *Dramatic News*, 17 June 1876, p. 3.

11. Obituary of G. H. Tyler, N.Y. *Clipper*, 23 Aug. 1884, p. 357.

12. N.Y. *Dramatic News*, 19 Feb. 1876, p. 6; 24 June 1876, p. 4; 26 Aug. 1876, p. 5; "Poor Fox!", 2 Sept. 1876, p. 5; 16 Sept. 1876, p. 5; "Clowns and Clowning." For Drs. Jelly and Brown-Séquard, see H. A. Kelly and W. L. Burrage, *American Medical Biographies* (Baltimore, 1920), pp. 621, 155–157.

13. "Poor Fox!" The place of McLean's in the development of the American insane

asylum is touched on in A. Deutsch, *The Mentally Ill in America* (Garden City, N.Y., 1937), pp. 105, 273 ff.; G. N. Grob, *Mental Institutions in America* (New York, 1973), pp. 51–55, 69–70; and D. J. Rothman, *The Discovery of the Asylum* (Boston, 1971), 147–49.

14. "George L. Fox at Home," unident. clipping, Lincoln Center.

15. "Death of George L. Fox," N.Y. *Times,* 25 Oct. 1877, p. 5; N.Y. *Dramatic News,* 16 Sept. 1876, p. 5; N.Y. *Clipper,* 16 Sept. 1876, p. 198.

16. "Poor Old Humpty Dumpty," unident. clipping, HTC.

17. "George L. Fox at Home."

18. "Humpty Dumpty's Widow," N.Y. *Dramatic News,* 9 Feb. 1978; W. S. Howard, *From Slavery to Prohibition: A Dramatic History of the Drama 'Uncle Tom's Cabin'* (unpub. typescript, Tex), p. 279.

19. N.Y. *Clipper,* 13 Jan. 1877, p. 334; "Death of George L. Fox," *N.Y. Times;* "The American Grimaldi"; N.Y. *Dramatic News,* 28 Apr. 1877, p. 4; "Fox," 28 Apr. 1877, unident. clipping, HTC.

20. "Humpty Dumpty's Widow."

21. "Give Humpty Dumpty a Benefit," N.Y. *Sun,* 16 Oct. 1877.

22. W. L. G., N.Y. *Herald,* 17 Oct. 1877.

23. "Death of George L. Fox," N.Y. *Times.*

24. Howard, pp. 279–80; unident. clipping 29 Oct. 1877, in scrapbook in author's collection; unident. clipping in extra-illustrated volume on *Booth's Theatre,* Player's Club; N.Y. *Clipper,* 3 Nov. 1877, 10 Nov. 1877, p. 263; "Death of George L. Fox," Cambridge *Chronicle,* 27 Oct. 1877, p. 4; *Cambridge Directory* 1877; "Death of George L. Fox," N.Y. *Times.*

25. "Humpty Dumpty's Widow."

26. N.Y. *Clipper,* 12 Dec. 1885, p. 612; unident. clipping, 31 Oct. 1911, W. C. Cawley Collection, Lincoln Center.

27. N.Y. *Clipper,* 15 Dec. 1877, p. 303; 12 Dec. 1885, p. 612; 4 Feb. 1888, p. 754; GPH, Tex.

28. "Sudden Death of Hon. James A. Fox," Cambridge *Chronicle,* 22 Dec. 1900, pp. 17–18; "Resolutions for ex-Mayor Fox," Cambridge *Tribune,* 29 Dec. 1900, p. 3.

29. Clippings in Tex and HTC; GPH papers, Tex; A. Downer, "Cordelia Howard," in *Notable American Women* (Cambridge, Mass., 1971) 2:224–25.

Epilogue: Fox's Legacy
(pp. 218–23)

1. "Geo. H. Adams," N.Y. *Clipper,* 22 July 1882, p. 281. Denier advertised one of his productions with the fake-Latin slogan, "Soc et tuum," indicating the dissemination of "Sock it to 'em" as a slang phrase by this time. (N.Y. *Clipper Annual for 1885,* p. 108).

2. N.Y. *Clipper,* 2 Apr. 1881.

3. "American Pantomime," N.Y. *Mirror,* 18 Feb. 1882, p. 6.

4. C. Smith, *Musical Comedy in America* (N.Y., 1950), p. 23.

5. "The Pantomime Season," N.Y. *Clipper,* 7 Jan. 1888, p. 694. See also M. B. Leavitt, *Fifty Years in Theatrical Management* (New York, 1912), p. 115, and "A noted Humpty Dumpty," unident. clipping (26 July 1923), HTC.

6. J. Claretie, *La Vie à Paris 1881* (Paris, 1882), p. 358.

7. See "The Pantomime in Paris," N.Y. *Sun,* 22 Nov. 1891, and the Epilogue to R. Storey, *Pierrots on the Stage of Desire* (Princeton, N.J., 1985), esp. pp. 292–94.

8. R. Grau, "Is a Revival of Pantomime at Hand?," *Theatre,* Apr. 1912, pp. 126,

128; H. Broun, "Films have killed the pantomime," *Dramatic Mirror*, 1 Feb. 1919, p. 157.

9. W. Winter, *Life and Art of Edwin Booth* (New York, 1893), p. 89, n. 2.

10. T. Walton, "'Entortilationists' (The Hanlon-Lees in Literature and Art)," *Life & Letters Today*, 29 (Apr.–June 1941), p. 36.

Appendix Two
(pp. 226–28)

1. Townsend Walsh, N.Y. *Dramatic Mirror*, 1 Nov. 1911.

2. A. W. Pendergast and W. Porter Ware, *Cigar Store Figures in American Folk Art*, p. 27.

3. Information from museum staff, letters to author from Ann Barton Brown, Research Associate, 7 Nov. 1977, 15 Nov. 1977, 31 Jan. 1978.

4. Letter to author from Ladd Macmillan, Curator of Arts and Crafts, Heritage plantation, 30 Jan. 1979, 31 July 1980; letter to author from Frederick Fried, 11 Aug. 1980.

BIBLIOGRAPHY

I. Manuscript and Typescript Works

Booth's Theatre. Extra-illustrated volumes. Walter Hampden-Edwin Booth Memorial Library, Player's Club, N.Y.

Connolly, Mary Ann. *The Boston Schools in the New Republic 1776–1840.* Unpub. M.A. thesis, Harvard University, 1963.

Cook, Philip H. *History of the Drama in Worcester.* Unpub. typescript. Library of the American Antiquarian Society, Worcester, Mass.

Croghan, Leland A. *An Abstract of New York Burlesque 1840–1870: A Study in Theatrical Self-Criticism.* Unpub. Ph.D. dissertation, New York University, 1967.

Draper, Walter Headen. *George L. Fox, Comedian, in Pantomime and Travesty.* Unpub. Ph.D. dissertation, University of Illinois, 1958.

Hofele, Ferdinand. *Bowery Theatre Property Lists.* Harvard Theatre Collection.

Howard, Walter Scott. *From Slavery to Prohibition: A Dramatic History of the Drama 'Uncle Tom's Cabin.'* Hoblitzelle Theatre Collection, University of Texas at Austin.

Howard Family Papers. Collection of G. P. Howard. Hoblitzelle Theatre Collection, University of Texas at Austin.

Irishman in Baghdad: A Musical Romance in Two Acts. Prompter's copy, Purdy's National Theatre, New York. Harvard Theatre Collection.

McDowell, Michael McEachern. *American Attitudes Towards Death, 1825–1865.* Unpub. Ph.D. dissertation, Brandeis University, 1977.

Old Bowery Theatre Account Book, 28 Apr. 1862–28 Nov. 1863. Hoblitzelle Theatre Collection, University of Texas at Austin.

Pantomime Scripts and Property Lists of George L. Fox, sold to James Bailey. McCaddon Collection. Princeton University Library.

Sankus, Patricia Helen. *Theatrical Entertainments and Other Amusements in Salem Massachusetts from the Colonial Period through the Year 1830.* Unpub. Ph.D. dissertation, Tufts University, 1981.

Tremont Theatre Account Books for 1839. Tremont Theatre Forfait [sic] *Books for 1840–[43]. Scrapbook of clippings 1827–32.* Harvard Theatre Collection.

II. Published Works

Adams, William Davenport. *A Book of Burlesques: Sketches of English Stage Travestie and Parody.* London: Henry & Co., 1891.

Aiken, George L. *Uncle Tom's Cabin; or, Life among the Lowly: A Domestic Drama in Six Acts.* New York: Samuel French, [n.d.].

"The American Grimaldi," N.Y. *Clipper*, 3 Nov. 1877.

"American Pantomime." N.Y. *Mirror*, 18 Feb. 1882, p. 6.

"An American Pantomimist," and "American and English Pantomime." New York *Mirror*, 18 Feb. 1882, pp. 6–7.

"Any Type Theater Building Banned by Law Passed 1806," Portland *Evening Express*, 25 June 1977.

Appleton, William W., "The Marvellous Museum of P. T. Barnum." *Revue d'histoire du théâtre* 1 (1963): 57–62.

Arthur, T. S. *Ten Nights in a Barroom.* Edited by C. Hugh Holman. New York: Odyssey Press, 1966.

Asbury, Herbert. *The Gangs of New York: An Informal History of the Underworld.* Garden City, N.Y.: Garden City Publishing Co., 1928.

Ball, Thomas. *My Threescore Years and Ten: An Autobiography.* Boston: Roberts Brothers, 1892.

Ball, William T. G. "The Old Federal Street Theatre." *The Bostonian Society Publications* 8 (1911): 43–91.

Bangs, Frank C. "Recollections of Players, II." New York *Dramatic Mirror*, 5 Feb. 1898, p. 24.

Bariskill, James M. "Newburyport Theatre in the Early Nineteenth Century." *Essex Institute Historical Collections* 93 (1957): 279–314.

Barker, Barbara. *Ballet or Ballyhoo: The American Careers of Maria Bonfanti, Rita Sangalli and Giuseppina Morlacchi.* New York: Dance Horizons, 1984.

Barnard, William F. *Forty Years at the Five Points: A Sketch of the Five Points House Industry.* New York: The Author, 1893.

Barnum, Phineas Taylor. *Struggles and Triumphs; or, The Life of P. T. Barnum, written by Himself.* Edited by George S. Bryan. 2 vols. New York and London: Alfred A. Knopf, 1927.

"A Benefit for G. L. Fox." N.Y. *Dramatic News*, 22 Jan. 1876, p. 4.

Bernard, Charles. "George L. Fox, King of Clowns." *The Circus Scrapbook* 12 (Oct. 1931): 6–9.

Biographical Sketch of Ossian T. Dodge. Boston: Wright & Potter, 1856.

Birdoff, Harry. *The World's Greatest Hit—Uncle Tom's Cabin.* New York: S. F. Vanni, 1947.

"'The Black Crook,' 'Humpty Dumpty,' and the Christmas Pantomimes." N.Y. *Clipper*, 20 Apr. 1872, p. 20.

Blake, Charles. *An Historical Account of the Providence Stage.* Providence, R.I.: George Whitney, 1868.

Blanchard, Edward Leman. *The Life and Reminiscences of E. L. Blanchard, with notes from the Diary of William Blanchard.* Edited by Clement Scott and Cecil Howard. London: Hutchinson, 1891.

Blayney, Glenn H. "City Life in American Drama, 1825–1860." In *Studies in Honor of John Wilcox.* Edited by A. D. Wallace and W. Ross, pp. 99–128. Detroit: Wayne State University Press, 1958.

Bode, Carl. *The Anatomy of American Popular Culture 1840–1861.* Berkeley and Los Angeles: University of California Press, 1959.

Booth, Michael R. "The Drunkard's Progress: Nineteenth-century Temperance Drama." *Dalhousie Review* 44 (1964–65): 205–12.

Bordman, G. *American Musical Theatre.* New York: Oxford University Press, 1878.

[Bowen, Abel]. *Bowen's Picture of Boston, or The Citizen's and Stranger's Guide to the Metropolis of Massachusetts, and its Environs. To which Is Affixed the Annals of Boston.* 3d ed. Boston: Otis, Broaders & Co., 1838.

Boyer, Paul. *Urban Masses and Moral Order in America, 1820–1920.* Cambridge, Mass.: Harvard University Press, 1978.

Brayley, A. W. *Schools and Schoolboys of Old Boston from 1636 to 1844.* Boston: L. P. Hager, 1894.

Broadbent, R. J. *A History of Pantomime.* (1901). New York: Citadel, 1965.

Broun, Heywood. "Films have killed the pantomime." New York *Dramatic Mirror*, 1 Feb. 1919, p. 157.

Brown, Daniel J. "Footlight Favorites Forty Years Ago: A Stroll Up Broadway," *Valentine's Manual of Old New York*, n.s., 6 (1922): 133–68.

Brown, T. Allston. *A History of the American Stage: Containing Biographical Sketches of Nearly Every Member of the Profession That Has Appeared on the American Stage, from 1733 to 1870.* New York: Dick & Fitzgerald, 1870.

————. *A History of the New York Stage from the First Performance in 1732 to 1901.* 3 vols. New York: Dodd, Mead, 1903.

————. "Kate Denin Wilson." N.Y. *Dramatic Mirror*, 23 Feb. 1907, p. 12.

————. "The Olympic Theatre." N.Y. *Clipper*, 22 Nov. 1890.

Browne, Julius Henri. *The Great Metropolis: A Mirror of New York.* Hartford, Conn.: American Publishing Co., 1869.

Bruchey, Stuart. *The Roots of American Economic Growth, 1607–1861.* New York and Evanston: Harper & Row, 1965.

Buntline, Ned [Edward Z. C. Judson]. *The B'hoys of New York: A Sequel to the Mysteries & Miseries of New York.* New York: Dick & Fitzgerald, [n.d.]

————. *The G'hals of New York: a Novel.* New York: Robert M. De Witt, [n.d.]

————. *The Mysteries and Miseries of New York: A Story of Real Life.* New York: Berford & Co., 1848.

Burnham, Charles. "Eventful Life of the Chatham Theatre." New York *Sun*, 6 May 1923.

————. "Historic New York Theatres No. 3: Niblo's Garden and Wallack's Lyceum." *Theatre*, May 1918, p. 294.

————. "New York's Historic Theatres No. 1: The Old Bowery." *Theatre*, Mar. 1918, pp. 160–62.

Burt, Col. Silas W. *My Memories of the Military History of the State of New York during the War for the Union, 1861–65.* Edited by the State Historian and issued as War of the Rebellion series—Bulletin, no. 1. Albany, N.Y.: J. B. Lyon, 1902.

Campbell, Mrs. Helen, Col. Thomas W. Knox, and Supt. Thomas Byrnes. *Darkness and Daylight; or, Lights and Shadows of New York Life.* Hartford, Conn.: Hartford Publishing Co., 1896.

Carboy, John [John A. Harrington]. "Theatric Reminiscences" in *Records of the New York Stage* [scrapbook, c. 1905, in the Harvard Theatre Collection]

Carson, Gerald. "The Great Meddler." *American Heritage*, Dec. 1967, pp. 28–33, 94–97.

————. "Sylvester Graham." In *The American Heritage Cookbook and Illustrated History of American Eating and Drinking.* New York: Simon and Schuster, 1964.

"The Case of George L. Fox." N.Y. *Dramatic News*, 22 Jan. 1876, p. 5.

Champfleury [Jules Fleury-Husson]. *Souvenirs des Funambules (1859).* Génève: Slatkine Reprints, 1971.

"Charles Burke." New York *Dramatic News*, 26 Nov. 1881.

"Charles Pope's Diary." *Educational Theatre Journal* 7:4 (Dec. 1955): 332.

Clapp, John Bouvé. "Boston Museum." Boston *Evening Transcript*, 16 May, 23 May, and 3 July 1903.

Clapp, William W. "The Drama in Boston." In *The Memorial History of Boston, Including Suffolk County, Massachusetts, 1630–1880*, edited by Justin Winsor, 4, pp. 356–82. Boston: Ticknor & Co., 1881.

————. *A Record of the Boston Stage.* Boston: James Munroe, 1853.

Claretie, Jules. *La Vie à Paris 1881.* Paris: Victor Havard, 1882.

"Clowns and Clowning." Cincinnati *Gazette*, 3 June 1883.

Coad, Oral Sumner, and Edwin Mims, Jr. *The American Stage.* New Haven: Yale University Press, 1929.

Coleman, John. *Players and Playwrights I Have Known: A Review of the English Stage from 1840 to 1880.* 2 vols. Philadelphia: Gebbie & Co., 1890.

Collins, Charles W. "Humpty Dumpty's Old Age." *The Green Room Album*, Oct. 1910, pp. 761–66.

Corbett, Alexander. "Boston Theatre 'Mystery House' Only Westerly End of Long Lobby." Boston *Globe*, 8 Mar. 1926.

Coveney, Peter. *The Image of Childhood: The Individual and Society: a Study of the Theme in English Literature*. Revised ed. Baltimore: Penguin Books, 1967.

Cowell, Emilie. *The Cowells in America being the Diary of Mrs. Sam Cowell during Her Husband's Concert Tour in the Years 1860–1861*. Edited by M. Willson Disher. London: Oxford University Press, 1934.

Cowell, Joseph. *Thirty Years Passed among the Players*. New York: Harper and Brothers, 1844.

Crane, Ellery Bicknell, ed. *History of Worcester County, Massachusetts*. New York: Lewis Historical Publishing Co., 1924.

Crapsey, Edward. *The Nether Side of New York; or, The Vice, Crime and Poverty of the Great Metropolis (1872)*. Montclair, N.J.: Patterson Smith, 1969.

Crawford, Mary Caroline. *Romantic Days in Old Boston: The Story of the City and Its People during the Nineteenth Century*. Boston: Little, Brown, 1910.

Cullen, Rosemary L. *The Civil War in American Drama before 1900: Catalog of an Exhibition November 1982*. Providence, R.I.: Brown University Library, 1982.

[Curtis, George William]. "Editor's Easy Chair." *Harper's* 74 (Mar. 1887): 643–44.

Daly, Joseph Francis. *The Life of Augustin Daly*. New York: Macmillan, 1917.

Day, Roy. "Charles Kemble Fox," and "George Washington Lafayette Fox." In *Dictionary of American Biography*, edited by A. Johnson and D. Malone, 6 pp. 566–67. New York: Charles Scribner's Sons, 1931.

Dearborn, Nathaniel. *Boston Notions: Being an Authentic and Concise Account of 'That Village,' from 1630 to 1847*. Boston: The Author, 1848.

"Death of George L. Fox." Cambridge *Chronicle*, 27 Oct. 1877.

"Death of George L. Fox." N.Y. *Times*, 25 Oct. 1877, p. 5.

"The Declining Days of the Old Chatham." N.Y. *Clipper*, 29 Jan. 1873, pp. 721–22.

De Leon, T. C. "Christmas Pantomimes." *Lippincott's* 3 (Jan. 1869): 36.

Denier, Antoine. *Denier's Parlor Pantomimes; or, Home Amusement for Old and Young, with a Memoir of the Author, by Sylvester Blecker*. New York: Samuel French, [c. 1864]

———. *Denier's Shadow Pantomimes; or, Harlequin in the Shades. How to Get Them Up, and How to Act Them*. New York: Samuel French & Son, 1868.

Denier, John. *Humpty Dumpty, a Pantomime in a Prologue and One Act . . . as Originally Played by George L. Fox*. New York: De Witt, [c. 1872].

Detmer, Josephine H., and Patricia McGraw Pancoat. *Portland*. Portland, Maine: Greater Portland Landmarks, Inc., 1973.

Deutsch, Albert. *The Mentally Ill in America: A History of Their Care and Treatment from Colonial Times*. Garden City, N.Y.: Doubleday, Doran, 1937.

DeVoto, Bernard. *Mark Twain's America*. Boston: Houghton Mifflin, 1967.

Disher, M. Willson. *Clowns & Pantomimes*. London: Constable, 1925.

"Doesticks, J. K. Philander" [Mortimer Thomson]. *Doesticks—What He Says*. New York: Edward Livermore, 1855.

Downer, Alan S., "Cordelia Howard," in *Notable American Women*, 2:224–25. Cambridge, Mass.: Harvard University Press, 1971.

Drake, Samuel Adams, ed. *History of Middlesex County, Mass.* 2 vols. Boston: Estes & Lauriat, 1880.

Dramas from the American Theatre 1762–1909. Edited with introductory essays by Richard Moody. Cleveland: World Publishing Co., 1966.

Draper, Walter Headen. "George L. Fox's Burlesque—*Hamlet.*" *Quarterly Journal of Speech* 50 (Dec. 1964): 378–84.

Dunn, Esther Cloudman. *Shakespeare in America.* New York: Macmillan, 1939.

Dunshee, Kenneth Holcomb. *As You Pass By.* New York: Hastings House, 1952.

Durham, Weldon B., ed. *American Theatre Companies, 1749–1887.* Westport, Conn.: Greenwood Press, 1986.

Dyer, Frederick H., comp. *A Compendium of the War of the Rebellion.* Des Moines, Iowa: Dyer Publishing Co., 1908.

"Edgar Allan Poe's Mother Made First Theatrical Debut Here [Union Hall, Portland]." Portland *Sunday Telegram and Sunday Press Herald,* 15 Nov. 1925.

Edgett, E. F. "Charles Burke." In *Dictionary of American Biography,* edited by A. Johnson and D. Malone, 3:280–81. New York: Charles Scribner's Sons, 1931.

Eliot, Samuel Atkins. *A History of Cambridge, Massachusetts (1630–1913).* Cambridge, Mass.: The Cambridge Tribune, 1913.

Ellis, Leonard Bolles. *History of New Bedford and Its Vicinity 1602–1892.* Syracuse, N.Y.: D. Mason & Co., 1892.

Engle, Gary D. *This Grotesque Essence: Plays from the American Minstrel Stage.* Baton Rouge: Louisiana State University Press, 1978.

"Famed as a Clown." Chicago *Chronicle,* 14 July 1904, p. 6.

Faulkner, Seldon. "The Octoroon War." *Educational Theatre Journal* 15:1 (Mar. 1963): 33–38.

"A Favorite Actor's Misfortune." N.Y. *Tribune,* 15 Nov. 1875.

Felheim, Marvin. *The Theatre of Augustin Daly.* Cambridge, Mass.: Harvard University Press, 1956.

Felt, Joseph B. *Annals of Salem.* 2d ed. Salem, Mass.: W. & S. B. Ives, 1849.

Ford, James L. *Forty-odd Years in the Literary Shop.* New York: E. P. Dutton, 1921.

Foster, Joseph C. *The Seven Dwarfs: Grand Spectacular Pantomime at the Bowery Theatre.* New York, 1869.

"Found—the Original Little Eva, Ex-Star, 84, Lives in Belmont." Boston *Sunday Advertiser,* 30 Oct. 1932.

"Fox in a Madhouse." N.Y. *Dramatic News,* 4 Dec. 1875.

"Fox in Pantomime." N.Y. *Dramatic News,* 30 Oct. 1875.

Fraser, Robert. "Decline of the Stage Clown." N.Y. *Herald,* 22 Sept. 1889.

Frow, Gerald. *"Oh, Yes It Is!" A History of Pantomime.* London: British Broadcasting Corporation, 1985.

Fülop-Müller, René. *The Motion Picture in America: A History in the Making.* New York: Dial Press, 1938.

"George L. Fox Insane." N.Y. *Dramatic News,* 20 Nov. 1875.

"G. F. [*sic*] Adams dead; famed as clown." N.Y. *Times,* 27 May 1935.

"Ghostly Pantomimes." *Household Words* 8:8 (1854): 399.

"Give Humpty Dumpty a Benefit." N.Y. *Sun,* 16 Oct. 1877.

Godfrey, Edward K. *The Island of Nantucket: What It Was and What It Is; Being a Complete Index and Guide to This Noted Resort, Including Its History, People, Agriculture, Botany, Conchology and Geography.* Boston: Lee and Shepard, 1882.

Goodale, Katherine. *Behind the Scenes with Edwin Booth.* Boston: Houghton Mifflin, 1931.

Gough, John B. *Autobiography and Personal Recollections, with Twenty-six Years' Experience as a Public Speaker.* Springfield, Mass.: Bill, Nichols & Co., 1869.

Grau, Robert. "Is a Revival of Pantomime at Hand?" *Theatre* (N.Y.), April 1912, pp. 126, 128.

Grimsted, David. *Melodrama Unveiled: American Theatre Culture 1800–1850*. Chicago: University of Chicago Press, 1968.

Grob, G. N. *Mental Institutions in America* (New York: Free Press, 1973).

Grossman, Edwina Booth. *Edwin Booth*. New York: The Century Company, 1895.

Grossman, Gerald N. *Mental Institutions in America: Social Policy to 1875*. New York: The Free Press, 1973.

Hagan, J. S. G. *Records of the New York Stage 1860–1870*. New York, 1877. [Extra-illustrated volume in Harvard Theatre Collection.]

Haggard, Howard W. *Devils, Drugs and Doctors: The Story of the Science of Healing from Medicine-Man to Doctor*. New York: Blue Ribbon Books, 1929.

Halline, Allen Gates, ed. *American Plays*. New York: American Book Company, 1835.

Halttunen, Karen. *Confidence Men and Painted Women: A Study of Middle-class Culture in America, 1830–1870*. New Haven: Yale University Press, 1982.

Harlow, Alvin F. *Old Bowery Days*. New York: D. Appleton, 1931.

Harris, Neil. *The Artist in American Society: The Formative Years 1790–1860*. New York: George Braziller, 1966.

––––––. *Humbug: The Art of P. T. Barnum*. Boston: Little, Brown, and Co., 1973.

Hayner, Rutherford. *Troy and Rensselaer County New York: A History*. 2 vols. New York: Lewis Historical Publishing Co., 1925.

The Heart of the Commonwealth; or, Worcester as It Is. Worcester, Mass.: Henry J. Howland, 1856.

Henderson, Mary C. *The City and the Theatre: New York Playhouses from Bowling Green to Times Square*. Clifton, N.J.: James T. White & Co., 1973.

Herring, Fanny. "Reminiscences of Fanny Herring." New York *Dramatic Mirror*, 12 July 1902, p. 3.

Hershkowitz, Leo. *Tweed's New York: Another Look*. Garden City, N.Y.: Anchor Press/Doubleday, 1977.

Hewins, Mary E. "The Giddy Gusher." N.Y. *Mirror*, 29 Jan. 1887.

Hewitt, Bernard. *Theatre U.S.A. 1665 to 1957*. New York: McGraw-Hill, 1959.

Hodge, Francis. *Yankee Theatre: The Image of America on the Stage, 1825–1850*. Austin: University of Texas Press, 1964.

Hofele, Ferdinand W., "Old Bowery," New York *World*, 8 Dec. 1901.

Hofstadter, Richard, and Michael Wallace, eds. *American Violence, a Documentary History*. New York: Vintage Books, 1971.

Horton, William E. *Driftwood of the Stage*. Detroit: Winn and Hammond, 1904.

Howard, George C. *Jack & Gill Went Up the Hill, the New, Original, Dazzling, and Gorgeous Comic Pantomime by G. L. Fox*. New York, 1866.

Howe, J. B. *A Cosmopolitan Actor: His Adventures All Over the World*. London: Bedford Publishing Co., 1888.

Hubbard, J. G. "The late G. L. Fox's first engagement." N.Y. *Clipper*, 10 Nov. 1877, p. 261.

"Humpty Dumpty Falls to His Death." New York *Sun*, 11 March 1917.

"Humpty Dumpty Interviewed—What He Said and How He Said It!" *Spirit of the Times*, 31 Jan. 1874.

"Humpty Dumpty's Widow." N.Y. *Dramatic News*, 9 Feb. 1878.

Hutton, Laurence. *Curiosities of the American Stage*. New York: Harper & Brothers, 1891.

––––––. *Plays and Players*. New York: Hurd and Houghton, 1875.

––––––. *Talks in a Library*. New York: G. P. Putnam's Sons, 1905.

Ireland, J. N. *Records of the New York Stage*. New York: T. H. Morrell, 1866–67.

Jackson, Charles O., ed. *Passing: The Vision of Death in America*. Westport, Conn.: Greenwood Press, 1977.

James, Henry. *A Small Boy and Others.* New York: Charles Scribner's Sons, 1913.

"James E. Hayes." N.Y. *Herald*, 8 May 1873.

Jennings, John J. *Theatrical and Circus Life; or, Secrets of the Stage, Greenroom and Sawdust Arena* . . . New York: William H. Shepard, 1882.

Johnson, Claudia D. "Burlesques of Shakespeare: The Democratic American's 'Light Artillery.'" *Theatre Survey* 21 (May 1980): 49–62.

———. "That Guilty Third Tier: Prostitution in Nineteenth-century American Theatres." In *Victorian America*, edited by D. W. Howe. Pittsburgh: University of Pennsylvania Press, 1976.

Judd, Dr. "Fifty Years Recollections of an Amusement Manager." *Billboard*, 5 Dec. 1903.

———. "The Pioneer Uncle Tomers." *Theatre* (N.Y.), 4 Feb. 1904, p. 44.

"Kate Denin." N.Y. *Dramatic Mirror*, 23 July 1910.

Kelley, Daniel. "Facts about the Olympic." N.Y. *Herald*, 24 April 1923.

———. "The Site of the [Olympic] Playhouse," N.Y. *Herald*, 2 April 1923.

Kelly, Howard A., and Walter L. Burrage. *American Medical Biographies.* Baltimore: Norman, Remington, 1920.

Kemble, Frances Anne. *Journal by Frances Anne Butler.* 2 vols. Philadelphia: Carey, Lea & Blanchard, 1835.

Knights, Peter R. *The Plain People of Boston, 1830–1860: A Study in City Growth.* New York: Oxford University Press, 1971.

Kouwenhouven, John A. *The Columbia Historical Portrait of New York: An Essay in Graphic History in Honor of the Triennial of New York City and the Bicentennial of Columbia University.* Garden City, N.Y.: Doubleday, 1953.

Kovacs, Katherine. "A History of the Féérie in France." *Theatre Quarterly* 8 : 29 (Spring 1978): 29–38.

Lane, Roger. *Policing the City: Boston 1822–1885.* Cambridge, Mass.: Harvard University Press, 1967.

"The late Clifton Tayleure." N.Y. *Clipper*, 25 April 1891.

Lawrence, W. J. "Pantomime in the United States," *Theatre* (London), 1 Feb. 1896, pp. 83–86.

Leavitt, M. B. *Fifty Years in Theatrical Management.* New York: Broadway Publishing Company, 1912.

Leech, Margaret. *Reveille in Washington 1860–1865.* New York: Harper & Brothers, 1941.

Leman, Walter M. *Memories of an Old Actor.* San Francisco: A. Roman, 1886.

Lening, Gustav. *Die Nachtseiten von New York und dessen Verbrecherwelt von der Fünften Avenue bis zu den Five Points.* New York: Friedrich Gerhard, 1873.

"Letter from New York." *Era*, 13 Apr. 1889.

Levine, Lawrence E. "William Shakespeare and the American people: A Study in Cultural Transformation." *American Historical Review* 81 : 1 (Feb. 1984): 34–66.

Levy, Lester S. *Grace Notes in American History: Popular Sheet Music from 1820 to 1900.* Norman, Okla.: University of Oklahoma Press, 1967.

Livermore, Mary A. *The Story of My Life or The Sunshine and Shadow of Seventy Years.* Hartford, Conn.: A. D. Worthington & Co., 1897.

Logan, Olive. *Before the Footlights and Behind the Scenes* . . . Philadelphia: Parmelee, 1870.

"Long Evening." Worcester *Daily News*, 26 Sept. 1850.

Lynch, Denis Tilden. *The Wild Seventies.* New York: D. Appleton-Century, 1941.

McCabe, John D., Jr. *Lights and Shadows of New York Life.* Philadelphia: National Publishing Co., 1872.

McCloskey, J. J. "The Old Bowery Theatre," New York *Dramatic Mirror*, Christmas, 1896, pp. 49–52.

McConachie, Bruce A., and Daniel Friedman, eds. *Theatre for Working-Class Audiences in the United States, 1830–1980*. Westport, Conn.: Greenwood Press, 1985.

Macdonald, Cordelia Howard, "Memoirs of the Original Little Eva." *Educational Theatre Journal* 8 (Dec. 1956): 267–82.

McGlinchee, Claire L., *The First Decade of the Boston Museum*. Boston: Bruce Humphries, 1940.

———. "The Marvellous in the Pantomime: Spectacles and Extravaganzas in the 19 C American Theatre." *Revue d'histoire du théâtre* 15 (Jan.–March 1963): 63–70.

McHale, Frank. "The Bowery Gods: Their Ways and Favorites." New York *Clipper*, 20 June 1873, p. 89.

McNamara, Brooks. "Scavengers of the Amusement World." In *American Pastimes*. Brockton, Mass.: Brockton Art Center, 1976.

McPharlin, Paul. *The Puppet Theatre in America*. Boston: Plays, Inc., 1969.

Macy, Obed. *The History of Nantucket* . . . 2d ed., 1880. Clifton, Mass.: Augustus M. Kelley, 1972.

Mandelbaum, Seymour J. *Boss Tweed's New York*. New York: John Wiley and Sons, 1965.

Marcosson, Isaac F. "Sawdust and Gold Dust: The Earnings of the Circus People." *Bookman*, June 1910.

Marks, Edward B. *They All Had Glamour from the Swedish Nightingale to the Naked Lady*. New York: Julian Messner, 1944.

"Marlowe." "Uncle Tom's Cabin," New York *Dramatic Mirror*, Christmas, 1905, p. vii.

Matthews, Brander. *A Book about the Theatre*. New York: Charles Scribner's Sons, 1916.

Mayer, David, III. *Harlequin in His Element: The English Pantomime, 1806–1836*. Cambridge, Mass.: Harvard University Press, 1969.

Mémoires et pantomimes des frères Hanlon-Lees. Preface by Théodore de Banville. Paris, RL, [1880]

Mencken, H. L. *The American Language: Supplement II*. New York: Alfred A. Knopf, 1923.

Miller, Douglas T. *The Birth of Modern America 1820–1850*. New York: Pegasus, 1970.

Minnegerode, Meade. *The Fabulous Forties 1840–1850: A Presentation of Private Life*. New York: G. P. Putnam's Sons, 1924.

Moore, Frank, ed. *The Rebellion Records: A Diary of American Events, with Documents, Narratives, Illustrated Incidents, Poetry, etc.* New York: G. P. Putnam's, 1861–68.

Mosier, J. L. H. "'Charley' Burke." New York *Times*, 30 Apr. 1905.

"Mr. Fox's Legacy." N.Y. *Dramatic News*, 15 Jan. 1876.

"Mrs. E. A. Eberle." New York *Dramatic Mirror*, 22 Oct. 1898.

Newport *Mercury* Editor. *Newport Illustrated in a Series of Pen and Pencil Sketches*. New York: D. Appleton, [1854]

The Night Side of New York: A Picture of the Great Metropolis. By Members of the New York Press. New York: J. Haney & Co., 1868.

Northall, William Knight. *Before and Behind the Curtain or Fifteen Years' Observations among the Theatres of New York*. New York: W. F. Burgess, 1851.

"Now Living in Poorhouse." N.Y. *Journal*, 21 Sept. 1916.

Nye, Russell B. *Society and Culture in America, 1830–1860*. New York: Harper & Row, 1974.

———. *The Unembarrassed Muse: The Popular Arts in America*. New York: The Dial Press, 1970.

Odell, George C. D. *Annals of the New York Stage.* 15 vols. New York: Columbia University Press, 1927–49.

———. "'A Midsummer Night's Dream' on the New York Stage." In *Shakespearean Studies by Members of the Department of English and Comparative Literature in Columbia University,* edited by J. B. Mathews and A. H. Thorndike. New York: Columbia University Press, 1916.

"Off the Stage, or, In Front of the Footlight." *Sporting Times and Theatrical News* 15 Oct. 1868.

Ordway, H. M. "The Drama in Lowell with a Short Sketch of the Life of Perez Fuller." In *Contributions of the Old Residents' Historical Association, Lowell, Mass.* Lowell: Morning Mall Press, 1883.

"Our Portrait Gallery. James W. Lingard. Actor and Manager. His Life, Death, and Burial," N.Y. *Clipper,* 16 July 1870, p. 114.

Paine, Albert Bigelow. *Thomas Nast: His Period and His Pictures.* New York: Macmillan, 1904.

Paine, Nathaniel. "The Drama in Worcester." In *History of Worcester County, Massachusetts . . .* compiled by D. Hamilton Hurd. 2 vols. Philadelphia: J. W. Lewis, 1889.

"The Pantomime in Paris." N.Y. *Sun,* 22 Nov. 1891.

"The Pantomime Season." N.Y. *Clipper,* 7 Jan. 1888, p. 694.

Parks, George S. "Old Stage Friends." N.Y. *Tribune,* 8 May 1923.

Phelps, H. P. *Players of a Century: A Record of the Albany Stage. Including Notices of Prominent Actors Who Have Appeared in America.* Albany, N.Y.: Joseph McDonough, 1880.

Phisterer, Frederick, comp. *New York in the War of the Rebellion 1861 to 1865.* Albany, N.Y.: Parsons & Co., 1890.

"A Pioneer in 'Uncle Tom.'" New York *Sun,* 7 Sept. 1902, p. 596.

"Poor Fox!" N.Y. *Dramatic News,* 2 Sept. 1876.

Power, Tyrone. *Impressions of America: During the Years 1833, 1834 and 1835.* 2 vols. Philadelphia: Carey, Lea & Blanchard, 1836.

Powers, James T. *Twinkle Little Star: Sparkling Memories of Seventy Years.* New York: G. P. Putnam's Sons, 1939.

Preston, Paul. "Pantomimes Ancient and Modern." New York *Clipper,* 8 May 1869, p. 36.

"The Ravel Brothers." *Ballou's Pictorial* 14:8 (20 Feb. 1858).

"The Ravel Family." Boston *Courier* 63 (15 March 1858).

Renauld, J. Booth. "Recollections of C. K. Fox." New York *Clipper,* 6 Mar. 1875, p. 385.

Renton, Herbert S. "The Clown in the Pantomime." *The Elks-Antler,* Jan. 1923, pp. 195–99.

———. "G. L. Fox as an Actor." New York *Herald,* 2 Feb. 1924.

———. "Humpty Dupmty [*sic*] and Others." New York *Sun,* 19 April 1929.

———. "Mimes as Actors." New York *Herald,* 12 Feb. 1924.

———. "More about Fox." New York *Sun,* 2 May 1929.

Rezneck, Samuel. "Social History of an American Depression, 1837–1843," *American Historical Review* 40 (July 1935): 662–87.

Robinson, Solon. *Hot Corn: Life Scenes in New York illustrated including the Story of Little Katy, Madalina, the Ragpicker's Daughter, Wild Maggie, &c.* New York: De Witt and Davenport, 1854.

Rothman, David J. *The Discovery of the Asylum: Social Order and Disorder in the New Republic.* Boston: Little, Brown, and Co., 1971.

Ryan, Pat M. "The Old Salem Theatre." *Essex Institute Historical Collections* 98 (Oct. 1962): 287–93.

Saxon, A. H. "P. T. Barnum's American Museum." *Seaport: New York's History Magazine* 20 (Winter 1986/87): 27–33.

Schultz, Stanley K. *The Culture Factory: Boston Public Schools 1789–1860.* New York: Oxford University Press, 1973.

Seitz, Don C. *The Dreadful Decade; Detailing Some Phases in the History of the United States from Reconstruction to Resumption, 1869–1879.* Indianapolis: Bobbs-Merrill, 1926.

Senelick, Laurence. "George L. Fox and American Pantomime." *Nineteenth Century Theatre Research* 7:1 (Spring 1979): 1–25.

———. "George L. Fox and Bowery Pantomime." In *American Popular Entertainment: Papers and Proceedings of the Conference on the History of American Popular Entertainment,* edited by Myron Matlaw. Westport, Conn.: Greenwood Press, 1979.

———. "Pepper's Ghost Faces the Camera." *History of Photography,* Jan.–Mar. 1983, pp. 69–72.

Seymour, William. "G. L. Fox as a Comedian." New York *Herald,* 5 Feb. 1924.

Shafer, Yvonne. "George L. Fox and the *Hamlet* Travesty." *Theatre Studies* 24/25 (1977–79): 79–94.

Shank, Theodore J. "Theatre for the Majority: Its Influence on a Nineteenth Century American Theatre." *Educational Theatre Journal* 11:3 (Oct. 1959): 188–99.

Sharp, James Roger. *The Jacksonians* versus *the Banks: Politics in the States after the Panic of 1837.* New York: Columbia University Press, 1970.

Shattuck, Charles H. *The Hamlet of Edwin Booth.* Urbana, Ill.: University of Illinois Press, 1969.

Shepard, Leslie, ed. *Encyclopedia of Occultism & Parapsychology.* 2 vols. Detroit: Gale Research Co., 1978.

Sherwood, Robert Edmond. *Here We Are Again: Recollections of an Old Circus Clown.* Indianapolis: Bobbs-Merrill, 1926.

Smith, Cecil. *Musical Comedy in America.* New York: Theatre Arts Books, 1950.

Smith, George B. "Memories of the Long Ago 1838–1925." *Bulletin of the Newport Historical Society* 56 (Jan. 1926): 1–13.

Smith, Henry Nash, ed. *Popular Culture and Industrialism 1865–1890.* Garden City, N.Y.: Doubleday, 1967.

Sowers, William Lee. "Pantomime in America." *Texas Review* (Austin, Tex.) 2 (1917): 235–47.

Spann, Edward K. *The New Metropolis: New York City 1840–1857.* New York: Columbia University Press, 1981.

Speaight, George. "Professor Pepper's Ghost." *Revue d'histoire du théâtre* 1 (1963): 48–56.

Stackpole, Edward A. "The Great Fire of 1846." *Proceedings of the Nantucket Historical Association* 52 (1946): 35–53.

Stebbins, Oliver B. "The Oldest Theatre Now in Boston." *The Bostonian* 1:2 (Nov. 1894): 113–30.

Still, Bayrd. *Mirror for Gotham: New York as Seen by Contemporaries from Dutch Days to the Present.* New York: New York University Press, 1956.

Stoddard, Richard. "Isaiah Rogers's Tremont Theatre, Boston." *Antiques* 105 (1974): 1314–19.

Stone, Henry Dickinson. *Personal Recollections of the Drama, or Theatrical Reminiscences, Embracing Sketches of Prominent Actors and Actresses, Their Chief Characteristics, Original Anecdotes of Them, and Incidents Connected Therewith.* Albany, N.Y.: Charles van Benthuysen & Sons, 1873.

Stone, Henry P. "Memories of Uncle Tom's Cabin," New York *Dramatic Mirror,* 28 Mar. 1901.

Storey, Robert. *Pierrots on the Stage of Desire*. Princeton, N.J.: Princeton University Press, 1985.

Stuart-Wortley, Lady Emmeline. *Travels in the United States etc. during 1849 and 1850*. New York: Harper & Brothers, 1851.

Swift, Mary Grace. *Belles and Beaux on their Toes: Dancing Stars in Young America*. Washington, D.C.: University Press of America, 1980.

Taylor, Robert Lewis. *Vessel of Wrath: The Life and Times of Carrie Nation*. New York: New American Library, 1966.

Tenney, W. J. *The Military and Naval History of the Rebellion in the United States with Biographical Sketches of Deceased Officers*. New York: D. Appleton, 1865.

Thwing, Annie Haven. *The Crooked & Narrow Streets of the Town of Boston 1630–1822*. Boston: Marshall James Co., 1920.

Ticknor, Howard Malcom. "The Passing of the Boston Museum." *The New England Magazine*, n.s. 28:4 (June 1903): 379–96.

Tompkins, Eugene, and Quincy Kilby. *A History of the Boston Theatre 1854–1901*. Boston: Houghton Mifflin, 1908.

"Tony Denier, H.D." New York *Dramatic Mirror*, 6 Jan. 1906, p. 14.

Townsend, Thomas S. *The Honors of the Empire State in the War of the Rebellion*. New York: A Lovell & Co., 1889.

Towse, John Ranken. *Sixty Years of the Theater: An Old Critic's Memories*. New York: Funk & Wagnalls, 1916.

Tracy, Joe. "The Late Geo. L. Fox, Greatest of All Clowns in Pantomime." *Five Grace Notes*, Christmas 1945.

Turner, Henry E. "Newport, 1800–1850," Newport *Daily News*, 24–25 Mar. 1897.

Tyrrel, Ian R. *Sobering Up: From Temperance to Prohibition in Antebellum America, 1800–1860*. Westport, Conn.: Greenwood Press, 1979.

"Uncle Tom among the Bowery Boys." New York *Times*, 27 July 1853, p. 1.

"Uncle Tom's Cabin: Its Early Days and the People Who Played In it." *New York Clipper*, 10 Feb. 1877, p. 365.

Vandenhoff, George. *Leaves from an Actor's Note-Book; with Reminiscences and Chit-Chat of the Green-room and the Stage, in England and America*. New York: D. Appleton, 1860.

Van Wyck, Frederick. *Recollections of an Old New Yorker*. New York: Liveright, 1932.

Wagner, Leopold. *The Pantomimes and All about Them: Their History, Preparation and Exponents*. London: John Heywood, [1881].

Walker, "Whimsical." *From Sawdust to Windsor Castle*. London: Stanley Paul, 1922.

Wallack, Lester. *Memories of Fifty Years*. New York: Charles Scribner's Sons, 1889.

Walton, Thomas. "'Entortilationists' (The Hanlon-Lees in Literature and Art)," *Life and Letters Today* 29 (Apr.–June 1941): 26–37.

The War of the Rebellion: A Compilation of the Official Records of the Union and Confederate Armies. Prepared under the direction of the secretary of war by Bvt. Lieut. Col. Robert N. Scott. 70 vols. Washington, D.C.: Government Printing Office, 1880–1896.

Watkins, Harry. *One Man in His Time: The Adventures of H. Watkins Strolling Player 1845–1863 from His Journal by Maud and Otis Skinner*. Philadelphia: University of Pennsylvania Press, 1938.

Weise, Arthur James. *History of the City of Troy, from the Expulsion of the Mohegan Indians to the Present Centennial Year of the Independence of the United States of America, 1876*. Troy, N.Y.: William H. Young, 1876.

———. *Troy's One Hundred Years 1789–1889*. Troy, N.Y.: William H. Young, 1891.

Welter, Rush. *The Mind of America 1820–1860*. New York: Columbia University Press, 1975.

Wemyss, F. C. "Supplement" to *The Guide to the Stage* . . . by Thomas Leman Rede. New York: Sam: French, 1864.

———. *Wemyss' Chronology of the American Stage, from 1752 to 1852.* (1852) New York: Benjamin Blom, 1968.

Werner, M. R. *Tammany Hall.* Garden City, N.Y.: Doubleday, Doran, 1928.

Willard, George O. *History of the Providence Stage 1762–1891.* Providence, R.I.: Rhode Island News Co., 1891.

Willson Disher, Maurice. *Clowns and Pantomimes.* London: Constable, 1925.

Wilmeth, Don B., and Rosemary Cullen, eds. *Plays of Augustin Daly.* Cambridge, Cambridge University Press, 1985.

Wilson, A.E. *Pantomime Pageant: A Procession of Harlequins, Clowns, Comedians and Principal Boys, Pantomime-Writers, Producers and Playgoers.* London: Stanley Paul, [1946].

Wines, Enoch Cobb. *A Trip to Boston in a Series of Letters to the Editor of the United States Gazette.* Boston: Charles C. Little and James Brown, 1838.

Winter, Marian Hannah. "Augusta Maywood." In *Chronicles of the American Dance,* edited by Paul Magriel. New York: Dance Index, 1948.

———. *Le Théâtre du merveilleux.* Paris: Olivier Perrin, 1962.

Winter, William. *Life and Art of Edwin Booth.* New York: Macmillan and Co., 1893.

———. *Other Days.* New York: Moffat, Yard, 1908.

———. *Vagabond Memories, being Further Recollections of Other Days.* New York: George Doran, 1915.

Woodward, W. E. *A New American History.* New York: Farrar & Rinehart, 1936.

III. Newspapers and Periodicals

Boston *Sporting Times and Theatrical News*
Boston *Transcript*
Cambridge *Chronicle*
New York *Clipper*
New York *Dramatic Mirror*
New York *Dramatic News*
New York *Herald*
New York *Sun*
New York *Times*
New York *Tribune*
Northern Budget
Porter's Spirit of the Times
Spirit of the Times
Theatre (New York)
Wilkes' Spirit of the Times

INDEX

Abbey, Henry Eugene (manager, 1846–96), 213, 218
Abbott, Charles (clown, 1842–74), 169, 209
Abby Aldrich Rockefeller Museum, 226
Abduction from the Seraglio (Mozart), 80
Academy of Music, New York, 103–4, 111, 134
Actress of All Work, The, 54
Acts and Boke of Martyres, The (Foxe), 2
Adams, George H. (clown, 1853–1935), 184, 212, 218
Adams, I. P. (entrepreneur), 33
Addams, John P. "Yankee" (actor, 1815–85), 21, 32, 38
After Dark (Boucicault), 151
Ahnfrau, Die (Grillparzer), 114
Aiken, Frank W. (actor, *b.* 1836), 3, 61, 63, 77, 79
Aiken, George L. (actor, 1830–76), 3, 5, 35, 38, 43, 54, 59, 61, 63, 72, 79, 82
Aiken, Lemuel G. (father of George, 1805–58), 3
Aiken, Susan Wyatt (mother of George), 3
Ainsworth, William Harrison (novelist, 1805–82), 76
A-Lad-In, 77
Alger, Horatio, Jr. (novelist, 1832–99), 52
Allen's Dramatic Agency, New York, 216
American Hotel, Troy, New York, 55
American Society for the Prevention of Cruelty to Animals, 154
American Society for the Promotion of Temperance, 26
American Theatre, Philadelphia, 126
Americus (violinist), 184
Anabasis (Xenophon), 33
Ancestress, or The Ghost of Destiny, The, 114
Ancient Briton, The (J. A. Stone), 6
Anderson, James "Irish" (stage-manager), 48–49, 58, 63, 73
Angel of Midnight, The (Brougham), 105
Angel of the Attic, The (T. Morton), 24
Annexation of Texas, or Uncle Sam's Courtship, The, 28
Antony and Cleopatra (Shakespeare), 93
Arch Street Theatre, Philadelphia, 17, 126, 129
Art Students League, New York, 166
Artful Dodger, or The Inventions of Lollypop, The, 28

Asphodel; or, The Magic Pen (Ravel), 72, 77, 94
Astor Place Riot, 46, 123
Althenaeum, Nantucket, 33–34
Atlas (Boston), 8
Aurilla, the North Wind; or, Spirit of the Air, 81
Auriol, Emma. *See* Denier, Emma Auriol

Baba, 214
Bacon, Peter (mayor of Worcester, Mass.), 43
Baker, Amos (schoolmaster), 8
Baker, Master (child prodigy), 4
Ballo in maschera, Un (Verdi), 12
Baltimore Museum, 17–18
Bamboozling! (Wilks), 34
Bannister, Mrs. Nathaniel Harrington (Amelia Green, actress, *fl.* 1817–53), 63
Baptistine (Harlequin), 115
Barnard, Frederick Augustus Porter (judge, 1809–89), 178
Barnum, Phineas Taylor (showman, 1810–91), 58, 115, 119–21, 124, 146, 154
Barnum's American Museum, New York, 68–69, 111, 115, 119–24, 129, 134
Barrett, George Horton (actor, 1794–1860), 22
Barrett, Lawrence (actor, 1838–91), 164
Barry, Thomas (actor, 1798–1876), 12, 19
Barrymore, William Henry (playwright, *d.* 1845), 12, 24
Bartholomew, William H. (clown, 1831–1917), 218, 220
Bateman, Ellen Douglas (actress, 1844–1936), 4, 168
Bateman, Kate Josephine (actress, 1843–1917), 4, 168
Battle of Booneville and New Union Tableaux, The (Seymour), 102
Battle of Buena Vista, The (Addams), 38
Battle of Bull Run, First, 102–3
Battle of Bunker Hill, The, 109
Battle of Gettysburg, 108
Battle of Lake Erie, The, 18
Beane, Fanny (actress, *b.* 1853), 167
Beane, George A. (pantomimist), 82, 167, 169, 180
Beecher, Lyman (preacher, 1775–1863), 15–16, 19, 26, 31